This book is about recent changes in the design of intelligent machines. New computer models of vision and navigation in animals suggest a different way to build machines. Cognition is viewed not just in terms of high-level "expertise," but in terms of the ability to find one's way around the world, to learn new ways of seeing things, and to coordinate activity. This approach is called situated cognition.

Situated Cognition differs from other purely philosophical treatises in that Clancey, who has built expert systems for twenty years, explores the limitations of existing computer programs and compares them to human memory and learning capabilities. He examines the implications of situated action from the perspective of artificial intelligence specialists interested in building robots and cognitive scientists seeking to relate descriptive models to neural and social views of knowledge.

Situated cognition

Learning in doing: Social, cognitive, and computational perspectives

GENERAL EDITORS: ROY PEA

JOHN SEELY BROWN

Situated cognition

On human knowledge and computer representations

WILLIAM J. CLANCEY
Institute for Research on Learning

CAMBRIDGE
UNIVERSITY PRESS

PUBLISHED BY THE PRESS SYNDICATE OF THE UNIVERSITY OF CAMBRIDGE
The Pitt Building, Trumpington Street, Cambridge CB2 1RP, United Kingdom

CAMBRIDGE UNIVERSITY PRESS
The Edinburgh Building, Cambridge CB2 2RU, United Kingdom
40 West 20th Street, New York, NY 10011-4211, USA
10 Stamford Road, Oakleigh, Melbourne 3166, Australia

First published in 1997

Printed in the United States of America

Typeset in Times Roman and Century Schoolbook

Library of Congress Cataloging-in-Publication Data
Clancey, William J.
Situated cognition: on human knowledge and computer
representations / William J. Clancey.
p.   cm. – (Learning in doing)
Includes bibliographical references and indexes.
ISBN 0-521-44400-4 (hard). – ISBN 0-521-44871-9 (pbk.)
1. Artificial intelligence.   2. Robots.   3. Cognition.
4. Knowledge, Theory of.   I. Title.   II. Series.
Q335.C5   1997
006.3 – dc20   96-35839
                                                     CIP

*A catalog record for this book is available from
the British Library.*

ISBN 0 521 44400 4 hardback
ISBN 0 521 44871 9 paperback

In memory of Konstantin Kolenda (1923–1991)
of Rice University, who taught me to converse
with philosophers past

Contents

Figures and tables

Figures

Tables

Series foreword

This series for Cambridge University Press is becoming widely known as an international forum for studies of situated learning and cognition.

Innovative contributions from anthropology; cognitive, developmental, and cultural psychology; computer science; education, and social theory are providing theory and research that seeks new ways of understanding the social, historical, and contextual nature of the learning, thinking, and practice emerging from human activity. The empirical settings of these research inquiries range from the classroom, to the workplace, to the high-technology office, to learning in the streets and in other communities of practice.

The situated nature of learning and remembering through activity is a central fact. It may appear obvious that human minds develop in social situations, and that they come to appropriate the tools that culture provides to support and extend their sphere of activity and communicative competencies. But cognitive theories of knowledge representation and learning alone have not provided sufficient insight into these relationships.

This series is born of the conviction that new and exciting interdisciplinary syntheses are under way, as scholars and practitioners from diverse fields seek to develop theory and empirical investigations adequate to characterizing the complex relations of social and mental life, and to understanding successful learning wherever it occurs. The series invites contributions that advance our understanding of these seminal issues.

Roy Pea
John Seely Brown

Acknowledgments

I began writing this book shortly after joining the Institute for Research on Learning in 1988, with the intention of explaining the situated cognition perspective to my home audience of AI researchers. At the time, my understanding and much of my inspiration came from philosophical writings. These influences have been supplanted by the robot designs and neurobiological models of the 1990s. Consequently, the philosophical works are underrepresented in both my presentation and citations – in the way steps in solving a mathematical problem are not represented in the proof. In particular, as an undergraduate, I was strongly taken by the writings of Ludwig Wittgenstein and Gilbert Ryle. Similarly, Hubert Dreyfus's *What Computers Can't Do* (1972) was pivotal in my decision to become an AI researcher (although many people at the time feared it would have the opposite effect!).

At Rice University I was introduced to situated cognition in 1972–1973 in courses taught by the cognitive anthropologist Stephen Tyler (specifically the course on "Language, Thought, and Culture") and a visiting sociologist from UC Irvine, Kenneth Leiter ("The Sociology of Knowledge"). Within the AI field, Terry Winograd and Fernando Flores (1986) made it possible to engage in this discourse; the visits of Phil Agre and Jeanne Bamberger to IRL influenced me very much. Several books and articles that I read at the same time shaped my reformulation of the relation of representations and memory: Bartlett (1932), Bateson (1988), Gregory (1988), Schön (1979), Tyler (1978), and Wilden (1987). Space limitations and respect for my readers' patience require that I leave the discussion of Vygotsky, Piaget, Freud, and related contemporary research for another time and place.

Several people have advised me over the years and taught me by example how to think about these issues. Their ideas and values are so bound up in my own that I tend to take them for granted: Konnie Kolenda, Bruce Buchanan, John Seely Brown, Alan Collins, and Jim Greeno. I especially thank my friends and diligent readers of the many early drafts of this manuscript: Mark Bickhard, Eric Bredo, Harold Cohen, Paul Compton, Paul Feltovich, Robert Hoffman, Bob Howard, Ali Iran-Nejad, Rick Lewis, Maja Mataric, John McDermott, John O' Neil, Rolf Pfeifer, Jeremy Roschelle, Israel Rosenfield, Valerie Shalin, Maarten Sierhuis, Peter

Slezak, Steve Smoliar, Luc Steels, Mark Stefik, Reed Stevens, Kurt van Lehn, Erik Vinkhuyzen (and the members of the AI group at the University of Zurich), Lorraine Watanabe, and Etienne Wenger.

I am indebted to Julia Hough of Cambridge University Press for her persistent support and flexibility as the topic and focus of this book have been refined. Local assistance in preparing the manuscript was provided by Susan Allen, Greg Caster, Charlene Taylor, and Anne Tourney. Funding was provided in part by grants from the Xerox Foundation, Digitial Equipment Corporation, and NYNEX Science and Technology, Inc.

Portola Valley, CA
October 1996

Introduction: What is situated cognition?

I shall reconsider human knowledge by starting from the fact that we can know more than we can tell.

Michael Polanyi, *The tacit dimension*, 1966, p. 4

Speaking is the alienation of thought from action, writing is the alienation of language from speech, and linguistics is the alienation of language from the self.

Stephen A. Tyler, *The said and the unsaid: Mind, meaning, and culture*, 1978, p. 17

This book is about the relation between human knowledge and computer programs. How can we build a robot that behaves like a person? How does the brain work? What is the relation between knowledge and culture? Do other animals think? These questions are posed by diverse scientific fields ranging from artificial intelligence (AI) to neurobiology, anthropology, and ethology. Each field brings different perspectives on the nature of knowledge. But now, after working in relative isolation over the past century, researchers in the cognitive sciences are increasingly reading each others' work and working together. The resulting approach, called *situated cognition*, emphasizes the roles of feedback, mutual organization, and emergence in intelligent behavior. Neuroscientists and computer scientists, in particular, are realizing the cybernetic vision of creating relatively simple, biologically inspired robots; their work reveals the dynamic nature of knowledge, an idea that philosophers and social scientists have been trying to explain for at least a century. In this book I analyze and compare the new robot designs with respect to contextualist studies of human experience. This exploration leads to a somewhat unexpected reformulation of how memory works, how conceptualizing is a form of physical coordinating, and how the symbols in programs, neural systems, and speech are related. This introductory chapter surveys the key ideas, explains the origins and goals of the book, and concludes with an outline for the reader.

Descriptions and coordinations

The theory of situated cognition, as I present it here, claims that every human thought and action is adapted to the environment, that is, *situated*, because what people *perceive*, how they *conceive of their activity*, and what

1

they *physically do* develop together. From this perspective, thinking is a physical skill like riding a bike. In bicycling, every twist and turn of the steering wheel and every shift in posture are controlled not by manipulation of the physics equations learned in school, but by a *recoordination* of previous postures, ways of seeing, and motion sequences. Similarly, in reasoning, as we create names for things, shuffle around sentences in a paragraph, and interpret what our statements mean, every step is controlled not by rotely applying grammar descriptions and previously stored plans, but by adaptively recoordinating previous ways of seeing, talking, and moving. All human action is at least partially improvisatory by direct *coupling* of perceiving, conceiving, and moving – a coordination mechanism unmediated by *descriptions* of associations, laws, or procedures. This mechanism complements the inferential processes of deliberation and planning that form the backbone of theories of cognition based on manipulation of descriptions. Direct coupling of perceptual, conceptual, and motor processes in the brain involves a kind of "self-organization with a memory" that we have not yet replicated in computer programs, or indeed in any machine.

Following the simple idea that knowledge consists of descriptive models – *descriptions of how the world appears* (such as what symptoms are associated with a given infectious disease) and *descriptions of how to behave* in certain situations (such as how a physician selects a set of antibiotics to cover a set of disease hypotheses) – cognitive science made rapid progress throughout the 1970s and 1980s.[1] This approach, often called *symbolic cognitive modeling,* supported by empirical studies, has greatly advanced our understanding of human expertise (especially in medicine and engineering). Cognitive studies have revealed how a beginner's reasoning differs from an expert's, how people learn from failures, and how a teacher selects examples to correct a student's misunderstandings. More generally, the descriptive modeling approach has revealed how people relate words and meaning when reading, how problem solvers opportunistically and strategically relate goals to plans and limited resources, how decision makers sort through ambiguous, uncertain data, and so on. Many useful programs incorporate descriptive models to automate routine operations throughout science, business, and engineering, including controlling manufacturing plants, auditing spreadsheets, discovering patterns in medical databases, and so on. Although perhaps not as ubiquitous as AI researchers imagined 20 years ago, "intelligent" assistants, instructors, and simulators have gradually transformed software engineering into the knowledge-based paradigm. Obviously, there is something valuable about the descriptive approach, and any revision to cognitive theory must build on it.

Broadly speaking, situated cognition is a philosophical perspective and an engineering methodology that acknowledges the value of descriptive models of knowledge as abstractions but attempts to build robots in a different way. In contrast to the *symbolic approach* (which I hereafter call the *descriptive approach*), the theory of situated cognition claims that when modelers equate human knowledge with a *set of descriptions*, such as a collection of facts and rules in an expert system, they are describing abstractly how the program should behave in particular situations, but they are not capturing the full flexibility of how perception, action, and memory are related in the brain. In the words of Alfred Korzybski, the map is not the territory: Human conceptualization has properties relating to physical coordination that make human knowledge different from the written procedures and word networks in a computer program. According to this theory, which has roots in the functionalist psychology of William James and Frederic C. Bartlett and in the pragmatist philosophy of Charles S. Peirce and John Dewey, the memory mechanism that coordinates human perception and action is quite different from the stored-description memory of descriptive models. Descriptions are indeed central to human behavior, but their role is not in *directly* controlling what we do (even as instructions). Rather, in our speech and writing, descriptions allow us to extend our cognitive activity into our environment, hold active and order alternative conceptions in our mental processing, and thus move beyond reactive, "unthinking" routines (see Chapter 9).

If you will permit me one more advance description of where this book is headed, here is a central question, one that is especially exciting and inspiring for today's robot builders: If human knowledge doesn't consist of stored descriptions, what then is the relation of what we say to what we do? Speaking must be seen not as bringing out what is already inside, but as a way of changing what is inside. Speaking is not restating what has already been posted subconsciously inside the brain, but is itself *an activity of representing*. Our names for things and what they mean, our theories, and our conceptions *develop in our behavior* as we interact with and reperceive what we and others have previously said and done. This causal interaction is different from the linear "describing what I perceive" or "looking for what I conceive." Instead, the processes of looking, perceiving, understanding, and describing are arising together and shaping each other. This is called the *transactional perspective*.

So there is a kind of twist in how neural processes and behavior develop: Neural processes are more flexible and adaptive in how they relate conception, percept, and deed than a body of descriptions allows, but the act of describing is nevertheless crucial for reorienting human behavior. The first step in unraveling this recursive relation is to distinguish between human memory and a body of descriptions. Understanding the nature of human memory as a recoordinating mechanism, we can then sort out the relative roles of neural categorization and representational manipulations in the environment (such as drawing and writing). As the chapter-opening quote from Tyler indicates, the very act of describing human knowledge changes what we know (and this is often good). But revered as a body of formalized thought, as in linguistics or knowledge engineering, descriptions partially obscure our actual experience (which is not good when scientists are trying to study imagery, rhythm, or other nonverbal modes of coordination). As the chapter-opening quote from Polanyi indicates, although words and diagrams are often pivotal, they are not the only means by which cognition proceeds.

In short, situated cognition is the study of how human knowledge develops as a means of coordinating activity *within activity itself.* This means that feedback – occurring internally and with the environment over time – is of paramount importance. Knowledge therefore has a dynamic aspect in both formation and content. This shift in perspective from knowledge as *stored artifact* to knowledge as *constructed capability-in-action* is inspiring a new generation of cyberneticists in the fields of situated robotics, ecological psychology, and computational neuroscience. Empirical studies are bringing together insights about interactions occurring at different levels inside and outside the brain.

Human knowledge is, of course, more complex than the bicycle-riding example suggests: Controlling sensorimotor skills, creating and interpreting descriptions (such as the parent's instructions about how to balance), and participating in a social matrix (such as becoming a "grown-up kid" by joining the gang down the block) are related and dynamically composed by *conceptual coordination.* These organizers of behavior occur in parallel, all the time, influencing each other. Three *forms of feedback* are thereby emphasized:

- *Short-term actions change the flux of sensory data* (forces and views are changed by forward motion of the bicycle).
- *Perception and conception are dynamically coupled* (whether the curb appears as a boundary or affords jumping depends on how threatening you conceive the traffic behind you to be).
- *Goals and meaning are reconceived as transformations made to the environment over time are reperceived* (accumulated bicycle ruts in hills of an abandoned lot might mark it for children as "a place to go ride your bike" or appear to the town council as an eroded landscape needing to be restored).

In *reexamining the nature of feedback*, situated cognition research explores the idea that conceptual knowledge, as a capacity to coordinate and sequence behavior, is inherently formed *as part of* and *through* physical performances. The formation of perceptual categorizations and their *coupling* to concepts provides material for reasoning (inference), which then changes where we look and what we are able to find.

In this book, I explain these ideas by reexamining the nature of descriptive cognitive modeling, interpreting biological evidence and philosophical arguments, and critiquing new robot designs. In elaborating the notions of feedback and causal coupling, I show how situated cognition is helping resolve age-old controversies about the nature of meaning and sheds much light on recent debates about symbol grounding, direct perception, and situated learning.

On comparing human knowledge and computer representations

To conclude this introduction, I provide some background for readers who may be unfamiliar with the history of descriptive cognitive modeling and introduce my comparative approach.

Scientific papers and books are ultimately personal statements, locating the author's developing thought along a path from what is now seen as naive toward what is viewed as a hopeful redirection. From 1974 to 1987, I was part of a community of AI researchers who devised computer programs that could diagnose diseases, engage in case-method discourse for teaching, and model students' problem-solving strategies.[2] Following the rubric of *knowledge-based systems*, we believed not only that knowledge could be represented in rules ("If there is evidence of bacterial meningitis and the patient is an alcoholic, then therapy should cover for diplococcus organisms"), but also that a body of such rules would be functionally equivalent to what an expert physician can do. We knew that the physician knew more, but we assumed that his or her knowledge simply consisted of *more rules*.

The assumption that human knowledge consists exclusively of words organized into networks of rules and pattern descriptions (*frames*) guided the creation of hundreds of computer programs, described in dozens of books such as *Building Expert Systems* (Hayes-Roth, Waterman, and Lenat, 1983), *Intelligent Tutoring Systems* (Sleeman and Brown, 1982), and *The Logical Foundations of Artificial Intelligence* (Genesereth and Nilsson, 1987). Certainly these researchers realized that processes of physical coordination and perception involved in motor skills couldn't easily be replicated by pattern and rule descriptions. But such aspects of cognition were viewed as *peripheral* or *implementation* concerns. According to this view, intelligence is *mental*, and the content of thought consists of networks of words, coordinated by an *architecture* for matching, search, and rule application. These representations, describing the world and how to behave, serve as the machine's knowledge, just as they are the basis for human reasoning and judgment. According to this *symbolic approach* to building an artificial intelligence, descriptive models not only *represent* human knowledge, they correspond in a maplike way to *structures stored* in human memory. By this view, a descriptive model is an explanation of human behavior because *the model is the person's knowledge* – *s*tored inside, it directly controls what the person sees and does.

The distinction between representations (knowledge) and implementation (biology or silicon), called the *functionalist* hypothesis (Edelman, 1992), claims that although AI engineers might learn more about biological processes of relevance to understanding the nature of knowledge, they ultimately will be able to develop a machine with human capability that is not biological or organic. This strategy has considerable support, but unfortunately, the thrust has been to *ignore the differences* between human knowledge and computer programs and instead to tout existing programs as "intelligent." Emphasizing the similarities between people and computer models, rather than the differences, is an ironic strategy for AI researchers to adopt, given that one of the central accomplishments of AI has been the formalization of *means–ends analysis* as a problem-solving method: Progress in solving a problem can be made by describing the difference between the current state and a goal state and then making a move that attempts to bridge that gap.

Given the focus on symbolic inference, cognitive studies have appropriately focused on aspects of intelligence that rely on descriptive models, such as in mathematics, science, engineering, and medicine – the professional areas of human expertise. Focusing on professional expertise has supported the idea that "knowledge equals stored models" and hence has produced a dichotomy between physical and intellectual skills. That is, the distinction between physical skills and *knowledge* is based on an assumption, which was instilled in many professionals in school, that "real knowledge" consists of scientific facts and theories. By this view, intelligence is concerned only with articulated belief and reasoned hypothesis.

But understanding the nature of cognition requires considering more than the complex problem solving and learning of human experts and their tutees. Other subareas of psychology seek to understand more general aspects of cognition, such as the relation of primates to people, neurological dysfunction, and the evolution of language. Each of these requires some consideration of how the brain works, and each provides some enlightening insights for robot builders.[3] In this respect, the means–ends approach I promote is a continuation of the original aim of cybernetics: to compare the mechanisms of biological and artificial systems.

By holding computer programs up against the background of more general studies of cognition, cognitive scientists can articulate differences between human knowledge and the best cognitive models. Although questions about the relation of language, thought, and learning are very old, computational models provide an opportunity to test theories in a new way – by building a mechanism out of descriptions of the world and how to behave and seeing how well it performs. Howard Gardner describes this opportunity:

Only through scrupulous adherence to computational thinking could scientists discover the ways in which humans actually differ from the serial digital computer – the von Neumann computer, the model that dominated the thinking of the first generation of cognitive scientists. (Gardner, 1985b, p. 385)

Gardner concludes from such comparisons that cognitive scientists should substantially broaden their view of mental processes. This book is in the same spirit, stepping out from what AI programs do to inquire how such models of cognition relate to human knowledge and activity. I frame strategies for bridging the gap and provide some advice for appropriately using the technology developed to date.

When I describe how descriptive cognitive models work and how they measure up to human capability, some readers may wonder if I am criticizing the programs they are now working on. They may say, "But we already know that," pointing beyond what they have done to the vision of what the programs could become (if only we add more rules, if only we attach a sensory apparatus, if only we can store the definitions of concepts more flexibly, and so on). For example, a colleague wrote to me about his program's design:

[The program's] LTM [long-term memory] is entirely unlike a stored list of descriptions which can be explicitly searched, examined, and interpreted. Rather, it is more like a network of active associative processes.

But what is meant by *active processes*? Is the network of stored descriptions active in the same sense that a neural network in the brain is active? In what sense is this program's engineered list of rules like human memory? A proper comparison of biological and artificial systems requires asking questions like this. Is my colleague's description a neuropsychological claim in the cybernetic style or a hopeful, metaphoric interpretation? How can we properly appraise what we have accomplished and what remains to be done, if we speak loosely about the processes we aim to replicate? In the exploration of this book, I am especially concerned with elucidating the relation between program structures and biological processes, and especially how biological processes are *active* in a way that most computer models are not.

An exposition of the differences between people and computers necessarily requires examples of what computers cannot yet do. Such descriptions are to some extent poetic – a style of analysis promoted by Oliver Sacks in books such as *The Man Who Mistook His Wife for a Hat* – because they cannot yet be programmed. This analysis irks some AI researchers and has been characterized as "asking the tail of philosophy to wave the dog of cognitive science" (Vera and Simon, 1993). Through an interesting form of circularity, descriptive models of scientific discovery shape how some researchers view the advancement of their science: If aspects of cognition cannot be modeled satisfactorily as networks of words, then work on these areas of cognition is vague, and comparative analysis is nonoperational speculation. Here lies perhaps the ultimate difficulty in bridging different points of view: The scientific study of human knowledge only partially resembles the operation of machine learning programs. In people, nonverbal conceptualization can organize the search for new ideas. Being aware of and articulating this difference is pivotal in relating people and programs.

Recent advances in the related fields of connectionism, robotics, artificial life, and others greatly broaden the field of AI by placing the brain, the environment, and computational mechanisms in new relations. There is no longer "just one game in town," as Jerry Fodor described cognitive science in 1975. But the fundamental identification of knowledge with representations of knowledge – manifested as the identification of *concepts with text, context with data, trouble with puzzles,* and *activities with tasks* – continues in knowledge engineering and computer applications in general.

For decades, several fields of research, notably ecological and social psychology, areas of cybernetics, and the sociology of knowledge, have drawn distinctions between human knowledge and computer models. But these disciplines have proceeded in relative isolation from the AI community. For example, in the 1970s the cyberneticist-anthropologist Gregory Bateson lived and worked in Palo Alto, California, but his existence and ideas were unknown to AI researchers developing the first expert systems at Stanford University a few miles away. I was one of these researchers and am still stunned when I reflect on the isolation of the cognitive sciences at that time. Even now, despite reading hundreds of related articles and books over the past decade, I never heard of Robert Shaw or possessed a paper by Michael Turvey until late 1993 – yet they have been writing about the robot-building implications of ecological psychology since the early 1980s.

With such divisions in background, reactions to situated cognition are equally diverse. For example, a psychologist examined my comparisons of computer programs and said, "The approach is mainly philosophical (and not empirical)." But to computer scientists, programming is an experimental method – it is "philosophical" synthesis that is often omitted. Similarly, computer scientists have asked me for arguments to support John Dewey's positions – and I am left wondering why Dewey's supporters haven't cared that such arguments are missing in his writing. Perhaps studying the situated cognition *debate* would reveal more about conceptual change (in both enthusiasts and conservatives) than our laboratory protocols have ever captured. I have concluded, as social construction theories of meaning suggest, that a textual exposition of controversial concepts cannot stand alone. This book is but one statement in what must become a dialogue that includes face-to-face conversation.

Like perhaps any attempt to articulate what people take for granted, situated cognition at first appeared to be nonsensical, unnecessary, old hat, already accomplished by others, a form of religion, or "fool's gold." A government sponsor of my expert systems research wrote to me in the late 1980s – before we had the neurological evidence and robot designs I present here – that "what you are saying is just mystical." Sometimes the debate has become heated. I think perhaps because AI researchers so often used words describing neuropsychological processes metaphorically, there was no way of describing the distinctions that now appeared important. If *representations* meant *descriptions*, what word should we use for perceptual categorizations? If *reasoning* meant formally relating tokens by rules of a calculus, how shall we refer to thinking?[4] If *neural networks* meant a form of recursive hash coding (a kind of memory store), what shall we call brain structures?

Most important, I am not arguing that descriptive modeling is wrong and situated cognition is right. Instead, I aim to reveal how different perspectives may be reconciled. I find that a "both-and" view (Wilden, 1972) is often helpful, both as a theory of causality and as a way of relating psychological theories (Chapter 10). For example, the *direct coupling* causal mechanism I describe involves processes that are *spatially distinguished but not independent in time* – an orthogonal alternative to the serial–parallel dichtomy (Chapters 6 and 12). Similarly, I aim for a combination of the descriptive, build-it-in approach to robot engineering (after all, people do learn by being told) and the emergent approach (robots based on methods of insect navigation appear to work better when they are told less). I am trying to be inclusive, respecting how well descriptive modeling fits experimental data – but with an eye for the range of cognition in the wild (Hutchins, 1995a).

My objective is to formulate and promote a broad approach to cognitive science that respects the biological, neuropsychological, and social sciences. My working assumption is that robot builders need to be reminded of the full range of animal cognition, the experience of human learning, the multiple modalities of thought, and the evolution of human language from noncognitive mechanisms. In general, such a net is too broad and ill-advised as an everyday scientific effort. But such a synthetic effort is justified once in a while. In particular, I aim to complement the discipline-crossing approach of neuroscientists like Gerald Edelman and Oliver Sacks by building on their work as a computer scientist.

In this book, I present and explain computer programs and neuroscience studies that have been most valuable to me, as an AI researcher and a cognitive scientist, in understanding what biologists and social scientists are saying about context, feedback, and dynamic processes. In this exploration, I have developed a very different view of the ideas of data, perception, memory, concept, meaning, comprehension – the whole nine yards – than I assumed as part of the team developing the Mycin medical expert system at Stanford University in the 1970s. Specifically, I now understand a bit better how knowledge is *conceptual in form* (and thus cannot be exhaustively described) and how human knowledge is inherently *social in conception* (and thus is bound to personal identity). The works of the situated robot builders I will describe, as well as the works of philosophers, psychologists, and neuroscientists now contributing to cognitive science, have cheered me in explaining such ideas. They have provided the alternative notions of memory, learning, and coordination that make this book not just a theoretical exploration, but a presentation of results stemming from the situated cognition perspective.

Reader's guide

This book has four parts:

- Part I, "Representations and Memory," introduces the main ideas about knowledge in terms of the central question "What should the robot designer put inside the robot?"
- Part II, "Situated Robots," shows how neuroscientists and robot builders use a transactional perspective to invent a new kind of perceptual-motor mechanism (summarized by the chapter titles).
- Part III, "Ecological Theories," places arguments about representations and situated robot designs within a broader *systems perspective* for understanding the nature of context and change.
- Part IV, "Symbols Reconsidered," shows how different views about the nature of symbols can be reconciled by distinguishing between coupling mechanisms and inference.

In organizing the book in this way, I aim to ground difficult philosophical questions in existing robot designs and biological data. The overall effect is to work up from simpler forms of sensorimotor coordination (by which programs accomplish more than we might expect) rather than to work down from expert human reasoning (where we are prone to read into programs conceptual capabilities they don't yet have). This provides the basis in Parts III and IV for understanding a noninferential kind of categorizing mechanism, described by terms like *transaction, structural coupling,* and *dialectic.*

Although I started writing this book in the 1980s with a narrow view of *representation* and *symbol,* I developed a different understanding when trying to bring the neural, social, and psychological viewpoints together. The resulting broader view of *representing* and *symbol systems* allows me tentatively to describe how human knowledge and symbolic inference in a program are related; in particular, I reformulate my earlier research, which I call here *heuristic coordination.* Another surprise (for me) is the conclusion that the researchers who held tenaciously to the idea of *symbols* in the brain were justified in doing so, but the physical nature, development, and reconstructive aspect of these symbol *systems* is quite unlike the labels and their manipulation in descriptive models. Specifically, I show that *reference* in human understanding is a *higher-order categorization,* thus revealing how classification couplings may come to *function* as symbols in inferential reasoning (Chapter 12).

If the reader likes to jump around, then I suggest especially reading about the memory controversy (Chapter 3, in which I show that this is not a "straw man" argument) and the reformulation of symbol systems (Chapter 13, in which I show that I am not throwing the baby out with the bathwater). The discussion of different interpretations of *situated* is central to the argument (Table 1.1 in Chapter 1); there I explain why I am focusing on only one aspect of situated cognition (the nature of perception and memory) and show how this relates to the idea of social cognition (which requires a separate book). Other central themes and discussions include the following:

- The idea of a knowledge base as a kind of map, semantic interpretation, and indexical representation (Chapters 2 and 5).
- The nature of *information,* surveyed in terms of the work of Heinz von Foerster, Gregory Bateson, Humberto Maturana, and John Dewey (Chapter 4).
- Neurobiological evidence of coupling systems (Chapters 4, 6, and 7).
- Everyday examples of perceptual–conceptual coordination (Chapter 9; see especially Figure 9.6).
- Analytic frameworks for understanding and building a coupling mechanism (Chapters 8 and 10).
- An explanation of Gibson's theory of perception, relating people, robots, and mechanisms (Chapters 11 and 12).

- How well-known controversies in cognitive science can be reformulated in terms of conceptual coordination (Chapter 14).

In the Conclusions chapter, I list heuristics for engaging in scientific research on the basis of what I have learned about conceptual change in explaining the idea of situated cognition.

Part I

Representations and memory

1   Aaron's drawing

To be truly artistic, a work must also be esthetic – that is, framed for enjoyed receptive perception. Constant observation is, of course, necessary for the maker while he is producing. But if his perception is not also esthetic in nature, it is a colorless and cold recognition of what has been done, used as a stimulus to the next step in a process that is essentially mechanical. . . . Mere perfection in execution, judged in its own terms in isolation, can probably be attained better by a machine than by human art. . . . The doing or making is artistic when the perceived result is of such a nature that its qualities as perceived have controlled the question of production. . . . If the artist does not perfect a new vision in his process of doing, he acts mechanically and repeats some old model fixed like a blue print in his mind.

John Dewey, *Art as experience: Having an experience*, 1934, pp. 47–50.

Plans, drawings, and interpretations

Aaron is a robot designed to produce original drawings. Harold Cohen is the artist and programmer who designed and has improved Aaron since the 1970s. Figure 1.1 is one of Aaron's drawings. As a robot designer, Cohen has a dilemma: He wants Aaron to produce original drawings, but would they be original if he stored in the program descriptions of the pictures Aaron will make? For example, if Cohen included in Aaron a grammar that specified wha*t types of drawings* Aaron will produce – describing, for example, anatomical properties of people and plants and how they might be arranged – would the result be Cohen's drawings or Aaron's?

In effect, Cohen's dilemma is to understand the relation between internal descriptions, which he formulates and builds into the program, and outside behaviors, which observers will abstract and interpret in Aaron's drawings. To be fair (and realistic), Cohen's goal is not to create a robot artist, but "to discover the minimum configuration under which marks are understood to be images" (private communication, March 1994). In particular, can Aaron produce drawings that appear three-dimensional if Cohen doesn't store three-dimensional descriptions of the world in Aaron's memory? The problem gets more complex if you imagine that Aaron plans its drawings by preparing a three-dimensional sketch in its working memory before it draws on paper. We're caught in a recursive conundrum: What produces the three-dimensional visualization if not a description of a three-dimensional sketch?

Figure 1.1. Aaron's drawing from the "Eden Suite." (Photograph reprinted with permission from Becky Cohen.)

Mechanisms versus descriptions of behavior

To partially resolve this conflict – requiring descriptions of drawings before they are produced – Cohen discovered that Aaron could produce drawings that observers interpret three-dimensionally by laying out its drawings two-dimensionally in terms of the placement of objects relative to the bottom of the drawing. This laying-out process creates an internal plan, which is generated and stored as data structures in the computer program. In this way, the *product* (what observers perceive) and the *mechanism* (what is inside the robot) are distinct. Aaron draws by sensing and responding to local, two-dimensional features in its evolving drawing, which we interpret three-dimensionally. Aaron's planning doesn't presuppose what it is supposed to produce. As Cohen describes it:

There are descriptions of how to make drawings. That's a separate part of the program; the two parts are interdependent. The strategy for making a drawing is constrained not only by what the program knows about the outside world, but also by how that knowledge is represented. That's one of the more interesting features of the program, and it isn't entirely simple. (Private communication, March 1994)

Cohen's design is based on the essential distinction between a mechanism and an observer's perception of patterns in the robot's behavior in some environment over time. The approach suggests that mechanisms can be simpler than the descriptions observers make of the resulting behavior, an idea expounded and developed by Braitenberg in his experimental designs for robots (which he calls *vehicles*):

> When we analyze a mechanism, we tend to overestimate its complexity. In this uphill process of analysis, a given degree of complexity offers more resistance to the workings of our mind than it would if we encountered it downhill, in the process of invention. . . . The patterns of behavior described in vehicles (just illustrated) . . . undoubtedly suggest much more complicated machinery than that which was actually used in designing them. (Braitenberg, 1984, pp. 20–21)

Descriptions of Aaron's drawings are global and historical. They incorporate how the mechanism has interacted with its environment over time – a perspective the mechanism doesn't necessarily need to produce its moment-by-moment behaviors.

The idea of designing a robot by distinguishing between inside mechanism and outside appearance is a new trend in AI. Other examples of such mechanisms are the *situated robot* designs presented in Part II. These robots can navigate effectively and swiftly, with far less complicated reasoning than required by the designs of the early robots of the 1960s. Situated robots, and programs like Aaron, demonstrate that alternative ways of relating mechanism, local behavior, and product over time are possible. Controlling behavior by consulting internal maps of the world and plans for how behavior should appear to an observer is just one possible mechanism.

We know, of course, that human cognition far exceeds the capabilities of such robots, which can only do simple things like finding a Coke bottle and putting it in the garbage. Indeed, Aaron isn't looking at its drawing in the world the way people do – it "sees" only its internal two-dimensional description. As Dewey emphasizes in the chapter-opening quote, people are observers of their own behavior. Their comments, in the forms of goals, plans, and strategies, influence what they subsequently perceive and how new behaviors are composed. In an unexpected twist, Cohen has shown that when procedures for making drawings take into account how the observer of the final product will see a drawing, it is quite possible to produce an aesthetic drawing without having eyes to see the result. In some sense, Aaron, the blind artist, is like Beethoven in his later years of deafness. Internal representing goes very far indeed in anticipating how the product will be perceived.

When interpreting Aaron's drawings, we are considering the robot's goals and beliefs. This process of describing other people or robots, or reflecting on our own behavior, involves being a historian of sorts – naming past events, segmenting and ordering sequences into units, explaining relationships. The example of Aaron reveals, as Braitenberg says, that descriptions of intention characterize a pattern in an *accumulated series of behaviors*, not necessarily the mechanisms producing individual actions.

Aaron's program versus what an artist knows

Understanding the relation of computer programs, robot behavior, and an observer's descriptions is difficult, for we must distinguish between:

- Storage of pattern descriptions in the robot's memory (such as descriptions inside Aaron that relate the length of human arms to the height of the body and to what extent these proportions emerge from implicit relations in Aaron's drawing procedures).
- Attributions an observer makes about Aaron's drawings (e.g., that they have a three-dimensional aspect).
- How people imagine experiences from memory (e.g., an emotional experience that is visualized as a raucous jungle).
- Claims about human memory.

Again, Cohen doesn't propose that we evaluate Aaron's work in comparison to that of human artists. Definitional arguments about *art* and *artist* are often unproductive. Nevertheless, by relating Aaron to people, we get some important insights into Aaron's design and capabilities, as well as Cohen's experience in using Aaron. For example, in relating Aaron to a human artist, we might find that it is a good model of how an artist previsualizes a drawing two-dimensionally but a poor model of human memory (regarding the storage of anatomical descriptions) and emotional experience. In this respect, my discussion is not a criticism of Aaron, but it deliberately steps beyond Cohen's goals to extract some general lessons.

Regarding the nature of Aaron's knowledge, Cohen tells us that in a more recent version, Aaron has acquired three-dimensional knowledge of the world (800 points for the body, 100 points for the head). In other words, Cohen stores three-dimensional maps of human anatomy in Aaron's memory. What is the relation of these three-dimensional maps and an artist's knowledge? How does storing facts in a robot relate to telling a person something? Is this how we teach people to become artists?

According to Cohen, a body of anatomical facts is what an artist "needs to know to build plausible visual representations of the external world" (McCorduck, 1991, p. 192). Yet, if we say that an artist knows the 800 points that characterize a human body, we don't mean that the artist could tell us these points. Cohen had to look them up in a book. Is it perhaps the case that a mechanism like Aaron, which produces drawings from *descriptions* of people, needs to have certain kinds of descriptions that people don't need?

Quite possibly "Aaron needs to know," or equivalently, "Cohen needs to store inside Aaron," certain descriptions because of the kind of mechanism Cohen is using, that is, the architecture of his robot. And quite possibly, the very preponderance of detailed data required by Aaron, which a human artist *doesn't know as descriptions*, is precisely the kind of experimental evidence that discounts Aaron as a psychological model (at this level) of how people draw. Of course, it remains to be shown whether a mechanism based on descriptions of the world and procedures for drawing could have the same *capability* as a human artist. Perhaps the descriptions Cohen stores are functionally equivalent to his own knowledge of human form. Thus, a colleague emphasized to me:

The fact that an artist cannot explicate the 800 points that characterize the human body does not imply that the knowledge is not there in some form; just not in a form that can be articulated.

To a neuropsychologist, the question then becomes "So what *is* the form of human knowledge?" Could inarticulate (presumably nonverbal) knowledge convey flexibility in recoordination and originality that a stored body of descriptions cannot provide? Might this be relevant for understanding the nature of human learning and creativity?

Confronted with such difficult questions, Cohen once replied:

You finish up saying to yourself, rather wearily, what's *wrong* with telling the computer what it's supposed to be interested in? Why do we have this red herring on the issue of autonomy, which of course everybody is aiming at: *"You can't really say the machine is autonomous as long as you tell it something."* Nonsense. Telling it something actually makes it an entity in the first place. (McCorduck, 1991, p. 182)

But, first, no human artist is *interested in* or able to use information about 800 points describing a body. If Cohen tried to tell his peers or students all 800 points, he'd bore them to death. Second, Cohen doesn't t*ell* Aaron anything; he stores descriptions in its memory. Aaron can't carry on a conversation at all. We can quibble about how we want to define autonomy, but surely only being able to follow orders would seem to be the opposite of what we expect of an agent with its own mind. Programming is perhaps something like giving commands, but it only vaguely resembles an apprentice learning from a mentor. Third, Cohen's critiques of Aaron's work and his steady improvements in the program reveal an artistic ability that Aaron lacks. Cohen's changing the vocabulary and theory of drawing surely justifies calling him a meta-artist, as he suggests. Obviously, reconceiving objectives is a crucial part of human intelligence. If Cohen built in more descriptions and procedures for *modifying the drawing knowledge*, would Aaron then have the learning capability of people?

The experience of an artist participating in a community

Harold Cohen, using Aaron, is an acclaimed artist. It makes little sense to quibble about whether Aaron is itself an artist, for this kind of philosophical discourse won't be (and historically has not been) helpful for understanding the questions about perception and representation raised here. But we can gain some insights into human knowledge by examining Cohen's relation to the larger community in which he shows his work. For example, as Cohen points out in his lectures, the notion of accuracy of rendition, for example, is a cultural value, not an exclusively personal experience. These values and appreciations are surely part of Cohen's cultural experience, as we see in the progression of Aaron's design, which by the early 1990s produced portraits of what appear to be particular people.

To state the obvious, Aaron has no values. It can neither see its own drawings nor learn from experience. Forming theories by reflecting on patterns in one's own drawings and those of the community is part of expertise – as surely Cohen manifests in his work. As a kind of expert system, Aaron differs from people in lacking this kind of learning through participation.

For Cohen, reflection and new theorizing is potentially part of every drawing experience. Aaron's drawings are based on parametrized objects and relations fixed before any drawing begins; the program has no "experiences" at all, for it has no memory of any work it has done. Cohen's coloring exhibits flexibility and innovation with each example we see. From our perspective, we say Aaron is drawing, and obviously it cannot experience anything because it cannot learn. But consider the irony: We talk about storing knowledge of the world in Aaron's "memory." But what kind of memory is not influenced by experience? What is it a memory *of?* Can human memory be thought of as having different compartments: facts about the world that we read or are told, episodes of firsthand experience, and feelings?

Figure 1.2 attempts to tease apart the different relations Aaron and Cohen have to the resultant drawings and the community of artists. Aaron interactively constructs a drawing by following the rules and descriptions of objects stored inside it. Cohen has many roles:

- Interpreting Aaron's drawings (to see if they make sense from his experience of how plants and people are arranged on the planet Earth).
- Selecting and coloring these drawings for exhibits.
- Reinterpreting why Aaron's code does what it does.
- Reconceiving what he wants Aaron to do and formalizing this in terms of further rules and descriptions.
- Participating in the community of artists and computer scientists by creating exhibits, redesigning Aaron, and lecturing about his work.

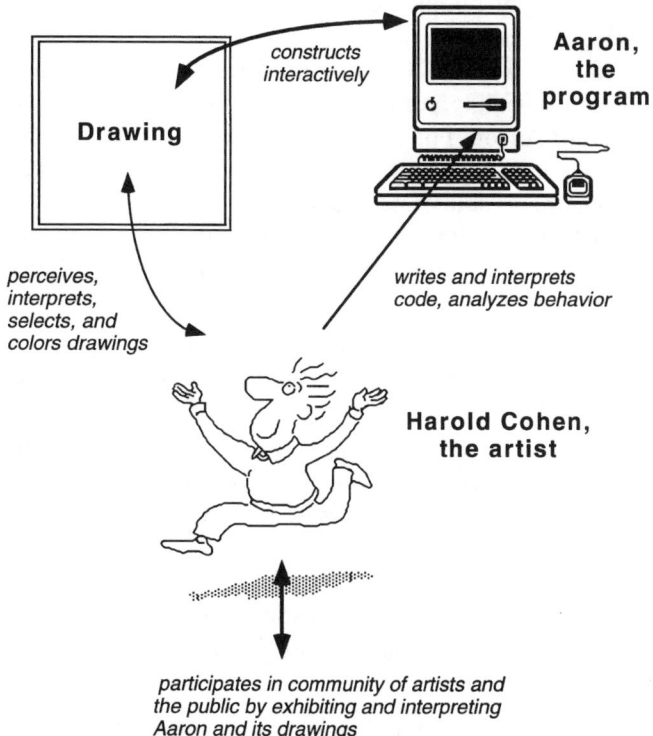

Figure 1.2. Relation of a person in a community of practice to a computer program and what it produces.

We see in this example so far that comparisons of human knowledge to computer representations are superficially easy to understand but potentially leave behind a great deal of human experience. We may say, "The computer is the artist, it does the drawing, its activities guided and determined by the program that lies in its memory (just as human artists' knowledge and skills lie in their memories)" (Herb Simon, quoted in McCorduck, 1991, p. 46). But this view plays fast and loose with what it means to be an artist, the activities of drawing, to what extent artistic knowledge consists of descriptions, and in what sense human memory is a storage place. When we say that "no humans achieve human competence without their human programmers and critics (parents, teachers, coaches) to guide them" (Vera and Simon 1993, p. 130), what are we suggesting about the relation between computer programming and human learning? Does such a summary statement adequately describe either Harold Cohen's activity in devising just a clever program or human tutelage? If we equate building Aaron with *guidance*, we partially obscure both the nature of computer tools and human learning.

Throughout Cohen and McCorduck's writing about Aaron are glimpses of another view, revealing perhaps how the human brain is quite unlike the mechanism of Aaron. For example, Cohen says, "Doing something in a structured way does not imply that one could say why one is doing it at all. Doing something deliberately does not imply that one is doing it rationally" (McCorduck, 1991, p. 124). Cohen here suggests that drawing is based on more than descriptions, more than explicit rules of thumb. Cohen adds:

If you're doing something that keeps you glued to it for 14 hours a day, every day, and there's nothing you want to do more than that, even though you don't quite know why you're doing it, or where you're going – there's passion.

Being passionate is part of being an artist. Cohen's enormous body of work, his vibrant pastel abstractions, his jungles of vines and dancing people all express his passion. And Cohen knows as much as any AI theoretician that Aaron is not passionate.

Part of being an artist or a scientist is knowing the boundaries of what you have accomplished and being sharp about what you are leaving out. Cohen summarizes the nonhuman nature of Aaron in his critique of the state of AI a few years ago:

Surely we are all aware that more people know the name of Dante than have ever heard of Fibonacci. That Bach has given more joy to more people than Isaac Newton ever did. And that Cezanne and Monet will be remembered long after Brunel's bridges have crumbled and Riemann has been forgotten. . . . Figuring out how AI is to encompass more of human life and human needs than can be measured in economic terms constitutes the greatest challenge to the field. (Cohen, 1988, oral presentation)

When we say that Aaron is an artist, what are we leaving out about *why people draw*? About *what people experience* when they see Cohen's beautifully colored versions of Aaron's drawings? About how and *why Cohen became an artist*? About how his work delights children and adults alike? What does Cohen or any artist know that Aaron does not? Could we inventory and finally capture what Cohen knows – what it means to be an artist – by *only storing more descriptions* inside the machine?

The structural and functional aspects of situatedness

To conclude this discussion of Aaron, I will organize my observations by a framework for understanding the situated nature of cognition.

Long before its usage in cognitive science, the term *situated* was prevalent in the sociology literature. The ideas are found, for example, in the

Table 1.1. *Three perspectives about situated cognition*

Perspective	Interpretation
(Functional form analysis)	
Social	Organized by interpersonal perception and action; conceptually *about* social relations (norms, roles, motivations, choreographies, participation frameworks)
(Structural mechanism analysis)	
Interactive	Dynamically coupled state–sensory–effector relations; reactive co-organization
Ready-at-hand	Physically coupled, nonobjectified connection ("seen through," without description)
(Behavioral content analysis)	
Grounded	Located in some everyday physical activity, an interactive spatial–temporal setting

writings of George Herbert Mead on the relation of knowledge, identity, and society in the 1930s and in a famous paper by C. W. Mills, "Situated Action and Vocabularies of Motive" (1940). Lucy Suchman (1987) brought these ideas to the cognitive science community in her study of how plans (such as instructions for using a photocopier) were used in actual behavior. Unfortunately, the overwhelming use of the term *situated* in AI research since the 1980s has reduced its meaning from something conceptual in form and social in content to merely "interactive" or "located in some time and place."

Situated has multiple useful meanings, which we can relate systematically by a framework of three views commonly used to describe complex systems (Table 1.1): *functional* (a choreographed activity, conceived as a social process), *structural* (a dynamically configured mechanism), and *behavioral* (a transactional process of transforming and interpreting materials in the world). There are quite a few new terms in this table; you can view it as an attempt to bring together and sort out the jargon used in different disciplines. I will first illustrate the three levels of analysis using the Aaron example.

Let's begin with the functional perspective of situated cognition. I have emphasized in this chapter that Harold Cohen's knowledge as an artist is pervaded by how he conceives his participation as an artist in our society. This conception constitutes a *choreography* by which he produces drawings, shows them, offers some for sale, writes and lectures about his work, and so on. That is, his knowledge is *functionally* developed and oriented. In engineering, *functional* may mean "working or operative"; in business one's function is a *job*. In the psychology of problem solving, a function is some cognitive goal, called a *task*. The social view of functionality emphasizes that Cohen's *intentional, purposive orientation* is with respect to the activities in which he is "being an artist." Even when he is alone, his choice about how to spend his time, what tools and results are valued, how to dress in his workshop, and what to do next are constrained by his understanding, his conception, of who he is within our society. We say, therefore, that his knowledge is inseparable from his identity; that is, Cohen's knowledge is *functionally situated* as that of a person who participates in our society in a certain way (Bannon, 1991; Wynn, 1991).

From the perspective of participation, an activity is not merely a movement or action, but a complex choreography of role, involving a sense of place, and a social identity, which *conceptually regulates* behavior. Thus, Cohen's conception of what he is doing, and hence the *context* of his actions, is always social – even when he is alone – because he conceives of himself as a person, as somebody (and indeed, some *body*). Professional expertise is therefore *contextualized* in the sense that it reflects knowledge about the community's activities of inventing, valuing, and interpreting theories, designs, and policies. This conceptualization of context has been likened to the water in which a fish swims; it is tacit, pervasive, and necessary.[1]

The second level of the situated cognition framework concerns *structural mechanism* – how perception, conception, and action are physically coordinated. In the example of Aaron, there are two examples of structural situatedness. The "interactive" aspect is perhaps most apparent in how observers perceive Aaron's drawings as three-dimensional because they conceive of the drawings as being about things in the world they have encountered. The dynamic coupling relation between perception and conception is mostly involuntary and subconscious. It requires quite an effort to look at Figure 1.1 and imagine that it is just an abstract set of lines, with no reference to trees or people. Deliberation (making inferences) doesn't help or appear to play a role. Thus human perception and meaning attribution arise together; they are coupled through experience and influence each other. (These ideas are discussed in detail in Part III.)

The "ready-at-hand" aspect of structural situatedness is illustrated by how Aaron draws on paper. Like a blind man with a cane, Aaron's drawing procedures don't require descriptions of the shape of the arm holding the paint or the height of the servomechanism on which the drawing tool is mounted. These connections and relations are implicitly integrated in the control programs that manipulate the drawing tool. An intermediate description or model of these devices is not required by the robot itself for certain kinds of manipulations. A key concern for robot builders in general is how such sensing and control develop. For example, neurophysiological studies (Chapter 4) indicate that neural structures responsible for sensorimotor mapping are capable of reorganizing themselves when an injury occurs.

The third level of the situated cognition framework relates cognition to spatial-temporal settings. Unlike the functional aspect, which broadly considers the meaning of action, or the structural aspect, which considers the internal mechanism, the behavioral aspect considers the local feedback and time-sensitive nature of action in place. For example, Aaron uses an internal representation of the drawing in order to modify locally how areas are placed, what lines are hidden, and so on. Individual changes are not planned in advance but constructed on the spot, at the time of drawing, to fit the local constraints. In this way, behavior is reflective and continuously adjusted. (Part II describes other robots with these properties.) In people, reperception of the drawing and descriptions of what is emerging play an important role, just as Cohen reflects on Aaron's output and adjusts the parameters or rewrites the rules to produce new effects (Chapter 9).

The three perspectives of the situated cognition framework are different ways of viewing human knowledge and behavior. Broadly speaking, the social sciences emphasize the functional and behavioral aspects, and neurobiology emphasizes the structural aspect. Using the framework, we can go back and sort out research programs to see what aspects have been considered or emphasized. For example, functional situatedness has been interpreted narrowly in most cognitive science models to correspond to business or professional views of work as procedural tasks. In contrast, functional situatedness concerns participation in a society from day to day – the manner in which a person spends time and makes decisions in different ways during the day, in the evening, at conferences, in meetings, on holidays, and so on. Similarly, the structural aspect has been modeled as a generally linear input–deliberation–output, without an adequate accounting of:

- The adaptiveness of perception (as in reading a poor fax transmission),
- Coordination by multiple conceptual organizers (as in playing an instrument while reading music and singing at the same time), or
- Conceptual control of perception (as in controlling figure–ground shifts in optical illusions).

To build a robot capable of learning and coordinating behavior like a human, we might attempt to understand better the three kinds of situatedness:

- How perceiving and moving are related (the structural view).
- How this physical coordination process is related to conceptualizing activities, whose content is inherently social (functional view).

- How subconscious processes of perceiving and conceiving relate to the inherently conscious process of representing in speech, text, drawings, and so on (the behavioral view).

These perspectives also help us understand why explanations of situated cognition by social scientists have been unsatisfactory for psychologists and AI researchers. First, experience with information processing predisposes researchers to suppose that situated refers to the data in the environment or that processing is specific to time and place, which are well-known ideas to anyone familiar with computer programming. Similarly, the term *social* and examples of meetings as activities suggest a behavioral interpretation of "surrounded by other people." Examples of improvisation, emphasized by situated cognition proponents, such as in shooting down rapids in a boat, suggest to a psychologist or an AI researcher the need for interactive, "dynamic replanning" and real-time, reactive movements – again, well-recognized ideas in process control and robotics. Indeed, rather than grasping the more profound claims about conception of *activity* and the mechanism of *conceptual coordination*, which suggest that all human behavior involves feedback and adaptation at multiple levels, we find some cognitive scientists in the late 1980s superficially proposing new methods for situated learning, such as using videos to teach a foreign language.

The failure to communicate the idea of situatedness was propounded by highly visible claims by social scientists in the 1980s that "knowledge is in the environment." Neural processes and individual understanding are thus made to appear inconsequential: "Learning is a process that takes place in a participation framework, not in an individual mind" (William F. Hanks, preface to Lave and Wenger, 1991, p. 15). Some social scientists suggest that opposing viewpoints are not merely wrong, they are dangerous: "Lave and Wenger . . . give us the opportunity to escape from the tyranny of the assumption that learning is the reception of factual knowledge or information" (ibid., frontpiece). Such an opening poses quite a barrier to the psychologists in the audience.[2]

In relation to the idea of situated action described by social scientists, situated cognition as I present it here is a broader inquiry, embracing all issues usually associated with cognitive psychology pertaining to memory, learning, and reasoning. Situated action is predominantly social analysis, relating behavior to *what* people conceive about their role (behavioral and functional analysis). Situated cognition is also concerned with conceptual structure (as in the relation of imagery and speech), the development of representational capability (as in learning mathematical notation), and how conceptualization occurs as neural processes (i.e., structural analysis). The implications for cognitive science are perhaps most obvious when we consider robot sensorimotor mechanisms and observer attributions (as in the story of Aaron), and this is why I have focused on situated robotics in this book.

Simplifying the situated cognition framework of Table 1.1, two ideas about conceptualization can be brought together:

- In people, physical recoordination usually involves conceptualization.
- Conceptual understanding of place, activity, role, and value is socially developed and constituted.

From the biological (structural) perspective, situated cognition is a theory of *how conceptual coordination occurs*; from the social (functional-behavioral) perspective, situated cognition can be viewed as *a theory of conceptual content* (socially constituted means that knowledge of activities – how to behave – is with respect to social relationships and purposes).

In its simplest terms, situated cognition presents the robot builder with a framework for inventing new kinds of mechanisms – a different kind of memory and controlling device – by which categorizing, associating, and sequencing behaviors are related. The difficult twist is that understanding the functional aspect of the framework requires a special notion of *goal-driven* that involves a kind of *subjectivity*. This subjectivity is not realized as possessing a subset of facts about the world or misconceptions, as in descriptive models; rather, it is a form of feedback between how the world is perceived and how the person conceives his or her identity. Conceptualizing situations, problems, and alternative actions inherently involves an aspect of self-reference in the perceptual-conceptual mechanism. That is, a person's understanding of "What is happening?" is really "What is happening *to me* now?" The impact of a new perception is not just "How does this change my knowledge of the world?" but also "How does this relate to who I am as a person?"

For example, referring again to Figure 1.2, the conceptual understanding of the activity of being an artist is simultaneously "What am I doing now?" and "Who am I in this social enterprise?" The local, minute-by-minute work of fiddling with Aaron is pervaded by Cohen's global understanding of what he will do with what he is making, the previous feedback he has received from colleagues and people at shows, and the intellectual questions he is addressing. Anticipated and reexperienced lectures and museum exhibits pervade his daily decision making. By conjecture, this understanding can be tacit (not mediated by descriptions) because of the way in which conceptualizations are coordinated in the brain. Thus, we have a different view not only of mechanism as dynamic, but also of mechanism as self-referential – hence the renewed interest in consciousness in cognitive science today.[3]

To summarize, cognition is *situated*, on the one hand, by the way conceptualizing relates to sensorimotor coordination and, on the other hand, by the way conceptualization, in conscious beings, is about the agent's role, place, and values in society. Thus, situated cognition is both a theory about *mechanism* (intellectual skills are also perceptual-motor skills) and a theory about *content* (human activity is, first and foremost, organized by conceptualizing the self as a participant-actor, and this is always with respect to communities of practice [Wenger, in preparation]). But the two aspects of functional situatedness and structural situatedness cannot be strictly separated: The conceptualization of *social action* involves a kind of internal feedback that permits people to conceive *that they are conceiving*. Put another way, people can be aware that they are engaging in activities; they can conceive of how they and others are paying attention. Internally, this conceptual ability includes being *aware* that we are juggling multiple perspectives at one moment, holding them active, naming them, weaving stories about them. Thus, we are aware that we are *deliberately* adopting a certain view of ourselves and our activity.

With the advent of modern computers, we have come to describe thinking as a sequential process of chaining descriptions in a symbolic model and to treat thoughts as storable objects. My objective in this book is to make us more aware of what the brain is doing and contrast this to what our programs are doing. In the case of Aaron and other programs based on stored descriptive models, this analysis will, at the very least, reveal the contribution people bring to bear in using these programs and why the programs work as well as they do.

Aaron illustrates the power of descriptive models in combination with a device for creating and modifying things in the world. By coupling a drawing mechanism to an internal description of how the world is changing – relying on local feedback – Cohen has minimized the need for predescriptions of how Aaron's drawings will appear. Recalling Cohen's goal of "discovering the minimum configuration under which marks are understood to be images," he leverages off the human ability to perceive three-dimensionality from two-dimensional layouts and thereby to reconstruct previously experienced conceptual relations of people, plants, rooms, and so on in Aaron's drawings. In the next chapter, we consider again the relation between descriptions, mechanisms, and observer attributions of meaning. In this case, the story of Mycin, people once again bring their implicit understanding to bear as they interpret the program's questions and rules and provide the necessary feedback that couples the program's models to what is happening in the world.

2   Mycin's map

Afterward, they'd got Rudy's foreman to let him off, and, in a boisterous, whimsical spirit of industrial democracy, they'd taken him across the street for a beer. Rudy hadn't understood quite what the recording instruments were all about, but what he had understood, he'd liked: that he, out of thousands of machinists, had been chosen to have his motions immortalized on tape.

> Kurt Vonnegut, *Player piano*, 1952, p. 9

It seems preferable to avoid calling the body of knowledge a memory.... Knowledge can only be created dynamically in time.

> Allen Newell, First Presidential Address to the American Association of Artificial Intelligence, 1980, in Newell (1982), pp. 101, 108

A simple introduction to knowledge representations

Mycin is a computer program developed in the 1970s by Ted Shortliffe and his colleagues. Mycin was designed to diagnose certain infectious diseases and prescribe appropriate antibiotic drugs. Mycin's memory, which we called a *knowledge base*, consists mostly of rules relating a patient's symptoms, laboratory tests, diseases, and drugs.

Here is a typical Mycin rule:

```
If:   (AND   (SAME CNTXT G001 G002)
             (SAME CNTXT G003 G004)
             (SAME CNTXT G005)
             (SAME CNTXT G006))
Then:
             (CONCLUDE* CNTXT G007 TALLY
                '((G008 400)
                  (G009 200)
                  (G010 300))))
```

The rule states that if Mycin has evidence that G001 has the value G002 and G003 has the value G004, and if G005 and G006 are true, then G007 is G008 with moderate certainty, G009 with weak certainty, and G010 with weak certainty. We call these G00X labels *clinical parameters*. To get information about a clinical parameter, Mycin applies additional rules or it asks the user. This process of asking for information about a particular patient and prescribing therapy for the patient is called a *consultation dialogue*.

When Mycin wants to get information about G005, for example, it prints on the computer screen "Has the patient undergone surgery?" Mycin's knowledge base contains the description

G005

PROMPT: (has * "undergone surgery?")

If you reply, "I'm not sure; the patient was supposed to be operated on last week," Mycin won't understand you. Mycin doesn't understand what an operation is. It is a kind of symbolic calculator, storing and manipulating labels like G005, which we call *symbols*. In general, the term *symbol* in computer programming refers to data expressed as strings of letters and/or numbers (e.g., "G005," "surgery," "CONCLUDE*"). *Symbolic programming*, involving networks of associations between symbols (like G010 and G007), is historically contrasted with numeric programming.

Described in this way, Mycin is easily understood as being a tool, a kind of calculator, that can help medical personnel diagnose and treat diseases. But as we saw in studying Aaron, the behavior of such a tool seductively invites anthropomorphic metaphors. And our language tends to be loose. We say things like "Mycin knows that neurosurgery can cause bacterial meningitis" and "Mycin diagnoses diseases." Many AI researchers in the 1970s and 1980s would say that, just as Aaron is an artist, Mycin is a medical expert. In this example, we will examine in more detail how Mycin is constructed and how its symbol network relates to human knowledge.

Mycin's knowledge base doesn't actually consist of symbols like G004 or people would find it too difficult to read the rules when debugging the program. The internal notation for rule number 512, stated earlier, is actually[1]

RULE512

```
IF:  (AND  (SAME CNTXT TREATINF MENINGITIS)
           (SAME CNTXT TYPE BACTERIAL)
           (SAME CNTXT SURGERY)
           (SAME CNTXT NEUROSURGERY))
THEN:
           (CONCLUDE* CNTXT COVERFOR TALLY
             '((STAPHYLOCOCCUS 400)
             (STREPTOCOCCUS 200)
             (E.COLI 300)))
```

Symbols like TREATINF and COVERFOR are neither English nor medical jargon. The programmers, called *knowledge engineers*, made up these names as abbreviations. Each symbol is an *atom* or primitive element in the Lisp programming language in which Mycin is coded. Each symbol

Table 2.1. *Definition of SURGERY in Mycin*

SURGERY	
PROMPT	T
TRANS	(* has "undergone surgery")
USED–BY	(RULE512)
ASKFIRST	T

has a list of properties and values that define how the parameter is to be used by Mycin. Lisp is designed to make it easy for a programmer to describe such networks of relations between symbols. Table 2.1 presents the internal data structure that describes the relation between the symbol SURGERY and other symbols in the Mycin knowledge base.

The symbols in the left column of the table are called *properties*. The right column gives the *value* for each property. In general, the value can be any expression in the Lisp programming language: another symbol, a string of characters, or a list of these. RULE512 is another symbol; IF and THEN are two of its properties.

At this point, it may be useful to summarize some terminology. The symbols in Mycin, called *production rules* (e.g., RULE512) and *clinical parameters* (e.g., SURGERY), along with their properties, are commonly called *knowledge representations* because they represent the knowledge of a human expert. Commonly, rules and parameters are simply called *knowledge*; hence the collection is called a *knowledge base*. The rules and clinical parameters are simply called *representations*. Until about 1990, in the AI community the term *representation* referred exclusively to some expression stored in a computer memory, consisting of networks of symbols. In effect, this symbolic approach to building intelligent robots assumes that Lisp expressions, knowledge representations, human knowledge, and internal representations are equivalent in form and functionality.

Mycin's rules and clinical parameter property tables are written in a *knowledge representation language* whose syntax specifies the structure of rules and parameters and what kinds of symbols are allowable (e.g., the fact that either T or a list of strings and symbols is an allowable value for a PROMPT property). In this sense, knowledge bases constitute a kind of text, different from a natural language like English and the programming languages in which they are encoded. A knowledge representation language is a disciplined way of using a programming language (including a set of special elements, such as rules and clinical parameters); a knowledge base is encoded in a particular knowledge representation language. We can show this as three levels:

Mycin's knowledge base
(rules and clinical parameters)

Mycin's knowledge representation
language

Lisp programming language

A rule is composed of *propositions* such as (SAME CNTXT TREATINF MENINGITIS), which is displayed in English as "The infection which requires therapy is meningitis." Each proposition is an expression in Mycin's knowledge representation language. TREATINF is a *symbol*, and the entire proposition in which it appears is a symbol structure. The symbol TREATINF, together with its properties and their values (Table 2.1), is frequently called a *frame*, *schema*, or *concept*. In this book, I refer to such expressions as *descriptions* because the people who wrote them intended them to describe objects and events in the world, including the reasoning processes of human experts.

Returning to Table 2.1, the properties in Mycin's knowledge base are used by a complex computer program written in Lisp, which controls how Mycin uses its rules and interacts with the user. We call this program Mycin's *knowledge base interpreter*, also known as an *inference engine*. Tables like Table 2.1 indicate to the interpreter how to ask people for information, how to display information, what rules use this information, and whether to ask for additional information before trying to deduce a value from rules.

Note that the programmer has devised a shorthand notation: The symbol T tells the interpreter that the PROMPT can be constructed from the TRANS property. On the other hand, the value of ASKFIRST, also T, means "Yes, you should ask the user about surgery before trying to infer information from rules." This is a simple example of how the network of relations in the knowledge base is a kind of code that makes sense only to people who know how the code is manipulated by the interpreter program. Put another way, representing knowledge in a computer program is a process of *encoding* concepts and their relations in symbols, with an under-standing of how these encodings cause the inference engine to operate in different ways.

Using the TRANS property of clinical parameters, Mycin can display its rules in a form that medical personnel can read:

Rule 512

If: The infection which requires therapy is meningitis,
     the type of the infection is bacterial,
     the patient has undergone surgery, and
     the patient has undergone neurosurgery,

Then:
Conclude that the organisms which might be causing the
infection are:
Staphylococcus (moderate evidence), *Streptococcus* (weak
evidence), and *E. coli* (weak evidence).

A special program generates these phrases by nesting TRANS strings,
negating verbs, and adding punctuation. The programmer's wording is replicated mechanically wherever the symbols appear (including syntactic
blunders; the phrase should be "that might be causing the infection"
because COVERFOR is a subset of organisms that the program is
considering).

Programs have been written to go in the opposite direction, from English
text to knowledge base symbols and properties. Programs for entering
new rules into Mycin can thus parse simple English phrases into the
internal notation of symbols and properties. Although the program can
recognize that "surgery" refers to SURGERY (the internal symbol),
Mycin doesn't understand what words like "undergone" or "requires"
mean. Other AI programs have been devised that represent the meaning of
such words, using more distinctions than the properties shown here for
defining SURGERY. For example, SURGERY might be defined as a kind
of medical procedure. But Mycin appeared to work well without such
refinements.

It should now be clear that the text of Mycin's rules (expressed in a coded
shorthand) is not just a physician's or knowledge engineer's description of
medical facts and reasoning but constitutes part of the *mechanism* for
diagnosing patients, explaining reasoning, and modeling students' reasoning. The text specifies what to do, in the sense that rules and properties are
interpreted literally – as pointers to other structures and switches for controlling the program's operation – not according to what the symbols mean
to human readers. In distinguishing between human knowledge and computer representations, this is certainly a provocative place to begin. When
we say, "Mycin understands the relation of surgery to bacterial meningitis,"
how is that different from the understanding of the physicians who collab-
orated with knowledge engineers in writing such rules?

A knowledge base is a kind of map

One way of understanding knowledge representations is to relate knowledge bases to maps. Consider a map of the Stanford University campus
(Figure 2.1).

A map is a kind of representation with a specific purpose; the Stanford
map is designed to help people find their way around the campus. In

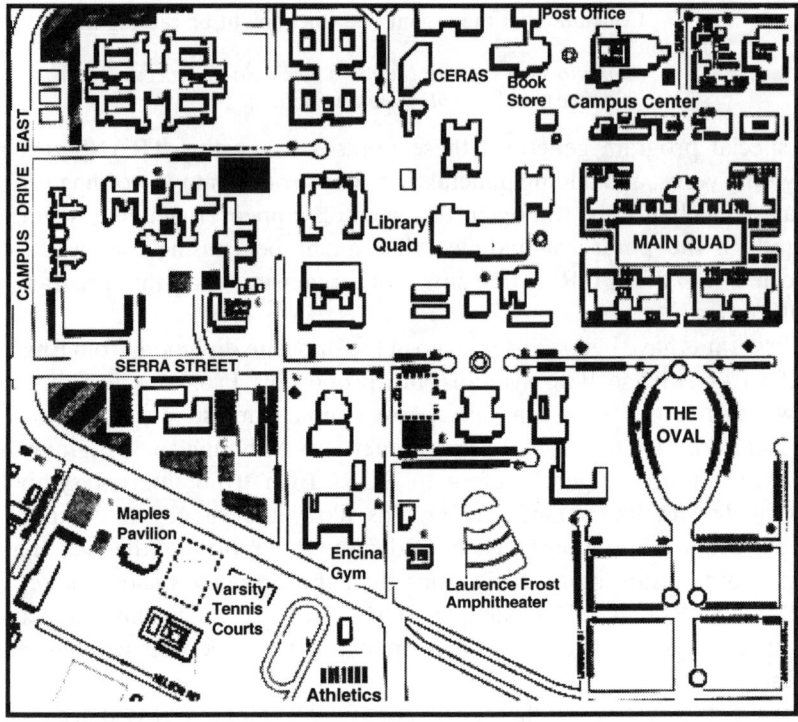

Figure 2.1. Map of the Stanford University campus (shading indicates different kinds of parking areas). (Adapted with permission.)

particular, this map is useful for finding buildings and parking places. If we wanted to drill for oil in this area of California, we'd need a different kind of map.

Similarly, knowledge bases are selective models of things in the world designed to help people do something. Mycin's network of symbols comprises models of patients, diseases, and drug therapies. In effect, Mycin's "expertise" consists of relating a model of a person to a model of disease to a model of therapies. For example, the fact that the patient is an alcoholic might suggest that *Diplococcus pneumoniae* is causing the symptoms of meningitis, which suggests that penicillin should be administered to the patient. This chaining of models is called *heuristic classification*. Many expert systems work this way.

General versus situation-specific models

When the Mycin program is running, two kinds of descriptions are in the program's memory: general descriptions such as RULE512 and situation-

Table 2.2. *Portion of Mycin's situation-specific model*

PATIENT-412	
AGE	((43 1000))
NEUROSURGERY	((YES –1000))
TREATINF	((UNKNOWN 1000))

specific descriptions, which are propositions about a particular patient. For example, situation-specific descriptions include "The age of Bill is 43" and "Bill has not undergone neurosurgery." Assuming that Bill is patient number 412, these situation-specific descriptions appear internally in the form shown in Table 2.2.

This is just a small part of the network of symbols that Mycin's interpreter constructs when diagnosing PATIENT-412. Other tables will record what questions have been asked, what information the user supplied, what rules have been applied, what information was inferred, and so on. As before, we see that this information is encoded in a language invented by the knowledge engineer. For example, ((YES −1000)) indicates that the value is "definitely not YES"; that is, PATIENT-412 has not undergone neurosurgery.

The situation-specific network of symbols and properties constructed by Mycin's interpreter is called a *situation-specific model*. In contrast, the symbols and properties in the knowledge base – consisting of hundreds of rules like RULE512 and hundreds of clinical parameters like SURGERY (Table 2.1) – constitutes the *general model*.[2] In effect, the situation-specific model is a kind of database of facts with time stamps. The general model is a set of principles that can be used to explain why these facts occur together (e.g., how Bill's headache is related to the organisms growing in his blood culture). Indeed, Mycin's ability to chain situation-specific models – relating facts about Bill and his life to facts about processes occurring inside his body to alternative therapy processes – is the reason we attribute knowledge and intelligence to the program.

The term *model* is used here in the ordinary scientific way in which a notation is devised to represent some phenomenon of interest in the world. The expressions in the situation-specific model are said to be true insofar as there is a correspondence between these descriptions and what we as observers take to be true in the world. Part of the difficulty in understanding the relation between human knowledge and computer representations is that many AI researchers in the 1970s and 1980s used the term *model* to refer to simulation models, not taxonomic models as in Mycin. It was common to say that "Mycin isn't model based." Both simulation models (describing the causal, spatial, and temporal relations between objects and events) and taxonomic models (which describe processes or structures more abstractly) are constructed as networks of symbols (terms in a language). Both are stored descriptions of how the world appears and how to behave to change the world.[3]

Searching a descriptive model

To continue our analogy of how a knowledge base is like a map, consider how we use the map of Stanford University to solve problems. The map is used to answer questions about our actions in the world, such as "Where should I park my car if I am going to the Center for Educational Research (CERAS)?" To use this map, we need to refer to the key. The key indicates how the objects on the map correspond to objects in the world. The key of the Stanford map indicates how different areas may be used by people (e.g., parking lots, athletic fields, pedestrian passages, bicycling routes).

Mycin's knowledge base also has a key for interpreting its rules and other representations. The key describes the syntax of rules as a set of *templates* for clauses. For example, in Mycin the premise (IF part) of RULE512 can be parsed using two basic templates: (SAME CNTXT PARM VALU) and (SAME CNTXT PARM). Using this key, Mycin's interpreter can determine that the first proposition in RULE512 – (SAME CNTXT TREATINF MENINGITIS) – requires that the infection be MENINGITIS (the "value" of the clinical parameter TREATINF). This enables Mycin to take apart its rules to apply them or "explain" how information was inferred or used, as well as to assemble new rules. We'll return to the issue of how having a key relates to understanding a map in a moment.

Besides a key, we need a process for using the map to solve practical problems. Examining the Stanford map, we see that we can draw certain inferences from it. For example, the bookstore and the post office are connected. The parking lots closest to the main quadrangle are several buildings away. In this way, we are using the map as a model of the world. This is precisely how Mycin's interpreter examines the knowledge base to find connections between descriptions of people, diseases, and drugs. With the addition of heuristic associations, like Mycin's rules, a computer program could use the Stanford map to give advice to someone about where to park a car and how to get from one point to another. With information about distances and traffic patterns, the program could provide advice about when to arrive on campus before a meeting.

The process of examining a descriptive model to apply it to a specific situation is so important in AI that the term *search* is readily recognized by any AI researcher as an area of research specialization. And just as descriptive models have been equated with knowledge, searching general models to construct a situation-specific model has been equated with *reasoning*.

Consider, for example, the process of answering the question "Where should I park if I am going to CERAS?" First, you might look on the map to find CERAS. Then you might look at the area around this building, examining its spatial relation to parking areas. To save time when solving problems like this, you might have examined the map ahead of time and created a list of parking areas, which you could now examine to see which is closest to CERAS. No matter how you search the map, you will be looking for a path connecting two objects – CERAS and a parking lot – that will be spatially related in some way.

Mycin diagnoses diseases and prescribes therapy in a similar way. To save time when giving advice during a consultation dialogue with a user, the program compiles an index relating symptoms, laboratory tests, diagnoses, and therapies (like compiling a list of buildings and parking areas on the Stanford map). Then, to answer the question "What is the proper treatment for this patient?" the program searches its knowledge base to find a path between the patient's symptoms and antibiotics. In Mycin this path is simply defined by its rules in the way RULE512 relates MENINGITIS to SURGERY, E.COLI, and then PENICILLIN.

Most medical knowledge bases today – two decades after Mycin's development – indicate spatial, temporal, and causal relations between symptoms, disease processes, and antibiotics. In Mycin, the relations are *logical* (conjunction, disjunction, negation, and implication) and *evidential* (by which degrees of certainty are combined). In other programs, the symbol CAUSES might be used to state "(CAUSES NEUROSURGERY E.COLI)"; that is, "Neurosurgery causes *E. coli*." An additional network of causal propositions might describe how this process occurs. But in any event, the inference process is essentially the same: The program's interpreter examines the general model to answer questions about how things in the world are related, creating a situation-specific model.

Now we are ready to consider the idea of interpretation. Consider a computer program whose knowledge base includes the Stanford University map. We can build a useful map-reading program that gives advice about parking, for example, with only superficial descriptions stored inside about what the terms on the map mean. By searching the network, the map-reading program might tell us where we can find art on campus. But just as Mycin doesn't know what surgery is, this map-reading program doesn't know what art is. Similarly, if we don't represent any relation between tennis, athletics, football, and a gym, the model will only indicate that they appear in adjacent areas of the campus. The program doesn't understand what a sports game is, but it could help you reserve a tennis court.

A program's ability to interpret a knowledge base is determined by the *relations* the knowledge engineer represents between different symbols. Relations might be stated directly in a rule or by a property table (Table 2.1) or they might be stated indirectly as generalizations such as "You can walk between connected buildings without getting wet." A program with a mixture of specific facts about the world (like the Stanford map) and a large collection of generalizations can answer a wide variety of questions and may amaze us by its ability to draw useful inferences.

Symbolic calculators like Mycin can make predictions about the weather, diagnose diseases, design complex computer circuits, plan recombinant DNA experiments, control chemical plants, and so on. All these programs work by constructing internally a situation-specific model from a general model. The general model represents how the system or process in the world is put together (its parts and structure), how it normally behaves, how its components function together, and how it might be operated. As such, descriptive modeling is a powerful technique in science, engineering, and business.

The map isn't the territory

AI researchers commonly call the expressions in a knowledge base *internal representations*, in contrast to expressions that appear on the computer screen or in a hardcopy printout of the program, called *external representations*. Obviously, there is an isomorphic relation (a one-to-one mapping) between the external and internal representations of Mycin's models. But what is the relation of Mycin's knowledge base to a physician's knowledge?

In the 1970s, and for many researchers today, it was common to suppose that a human expert writing down a rule like RULE512 is creating an external representation of linguistic expressions stored in his or her memory. That is, something like RULE512 was stored – in the form of linguistic symbols – in the brain before the rule was ever written down or uttered. By this view, knowledge representations in a computer program are assumed to have a one-to-one correspondence to human knowledge. From here it is but a short leap of logic to conclude that Mycin is an expert because, like an expert physician, "it has medical knowledge stored in its memory."

As should now be obvious, descriptive models bear no necessary relation to human knowledge. Indeed, even though many people can readily spout a wealth of rules and relations about their area of expertise, "extracting facts and rules from an expert's head" is a poor characterization of the work involved in creating a program like Mycin. Very often creating a knowledge base requires inventing new terminology and developing an understanding of causal, temporal, and spatial relations that exceeds what anyone has known before. Creating a knowledge base is often a scientific effort of empirically constructing and testing models. What then is the relation between human knowledge and the symbols and descriptions in a computer's knowledge base?

When I show you a map of the Stanford University campus, it isn't necessary to say, "This is not Stanford University; this is a representation of the campus. It isn't the campus itself." But in the mid-1980s, when I showed knowledge engineers RULE512 and said, "This is not the expert's knowledge; this is a representation of knowledge. It isn't knowledge itself," I was confronted by nervous chuckles and strange stares. To the knowledge engineer creating Mycin and many other expert systems, the map is the territory: A representation is knowledge because human knowledge consists of representations stored in the brain. Just as there is a one-to-one mapping between Mycin's internal coding of RULE512 and how the rule is displayed on the screen, surely there must be a one-to-one mapping between a person's knowledge (long-term memory) and what he or she says about the world. The reformulation of concepts, memory, and action in situated cognition (Table 1.1) leads us to question this point of view.

Models, such as the Stanford map or Mycin's knowledge base, are tools created and used by people. Descriptive models can be used to *represent* knowledge, as in expert systems and the student models of an instructional program. But when people use tools, when they interpret what a word or a rule means in an ambiguous situation, they are doing something more and different from Mycin's process of searching its map. Behind my questioning is the puzzle: What enables people to create a program like Mycin and use it as a tool? How is this process of creating and interpreting models different from what Mycin does?

Explaining rules

If we systematically replace all the symbols in Mycin's rules by nonsense labels (for example, replace E.coli by G009), the program will work exactly as before. But to the knowledge engineer who modifies the program, the result would be as chaotic as jumbling the names in a phone directory. In this section, I consider how the meaning of the rules – why they are believed to be true by knowledge engineers – inherently lies outside the program. I am not referring to an arbitrary outside observer's opinion, but rather to the understanding of the people who create the program – and having such understanding is crucial for them to construct a coherent model that works. Perhaps surprisingly, the meaning of Mycin's symbols and rules changes over time with the experience of the physician experts and knowledge engineers who build the program: What a given rule means to the designers can change, despite the fact that the rule is not modified in any way. What the symbols refer to and why the model is believed to be accurate can change. In effect, what the designers say the program "knows" is not just the symbols and rules stored inside. So in some paradoxical way – revealing conceptual confusion – *what the designers claim the program knows may not influence its behavior.* Although this is not surprising in people (a child may do something he knows is wrong), it seems rather odd for a device that supposedly operates by manipulating knowledge that people have put inside. If knowledge is what observers say symbolic structures *mean*, how can we say that "Mycin's knowledge causes its behavior"? This puzzle arises because we have equated descriptive models with knowledge. Mycin's stored descriptions do cause its behavior, but in people knowledge includes conceptual relations that are not all reducible to words. The puzzle is solved when we distinguish the product (the knowledge base) from the process that enables it to be created and used.

To illustrate how describing and meaning are related, let's begin with a simple Mycin rule: "If the patient is less than 7 years old, then do not prescribe tetracycline." Most readers will know what all the words mean but will still not understand why the rule is correct. In what sense does Mycin understand this rule? If Mycin doesn't understand the rule, how can it be said to be *reasoning*? We say that this is one of the rules that Mycin "knows." This is knowing in the sense of memorizing, not understanding and interpreting. The rule concerning tetracycline and the age of a patient is *a representation* of what expert physicians know.

Why would Mycin need to know why its rules are correct? First, applying a rule to a specific situation may require interpreting it in a flexible way. Tetracycline discolors the permanent teeth of a child if they are growing when the drug is administered. A physician or nurse may detect that this child's permanent teeth are still growing, even though he is a few months over the age of 7, so tetracycline still shouldn't be prescribed. That is, Mycin isn't *reasoning about* its medical rules; it is applying them blindly. But in the parlance of descriptive cognitive modeling, reasoning includes any manipulation of symbol structures that creates situation-specific models from general models. The distinction between symbolic calculators and human reasoning is thereby blurred.

How often do medical physicians reconceive the meaning of terminology to fit new circumstances? Are Mycin's rules supposed to correspond to inaccessible neural processes in the expert's head or to words on paper that are comprehended and interpreted by people? When people do reconfigure models on the fly, are they drawing only on other descriptive models? Such questions were not considered in the development of Mycin when we simply assumed the following: The rules are knowledge, knowledge is stored in the program's memory, knowledge is stored in the expert's memory, and knowledge is what makes an agent intelligent.[4]

Understanding what a model *means* is especially important when it is augmented to cover additional cases. For example, at one time, there was a rule in Mycin that said, "If there are two positive cultures from a nonsterile site, then the organisms found on these cultures are significant." A culture is a laboratory test designed to reveal whether organisms are present in a sample taken from a patient by providing a medium for bacterial growth and allowing time for the organisms to grow. When a sample of material is taken from a nonsterile site, such as the sputum or skin, organisms normally found there may be included in the sample. Heuristically, the fact that two samples resulted in the growth of organisms on the culture suggests that the culture has not been contaminated by normal flora, but represents organisms causing an infection. To show this graphically:

Rule 1:

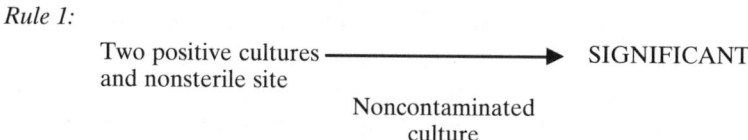

Later, Mycin's knowledge base was extended to handle other kinds of infections. The physicians and knowledge engineers wanted to include a rule to ensure that when organisms associated with cystitis (a urinary tract infection) were found, antibiotic drugs were prescribed by the program unless there was evidence of pyuria (pus in the urine). Examining the network of symbols and rules, the knowledge engineers found that they could codify this effect by writing a new rule for the symbol SIGNIFICANT as follows:

Rule 2:

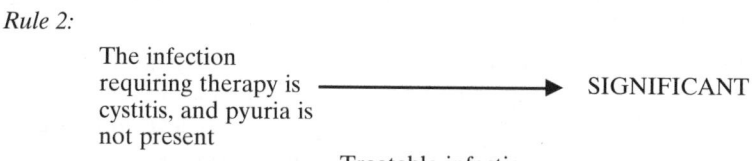

Here no culture is involved. SIGNIFICANT is now interpreted to mean "evidence of an infection that should be treated." Crucially, this meaning of SIGNIFICANT subsumes the earlier interpretation: Growth of a noncontaminated culture is also evidence of an infection that should be treated. The meaning of SIGNIFICANT in Rule 1 has changed even though the rule itself has not been modified. In effect, in order to reuse the symbol SIGNIFICANT in a different context, the designers of Mycin generalized its meaning. Although the UPDATED-BY property of SIGNIFICANT now points to both Rules 1 and 2, there is no record in the program that people have reconceived what the symbol SIGNIFICANT means.

To summarize our example, from the perspective of people interpreting the knowledge base, the meaning of SIGNIFICANT depends in part on the set of rules that can be used to infer information about it. Two points stand out:

- We call the SIGNIFICANT rule a knowledge representation, but what is represented is as much in our interpretive commentary – what we say about the rule in context – as in the rule description itself.
- The meaning of symbols in the knowledge base cannot be determined by examining rules in isolation. Meaning is not a tablelike mapping from names to things, but concerns how people interpret objects and events in the context of actions they may take.

What SIGNIFICANT means or why the individual rules are valid has no effect on Mycin's behavior per se. The program is only a symbolic calculator, manipulating its inputs and rules as surely as a numeric calculator makes algebraic and numeric manipulations without knowing whether 685,000 is a mortgage or the cost of a truck full of garlic. We do not attribute knowledge of mathematics to a calculator, so why do we attribute knowledge of medicine to Mycin? If Mycin were a model of neural processes, it might not make sense to ask, "What do the symbols mean?" But Mycin's knowledge base is a medical model – a description of disease processes and therapies. A person using such descriptions without knowing what they mean would be quickly uncovered as a charlatan. Only the certification of Mycin as a map for a narrow range of well-defined problems allows us to view it as competent at all.

On the other hand, it is important to acknowledge that attributing knowledge to Mycin is crucial when creating and using the program. As Newell explained in his famous *knowledge-level analysis*, knowledge is attributed by people as part of an explanation of a program's rationality. When people attempt to understand a sequence of questions asked by Mycin, they attribute knowledge to Mycin. These attributions are essential for interacting with the program and gaining confidence in its validity as a model of patients, diseases, and therapies.

Fodor (1980) has referred to what researchers actually do as *methodological solipsism* by virtue of developing a machine that lives only in a "notational world":

People who do machine simulation . . . often advertise themselves as working on the question [of] how thought (or language) is related to the world. . . . Whatever else they are doing, they certainly aren't doing that. The very assumption that defines their field – viz., that they study mental processes qua formal operations on symbols – guarantees that their studies won't answer the question how the symbols so manipulated are semantically interpreted. . . . If the programmer chooses to interpret "Robin Roberts won 28" as a statement about Robin Roberts (e.g., as the statement that he won 28 [games of baseball]), that's all well and good, but it's no business of the machine's. The machine has no access to that interpretation, and its computations are in no way affected by it. The machine doesn't know what it's talking about, it doesn't care; about is a semantic relation. (p. 65)[5]

Fodor accurately describes the practice of descriptive cognitive modeling; but he misses how a user's interpretation of Mycin's questions affects the machine's computations by changing the data available to it. The preservation of "aboutness" – Mycin's coupling to the world – occurs by virtue of human comprehension and manipulation of clinical parameters. The construction of an accurate situation-specific model is a joint effort. To underhand how a *user makes Mycin into a representational system*, we must distinguish further between different kinds of interpretation.

Syntactic and semantic interpretation

Many people have noted that the word *interpret* is used in strikingly different ways when talking about a rule in a knowledge base. The distinction is summarized by saying that Mycin interprets its rules syntactically, but people interpret them semantically.

When Mycin interprets Rule 1 and Rule 2, it need only match the symbols and their associated properties, without regard for what they refer to in the world. Our thought experiment of replacing all of Mycin's clinical parameters by nonsense symbols demonstrates that the process of interpretation by searching networks and matching symbols is purely syntactic. Mycin interprets Rule 1 by using the *formal properties* of the symbol SIGNIFICANT (see Table 2.1). When we say, "Mycin follows a rule," we mean that it does so literally. By common use of the terms, we would say that Mycin's *use* of rules is *mechanical*, not intelligent.

When people read Mycin's rules and say what SIGNIFICANT means in the broad world of medicine, they are interpreting semantically. A human observer semantically interprets a representation by providing a commentary about it, indicating what the symbols refer to, why the network is correct, and how it came to have its present form. We interpret Rule 2 semantically by supplying a context for understanding the disease process, relating the rule to Rule 1, explaining why Rule 2 was added to the knowledge base, and so on. We might say, "This is one of a dozen rules that interpret culture results as possible evidence of disease. Rules relevant to cystitis were added later, broadening the meaning of SIGNIFICANT." What SIGNIFICANT means is conceived through our interests, our sociohistorical background, and our intentions in creating Mycin – all of which lie outside the program itself.

When we say that Mycin has *representations* stored inside, we are claiming that the symbol structures of its knowledge base are meaningful to us. This is because Mycin's representations are descriptions of the world and must be if the program is to diagnose diseases and construct therapy plans. Lisp atoms like TREATINF have meaning – *they are symbolic* – precisely because a person can give them a semantic interpretation. The idea of symbolic programming originated in this interpretive process. The constructs in descriptive models are necessarily meaningful to the human designers. The very idea of a descriptive model is that the terms and relations refer to things in the world that the model is about.

The idea of symbol systems divides into two paths here, as I will discuss in detail in Part IV. One path of development extends the definition of symbol to mean "any pattern that denotes" and broadens the idea of denotation to mean any inherent "distal access" to some other internal or external process (a definition promoted by Allen Newell [1990]). By this extension, the pattern may not be a static thing, but rather structural changes within a system over time, as occur in visual processing (Chapter 4). By this view, some structure-processes are representations by virtue of *how they function internally*. For example, CULTURE-1 is a symbol that Mycin uses to designate records it has accumulated about what we call "the first culture we told Mycin about." Mycin's use of CULTURE-1 as a pointer is called a *syntactic relation*; any shape or form could be substituted – it is just a pattern that denotes.

The second path of development considers that denotation or *reference* is conceptual, as illustrated by the interpretation of what SIGNIFICANT means to human readers. Internally, the relation between SIGNIFICANT and the conceptualization of its meaning is more than a pointer. There must be a *conception* of the idea that a name could have a meaning, that meaning (in this case) is a relation between a formal name and a process in the world, and indeed, even that there are objects in the world that can be described. The human's use of CULTURE-1 as a name is called a *semantic relation*, and the label is conventional. Such denotation requires that the agent *understand what reference is*.

These two perspectives are useful, but they have been confused by descriptive cognitive modeling. Paraphrasing Bertrand Russell, researchers who identify the two kinds of denotation (or interpretation) say that there are "representations all the way down," such that there is no difference between neural categorizations and TREATINF. By this view, the internal–external distinction doesn't matter. All reasoning is just *symbol manipulation*, subconscious or not. For example, "case-based" models of memory suggest that past experience is stored as descriptions of events and that people comprehend text only by referring to such remembered descriptions. By this view, the process of commenting on what words mean is another sy*ntactic* process of indexing and assembling stored definitions and properties, at ever smaller grain sizes of meaning and attribution.

The alternative perspective on denotation is that people draw on more than other descriptions when they understand and generate text like Mycin's rules. What other means of representing the world and behavior might exist in the brain? This is the fundamental question I want to press, one that goes unasked when cognition is equated with the inferential processes of descriptive models. As Newell states in the opening quote of this chapter, we should perhaps think of knowledge not as a stored body of things, but rather as a capability constructed in action. We will find that the process of perceptual-motor coordination is key to understanding how knowledge develops and what it accomplishes.

In the development of my thinking about situated cognition – in considering the nature of explanation of rules, conceptual broadening, and deliberate structuring of knowledge bases – I concluded that understanding the nature of human memory as a coordinating mechanism is central if we are to properly relate human knowledge and computer programs. I discovered that the limitations of the stored traces or engram theory of memory have been of central concern in psychology for 100 years; indeed, criticisms of descriptive cognitive modeling were in print in the 1970s, even as we were creating Mycin. I review the history of this controversy in the next chapter and show how it leads to the experimental designs of situated robots and new biological models.

3   Remembering controversies

I think that human knowledge is essentially active. To know is to assimilate reality into systems of transformations. . . . I find myself opposed to the view of knowledge as a copy, a passive copy of reality. . . . Knowing an object does not mean copying it – it means acting upon it.

Jean Piaget, *Genetic epistemology*, 1970, p. 15

For the genetic epistemologist, knowledge results from continuous construction, since in each act of understanding, some degree of invention is involved.

Ibid., p. 77

This chapter discusses an enduring controversy about human memory: the distinction between a storage place and the ability to reconstruct or reenact some behavior. A central tenet of descriptive cognitive modeling is that human *long-term* memory can be replicated by a collection of stored statements in some language, such as Aaron's anatomical maps of the human body and Mycin's disease taxonomy. To understand criticisms of this claim, it is helpful to understand the historical nature of the debate: What have been the essential objections? What is the evidence for these claims? What is proposed instead?

Researchers have different attitudes about this scientific debate. Some people, like myself, are fascinated to find that the very issues that grip us today were clearly discussed and argued 100 years ago – with insightful observations about the directions psychology should take. Other people find historical statements to be either obviously irrelevant (because there were no computer models back then) or merely expressions of opinion (because they are often philosophical). I agree that the weight of the argument should rest, where possible, on the models and methods of today (which I present in Chapter 4 and Part II). Nevertheless, I believe that the scholarship of cognitive science and AI needs to be improved, and this entails at least laying out the historical trends and opposing camps.

My presentation has four parts: a brief overview of claims by early psychologists, a selection of published claims about descriptive cognitive modeling starting with the information processing psychology of Newell and Simon, discussion of the reactions to this work by the contextualists and connectionists, and finally, an appraisal of connectionist models. My presentation establishes that the debate about memory has persisted throughout the history of psychology. How memory works is a very difficult theoretical issue involving the nature of self-organizing processes, recurrent-reconstructed processes, and modularization as structures that codefine each other.

Arguments for memory as a dynamic process, against structure storage

For decades many well-known psychologists and philosophers argued that the formation of a habit, being reminded, and what is remembered should not be equated. Learning and remembering are more than storing and retrieving something. A historical review might begin with the famous psychology text of William James (1892):

Memory proper, or secondary memory as it might be styled, is ... knowledge of an event, or fact, of which meantime we have not been thinking, with the additional consciousness that we have thought or experienced it before. ... [P]sychical objects (sensations, for example) simply recurring in successive editions will remember each other on that account no more than clock-strokes do. No memory is involved in the mere fact of recurrence. (p. 252)

In the notes to this page James wrote, "Faculty view. Ideas not *things* but processes | No reservoir" (p. 452). James viewed an idea as a process; the experience of remembering is the experience of being aware that a reactivation or recomposition of a previous experience is occurring. That is, the mere construction of a habit, a recurrence, is different from the human experience of perceiving that "this is the same as what I experienced (or did) before." This awareness of the past, James's *memory proper*, is better called *remembering*.

Forty years later, Frederic Bartlett was still struggling to articulate the theory of memory suggested by James. Neurobiological data were now available, and there was apparently much talk about the idea of schemas (introduced by Bartlett's teacher, the neurologist Henry Head). Bartlett (1932) argued that a schema should not be viewed as a memory-thing, as a neural path or "trace" that is simply reactivated:

Remembering is not the re-excitation of innumerable fixed, lifeless and fragmentary traces. It is an imaginative reconstruction, or construction, built out of the relation of our attitude towards a whole active mass of organised past reactions or experience, and to a little outstanding detail which commonly appears in image or in language form. (p. 213)

Remembering is a conscious process of recollecting a previous experience. This process is imaginative and involves an emotional attitude about the experience. What is constructed is the relation between past experience and a detail in our present experience. The past experience exists (neurally) as "a whole active mass" and is organized. Reconstructing experience – remembering – involves establishing a new (physical) coordination, which reuses previous perceptions, ways of talking, and conceptions. Thus, remembering is not retrieving one thing but *reestablishing a relation*, a way of coordinating perception, words, ideas, and actions.

Bartlett emphasized that even practiced behavior is always adapted to the present complex of active postures and orientations, not merely a process of executing a stored program:

Suppose I am making a stroke in a quick game, such as tennis or cricket. . . . I do not, as a matter of fact, produce something absolutely new, and I never merely repeat something old. The stroke is literally manufactured out of the living visual and postural 'schemata' of the moment and their interrelations. (p. 202)

It is with remembering as it is with the stroke in a skilled game. We may fancy that we are repeating a series of movements learned a long time before from a text-book or from a teacher. But motion study shows that in fact we build up the stroke afresh on a basis of the immediately preceding balance of postures and the momentary needs of the game. Every time we make it, it has its own characteristics.

There is no reason in the world for regarding these [traces/schemata] as made complete at one moment, stored up somewhere, and then re-excited at some much later moment. (p. 211)

Bartlett is sometimes credited in the AI and cognitive science literature with introducing the term *schema* as it has been used in descriptive models, to refer to a prototypical *description* of some object or concept. Ironically, he specifically argued against this term because it suggested an isolated, held-in-place configuration:

I strongly dislike the term 'schema.' It is at once too definite and sketchy. . . . It suggests some persistent, but fragmentary, 'form of arrangement,' and it does not indicate what is very essential to the whole notion, that the organised mass results of past changes of position and posture are actively doing something all the time. . . . (p. 201)

That is, the structures involved in remembering – the neural reconstructions – should be thought of as processes that are *doing something*, not as static things or arrangements.[1]

Bartlett here adopts the perspective of a biologist, a position earlier promoted by James and John Dewey:

Everything in this book has been written from the point of view of a study of the conditions of organic and mental functions, rather than from that of an analysis of mental structure. It was, however, the latter standpoint which developed the traditional principles of associationism. The confusion of the two is responsible for very much unnecessary difficulty in psychological discussion. (p. 304)

By *functions*, Bartlett was striving for a psychological theory that viewed the organism as a whole, within its everyday experience of perceiving and acting in some context. That is, theories of psychological capability should be grounded in the transactions sustained by the organism in its environment, not reduced to local processes happening inside the brain.

The associationism Bartlett opposed is essentially the stimulus–response theory of early psychology. In associationism, remembering is explained by the idea that a stimulus causes the reactivation of other perceptions and ideas. These linkages or *traces* are means by which a response is recalled or a stimulus is recognized. In contrast, the emphasis on mental function emphasizes that associations are not isolated but part of perceptual-motor "circuits" and that remembering, as engaged in by a person, is a complex, constructive process of relating details, emotions, and previous coordinations, not just a simple associative pair. In this respect, Bartlett's theory of remembering is an argument in favor of the internal categorizing, comparing, and composing in descriptive cognitive models – and hence an argument against a simplistic view of association, which later became the black box of behaviorism.

But in regard to how the memory mechanism is modeled, descriptive cognitive models resemble more the stimulus–response and stored-trace mechanism of associationism than functional coordination, circuits, and the "doing something all the time" character of biological processes. Simply put, the descriptive approach replaces a simple associationism by a complex associationism, including a variety of hierarchical structures and buffers for posting long-term and transitory results.

Bartlett's views about the debate about memory are revealed especially by the following passage, in which he asks, "Why is it, although everybody now admits the force of the criticism of associationism, the associationist principles still hold their ground and are constantly employed?" (p. 307).

First, it is because the force of the rejection of associationism depends mainly upon the adoption of a functional point of view; but the attitude of analytic description is just as important within its own sphere. . . . (pp. 307–308)

That is, to understand what Bartlett is saying, one must adopt a different perspective on what remembering *does*. Nevertheless, Bartlett agrees that there is a place for analytic description, and he elaborates why:

Secondly, it is demonstrable that every situation, in perceiving, in imaging, in remembering, and in all constructive effort, possesses outstanding detail, and that in many cases of association the outstanding detail of one situation is taken directly out of that, and organised together with the outstanding detail of a different situation. . . . (p. 308)

That is, perceptual categorizations (details) persist in our experience – they can be stably reconstructed – and can be recomposed in different conceptualizations. The way words are used in scientific models especially has this character of repeated statements and relations:

Thirdly, we have seen how to some extent images, and to a great extent words, both of them expressions often of associative tendencies, slip readily into habit series and conventional formations. They do this mainly in the interest of intercommunication within the social group, and in doing it they inevitably take upon themselves common characteristics which render them amenable to the general descriptive phrases of the traditional doctrines of association. (p. 308)

Not only details, but also sequences of understanding and behavior, such as phrases in a language or symptom-disease-treatment patterns, persist and are recomposed in subsequent behavior. These *habit series* are what observers represent in associative networks of descriptive cognitive models.

In various senses, therefore, associationism is likely to remain, though its outlook is foreign to the demands of modern psychological science. It tells us something about the characteristics of associated details, when they are associated, but it explains nothing whatever of the activity of the conditions by which they are brought together. (p. 308)

Models describing patterns of behavior (such as the grammatical models of natural language systems) are useful, but they do not explain the internal recoordination process (the functional conditions) by which categorizations are brought together and habits are formed.

Descriptive cognitive models that relate remembering and problem solving, emphasized in the *case-based reasoning* approach of Roger Schank and his students (Kolodner, 1993), significantly improve upon the simple stimulus–response view of associationism. However, such models again do not have the functional or active character of biological processes that Bartlett emphasized. To understand what issues descriptive cognitive models do not address, let's first consider what researchers have claimed about the stored memory.

How descriptive modelers talk about symbols and representations

As I discussed in Chapter 2, the descriptive modeling literature often equates

> knowledge
> knowledge representations
> representations
> mental models
> knowledge base
> concepts

For example, the following recently appeared in *AI Magazine*:

The situationalists are attacking the very *idea* of knowledge representation – the notion that cognitive agents think about their environments, in large part, by manipulating internal representations of the worlds they inhabit. (Hayes, Ford, and Agnew, 1994, p. 17)

In this use of the term *knowledge representation*, it is unclear what idea is being defended: that human knowledge is "representational" because it describes the inhabited world; that subconscious (internal) processing is indistinguishable from the manipulations of conscious speaking, writing, and drawing; or that the only kind of representations in the brain are like the descriptions found in expert systems.

The last identification is the error made in referring to Mycin's map as being isomorphic to the a priori knowledge of an expert: No distinction is made between what the expert knew before the knowledge engineers began their work and the product, a descriptive model of disease and the diagnostic process. Cognitive psychology has pressed this view to the extreme: A representation of knowledge – *a scientist's representation of a subject's knowledge* – is not just a description in a model but literally something manipulated internally in the subject's brain. For example, in commentary presented at an AI symposium in 1988, Zenon Pylyshyn said that the computational view hypothesizes that the scientist's model and the subject's knowledge are equivalent in both notation (knowledge representation language) and architecture (the knowledge base interpreter and the relation of sensation and models to motor processes):

The choice of both notation and architecture are central empirical issues in cognitive science, and for reasons that go right to the heart of the computational view of mind. It's true that in the physical sciences, theoretical notation is not an empirical issue. But in cognitive science our choice of notation is critical precisely because the theories claim that representations are written in the mind in the postulated notation: that at least some of the knowledge is explicitly represented and encoded in the notation proposed by the theory. The architecture is likewise important because the claim is that these are literally the operations that are applied to the representations. . . . In cognitive science, theories claim that the mind works the way the model does, complete with notation and architecture. What is sometimes not appreciated is that computational models are models of what literally goes on in the mind. (Pylyshyn, 1991, p. 221)

Sometimes human knowledge and descriptions in a model are equated quite deliberately, as in Zenon Pylyshyn's frank statement; other claims about concepts, mental models, and knowledge bases become so ingrained that scientists do not reflect upon them. George Lakoff (1987) provides perhaps the best historical review of the paradigm:

The traditional view is a philosophical one. It has come out of two thousand years of philosophizing about the nature of reason. It is still widely believed despite overwhelming empirical evidence against it. . . . We have all been educated to think in those terms. . . .

We will be calling the traditional view *objectivism* for the following reason: Modern attempts to make it work assume that rational thought consists of the manipulation of abstract symbols and that these symbols get their meaning via a correspondence with the world, objectively construed, that is, independent of the understanding of any organism. . . .

A collection of symbols placed in correspondence with an objectively structured world is viewed as a *representation* of reality. . . . Thought is the mechanical manipulation of abstract symbols. The mind is an abstract machine, manipulating symbols essentially in the way a computer does, that is, by algorithmic computation. Symbols that correspond to the external world are internal representations of an external reality. . . .

Though such views are by no means shared by all cognitive scientists, they are nevertheless widespread, and in fact so common that many of them are often assumed to be true without question or comment. Many, perhaps even most, contemporary discussions of the mind as a computing machine take such views for granted. (pp. xii–xiii)

Since the late 1980s, with the airing of alternative points of view, some AI researchers have argued that situated cognition claims about the descriptive approach were all straw men, or that only expert systems were based on the idea that human memory consisted of a storehouse of descriptions (Hayes et al., 1994). With the tacit identification of models and knowledge now so baldly presented, some people have doubted that anyone could have ever believed such things. But certainly, the idea that knowledge equals representation of knowledge is clear in the expert systems literature of the early 1980s:

Knowledge is seen to be of paramount importance, and AI research has shifted its focus from an inference-based paradigm to a knowledge-based paradigm. Knowledge is viewed as consisting of facts and heuristics. (Davis and Lenat, 1982, p. xvi)

Given this view of human knowledge, reasoning could be automated by extracting knowledge from experts, capturing it in written form, and disseminating it in expert systems. The economic benefits were obvious and motivated some of the excitement:

Traditionally the transmission of knowledge from human expert to trainee has required education and internship years long. Extracting knowledge from humans and putting it in computable forms can greatly reduce the costs of knowledge reproduction and exploitation. (Hayes-Roth, Waterman, and Lenat, 1983, p. 5)

Going in the other direction, to use expert systems for teaching, the psychological claims are fully visible:

Much of what constitutes domain-specific problem-solving expertise has never been articulated. It resides in the heads of tutors, getting there through experience, abstracted but not necessarily accessible in an articulatable form. (Sleeman and Brown, 1982, p. 9)

They [knowledge-based programs] approach teaching from a subset viewpoint: expertise consists of a set of facts or rules. The student's knowledge is modelled as subset of this knowledge. (Goldstein, 1982, p. 51)

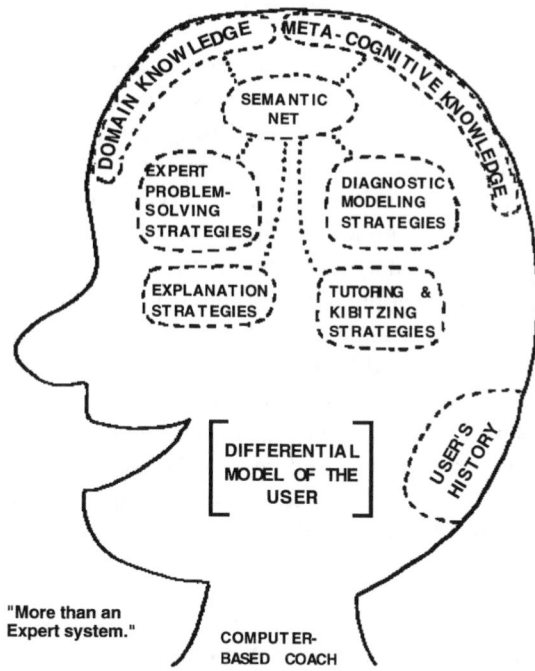

Figure 3.1. A naive theory of coaching: Knowledge sources for intelligent tutoring. (Slide reprinted with permission from an unpublished tutorial presented by John Seely Brown, National Conference on Artificial Intelligence, 1984.)

The processes of the student are divided into two homunculi – a problem solving specialist and a learning specialist – with the [genetic] graph serving as the student's basic memory structure for procedural knowledge. (Ibid., p. 71)

In these remarks we see clearly how stored facts and rules are referred to as *knowledge* and equated with *student knowledge* – indeed, the relation is that of a *subset*. Similarly, the AI researcher suggests that a network of words can serve as "the student's basic memory structure." Indeed, reasoning is explicitly described in terms of two agents inside the brain (homunculi) sending messages to each other. Figure 3.1 illustrates how this community, of which I was a part, conceived of the brain and computer programs.

The diagram shows the components of a computer-based coach. A semantic net (descriptions) stores and organizes the subject (*domain knowledge*) and *meta-cognitive knowledge* (e.g., how to monitor and improve your own problem solving) and various strategies for modeling the student, explaining reasoning, and tutoring. The *differential model of the user* is another network, showing which portions of the expert model have been exhibited in student behavior and which portions the student might not know.

At the time, circa 1977–1984, John Seely Brown, an eminent cognitive scientist who cofounded the intelligent tutoring system approach, emphasized that such a computer coach would need to be more than an expert system. In my own work, as Brown's student, I emphasized that an expert system's rules for medical diagnosis needed to be organized and annotated with *additional models*. For example, the disease taxonomy should be represented separately from the diagnostic procedure; the rules should be explained in terms of causal models of pathophysiology. With some prescience, Brown labeled his diagram *a naive theory of coaching*, referring to the abstract character of the listed knowledge sources and questioning the adequacy of a differential model for understanding a student's conceptions. Today I would say as well that the naive part of the theory is viewing these knowledge sources as structures stored inside the head of the human teacher. In short, this diagram clearly identifies descriptive models with brain structures – with the "user's history" visualized as a kind of Broca's area in the back of the brain.

The psychological view of a physical symbol system

A distinction is often drawn between knowledge engineering and the modeling of memory and natural language in cognitive psychology and linguistics. But in the decade starting about 1975, knowledge engineers viewed the expert system approach as consistent with all the other subareas of AI, revealing the broad applicability of Allen Newell and Herb Simon's physical symbol system hypothesis :

A consequence of the prominence of the physical symbol system hypothesis is the recent emergence of the representation of knowledge as one of the most central enterprises of the field. Almost every AI project of recent vintage – from natural language understanding to visual perception to planning to expert systems – has employed an explicit symbolic representation of the information in its domain of concern. General languages for representing arbitrary knowledge are becoming a focus in this preoccupation with using symbols for facts and metainformation for a given domain.... One of the working hypotheses in this field is that knowledge is representational; that is, "knowing" consists in large part of representing symbolically facts about the world. This lends support to Newell's physical symbol system hypothesis.... (Hayes-Roth et al., 1983, pp. 45–46)

Notice how the claims go beyond saying that "knowledge is representational" to argue that knowledge is "explicit" and "symbolic," which in expert systems means that knowledge is represented descriptively as rules or other associational patterns. The symbols are not just arbitrary patterns (symbols), they are *meaningful encodings*:

It is sufficient to think of symbols as strings of characters and of symbol structures as a type of data structure.... The following are examples of symbols: Apple, Transistor-13, Running, Five, 3.14159. And the following are examples of symbol structures: (On Block1 Block2) (Plus 5 X) (Same-as (Father-of Pete) (Father-of (Brother-of Pete))). (Ibid., p. 61)

Although it is true that this point of view remained controversial among philosophers and even among psychologists (as I will show in the next section), it was the dominant means of modeling cognition throughout the 1980s. The assumption that human memory is a place where descriptions are stored was either taken for granted or treated as a psychological issue of little relevance to creating intelligent machines. The identification of knowledge with computer programs prevailed and was characteristic of the symbol-modeling paradigm: As Mark Stefik said earlier, "It is sufficient to think ... of symbol structures as a type of data structure."

The broad acceptance of this approach is amply illustrated by Michelene Chi's introduction to *The Nature of Expertise*:

There is now a cognitive science related to the representation and execution of expert performance. This science has developed a technology in the form of programs for performing tasks formerly done only by experts. Although this technology is still primitive, it represents an important contribution of fundamental research on the nature of representation in memory. Behind this technology is a better understanding of what it means to be an expert. Expertness lies more in an elaborated semantic memory than in a general reasoning process. Such knowledge is present not only in the performance of unusual people, but in a skill like reading which is widely distributed in most of us. We are beginning to understand the nature of the propositional network underlying such representation. The expert has available access to a complex network without any conscious representation of the search processes that go on its retrieval. (Chi, Glaser, and Farr, 1988, p. xxxv)

In interpreting such statements, it is important to examine what the researchers are arguing against. Here the advance is realizing that "expertness lies more in an elaborated semantic memory than in a general reasoning process." At the time, we often said, "Knowledge is power." To build a humanlike robot, we would have to put inside a lot of task-specific knowledge. This is the lesson of Mycin, as well as of Aaron. Reasoning means not just being "smart" but also knowing a lot about specific things. Broadly viewed, this is consistent with the situated cognition emphasis on interactive experience; the problem is the emphasis on stored descriptions and verbal concepts.

Notice how representations are viewed as *things* in the preceding quotes. This research community believed that human knowledge consisted of representations that are literally stored in a *semantic memory* consisting of a complex network that is subconsciously *searched*. This is precisely what the physical symbol system hypothesis claims: that there is a correspondence between a knowledge base, searching, and matching performed by a computer and comparable structures and processes in the human. More generally, this is the hallmark of the information-processing approach, which is especially obvious in models of natural language processing:

The comprehension model is an information-processing model: It identifies certain processes and mechanisms (a short-term memory buffer, cyclical processing, memory retrieval) that interact to produce comprehension. (Miller, Polson, and Kintsch, 1984, pp. 4–5)

Newell and Simon (1972) explicitly rejected the idea that their models were just abstract descriptions. They claimed the body of descriptions to be literally the stuff out of which cognition arises:

The theory posits a set of processes or mechanisms that produce the behavior of the thinking human. Thus the theory is reductionistic; it does not simply provide a set of relations or laws about behavior from which one can often conclude what behavior must be. (The elementary processes and their organization, of course, are not explained: reduction is always relative.) Thus, the theory purports to explain behavior – and not just to describe it, however parsimoniously. (We are aware that some would dispute such a distinction, viewing all causal explanations as simply descriptions.) (p. 9)

As a testimony to their thoroughness and scholarship, Newell and Simon (1972) acknowledge here that some would view their models "as simply descriptions." But, with behaviorism as *their* antagonist, they insist instead that their programs replicate *physical processes* occurring in the brain:

The processes posited by the theory presumably exist in the central nervous system; they are internal to the organism. As far as the great debates about the empty organism, behaviorism, intervening variables, and hypothetical constructs are concerned, we take these simply as a phase in the historical development of psychology. Our theory posits internal mechanisms of great extent and complexity, and endeavors to make contact between them and visible evidences of problem solving. That is all there is to it. (pp. 9–10)

Newell and Simon didn't question how computer programs differ from "elementary" neural processes, viewing neurons and computer circuits as merely different substrates on which the programs run. Instead, they couched the correspondence between the brain and their models as a comparison between "human programs" and their models:

We confess to a strong premonition that the actual organization of human programs closely resembles the production system organization. . . . (p. 803)

Newell's *Unified Theories of Cognition,* a masterful synthesis of psychological experimentation and computer modeling, depicts a more recent version of the production system architecture (Figure 3.2). In contrast with the pedagogically humorous portrayal of knowledge in Figure 3.1, this diagram is intended to be a psychological model. That is, Figure 3.2 makes

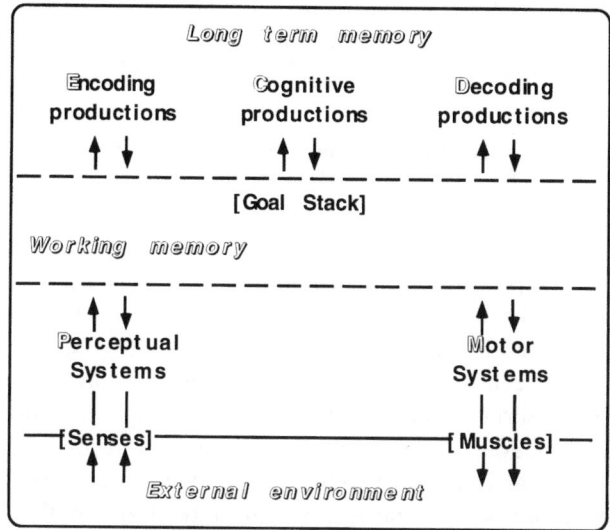

Figure 3.2. The total cognitive system. (Reprinted with permission of the publishers from *Unified Theories of Cognition*, p. 195, by Allen Newell, Cambridge, Mass.: Harvard University Press, Copyright © 1990 by the President and Fellows of Harvard University Press.)

specific claims about the "total cognitive system" of memory, perception, physical coordination, and learning.

In particular, long-term memory is the place where symbol structures are stored, modeled here as a collection of production rules. These rules can be put away and retrieved unchanged. In robots based on this LTM architecture, these rules are written in a language that relates the perceptual and motor systems through encoding and decoding productions. For example, symbol structures include symbols that designate turning and moving Aaron's drawing instrument, which are decoded to the corresponding signals for moving the drawing apparatus itself. Similarly, in robots with perceptual systems, objects are recognized by mapping predetermined input signals (senses) to encoding productions. David Marr (1981) summarized this descriptive approach for creating a situation-specific model from perceptual categorizations. His example involves a story relating a newspaper to a buzzing fly:

When the newspaper is mentioned (or, in the case of vision, seen), it is described not only internally as a newspaper and some rough 3-D description of its shape and axes set up, but also as a light, flexible object with area. . . . (p. 138)

In a stored description model, perceptual and motor systems are distinct from memory; they are like the peripheral input and output devices of a complex computer system. *Cognitive productions*, such as rules relating objects to their functions in different scenarios, relate perception and action through working memory, where descriptions of the world and descriptions of possible actions are posted:

Note that a description of fly-swatting or reading or fire-lighting does not have to be attached to the newspaper; merely that a description of the newspaper is available that will match its role in each scenario. (Ibid.)

The process of manipulating descriptions – via deductive inference, specialization, and composition – to accomplish goals is called *deliberation*. Thus, perception and action coordination is *mediated by a descriptive model of the world* generated by deliberation. Single-step or "immediate" reflexive behavior may occur by direct links between perceptual and motor systems. But most serial behavior involves multiple cycles of production firing and use of the goal stack and working memory to represent states of the world and alternative plans of what to do next. The perceptual, central cognitive, and motor systems bear a linear causal relation, but they operate independently, whether their operation is serial or parallel. In particular, perception and deliberation are possible without motor action. *Perceiving and moving are distinct from remembering,* which happens at a different time. Learning occurs by modifying the three kinds of productions in long-term memory.

The stored-schema view takes hold

By the mid-1970s, most cognitive modeling was based on the idea that human long-term memory was literally a storehouse of descriptions. Marvin Minsky's knowledge-representation architecture called *frame theory,* although far more complex than the simple associations of Mycin's rules, was nevertheless based on a storage and matching mechanism. As a framework for describing concepts and their relations, frame theory proved to be highly influential in the design of modeling languages:

Here is the essence of the frame theory: When one encounters a new situation (or makes a substantial change in one's view of a problem), one selects from memory a structure called a *frame.* (Minsky, 1977, p. 355)

Psychologists familiar with the term *schema* identified Henry Head's neurological notion of schema with the stored structures of descriptive models:

For many theorists who use it, the term *schema* has come to be synonymous with the term *long-term memory structure.* The schema-is-a-structure assumption is clearly evident in the cognitive scientific literature and needs no elaboration. . . . Schemata are generally claimed to be pre-existing knowledge structures stored in some location in the head. (Iran-Nejad, 1987, p. 111)

The vast majority of cognitive psychology theories of memory of the 1970s were based on the idea that descriptions are literally stored in the brain. Faced with difficulties, researchers generally produced only variations of a storage model. As one example of a difficulty with the store-and-retrieve model, Elizabeth Loftus showed how witnesses in court trials as a matter of course reconstructed their experience, weaving a story that elaborated and filled in details – a process of *recategorization*, not just confabulation. Cognitive psychologists seeking to model these processes nevertheless continued to view speaking as a process of subconsciously manipulating text, the "contents" of memory, the reservoir-of-experience metaphor that James cautioned against. Notice how even here the written word dominates; the active aspect of remembering is viewed as rewriting:

Elizabeth Loftus has established a "rewriting" effect during question answering. . . . But these phenomena cannot be simulated in a system that treats question answering as a purely passive retrieval process. Memory alterations can only occur if the retrieval process somehow acts on memory, to refine or alter its previous contents. (Lehnert, 1984, p. 36)

Perhaps nowhere are the assumptions of descriptive modeling more clear and the difficulties more severe than in models of speaking and comprehension. But theories were always repaired by reformulating what descriptions were stored and how they were modified before action occurs. For example, the linguist Joan Bresnan reminded her colleagues that they all operate within the paradigm that knowledge consists of stored descriptions, and, by assumption, this is not the source of their difficulties. Rather, the controversies question whether the most abstract theories properly characterize the underlying processes by which such structures are modified through experience and applied:

The cognitive psychologists, computer scientists, and linguists who have questioned the psychological reality of grammars have not doubted that a speaker's knowledge of language is mentally represented in the form of stored knowledge structures of some kind. All theories of mental representation of language presuppose this. What has been doubted is that these internal knowledge structures are adequately characterized by transformational theory. (Bresnan and Kaplan, 1984, p. 106)

The citations I have given could be augmented a thousandfold by a cursory glance through conference proceedings and journals of the 1970s and early 1980s. By the mid-1980s, perhaps with the opposing voice of connectionism in the background, or perhaps just by reaching a state of maturity and stability that suggested taking stock of progress, researchers began to reflect more on the assumptions of the stored descriptions approach and were surprised to see how far the theories had gone. George Mandler, a psychologist from before the days of computer programming, offered thought-provoking criticisms in 1984 in a workshop called "Methods and Tactics in Cognitive Science." He questioned whether the debates about kinds of descriptions weren't perhaps less important than reconsidering what was meant by representation, knowledge, and process:

> The central themes that emerged during those 5 years [1955–1960] and that mark the cognitive sciences are the concepts of representation and process. They are the primary foci of all the relevant disciplines, and it is symptomatic of our acceptance and their importance that we rarely hear anybody question these two foundations. . . . We are more concerned about distinctions between analogic and propositional representations or between declarative and procedural knowledge. (p. 306)

The editors of this same volume pointed out that the debates were now narrowed, for example, to whether knowledge consists of stored descriptions about the world and behavior (*declarative* propositions) or procedures describing what to do when. Miller, Polson, and Kintsch (1984) lamented the terminological proliferation and more seriously how models were interpreted as psychological phenomena, that is, as brain *mechanisms*:

> We have only to invent three more terms like "schema" and cognitive science will be ripe for Nobel Prizes. . . . More interesting, and perhaps more serious, is the confusion between purposive and mechanistic language that characterizes much of the writing in cognitive science. As if it were the most natural thing in the world, purposive terminology has been imported into an information-processing framework: subgoals are stored in short-term memory; unconscious expectations are processed in parallel; opinions are represented propositionally; the mind contains schemata. . . . (p. 6)

Here Miller et al. call their audience to consider more clearly the distinction between human experience and computer programs. Without question, terms previously used only to describe people are now viewed as appropriate for characterizing programs, and views of people are now pervaded by talk of computational mechanisms.

Certainly, one can find throughout the philosophical AI and psychology literature more balanced treatments, especially by the 1990s. Ryszard Michalski, a distinguished specialist in machine learning, provides the following appraisal in the *Encyclopedia of AI*, explicitly distinguishing between human concepts and the descriptions in descriptive models:

> An intelligent system must be able to form concepts, that is classes of entities united by some principle. Such a principle might be a common use or goal, the same role in a structure forming a theory about something, or just similar perceptual characteristics. . . .
>
> In research on concept learning, the term "concept" is usually viewed in a narrower sense . . . namely, as an equivalence class of entities, such that it can be *comprehensibly described* by no more than a small set of statements. This description must be sufficient for distinguishing this concept from other concepts. (1992, p. 248; emphasis added)

Unfortunately, a great deal of crosstalk developed in the late 1980s as the term *representation* was broadened to include more than descriptions such as rules, frames, or schemas. This era of questioning was heralded by Winograd and Flores's book, *Understanding Computers and Cognition* (1985) and by the contemporary rise of connectionism. As the preceding quotes reveal, before this time knowledge was equated with comprehensible descriptions, a mental model was equated with the data structure manipulations of a computer program, and *all representing in the brain* was reduced to a vocabulary of symbols composed into relational networks. Consequently, when situated cognition researchers such as Rod Brooks denied in the late 1980s that mental representing is a process of manipulating word networks, their colleagues interpreted this as claiming that there are "no internal representations" *at all* (Hayes et al., 1994) or "no concepts in the mind" (Sandberg and Wielinga, 1991). Instead, the distinction, as Michalski takes pains to express, is that human concepts cannot be equated with descriptions such as "semantic nets."

Given that so little was known about neural processes during the 1970s and 1980s, studying the relation of descriptive models to neural processes was more often undertaken by philosopher-psychologists seeking to synthesize the cognitive sciences. Consistent with Newell and Simon's statement cited earlier, Daniel Dennett (1984) said, "No one supposes that the model maps onto the process of psychology and biology all the way down." The taken-for-granted assumption was that the mechanism – how "programs" are *implemented* in hardware – is irrelevant. Carbon-based structures should be replaceable by a hardware of silicon and electrons, just as we can build a watch from metal and diamonds or on a computer chip. Howard Gardner (1985b) makes this point clearly:

If there was to be an identity, it obviously could not reside in the hardware, but, as Putnam pointed out, might well occur in the software: that is, both human beings and machines – and any other form of intelligent life, from anteaters to Antipodeans – could be capable of realizing the same kinds of program. Thus, the equation occurs at a much higher level of abstraction – a level that focuses on the goals of cognitive activity, the means of processing at one's disposal, the steps that would have to be taken, the evaluation of steps, and the kindred features. (p. 78)

Just as the essence of timekeeping is in counting and displaying an accumulation of seconds, the essence of reasoning should be formalizable as goals, knowledge, and steps of inference, which might be represented and manipulated by a variety of physical devices. *Computation* is what these devices do – comparing, storing, combining – and the process of thinking as a manipulation of descriptions is hence *computational*. How the computations are actually accomplished is immaterial (so to speak). Descriptive modelers repeated this point to each other, emphasizing that they were only committed to the brain's representing the same information as computer programs, not that the physical structures are identical:

> Human thinking (cognition) can be regarded as a *computational* process. The basic notion is that human thought (including perception, understanding, and even perhaps emotion) is *the result* of the manipulation of information – homologous to data structures that might be employed in computers. [Note: Clearly there is no assumption of literal similarity in data structures, only a representational equivalence. (There are many obvious differences between computers and brains, e.g., computers are composed of silicon-based memory. . . .)] (Evans and Patel, 1990, p. 10)

Given this stance, it is perhaps not surprising that the most persuasive, head-turning arguments of situated cognition by today's roboticists and neurobiologists question whether the present-day stored-program mechanism is indeed equivalent in capability to neural processes. That is, is the "hardware" equivalent? Just as an electronic computer watch is more accurate than a pendulum-regulated device, and a computer chip may offer a wealth of more calculations than a sundial (such as the time of the next solar eclipse), might a biological mechanism afford kinds of comparisons and forms of memory that our present-day electronic computers cannot practically replicate? The contextualists tried to show what memory did, and the connectionists tried to show how.

"Actively doing something all the time": From associationism to contextualism

Throughout the 1960s and 1970s, the contextualists were psychologists who were still struggling against Bartlett's nemesis – the associationist view of memory. Contextualism holds that comprehending and remembering are forms of problem solving – not simply storing and retrieving stimuli. In many respects, the descriptive cognitive modeling approach developed this perspective very well, particularly in the line of work on story understanding, memory *scripts*, and case-based reasoning. So in assessing the stored-description approach, we need to acknowledge in what respect Bartlett's objections about stored traces were heeded and in what respect his advocation of an *active memory* was not realized. We find that the main contribution of contextualism, in suggesting a better mechanism for memory, is in showing how perception must be considered not as a separate module, but as integral to the comprehending and remembering process. This discussion, and the consideration of connectionism that follows, thus serve as a bridge to the new perceptual models discussed in the remainder of this book, especially Part III.

To begin, let's consider the summary provided by James J. Jenkins, a psychologist, who made the transition from associationism to contextualism:

The associationist believes in some kind or kinds of basic units. (The number is not important.) He believes in some kind or kinds of relations between units. He holds that the more complex behaviors are the same "in kind" as simple behaviors. He believes that explanation consists of an explication of mechanism. He believes that behavior *is* automatic and for any kind of complex behavior, he relies on memory. (1974, p. 786)

Jenkins outlines the origins of the alternative point of view, contextualism – a shift from stored units to experienced *events:*

The term contextualism is not highly familiar to American psychologists, but it is an American philosophical position that has been intimately intertwined with American psychology for three quarters of a century. Another name for it is *pragmatism*, and it has its roots in William James, C. S. Peirce and John Dewey. . . .

Contextualism holds that experience consists of *events*. Events have a *quality* as a whole. By quality is meant the total meaning of the event. The quality of the event is the resultant of the interaction of the experiencer and the world, that is, the interaction of the organism and the physical relations that provide support for the experiences. The relations can be thought of and analyzed into *textures*. A texture in turn consists of *strands* lying in *context*. (Ibid.)

These ideas are illustrated in a 1971 experiment conducted by John D. Bransford and Jeffrey J. Franks. Subjects are given a list of sentences, asked a comprehension question after each one, and afterward given another set of sentences and asked to indicate which ones they heard previously. Example sentences in the "acquisition phase" are as follows:

- "The girl broke the window on the porch." (pause 5 seconds) "Broke what?"
- "The large window was on the porch." (pause) "Where?"
- "The girl who lives next door broke the window on the porch." (pause) "Lives where?"

The list actually consists of four interrelated groups of sentences (of which one group is illustrated here), comprising four stories. The "test phase" includes sentences such as these:

- "The girl who lives next door broke the window."
- "The girl who lives next door broke the large window on the porch."

In constructing this experiment, Bransford and Jenkins sought to overturn the usual approach by which stimuli were either nonsensical or chosen to allow discrimination of events by the subject – the association assumption being that you had to present stimuli that could be learned if you wished to study memory. Bransford et al. realized that their experimental protocols were set up to observe the very phenomenon they sought to prove:

Everyone realizes the importance of constructing experimental lists so as to avoid unnecessarily "confusing" the subjects. And it hardly seems surprising that given a "confusable" list, the subjects *do* make "mistakes." But what do these obvious facts indicate about the nature of remembering? In particular, what do they indicate about the notion that an input results in a relatively independent, stored trace? (Bransford, McCarrell, Franks, and Nitsch, 1977, p. 462)

The experiments showed that subjects couldn't recognize very well which of the test sentences had been experienced before. Subjects estimated that between 5% and 80% of the test sentences were presented earlier, but none were. Furthermore, when test sentences mix the four stories ("The scared cat running from the barking dog broke the window"), they correctly reject the sentence with certainty. The conclusion is that what is remembered depends on the context – or better, what is *experienced* depends on the context. Isolated sentences are not merely noted and stored; rather, the subject experiences a relationship between a given sentence and the total set of acquisition *experiences*, the textures of the four stories. " 'Context' is not simply a variable to be manipulated" (ibid.); it is constructed by the subject, in an ongoing manner. Jenkins (1974) observes:

The quality of each of the events is indeed the total meaning of the complex sentence. Once the fusion of the strands into events has occurred (particularly since the strands are heard over and over again in various combinations), the subject cannot perform an analysis to recover the exact pattern of input that furnished support for the construction that he made. (p. 790)

In contrast, associationist experiments were designed to make "subjects look like 'exact copy' mechanisms that simply store traces" (Bransford et al., 1977, p. 462). Bransford et al. conclude:

Our purpose is not to deny the importance of *remembering*. . . . But we question the fruitfulness of assuming that a concept of *memory* underlies these events. [C]urrent uses of the term memory involve tacit or explicit assumptions . . . that memory can be broken down into a set of *memories*, that these consist of relatively independent *traces* that are stored in some *location*, that these traces must be *searched for* and *retrieved* in order to produce remembering, and that appropriate traces must be "contacted" in order for past experiences to have their effects on subsequent events. (Ibid., p. 431)

[In associative models] . . . the problem of remembering begins where the parsers stop. (Ibid., p. 444)

[W]e believe it unfruitful to separate problems of remembering from problems of comprehending and perceiving. (Ibid., p. 454)

This is the key point: Experience cannot be viewed as isolated stimuli that are presented to people. Rather, what is experienced is a construction of the person (called the "quality of the event"), "the result of the interaction of the experiencer and the world" (Jenkins, 1974, p. 787). And what is constructed is a kind of gestalt or integrated whole, a meaning. Recall and recognition experiments designed to test comprehension and memory also result in constructed experiences, as probes are related to the "global characteristics of the set of acquisition experiences as a whole" (Bransford et al., 1977, p. 463). The idea that primitive features and relations are simply detected in the input and then used to index into an existing network of connections does not hold up when we examine memory for *meaningful experience*. Put another way, the subject's experience cannot be equated with the observer-experimentalist's view of stimuli. Experience is relational within a context conceived by the subject.

Jenkins (1974) concludes:

[T]he phenomena disclosed by these experiments pose formidable problems for storage theories of memory. (p. 792)

[W]e should shun any notion that memory consists of a specific system that operates with one set of rules on one kind of unit. . . . (p. 793)

Apart from the belief that the construction of the mind is attributed to the past, he [William James] saw nothing to set memory apart from perception, imagination, comparison, and reasoning. Such a claim is unsettling because it says: *Memory is not a box in a flow diagram*. It is also threatening because it seems to demand an understanding of all "the higher mental processes" at once. Yet, that is what the data in our experiments suggest. To study memory without studying perception is . . . pushing all the difficult problems out of memory into the unknown perceptual domain for someone else to study. (pp. 793–794)

In repeatedly referring to perception, Bransford, Jenkins, and others relate contextualism to J. J. Gibson's theories, which I discuss at some length in Part III. The point of relevance here is that contextualism suggests that some kind of *transformation* is occurring during what we call *comprehension*, and this transformation apparently constructs some kind of holistic view of what is happening to the person. Borrowing from Gibson, Bransford suggests that subject is learning or becoming "attuned" to "invariant information" in the set of experiences (the strands). As expressed by the opening quotes of this chapter, this is essentially the Piagetian view of learning.[2]

From the point of view of descriptive cognitive modeling, it is all too easy to shirk off these observations as poetic specifications for what descriptive models already do. A descriptive cognitive modeler would say that the so-called gestalt is just a complex web of stored concept descriptions constituting a story or script. The individual sentence stimuli are interpreted in light of this evolving story, and new information is integrated into the web. The result – in the descriptive model as well – is not a set of isolated sentences but an integrated understanding. Test sentences can be parsed with respect to this network, so it is easy to detect discrepant terms, relations, or events. In effect, this is Schank's theory of *memory organization packets* and the mechanism of case-based learning and problem solving.

At this level of analysis, descriptive models of memory and learning in the 1980s fit contextualism rather well. Anticipating this (and having to handle similar objections), Jenkins (1974) responded in two ways. First, he emphasized that associationism (and here we would add descriptive modeling) "presupposes fundamental units and relations out of which all else is constructed" (p. 794). By saying human experience consists of *events*, Jenkins calls our attention to the fact that the way we break down experience into named objects and relations is not isomorphic to the experience itself. Descriptions are reifications – they make objects out of experience. Isomorphs exist *between descriptions* (Langer, 1942; Maturana, 1983; Tyler, 1978). Experience has a "quality as a whole" because it is not *produced by* a particular ontology of objects and relations. Instead, interaction *constructs an ontology*, which is partially what we experience.

In contrast, case-based reasoning programs have within them *modeling languages*, with some knowledge-engineered ontology of objects, events, and relations. Some set of primitives may suffice for a given set of stimuli within an observer's interest, for example in studying story understanding in a classroomlike setting. But what subjects experience – the events they construct – are prone to change in different settings. In Dewey's terms, the constructed conception of relationships is *functional* with respect to the subject's interests. Experiments narrow and attempt to restrict these interests. Consequently, to understand better how memory, perception, and reasoning are related, "Contextualism stresses relating one's laboratory problems to the ecologically valid problems of everyday life" (Jenkins, 1974, p. 794).

Hence, we have two claims, one concerning mechanism, the other methodology. First, contextualism claims that there is no set of primitive features. Meaningful features used by the subject may be recurrent and stable, but they are constructions developed during the course of the experimental trial. Second, to reveal the extent and functional character of this contextual effect, one must depart from contrived laboratory experiment to study people in their everyday lives. So here again, recalling the framework of Table 1.1, we have the structural and functional aspects of situated cognition. To realize the full force of these arguments, as I believe they are relevant to replicating human intelligence, we must go back a step from memory to perception. We must examine what assumptions have been made about perception in storage models of memory, how these are addressed by early connectionist models, and what neurobiology is revealing about brain mechanisms. I consider these issues in turn in the remainder of this chapter.

Classical memory: Stored traces and isolated modules

Israel Rosenfield (1988) has written a history of how classical memory research, starting in the 19th century, promoted the storage metaphor of descriptive cognitive modeling. He describes how recognition of shapes is modeled in terms of features stored as "fixed images":

[A]cquired knowledge is stored as fixed images in specific centers, just as the nineteenth-century neurologists believed. . . . The world is knowable, according to this view, only if it is already known: the recognition of a shape is possible only if there is a fixed image of that shape already stored in the brain. (p. 112)

Seeing, they [descriptive cognitive modelers] argued, requires first knowing what one is looking for. (p. 115)

Nobody pretended to understand the mechanisms that created the fixed images. That is a physiological question; its resolution would tell us little or nothing about the nature of memory. (p. 15)

The idea that knowledge is stored as traces or fixed images suggests that there is a *memory module* (where the stuff is stored), apart from other kinds of processors such as perceptual categorizers, reasoning procedures, and so on (cf. Figure 3.2). Although there is strong evidence that areas of the brain are functionally specialized, the storage view appears to suggest that these functions are independently operating (in serial or parallel) and that their products either chain together or are composed. Rosenfield is arguing against the idea of localization or *functional independence* of perceptual memory – the same neural mechanism contextualists were arguing against at the conceptual level.

Classical memory experiments in the laboratory suggested that different kinds of verbal memory were stored (located) in different places in the brain. Such a storage model, isolating verbal categories into modular, separately existing units, presupposes that the brain actually operates on the stimuli, rather than constructs the sensory features in the first place:

A hidden and unquestioned assumption of the localizationist view is that there is some specific information in the environment that can become the fixed memory images. But if recognition depends on context, it is the *brain* that must organize *stimuli* into coherent pieces of information. . . . (p. 63)

Using the contextualist argument, Rosenfield emphasizes that experimental settings, with deliberately well-defined and distinguishable probes, shows the brain to be a sorting and storage device:

Functional specializations, suggested by the study of clinical material must be illusory, for what is implied is not that the brain creates our perceptions out of ambiguous stimuli but that it *sorts* neatly packaged information coming from the environment. (Ibid.)

The effects are "illusory" because other experiments show that what is perceived depends on the ongoing context, as constructed by the subject. The world does not present itself as meaningful features. To predigest the world for a person or a program by supplying readily labeled things and events is to bypass the essential problem that memory must address. A proper study of perception must begin at the level below that of independently meaningful probes.

To this end, Rosenfield cites experiments that establish that "sounds are categorized and therefore perceived differently depending on the presence or absence of other sounds." For example, there is "a trade-off between the length of the *sh* sound and the duration of the silence [between the words of "say shop"] in determining whether *sh* or *ch* is heard" (p. 106). In fact, "lengthening the silence *between* words can also alter the *preceding* word" (p. 107). For instance, "if the cue for the *sh* in 'ship' is relatively long, increases in the duration of silence between the words ["gray ship"] cause the perception to change, not to 'gray chip' but to 'great ship.'" Hence, phonemes are not *given* but constructed within an ongoing context of overlapping cues. "What brain mechanism is responsible for our perceptions of an /a/, if what we perceive also depends on what came before and after the /a/?" (p. 110). In no sense does an /a/ exist somewhere *in isolation* in the brain.

The basic claim is that "the categorizations created by our brains are abstract and cannot be accounted for as combinations of 'elementary stimuli.'" There are no innate or learned primitives like /a/ to be found in the brain; that is, there are no primitive *descriptions of features* in the brain that can be combined. Instead, patterns of brain activity correspond to *constructed organizations of stimuli*. Our perception depends on past categorizations, not on some absolute, inherent combinations of stimuli (such as the frequencies of sounds) that are matched against inputs (p. 112). Stephen Smoliar (1992) gives a related example from music, revealing how perceptual categorization is inherently *sensory change in time*, not matching descriptions:

A chord may be perceived as an instance of the category **G-major-triad-in-root-position.** However, suppose that chord is then followed by an instance of the category **C-major-triad-in-root-position.** The sequence of the two chords may then be perceived as an instance of the category **dominant-tonic-cadence.** As a result, the first chord will now *also* be perceived as an instance of the category **dominant**, while the second will be perceived as an instance of the category **tonic.** . . . **Dominant** does not delimit a set for which there are necessary and sufficient conditions which may be invoked as the criteria for membership. (pp. 42–43)[3]

To provide an idea of where I am heading, let me review the hypotheses about neural mechanism suggested by this memory debate: What we call memory is an ability to *act similarly* to the way we have acted before, to reenact, sequence, and compose *past interactions*. We have a memory for coordinated, interacting processes, not for descriptions of them per se. These processes correspond to the activation, recategorization, and coordination of perceptual-conceptual-motor sequences and other temporal relations, including rhythm and simultaneity. Neurological structures are biased to reorganize themselves; so, with respect to speech performance, we can say a phrase, or write it, or spell it again. Thus, we speak in *ways* we have spoken before, giving the appearance of retrieving statements from a storehouse. But each new behavior is an adaptation of a previous coordination, not a literal replaying of stored control signals or mere execution of an isolated procedure. On making sounds again, we change the inflection as well as the intention, the meaning of the words. The key idea is that all of this is happening at the same time, such that the different levels of organization are affecting each other simultaneously (as well as sequentially in our conscious thought).

In moving from these observations to claims about concepts and problem solving, two hypotheses are made: First, conceptual categorizing is built on a similar mechanism, such that concepts cannot be defined by necessary and sufficient conditions either. Second, conceptual processes are coupled to perceptual processes in a way similar to the way sensory stimuli and perceptual categories are related, such that perceiving is not in general a module providing input to conceiving, but the possible organizations at any time are codetermined.

How might categorizing be always adapted, arise from nondescriptive elements, and yet build on what has been experienced before? Connectionism is an effort to build such a mechanism.

What's wrong with simple connectionism?

Connectionism is the name for a variety of computational methods based on representing information in a large network of parallel processes, loosely inspired by (and informally called) *neural networks*. These methods were developed in the 1980s, especially to address the learning limitations of a localized memory architecture. In general terms, a *simple connectionist program* constructs a memory for input–output pairs, such that what is retained is not independently stored units or descriptive logs of what has occurred, but rather a cumulative record of the *relations* between features in the input and corresponding outputs. Simple connectionism is thus a step in the direction of the contextualist view of memory as a gestalt or an integration of stimuli over time. In recent years, as our understanding of different architectures has improved, simple connectionism has been criticized for the way it recapitulates the stored-description approach.

The shortcomings of simple connectionism should now be obvious: What is learned are not internally constructed *experiences* but input–output pairings provided by the experimenter, and what is related are not *interacting processes* but predefined features by which inputs are described. In contrast, contextualists argued that learned associations are not presupplied outputs, but contrasts and distinctions functionally meaningful to the subject. Furthermore, in simple connectionist models, the categories to be learned (from the observer's perspective) are already implicit in the features by which an experimenter defines the inputs for the program. Storing a sequence of inputs with given outputs, and indeed, not requiring motor action at all, places simple connectionist learning squarely back in the associationist camp.

On the other hand, by the use of a "hidden layer" and feedback, simple connectionist networks do not merely store input–output pairs. An internal structure is developed that abstractly organizes the pairs. Studies of this structure reveal hierarchical patterns similar to those built deliberately into descriptive cognitive models (Elman, 1989). Hence, simple connectionism seeks to address the claim of Bartlett and the contextualists that learning is integrating and *relating*, "acquiring structure," not merely filing away. James McClelland (1991) summarizes this contribution:

> There is something basically associationist about connectionist networks that we work with today. They produce outputs in response to inputs. One of the key themes of work with these networks is the observation that they acquire structure – knowledge of regularities in the input and outputs and in the relations between them – through learning to produce particular outputs in response to particular inputs. (p. 42)

Thus, simple connectionism raises the possibility that a sequence of associations learned over time "could be the foundation of the sort of organized behavior calling for schemata-like notions" (Patterson, 1991, p. 36). As Mandler (1962) put it, "Cognitive characteristics of the organism may be developed out of associationist processes" (p. 416; cited in McClelland, 1991, p. 42). Thus, one response to the "build it in" excesses of descriptive cognitive modeling has been to return to the simple associations that inspired production rules, frames, and other schema modeling languages in the first place, but to replace the direct linking of items with a mechanism that relates the *history* of previous inputs (as encoded in weights in the network) to the current stimuli. Thus, there is some attempt to model experience as a cumulative, contextual effect and not as discretely stored and tagged events.

A survey by Dave Cliff (1991, pp. 32–34) provides a useful summary of the key problems with simple connectionism:

- *Biological implausibility:* "Connectionist 'models' do not correspond sufficiently closely to real neural systems to be regarded as models in the usual sense."
- *Information processing:* "The nervous system should not be treated as an input–output device.... Most connectionist models ... treat the

neural function to be modeled as being implemented in a 'pipeline' processor."

- *Designed ontology:* "Unless the network is involved in the first states of vision or hearing, the input vectors have to be prepared 'off-line,' invariably by humans rather than by other connectionist networks. That is, connectionist networks rely only on pre-processed information and are thus susceptible to the same problems as beset the microworld studies of the symbolic paradigm.... A model's performance depends crucially on the input and output representations chosen by the modeler."
- *Sensorimotor isolation:* "Connectionism exists within a biological vacuum.... If neurons are appropriately located relative to the sensorimotor system then activation patterns over a network of neuron[s] are meaningful *in themselves*. That is, the activation patterns do not have to be 'given meaning' in the same way that symbol-strings do."

Similar arguments have been made by Francis Crick, George Lakoff, Paul Smolensky, Heinz Pagels, Mark Bickhard, Jerry Fodor, Zenon Pylyshyn, and many others since the late 1980s (see also Lloyd, 1989, p. 97).

The difficulty of modeling human memory is only underscored by the failure of simple connectionism efforts to go beyond the ontological limits of stored description models, given that connectionism was devised to address this very issue. A related analysis is provided by Paul Verschure (1992, pp. 653–658) who argues that "subsymbolic connectionism does not fulfill its promise to solve the mind–brain dilemma, but still constitutes, in essence, a symbolic approach." He describes NETtalk, a connectionist program developed by T. J. Sejnowski and C. Rosenberg that learns how to talk:

The input layer of NETtalk consists of 7 identical groups of 29 units each. The letters of the alphabet plus 3 extra features representing word boundary and punctuation are coded in every group by a special unit.... Every unit of the output layer represents one of 23 articulatory features or one of 3 features representing stress and syllable boundaries. The network learns, by means of back propagation, to associate the letter coded for by the active unit of the fourth group of the input layer with a specific set of articulatory features represented by a specific pattern of active output units. The other 6 groups of the input layer provide a context.... NETtalk is able to learn to correctly pronounce 95% of the presented words after training 50,000 words. It could correctly generalize to new cases in 78% of the test words. (p. 654)

Analysis of the learned associations in the network showed that "patterns of the hidden units could be understood as separating two main features: vowels and consonants." Thus a "symbolic" distinction was claimed to have emerged from the back propagation process (the method by which strengths between layers are modified to represent relations between the input and the desired output). It is precisely this effort to find meaning in the patterns that Cliff and Lakoff claim is misguided.

Verschure points out that the articulatory features of the output layer constitute a predetermined encoding that distinguishes vowels from con- sonants. This encoding of 24 features has been created by linguists over time and constitutes a representation specially suited for the task of articu- lating vowel and consonant distinctions. Thus, it is no surprise that an internal mapping developed that distinguishes between vowels and conso- nants, given that words are input to the system, *along with the desired output*. According to Verschure, the real work is in the creation of the 24- feature category system for pronunciation, plus the preparation of the 50,000 input–output pairs constituting correct behavior associations. In this respect, a parallel–distributed processing (PDP) machine constitutes a clever hash-coding scheme: The person outside represents an item as a vector of features, which are numerically reconfigured for efficient storage. The memory's distributed nature does not change the fundamental encod- ing nature of the architecture.

Put another way, the representation of the domain of speech in terms of characters and articulatory features, plus the mappings of correct pronun- ciation associations, constitutes a *domain ontology* that is built into the program by the designers. The "subsymbolic" regularities found in the network after learning are already present implicitly in the design of the network and the data set. Hence, the very limitation we found at the conceptual level of Aaron and Mycin is replicated here in these models of perception: Mycin can produce an infinite variety of consultation dialogues, but the clinical parameters and their relations predetermine the situation- specific models it can produce. Similarly, although the variety of drawings that Aaron can produce is infinite, the kinds of elements and their relations are bounded by the ontology of the stored descriptions of anatomy, plants, and so on. This suggests that the work accomplished by the brain in con- structing meaningful patterns – at any level of analysis – has not been completely understood.

Rosenfield (1988) made similar observations in critiquing Rummelhart's early programs for learning the colors of flowers. The machine's ability to associate a color with an unknown flower originates in the programmer's *encoding* of the flower in terms of codes similar to those already learned. For example, the programmer provides as input specific codes correspond- ing to an a priori *parameterization* of objects into sizes and colors. The machine does not encounter flowers and colors as they occur in the world but is supplied with a *description* (p. 148):

Real generalization creates *new* categories of information . . . from the organism's point of view, the consequence of unforeseen elements in the environment. (p. 149)

A PDP researcher might claim that the preloading of the net, using a predetermined scheme of primitive features, in a teaching phase is just a way to start the research. But a continuation of the idea that the world presents itself as objective features, that reality can be coded, and that memory is storage of encodings is for contextualists just a continuation of the stored trace and "knowledge as true belief" view of descriptive modeling. The training approach begs several questions:

- Why does an organism *attend* to particular stimuli at all?
- "How do we create new ways of viewing the present, new *kinds* of generalizations?" (Rosenfield, 1988, p. 152)
- "How [do] patterns of activity acquire significance in a particular context?" (Ibid., p. 153)

Such questions resurrect the traditional nature–nurture dichotomy: The features and interests are either built in (developed in evolution and hence part of the mechanism itself) or they are inherent in the environment and learned. For example, how do children acquire the idea of past tense? (ibid., p. 153). Possibly the answer lies somewhere between these positions: A species-specific organizing process *creates useful distinctions* (features). Thus, the primitive units are not input, nor are they built in as primitives. Instead, the organizing process itself constructs patterns that constitute experience. Hence what is experienced and experience per se are circularly defined; in Gregory Bateson's terms, the developed system of distinctions is tautological. This is the approach of the situated roboticists and ecological psychologists. I conclude this discussion by introducing some of the problems and successful angles of attack.

First, consider the fundamental problem of perceptual learning, as posed by even a simple robot system. In Khepera, for example, a commercially available device, the infrared sensors may be in a combination of 1000^8 possible states. A robot's actions are able to distinguish only a small part of this sensory space: Many combinations are equivalent, and somehow generalizations must be easily formed and reactivated, or every sensory grouping will appear unique. The simplest approach is to predefine which states are functionally useful. For example, in Toto, a robot developed by Mataric (Chapter 5), features are built in to distinguish boxes from doorknobs or whatever else might be placed in an office environment. How could a robot learn features by generalizing sensory data from the actual objects it encounters?

One approach, promoted by Gerald Edelman and George Reeke (Chapter 7), is to induce discriminatory relations in the space of perceptual categorizations by projection from the space of useful actions. In shorthand form:

values –(reinforce)→ a space of actions –(induce)→ perceptual categorizations –(competitively selected within)→ space of sensory states.

That is, values and hence actions "tie down perception" (Rolf Pfeifer, private communication). Such a theory of perception isn't grounded in a vocabulary of primitive descriptions, but instead demonstrates how a certain mechanism functionally reduces a huge state space of *sensory data* to distinctions of value.

Mark Bickhard's analysis comes from the other direction, emphasizing that the *possibility of error* must be inherent in representational systems. A mere encoding of given inputs and outputs simply *records* a given association. An agent that encodes associations cannot be mistaken in how it discriminates input, for it is creating no criteria for itself of what constitutes a feature and what outputs are of value. Categorization cannot be just memorizing associations, but *actively constructing distinctions* and learning by feedback:

> Representational correspondences are intrinsically atemporal. . . . Encodings do not require any agent in order to exist; they are not dependent on action – however much it may be that action is taken to be dependent on (interpreting them). . . . Interactive representation cannot exist in a passive system – a system with no outputs. . . . Action and representation are not, and cannot be distinct modules. (Bickhard, in press, p. 8)

To restate these criticisms of what Bickhard calls *encodingism*, to which simple connectionism falls prey: We must distinguish the translational coding and categories of human languages from the internal biological processes by which sensorimotor coordination occurs. In short, the experimental setting of simple connectionism repeats the same shortcomings of associationism in not confronting the problems and accomplishments of everyday life. The fundamental failure of the stored-descriptions approach is in viewing the information-processing model of reasoning literally as a *complete mechanism of the brain*, suggesting that referential and inferential processes involving storage, matching, and composition, which obviously occur in serial, conscious behavior, account for *every aspect* of perception, memory, real-time movement, and intentionality.

In particular, models based on already formed descriptions (such as parameters in rules or procedures) cannot explain the evolution of language from a nondescriptive basis. This alone reminds us that other, nondescriptive-based mechanisms are operating in animals, and suggests that similar mechanisms are still operating and providing a basis for human cognition. Rejecting the stored-description approach as the foundation of cognition is tantamount to saying that knowledge is not fundamentally a copy of reality or behavior; memory is not a trace or record of encountered objects. Instead, knowing and remembering are constructive operations based on internal value as well as feedback. This situated approach assumes a complex interplay between nature and nurture, inside and outside, construction and world, and neural and social. The study of human memory suggests that this relating, coordinating process occurs by a mechanism that is interactive and historical, operates on many levels of organization simultaneously, and involves feedback in a way different from the serial and parallel architectures of computational systems.

With these observations and speculations in mind, we now turn to some neurobiological evidence and alternative perceptual-memory architectures that show how categorizing is possible without receiving input in terms of features that already carve up the world. The central question becomes "What is the nature of information?"

4   Sensorimotor maps versus encodings

For the animal, there is no such thing as up and down, front and back, in reference to an outside world, as it exists for the observer doing the study. There is only an internal correlation between the place where the retina receives a given perturbation and the muscular contractions that move the tongue, the mouth, the neck, and, in fact, the frog's entire body.

> Humberto R. Maturana and Francisco J. Varela, *The tree of knowledge: The biological roots of human understanding*, 1987, pp. 125–126

From an engineering perspective, all the questions about representations and memory can be rephrased as a simple question: What should a robot builder put inside the head of a robot? If knowledge is somehow improvised in interaction, subjectively functional, and coupled to perceptual experience, can memory be just a place where descriptions of the world and behavior are stored? Each of the descriptive modeling approaches to learning, especially "learning by being told," must assume that the world can be parametrized in some objective, useful way – primitives by which all facts and plans will be categorized. Or if such parameters are learned and subjective, all such models beg the question of how a representational foundation is constructed within the organism, for they either build in descriptions or supply descriptions as input. Thus, the question "What is knowledge?" becomes "What is memory?" and then "What is perception?"

In this chapter, I present recent work in neurobiology that shows how a representing capability may develop in sensorimotor coordination. Although the mechanism still has primitives, these are not features of objects or events in the world. Indeed, what is learned is not a description of the world or behavior, but a *coupling* between sensory stimuli and motor systems, developed through feedback during the organism's functioning. In moving to the sensorimotor level, we find that our questions about memory and perception finally settle on the question "What is information?" I begin with the philosophical analyses of Heinz von Foerster and Gregory Bateson, and then show how they are supported by Michael Merzenich's recent study of the owl monkey's sensorimotor maps. With this empirical grounding, I explain Humberto Maturana's theory of structural coupling, contrasting the idea of instruction with learning in a tautological system.

Finally, I show how John Dewey originally formulated the coupling idea in his critique of stimulus–response theory 100 years ago.

Von Foerster and Bateson: Descriptions of information

The idea that information is a physical substance is fundamental to information processing psychology. Following ideas developed in early data processing, information is viewed as some*thing* that can be stored, coded, matched, and displayed. In information processing psychology, information is treated synonymously with the idea of descriptive representation: Information consists of the names of things or events (e.g., "The patient's name is Bill"), numeric values or qualitative abstractions of parameters (e.g., "The patient's pulse is low"), and even causal explanations for observations (e.g., "We have been informed that the president has ischemia"). Indeed, the idea of *information* is often conflated with the ideas of *data*, *representation*, *model*, and *knowledge*, so the only distinctions are what is input and what is output in a given situation.

Criticisms of information processing terminology were raised by two of the most famous cyberneticists, Heinz von Foerster and Gregory Bateson. They recalled an earlier theoretical approach that attempted to do justice to both biological and computer systems rather than reformulate mental processing in computational terms. At a conference in 1969, Heinz von Foerster described how computer engineers in the 1950s began to use cognitive terms to describe machine operations:

Although it is quite possible, and perhaps even appropriate, to talk about a "proud IBM 360-50 system," the "valiant 1800," or the "sly PDP 8," I have never observed anyone using this style of language. Instead, we romanticize what appears to be the intellectual functions of the machines. We talk about their "memories," we say that these machines store and retrieve "information," they "solve problems," "prove theorems," etc. . . . (1970, p. 28)

For example, Newell and Simon used such language in naming the General Problem Solver, a system by which situations and desired states could be modeled using predicate calculus descriptions, manipulated in turn by an inference engine using means–ends analysis. Von Foerster especially objected to the adoption of anthropomorphic terms by biologists in the 1960s:

In the last decade or so something odd and distressing developed, namely, that not only the engineers who work with these systems gradually began to believe that those mental functions whose *names* were first metaphorically applied to some machine operations are indeed residing in these machines, but also some biologists – tempted by the absence of a comprehensive theory of mentation – began to believe that certain machine operations which unfortunately carried the *names* of some mental processes are indeed functional isomorphs of these operations. (Ibid.)

That is, scientists began to treat the operations of computer programs as indistinguishable from naturally occurring memory, perception, learning, and so on in animals. This criticism was especially valid in the 1960s before the development of integrated *active* models of memory and learning, when the term *computer memory* meant just a store. Nevertheless, von Foerster's experience in drawing these distinctions sounds eerily similar to what early proponents of situated cognition experienced a decade later:

> The delusion . . . is so well established in these two professions that he who follows Lorenz's example and attempts now to "de-anthropomorphize" machines and to "de-mechanize" man is prone to encounter antagonisms similar to those Lorenz encountered when he began to "animalize" animals. (Ibid., p. 29)

The difficulty then, as now, is to articulate how the named functions, reified as a mapping between descriptions of machines and descriptions of animals, could otherwise be organized and operating:

> This reluctance to adopt a conceptual framework in which apparently separate higher mental faculties as, for example, "to learn," "to remember," "to perceive," "to recall," "to predict," etc. are seen as various manifestations of a single, more inclusive phenomenon, namely "cognition," is quite understandable. It would mean abandoning the comfortable position in which these faculties can be treated in isolation and thus can be reduced to rather trivial mechanisms. (Ibid.)

Von Foerster claims that processes that operate together in the service of one, whole organism are reduced in early information processing psychology to functions studied and modeled independently:

> Memory, for instance, contemplated in isolation is reduced to "recording," learning to "change," perception to "input," etc. In other words, by separating these functions from the totality of cognitive processes one has abandoned the original problem and now searches for mechanisms that implement entirely different functions that may or may not have any semblance with some processes that are, as Maturana pointed out, subservient to the maintenance of the integrity of the organism as a functioning unit. (Ibid.)

Although one may object that the models of the late 1970s didn't separate memory, learning, and problem solving in this way, perception was still separated out until the incorporation of connectionist models in the 1980s. Furthermore, von Foerster's objections about problem-solving terminology remain valid, and are precisely those raised by social scientists who show that the operation of most computer models is not embedded in social function, in the manner of a person conceiving and coordinating activity over time (illustrated by the discussion of Harold Cohen as an artist versus Aaron's operation):

> If "memory" is a misleading metaphor in recording devices, so is the epithet of "problem solver" for our computing machines. Of course, they are no problem solvers, because they do not have any problems in the first place. It is *our* problems

they help us solve like any useful tool, say, a hammer which may be dubbed a "problem solver" for driving nails into a board. The danger in this subtle semantic twist by which the responsibility for action is shifted from man to machine lies in making us lose sight of the problem of cognition. By making us believe that the issue is how to find solutions to some well-defined problems, we may forget to ask first what constitutes a "problem," what is its "solution," and – when a problem is identified – what makes us want to solve it. (Ibid., p. 30)

Thus, recalling the framework I introduced in Table 1.1, on the one hand von Foerster attacks the theories of *mechanism* that linearize and separate perception and memory, and on the other hand he attacks the theories of *function* that reduce desires, responsibility, and problems to puzzles.

In some respects, the term *information* cuts across these levels of analysis, for the idea of information suggests to von Foerster something that both changes the agent and is meaningful to the agent:

Another case of pathological semantics . . . is the widespread use of the term "information." This poor thing is nowadays "processed," "stored," "retrieved," "compressed," "chopped," etc., as if it were hamburger meat. Since the case history of this modern disease may easily fill an entire volume, I only shall pick on the so-called "information storage and retrieval systems". . . . Of course, these systems do not store information, they store books, tapes, microfiche or other sorts of documents, and it is again these books, tapes, microfiche or other documents that are retrieved which only if looked upon by a human mind may yield the desired information. (Ibid., p. 30)

I believe von Foerster would agree today that the term *construct* rather than *yield* is more appropriate here. He wishes to distinguish passively existing data from an internal categorization that is functioning as part of a larger cognitive system. At one level, this is the distinction I have drawn between a descriptive model such as Mycin's map and the human experience of comprehending it. Von Foerster objected to the early terminology because there was no active processing that created information, only a place where descriptions were stored:

Calling these systems "information storage and retrieval systems" is tantamount to calling a garage a "transportation storage and retrieval system." By confusing vehicles for potential information with information, one puts again the problem of cognition nicely into one's blind spot of intellectual vision, and the problem conveniently disappears. If indeed the brain were seriously compared with one of these storage and retrieval systems, distinct from these only by its quantity of storage rather than by quality of process, such a theory would require a demon with cognitive powers to zoom through this huge system in order to extract from its contents the information that is vital to the owner of this brain. (Ibid.)

A cognitive scientist may easily object that the 1970s models of reading comprehension, for example, address von Foerster's complaint. His mention of a demon raises the well-known homunculus objection: A memory system consisting of descriptions alone would require an entire human being inside to read and interpret what the descriptions mean. (Searle presents a form of this objection, which I discuss in Chapter 14.) Von Foerster's paper ends at this point, and he admits being unable to resolve the dilemma. In some respects, his view of information is not very different from the information processing view when he speaks about "extracting" information from the contents of a store. He believes that something else is going on when we comprehend text to "yield information." He criticizes the match, filter, and reassemble view, yet his own language offers no alternative. The information processing models of the 1970s do indeed sound like what he was looking for. No homunculus is necessary when information, knowledge, and memory are identified with a flow of symbols carrying meaning, such as texts. Indeed, this is the allure of the descriptive modeling perspective: With all information processing flattened to word manipulation, except for the modulation and control of sensory and motor input–output, no other coordination processes are required.

How can we conceive of information as something dynamic, a relation within and between cognitive processes, not something *inherent* in a thing? Bateson (1972) developed this idea in his *ecological approach* to epistemology:

It is flatly obvious that no variable of zero dimensions can be truly located. 'Information' and 'form' resemble contrast, frequency, symmetry, correspondence, congruence, conformity and the like in being of zero dimensions and therefore are not to be located.

The contrast between this white paper and that black coffee is not somewhere between the paper and the coffee. . . . Nor is the contrast located between the two objects and my eye. It is not even in my head. Or, if it be, it must also be in your head. . . . In fact information and form are not items which can be localized. (p. 409; figure not in original text)

Bateson's analysis implicitly distinguishes between information and descriptions of information. Two basic properties of descriptions (e.g., words, rules, blueprints, semantic nets) – dimensionality and location – do not apply to information when it is viewed as an analytical term. Bateson treats *form*, meaning *pattern*, similarly because patterning is itself a relation with respect to some larger *functional context*. To say that something is a pattern, such as a configuration of trees on a hillside or strokes made by a pen on paper, is to detect a difference, a frequency, a symmetry, a correspondence, or the like relative to some larger universe of items or events. This detection doesn't necessarily involve anything as complex as human conception and description. This notion of pattern is also simpler than Newell and Simon's definition of symbol, "any pattern that denotes," which views information as a physical substance, residing in physical forms that carry it. Indeed, at this level of creating distinctions, one is beginning to consider how symbols themselves are created.

Von Foerster, Gregory Bateson, and the biologists and ecological psychologists we will consider subsequently (Chapter 11) strive for a theory of information (and hence of *cognition* or *mind*) that doesn't identify knowledge with scientific models (in the way Mycin's map is called knowledge). Indeed, a biologically oriented epistemology necessarily evokes mechanisms that existed prior to the evolution of the human species. In considering the cognition of insects or other mammals, ecological psychologists view information as a primitive notion that has nothing specifically to do with meaning or language.

The best way to understand what von Foerster and Bateson were saying is to jump ahead a decade to neural studies of sensorimotor learning involving the hand of a monkey. From this experimental work, we will then be able to understand Maturana's related claims about information and instruction. This will give us a dramatically different view of representing, one that is biologically based, and sets the stage for the memory and coordination mechanisms presented in subsequent chapters.

The owl monkey's map

Figure 4.1 shows areas of a monkey's brain (parietal cortex) and hand. Michael Merzenich and his associates have established that different areas of the monkey's brain become activated when certain areas on the monkey's hand are touched. In this "sematosensory map . . . the location of a tactile stimulus is represented as a spot on a map" (Steels, 1990a, p. 72). The left side of the diagram, showing the part of the brain, is the tactile map. Like a geographic map, a tactile map is analogical: Rather than specifying the locations of areas of the hand by descriptions, such as by stating that "The thumb is next to the first finger" or perhaps (NEXT-TO THUMB FIRST-FINGER), contiguous areas in the hand are represented as contiguous areas in the brain. For example, the relations between the areas of the hand labeled P_1, P_2, and so on have corresponding areas in the brain, bearing the same ordering and contiguity.

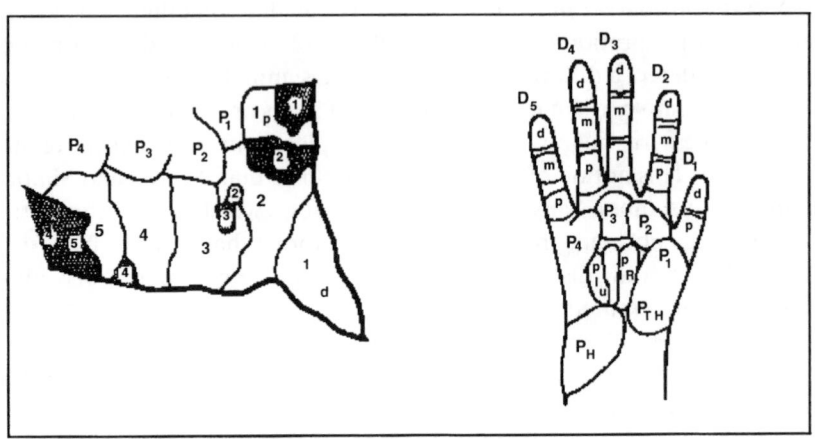

Figure 4.1. Sensory map (left, about 5mm wide) of the hand of a monkey. (Reprinted with permission from Steels, 1989, Figure 3, p. 73; adapted from Demazeau, Bourdon, and Lebrasseur, 1989; see also Merzenich, Kaas, Wall, Nelson, Sur, and Felleman, 1983a.)

It is tempting to view the internal "map" as having the same relation to the hand as the map of the Stanford campus bears to buildings and roads out in the world. Indeed, Figure 4.1 functions in this way to brain-map makers. But to understand neural functioning, we must distinguish how Figure 4.1 was created and how the neural distinctions (*described* by the left side of Figure 4.1 and boundaries drawn on the hand) were constructed.

To begin, consider that the symbols like P_1 and P_2 in Figure 4.1 don't actually appear in the monkey's brain. Similarly, the lines demarking areas of the monkey's brain, labeled P_1 and so on, don't appear in the brain. Unlike the names of roads and buildings on the Stanford campus map (Figure 2.1), the symbols and boundaries in Figure 4.1 exist only as part of *our description* of the relation between the monkey's brain and the monkey's hand.

More specifically, Figure 4.1 was constructed by stimulating parts of the monkey's hand. It is a map of how *two processes* – stimuli in the hand and neural activation in the brain – are related. These processes are related because the nervous system physically connects the hand to the brain. Figure 4.1 describes the relation between the processes of stimulation and neural activation. Actually, there is no huge bundle of nerves that links every conceivable spot of the area labeled P_3 on the palm, for example, to every spot in the area labeled P_3 in the brain. Instead, the map says that if you touch area P_3 on the palm, you will observe activation somewhere within the area of the brain labeled P_3. That is, Figure 4.1 describes "what happens when" rather than merely "the hand there is connected to the brain here." The two halves of Figure 4.1, separated by a white space, do not show how processes involving nerve stimulation and neural activation *are occurring within a single, connected physical system*, the monkey's body.

Dynamic, systemic processes of representing

When we look at Figure 4.1, we might view the right side, the description of the monkey's hand, as being something in the world, which the left side, the description of the monkey's brain, is about. The figure gives the impression of a *correspondence*, a mapping between language and the world, like the relation between the Stanford map and the university. But that is not how the neural maps that the diagram portrays develop and function.

It is true that the left side of the diagram can be viewed as being *about* the right side of the diagram (in the sense that we are expected to interpret the area labeled P_4 in the brain map as referring to the area labeled P_4 in the hand map). But this view of Figure 4.1 distorts the nature of *representing* occurring in the monkey's brain. As observers detecting neural activations through our instrumentation of the monkey's brain, we may say, "Ah, this area of the brain, P_4, represents this area P_4 of the hand." But actually, the diagram portrays just a *correlation of processes* in one physically closed system (the monkey's nervous system), which we have cut into parts, labeled, and observed at different times. The analytic, linguistic process of describing (what a person does in creating Figure 4.1) should not be equated with physical processes occurring inside a nervous system (when part of the monkey's brain becomes activated and activates other areas of the brain).

Maturana emphasizes the linguistic aspect of modeling, which occurs when we create Figure 4.1, the Stanford map, Mycin's knowledge base, or Aaron's anatomical database:

The basic operation that an observer performs (although this observation is not exclusive to observers) is the operation of distinction; that is, the pointing to a unity by performing an operation which defines its boundaries and separates it from a background. (1975, p. 325)

We usually speak and provide explanations for perceptual phenomena as if we as observers and the animals that we observe existed in a world of objects, and as if the phenomenon of perception consisted in grasping the features of the objects of the world, because these have the means to permit or specify this grasping. (1983, p. 60)

In explaining how the monkey can sense objects and move its hand, we relate features in one realm (the hand) to features in another (the brain). The continuous maps depicted in Figure 4.1 are *scientific constructions* from a discrete set of 172 probes: "Boundaries between the cortical areas of representation for different skin sectors were constructed by halving the distance between adjacent penetrations with different receptive fields" (Merzenich et al., 1983a, p. 35). This is not to say that the monkey's brain is not creating distinctions in a broad sense; the boundaries shown in Figure 4.1 accurately describe sharp discontinuities in the way neurons respond to stimulation (Merzenich, Kaas, Wall, Sur, Nelson, and Feldman, 1983b, p. 659). But Maturana warns us that we, as observers trying to explain perception, easily confuse our analysis with the work of the system we are studying: Our diagrams and descriptive models in general tend to view perception as a process of *mapping features to one another* rather than explaining *how the perceptual process itself creates features*.

Indeed, a developmental view reveals that the areas we label P_1, and so on, and encompassing neural processes that categorize the activation of these areas, are not hardwired but created and sustained as a process of ongoing, systemic differentiation.[1] Not only are neural areas not labeled and associated by tables or other data structures, the evidence suggests that the association of tactile stimulus and internal activation is dynamically maintained, through stimulation itself and continues to change in an adult monkey:

Map features . . . are the product of dynamic cortical processes. Our results fully support that conclusion for the sematosensory cortex, but we add the provisos that such dynamic processes are not fixed *in situ*, and that these resultant movements manifest a principal cortical process. . . . (Ibid., p. 660)

That is, sensory representations are not static structures, nor are they fixed procedures; the dynamic relations between skin surfaces and *cortical receptive fields* appear to be organized by a kind of *projection filter* onto the cortical areas. Most important, when nerves are severed between skin and cortex, the *receptive fields reorganize*. Amazingly, "the sites of representation of given field surfaces move across the cortical map as it reorganizes" (ibid., p. 661). That is, cortical areas are found to respond to different tactile areas and the *entire map is reorganized*, "including boundaries between more distant digits," as if one reshaped California and modified the Washington–Canada border as well (Calvin, 1988, p. 1802). "These changes strongly suggest that normal sematosensory cortex is subject to territorial competition, to a self-organizing force that can alter its topography" (Merzenich et al., 1983a, p. 50).

Furthermore, changes apparently occur as a product of dynamic processes operating at all levels, not just in the receptive fields. Merzenich et al. conclude that the mechanisms operating here are quite unlike prevalent descriptive models and may be just as important in perceptual-motor coordination:

These results are completely contrary to a view of sensory systems as consisting of hardwired machines, essentially established through a critical period of development, and static thereafter. That is, while anatomical wiring may or may not be static, and almost certainly limits distances across maps over which reorganization can occur after that early critical stage of brain development, dynamic modification of local map detail occurs throughout life. It is reasonable to suppose that such alterability is relevant to learning, recognition, and the acquisition of tactile skill. (1983b, p. 662)

Maturana characterizes such systems as *autopoietic*: The network of components and relations that constitute the system is continuously regenerated in the operation of the system itself. A fundamental characteristic of such systems is that they are not *in*-structable in the manner of computer programs, which match inputs against internally stored structures. Rather, the structure-sustaining processes of a sematosensory map are *internal differentiations*, not forms accepted from outside. Bateson referred to such relations as *tautological*; related analyses of such mechanisms use the term *dialectic* (Chapter 10). That is, the structural forms and relations are *mutually defining*, such that the function of a part (what an observer might call its *meaning*) depends on the normal operation of the system as a whole.

Theories of information processing that view representing as synonymous with symbol structure manipulation only vaguely characterize how processes of representing – processes detecting differences that functionally make a difference – develop in the sensorimotor processes of the brain. Given the dynamic aspects of higher-order mental processes of categorizing and reasoning – as opposed to sensory maps, which had been viewed as hardwired or static – it seems reasonable to hypothesize that conceptual and procedural representing in the brain has *at least* the plasticity now observed in sensory maps. That is, although there are perhaps significant, gross differences in the way sensorimotor and conceptual processes are neurally formed, the "openness" of perceptual recognition and metaphorical uses of concepts suggests a mechanism of adaptability-in-use, similar to what is observed in sensory map construction. Consequently, in addition to philosophical arguments about the "openness" of meaning and knowledge "construction," we now have biological evidence of a kind of learning mechanism that descriptive cognitive models do not replicate.

Maturana: In-formation versus in-struction

At this point, it is useful to consider a related analysis by Humberto Maturana, a biologist who strongly influenced von Foerster as well as Winograd and Flores's later critique of descriptive modeling. Complementing Bateson's cybernetic view (the zero-dimensionality of information),

Maturana (1970) criticizes the idea that sensory information is a kind of input that "instructs" an organism about perceptual features. He presents a profoundly ecological perspective, common to the cybernetic-biology approach, which takes the total system of organism-in-its-environment to be the phenomenon to be understood:

> Living systems are units of interactions; they exist in an environment. From a purely biological point of view they cannot be understood independently of the part of the environment with which they interact, the niche; nor can the niche be defined independently of the living system that occupies it. (p. 5)

This philosophical stance places the organism, observer, and world in a relation quite different from the one assumed in descriptive cognitive models:

> When an observer claims that an organism exhibits perception, what he or she beholds is an organism that brings forth a world of actions through sensory motor correlations congruent with perturbations of the environment in which he or she sees it [the organism] to conserve its adaptation.
> The phenomenon connoted by the word perception cannot be one of grasping features of an independent object world. (1983, p. 60)

"Bringing forth a world of actions" emphasizes the organism's *active construction* ("bringing forth") of functionally relevant features (called *affordances* by J. J. Gibson; see Chapter 11). The process is not that of "grasping (pre-existing) features" but of *making* distinctions. *Making* is to be taken literally here as a physical, *formative* process. The term *world* in "world of actions" emphasizes that the constructed features are relevant to action, such that perceiving a world is distinguishing "possibilities for action" – not naming or identifying per se, but recognizing "circumstances to act with or upon." Dewey called this view of categorizing *instrumentalism*. In contrast, Aaron's knowledge of body postures is not felt or enacted, but is *described* in a parametrized model of parts and orientations, consciously created by a perceiving, speaking person.

To explain further the perceptual learning mechanism, Maturana claims that a perceptual system in biology is *composite*; it "interacts through the operation of the properties of its components." That is, the components are not merely physically linked, like gears and levers, but are emergent properties functionally related. In Bateson's terms, biological processes relate not just through the dimensional physics of force and mass, but also through their operational qualities, which are *relationally determined* in space and time within a *system* of components. Such qualities include "contrast, frequency, symmetry, correspondence, congruence, [and] conformity." For example, in a composite system, modules operating in parallel may be tuned through negative feedback to accentuate their opposing outputs (a process by which contrast boundaries are detected in the visual system).

A composite system is *structure determined* in the sense that "its interactions can only trigger in it structural changes determined in its structure without specifying them" (Maturana, 1983, pp. 62–63). The parts don't describe or encode future states by which one component "specifies" how the whole will change; instead, components are operating within a space of configurations of the whole by which all components are mutually configured. There is no locus of control or specification. Put another way, Maturana says that the perceptual system is "informationally closed." Interaction with the environment is not mediated by encodings that pass from outside to inside; rather, the environment is "directly perceived" (Gibson's term).

Understanding the ideas of *information closure* and *direct perception* is essential for understanding the kind of memory-coordination mechanism Merzenich has uncovered. I devote Part IV to unraveling what *direct* means. I show a way of broadening the idea of *symbol* to distinguish between inferential processes (Figure 3.2) and *direct coupling* of subsystems (Chapters 12 and 13). Here I provide a first-pass introduction to the ideas.

To explain the idea of direct perception, Winograd and Flores (1986) paraphrased one of Maturana's examples:

When light strikes the retina, it alters the structure of the nervous system by triggering chemical changes in the neurons. This changed structure will lead to patterns of activity different from those that would have been generated without the change, but it is a misleading simplification to view this change as a perception of the light. If we inject an irritant into a nerve, it triggers a change in the patterns of activity, but one which we would hesitate to call a "perception" of the irritant. Maturana argues that all activity of the nervous system is best understood in this way. The focus should be on the interactions within the system as a whole, not on the structure of perturbations. (p. 42)

"Perception of light" is the observer's perspective. To understand how the nervous system works, so that we might replicate it, we must adopt a more myopic view. From the nervous system's perspective, perception is changing internal relations (as in the adjustments of the monkey's sematosensory maps), not creating and storing structures that stand for something happening outside. From this perspective, the *structure* of the perturbations doesn't matter. Indeed, structures participating in and reconstructed by perceptual recognition will change with every experience – an idea that is modeled in terms of chaotic attractors in Freeman's model of odor recognition (Chapter 6).

The states of a structurally determined system are not directly modified by the medium, but only changed through the mutually determined properties of the components. In this respect, a structure-determined system "does not admit instructive interactions. . . . [A]ll that takes place in the operation of the nervous system are changes of relations of activity between its component elements" (Maturana, 1983, pp. 63, 65). The idea of direct perception has been misunderstood from an objectivist perspective as suggesting that the world is somehow directly mapped inside – suggesting perhaps that sensation is not complex, that it converts complex objects and qualities into direct signals, or that the agent perceives only whole entities. Instead, the direct aspect is from the viewpoint of the system itself, whose boundaries admit no *insertion* of neural structures or other *forms* that might be input and placed in buffers to be processed. The only *formative* changes are occurring internally as the system is perturbed by signals, flux, or whatever energy changes are detected at the sensory surface.

In this interpretation of Gibson's idea of direct perception, *directness* means that the internal structures constitute and sustain their own space of configurations without *mediating* "stuff," such as symbol strings representing the world. At this level of processing, outside stuff is neither brought inside directly nor mapped onto internal codes. Internal structures operate on their own changing properties. Higher levels of processing may *categorize* sensory configurations, but these are again only internal correspondences or relations between internal structures. Perception is direct because it involves neither *input* nor *reference* to outside stuff. Only when an agent *conceives of a relation* between categories (e.g., as in talk about stuff in the world) do the notions of reference and correspondence, and hence meaning, operate – only then can there be *inferences*. A perceptual system operates in a different way.

Bateson described a perceptual representational system as tautological because the structures are *mutually formed*, as a set of differentiations, functionally constructed through feedback in action. This is to be contrasted again with the view that representing is copying the world or setting up a map that corresponds to what is in the world. Talk about correspondences characterizes the scientific process of creating geographical maps, anatomical charts, and models in expert systems, but it doesn't fit the operation of a perceptual system. This analysis fundamentally changes the notion of information. As the contextualist Robert Hoffman says in summarizing the descriptive modeling point of view: "Information is supposed to be real and representations are supposed to carry it" (Hoffman and Nead, 1983, p. 544). Thus internal representations in perceptual systems are not merely carried or mapped into the system on a flow of symbols; the functionality of representing can develop in another way by structural coupling. Ultimately, this analysis leads us to reformulate how internal structures come to *function as symbols* in the brain (Chapters 12 and 13).

Maturana's (1980) notion of *information closure* is not to be confused with the openness of the nervous system to change. The system is open to structural changes and becomes coupled to its *medium* (the environment). The historically developed complementarity of the organism-and-its-environment is called *structural coupling*. Perceptual learning is therefore not like the idea of learning by being instructed:

> Any description of learning in terms of the acquisition of a representation of the environment is, therefore, merely metaphorical and carries no explanatory value. Furthermore, such a description is necessarily misleading because it implies a system in which instructive interactions would take place, and such a system is, epistemologically, out of the question. In fact, if no notion of instruction is used, the problem becomes simplified because, then, learning appears as the process of continuous ontogenic structural coupling to its medium. . . . (p. xviii)

Observers may observe trends and describe them, but these trends are inherent in the historical interactions and are not driven by such descriptions:

> Accordingly, the significance that an observer may see a posteriori in a given behavior acquired through learning plays no part in the specification of the structure through which it becomes implemented. Also, although it is possible for us as human beings to stipulate from a metadomain of descriptions an aim in learning, this aim only determines a bias, a direction, in a domain of selection, not a structure to be acquired. This latter can only become specified during the actual history of learning (ontogenic structural coupling) because it is contingent upon this history. (Ibid.)

To explain this point of view, Maturana prefers not to talk about the operation of structure coupling in terms of causality:

> The notion of causality is a notion that pertains to the domain of descriptions, and as such it is relevant only to the metadomain in which the observer makes his commentaries and cannot be deemed to be operative in the phenomenal domain, the object of the description. (Ibid.)

Talk of instruction and subsequent behavior adopts the perspective of the teacher attempting to change the organism. "Instructive interaction" is based on a particular *punctuated view*: teacher, information, organism, memory, perception, interpretation, action. In seeking a different word than *causality*, Maturana is pointing to an understanding of change that doesn't begin with "here the organism" and "here the environment." He considers how the organism's interactions within a medium establish a *perceived niche* (1983, p. 64), which constitutes the environment from the organism's point of view. Rather than saying that "This probe causes this behavior," we consider how the existence of a probe becomes constructed by the organism in a process of self-reorganization.

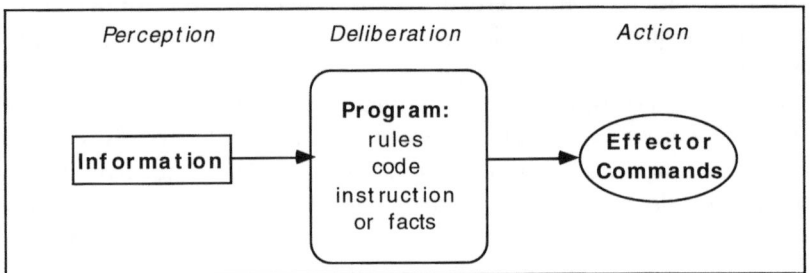

Figure 4.2. Information processing view of information as instructive.

Structural coupling adopts the perspective of the organism *functioning as a whole* with a changing environment. This *structure determinism* is based on a new kind of punctuated view: signal, internal correlation circuit, reactivation, coordination. By this view, it is the structure of the organism that "determines that it may be perturbed and *how* it will be perturbed by other objects" (Dell, 1985, p. 8). (This is essentially Gibson's notion of dispositional properties and affordances; see Chapter 11.) Saying that the learning system is *operationally closed* avoids placing scientists as describers between the world and the organism. The resulting theory of change is mechanistic in the sense of characterizing physical structures *within the organism* that are changing over time. And necessarily, such a mechanism does not admit *descriptions* of reorganization imposed from outside. The exchange of information occurs not as a transfer, but as a coupling between the nervous system and its medium. Furthermore, structural coupling is occurring all the time; even apparently stable behavior is actively reconstructed:

For a learning system there are no trivial experiences (interactions) because all interactions result in the selection of a structural change, even when the selected structure leads to the stabilization of a given behavior. (Maturana, 1978, p. 45)

To summarize, Figure 4.2 contrasts stored-symbol systems and structure-determined systems more explicitly. By the information processing view, information is of something coded, existing objectively in the environment as patterns, such as numbers or names in a database, signals output from a measurement instrument, speech, diagrams, and so on.

A computer system controlled by a descriptive model is structurally open: It is *in-structable*. Information consists of *structures that come in.* Input data and instructions are physical structures that literally match internal tags and their descriptions. For example, the letter A printed on paper, **A**, can be recognized as the letter A. Information may consist of verbal descriptions (such as the answers to Mycin's questions) or coded structures (such as the numeric ASCII notation that encodes the alphabet). Video cameras allow less structured input, but these are parsed by descriptions of objects and properties stored in the general model. So again, input is viewed as a *mapping* between "what is out there" and internal, preexisting descriptors (either models or primitives).

In contrast, a biological system is structurally closed. The system's history determines what produces an informative configuration and what is just noise. The system's history determines what is a *pattern* in the environment. The correlations a scientist-observer discovers between signals and internal structure do not *represent* these signals in the same way a descriptive model represents the world (e.g., Figure 4.1) (Dell, 1985, p. 10). The learning process by which the organism is physically changed during interactions with the environment is perhaps best viewed as *selective*. The internal structure of the organism *determines* the response, but the environmental interaction selects for different responses over time (ibid., p. 8). Learning is thus incremental and evolutionary, involving feedback and internal adjustment. The emergent organizations in the brain are *sensorimotor relations*, not coded transformations of detected signals in isolation. Perceptual information has no existence as information apart from categorizing and movement-oriented processes.

The biological studies of Merzenich and Maturana show that the information processing metaphor of input and output is not adequate for understanding the perceptual aspects of cognition. This raises questions about theories of conceptualization (as in comprehending a problem description) that suppose that information is given to a subject:

We all too often believe that information and communication can determine and specify how a living organism will behave. This is not the case. So-called "information" does not and cannot instruct the behavior of a living system. What we typically label as information is merely something which we observe to be interacting with the system. (Ibid., p. 6)

But relating Maturana's theory of perceptual systems to higher-level conceptual and reasoning requires some care. For example, text and diagrams have a tangible, conventional organization that speech and visual signals lack. An alternative definition of information must account for how stable, coherent conceptual systems develop within a community.

In particular, we must not adopt Maturana's either/or terminology wholesale. In making statements like "science cannot deal with systems that admit instructive interactions" (1983, p. 63), Maturana rejects terms like *information*, *control*, and *hierarchy* without making clear that they have value in describing and designing systems viewed in isolation, such as computers. Similarly, his rejection of *causality* is less useful than showing how the notion of structural coupling broadens our view of spatial and temporal interaction. Maturana's language gives the reader the impression that his view is objectively superior. Saying that "regulation" is "merely an observer's description" (Dell, 1985, p. 14) unnecessarily makes descriptive explanations appear inherently inferior. Obviously, it is nonsensical to equate science with a particular scientific approach (see the Conclusions, for further discussion of this pitfall).

Similarly, Maturana and Varela (1987) insist that the nervous system is not "representational" because the "structural state specifies what perturbations are possible and what changes trigger them" (p. 69); hence there are no preexisting inputs to represent. This properly rejects the view of perceptual representation as description or encoding, but there is no reason to say that the sensorimotor maps in the owl monkey's brain are not representational. Here representing involves recurrent transformational processes over time and space between different sensory systems; higher-level coordinating processes are categorizing these correlations and thus representing internal state (cf. Edelman's model in Chapter 6).

When we trumpet the exclusive value of one view (e.g., "Cognition is a biological phenomenon and can only be understood as such" [Dell, 1985, p. 5; Maturana, 1980, p. 7]), we are forced into absurd positions. For example, in failing to acknowledge the different domains of biological and computer systems, Dell (1985), following Maturana, concludes that computers are closed in the same fashion, and hence that there is no such thing as information (p. 6)! Clearly, it is of little value to say to a banker, "There is no such thing as data going into your computers." We will not improve our understanding of humans and computers if we insist on applying a single terminology of explanation uniformly in all domains. We must hold multiple perspectives aloft and compare them. Furthermore, robot engineering must rely partly on the methods of descriptive modeling to succeed (see Chapter 8).

Dewey: Coordination memory

John Dewey, an American philosopher-psychologist and moralist, presented an incisive critique of stimulus–response theories in his famous 1896 paper, "The Reflex Arc Concept in Psychology." Although Dewey's point of view contributed mightily to everything presented in this chapter so far (as well as to contextualism, described in Chapter 3, and ecological psychology, considered in Chapter 10), I have deferred discussing it until now. Dewey's presentation is based on insightful observation and analysis, without much data; Merzenich's and Maturana's biological evidence provides a setting for understanding what Dewey was pointing to 100 years ago. With the idea of structural coupling in mind, we may better interpret Dewey's claims and find further guidance. Here I focus on Dewey's analysis of sensorimotor coordination; the broader idea of *transaction* is developed in Chapters 8 and 9.

In criticizing early stimulus–response theories of behavior, Dewey (1896) sought a mechanism without linear causal linkage between perception and action. Dewey argued that subsystems in the brain co-organize each other; that is, they are mutually constraining but separately coherent. Dewey's view of functional differentiation, co-organization, and sensitivity to frame of reference confusions foreshadowed the analysis and theories of von Foerster, Bateson, and Maturana. Specifically, Dewey believed that a linear analysis of sensorimotor coordination into discrete systems artificially breaks apart the organism's experience into units and distorts the nature of coordination. Dewey's characterization of how "sensation, idea, and action" are separated in stimulus–response theories eerily sounds like an attack on the architecture of today's descriptive cognitive models (cf. Figure 3.2):

The older dualism between sensation and idea is repeated in the current dualism of peripheral and central structures and functions; the older dualism of body and soul finds a distinct echo in the current dualism of stimulus and response. Instead of interpreting the character of sensation, idea, and action from their place and function in the sensorimotor circuit, we still incline to interpret the latter from our preconceived and preformulated ideas of rigid distinctions between sensations, thoughts, and acts. The sensory stimulus is one thing, the central activity, standing for the idea, is another thing, and the motor discharge, standing for the act proper, is a third. As a result, the reflex arc is not a comprehensive, or organic, unity, but a patchwork of disjointed parts, a mechanical conjunction of unallied processes. . . . What is wanted is that sensory stimulus, central connections and motor responses shall be viewed, not as separate and complete entities in themselves, but as divisions of labor, functioning factors, within the single concrete whole, now designated the reflex arc. . . .

What shall we term that which is not sensation-followed-by-idea-followed-by-movement . . . ? Stated on the physiological side, this reality may most conveniently be termed co-ordination. (p. 137)

Thus Dewey rejects the idea of a reflex as arcing between stimulus and action, mediated by something inferential like thought. Coordination should be viewed as a functioning whole, a system with divisions of labor, operating together. Dewey emphasizes that there is not simply a stimulus event, but also *an already coordinated activity of perceiving*:

We begin not with a sensory stimulus, but with a sensorimotor co-ordination, the optical-ocular. . . . In a certain sense it is the movement which is primary, and the sensation which is secondary, the movement of body, head, and eye muscles determining the quality of what is experienced. In other words, the real beginning is with the act of seeing; it is looking, and not a sensation of light. (pp. 137–138)

All activity involves physical coordination; separating perception and action as discrete, independently operating processes of different kinds, causally related in a linear way, is inaccurate. Both are always *already* interacting within ongoing coordination:

> The reflex arc idea is defective in that it assumes sensory stimulus and motor response as distinct psychical existences, while in reality they are always inside a co-ordination and have their significance purely from the part played in maintaining or reconstituting the co-ordination.... The arc ... is virtually a circuit, a continual reconstitution, [the reflex arc idea] breaks continuity and leaves us nothing but a series of jerks, the origin of each jerk to be sought outside the process of experience itself.... No matter how much it may prate of unity, it still leaves us with sensation or peripheral stimulus; idea, or central process (the equivalent of attention); and motor response, or act, as three disconnected existences, having to be somehow adjusted to each other.... (p. 139)

By conceiving of stimulus, idea, and motor processes as existing apart, scientists need to develop mechanisms for relating them. For example, this is precisely what the *blackboard architecture*, a common control mechanism in descriptive models, seeks to do. Such a central posting or pipeline requires that the results of modules be packaged as "messages" in some sort of encoding so that constructions can be compared, combined, and decided among. Thus, the separation of functionality itself forces on the theoretician the very idea of descriptive encoding, by which modules may communicate. Such a formulation to some extent fits sequential, inferential reasoning, but it doesn't fit sensorimotor coordination. In an alternative mechanism, suggested by Dewey, the organization of a module playing a role within a coordination arises within the totality, such that the development of a response directly (without inferential steps depending on a categorization of reference) constructs what the stimulus is perceived to be.

As an example, Dewey analyzes how we respond to a sound. The quality, *what is experienced*, depends on how we are already coordinating our activity:

> If one is reading a book, if one is hunting, if one is watching in a dark place on a lonely night, if one is performing a chemical experiment; in each case, the noise has a very different psychical value; it is a different experience....
>
> What proceeds the "stimulus" is a whole act, a sensorimotor co-ordination ... the "stimulus" arises out of this co-ordination; it is born from it as its matrix; it represents as it were an escape from it.
>
> Unless the sound activity had been present to some extent in the prior co-ordination, it would be impossible for it now to come to prominence in consciousness.... We do not have first a sound and then activity of attention, unless sound is taken as mere nervous shock or physical event, not as conscious value. The conscious sensation of sound depends upon the motor response having already taken place. (p. 140)

Again, reacting is not merely a motor activity, but another coordination:

> The running away is not merely motor, but is sensorimotor, having its sensory value and its muscular mechanism. It is also a co-ordination.... The motor reaction

involved in running is, once more, into, not merely to, the sound. It occurs to change the sound, to get rid of it. . . . What we have is a circuit; not an arc or a broken segment of a circle. . . . Indeed, the movement is only for the sake of determining the stimulus, of fixing what kind of stimulus it is, of interpreting it. (pp. 140–141)

In effect, our separation of experience into stimulus and response is a matter of perspective; they always occur together in coordinated form; they are not physical structures, phases, or events that need to be brought together by an intervening mechanism (except in descriptive analysis):

Sensorimotor has validity only as a term of interpretation, only, that is, as defining various functions exercised.

Stimulus and response are not distinctions of existence, but teleological distinctions, that is, distinctions of function, of part played, with reference to reaching or maintaining an end. There is simply a continuously ordered sequence of acts, all adapted in themselves and in the order of their sequence. . . . The end has got thoroughly organized into the means. In calling one stimulus, another response, we mean nothing more than that such an orderly sequence of acts is taking place. In other words, the distinction is one of interpretation. . . . It is only when we regard the sequence of acts *as if* they were adapted to reach some end that it occurs to us to speak of one as stimulus and the other as response. Otherwise, we look at them as a *mere* series. (p. 144)

We may distinguish an experience as being a stimulus because, in the sequence of our acts, it leads to a problematic situation. But the response will define what the stimulus is, it will give meaning to it, it will interpret it. Meaning and response arise together:

The sensation or conscious stimulus is not a thing or existence by itself; it is that phase of a co-ordination requiring attention because, by reason of conflict within the co-ordination, it is uncertain how to complete it. Now the response is not only uncertain, but the stimulus is equally uncertain; one is uncertain only in so far as the other is. (p. 145)

They are therefore strictly correlative and contemporaneous. The stimulus is something to be discovered; to be made out. . . . As soon as it is adequately determined, then and only then is the response also complete. To attain either, means that the co-ordination has completed itself. Moreover, it is the motor response which assists in discovering and constituting the stimulus. It is the holding of the movement at a certain stage which creates the sensation, which throws it into relief. (p. 147)

As an example, Dewey tells the story of a child looking at a light to determine if this is the "seeing-of-a-light-that-means-burning-when-contact-occurs." In effect, how an experience is categorized depends on the ongoing sequence in which it becomes a part; a child who has been previously burned interprets seeing the light to mean "seeing-a-light-that-means-burning-when-contact-occurs."

More broadly, Dewey's analysis suggests the following key property of the mental architecture: Sequences of acts are *composed* such that subsequent experiences categorize and hence give meaning to what was experienced before. Categorization of perceptual details thus arises together with the ongoing categorization of "what I am doing now." Meaning is not recorded as stored facts about concepts, but is inherently the experience of a perceptual detail within an ongoing sequence of interactions (i.e., perception–action coordinations). Chapter 9 elaborates on how Dewey's analysis of coordination relates to mental operations that include inferential (symbolic) reasoning; I argue there that conceptualizations, as kinds of categorizations, have the same dynamic, nonlocalized character as sensorimotor coordinations.

Because categorization combines perceiving and moving, categories are *relational*, and hence not in general identifiable with named descriptions and isolated actions. The nature of *nondescriptive relation* is perhaps most familiar in understanding how the body sustains and changes posture. Rosenfield (1992) argues that all categories, including more complex conceptualizations of personality and speech are, like posture, dynamically reconstructed from previous coordinations:

[There is no] dictionary of all the words I know stored in my brain, waiting for me to use them. I create my language, and my sense of myself, more dynamically, just as I move around bodily in space. My sense of "posture" is not stored in my brain, but, rather, the ability to create one posture from another is, the ability to establish relations. And the senses of self and speech, like posture, are constantly evolving structures; what I just said determines, in part, what I will say. Just as one posture gives rise to another and one sentence gives rise to another, one expression of my personality gives rise to another.

Memory, too, comprises the acquired habits and abilities for organizing postures and sentences – for establishing relations. (pp. 122–123)

Henry Head (1920) used this same example of flexible, remembered relations when introducing the notion of *schemas*:

Every recognizable change enters into consciousness already charged with its relation to something that has gone before. . . . For this combined standard . . . we propose the word "schema". . . . Every new posture of movement is recorded on this plastic schema, and the activity of the cortex brings every fresh group of sensations evoked by altered posture into relation with it. (pp. 605–606; quoted in Rosenfield, 1992, pp. 48–49)

According to Head, what is organized are the continuous series of *dispositions*, the *changes over time*, the *relation to what has gone before*: "The unit of consciousness, as far as these factors in sensation are concerned, is not a moment of time, but a 'happening'" (ibid., p. 49). Rosenfield nicely summarizes this:

Awareness is change, not the direct perception of stimuli. Conscious images are dynamic relations among a flow of constantly evolving coherent responses, at once different and yet derived from previous responses that are part of an individual's past. (1992, p. 85)

To understand this nondescriptive notion of a schema, consider the movement of limbs in space. The places and orientations of our limbs, eyes, and fingers are infinite. Yet, we can model these relations descriptively. We can define points and parameterize space as a coordinate system, thus categorizing the locations of sensory surfaces. By doing this, we can effectively describe human motions, mimic motions in animated simulations, and effectively control robotic behavior. We do all this linguistically, in terms of objects, places, and angles we have defined in our modeling endeavor. The resulting parametrization has some degree of precision determined by the categories and scales we have chosen. The possible space of descriptions, learned behaviors, and control will be bound by the grain size of these representational primitives. For a stable environment with specified goals, a given model may fit satisfactorily. But more refined coordination descriptions will require finer distinctions – changing the representational language. As engineers, we can iterate in this way until we reach a satisfactory model for the purposes at hand.

In contrast, the idea of nondescriptive coordination pioneered by Dewey, Head, and Bartlett is that the neural system achieves increasing precision in real time *as part of its activity*. Learning to be more precise occurs internally, as part of active coordination. Certainly, behavior is limited by experience and determined by the neural repertoire. But limitations to perception and coordination are quite different from the ontological boundedness of descriptive models, such as Aaron's ability to draw. Boundedness in animal behavior is determined by prior coordinations, not *descriptions* of those coordinations, either in *terms* of the agent's body parts or places in the world. By hypothesis, this direct recomposition of prior sensorimotor coordinations provides a "runtime" flexibility that a mechanism of matching and instantiating descriptions of the world and behavior does not allow. Such a dynamic view of coordination is supported by the neurophysiological evidence of Merzenich and others presented earlier in this chapter.

Returning to the robot builder's dilemma of what to put inside the robot, the dynamic systems perspective suggests new ways of viewing mechanisms and relating subsystems in a robot. The role of feedback, both internally and with the environment, is central. Part II presents robot experiments based on the cybernetic approach that are intended to provide a new foundation for understanding cognition.

Part II

Situated robots

5 Navigating without reading maps

The ability of bees to use the sky as a directional reference, to measure flight distance, and to integrate directions and distances flown means that the radial coordinates of each foraging site within a colony's considerable flight range can be successfully communicated to recruits that have never flown there before. A map-based system, by contrast, would be limited by the extent to which the dancer and the recruit overlap in their experience of the landscape.

> Fred C. Dyer and Thomas D. Seeley, On the evolution of the dance language. *The American Naturalist*, 133(4):580–590, 1989

If animal memory is not a place where descriptions are stored, then some psychological phenomena previously thought to be explained by descriptive cognitive models need to be reconsidered: How is physical coordination and behavior sequencing possible without stored procedures? How is attention possible without words to describe goals and features? Could a robot develop its own criteria for what is interesting and what is an error, so that it is not bound by the designer's ontology?

In the past decade, a new generation of robot builders has sought to address these questions synthetically by building robots without maps of the world stored inside. Using architectures based on layering of situation-action mechanisms (which I will describe in detail), these robots speed from place to place and interact in a variety of tasks, including collecting ore samples and charging their own batteries. Generally, the robots I describe are the first examples of their kind; more capable systems are being designed every month.[1] My purpose is not to present the state of the art for its own sake but, more fundamentally, to reveal what problems are being addressed and how progress is made.

Exploration of alternatives to the stored description approach to modeling human intelligence and constructing robots, called variously *situated robotics* or *situated automata*, begins by not building maps of the world into the robot. By a *map* I mean something like Aaron's anatomical database or Mycin's symptom, disease, and drug taxonomies – a collection of *descriptions* of the world or behavior in some language, either statements or procedures. One research goal of situated robotics is to develop a theory of spatial learning without predefining categories in the robot's architecture. How can such a robot navigate in a novel environment without having a map? What is a landmark if not a description of a thing? Could learning mechanisms involved in path finding and trail making provide a foundation for higher-order cognition?

As for most attempts to invent something new, the first efforts of situated robotics don't entirely meet the objectives. Nor do the methods entirely break with the stored-description approach. But a new kind of engineering effort has begun, through which we can better understand the assumptions of the descriptive modeling approach and what more is required to replicate human capability. The obvious handicaps of situated robots are as interesting as their fascinating movements, suggesting basic clues about the nature of concepts and language. Lacking the ability to conceive coordinated activity and associate experiences, the situated robots presented in this chapter only vaguely resemble humans finding their way in a strange place. On the other hand, these robots do resemble, and are inspired by, the abilities of bees, ants, and cats to navigate and remember places. By such comparisons, we can understand more clearly that the ability to describe the world, although central to human experience, is not necessary for some aspects of cognitive behavior.

Parallel, layered machines

Some of the earliest and most well-known examples of situated robots were invented by Rod Brooks and his colleagues at MIT. Brooks was especially irked by the dilemma of AI research in the early 1980s: The community was striving for automated physicians and engineers, but hadn't yet created a program that could tie its own shoes or go down to the store and buy a quart of milk. A 3-year-old child could speak and learn better than any computer program. Carrying this idea further, Brooks suggested in 1986 that we lower our sights and aim for insect-level intelligence first.

Banishing maps from his programming repertoire, Brooks aimed for a robot that could avoid obstacles, find doorways, and identify simple objects like Coke bottles. Instead of drawing an internal map of the world and examining it to plan its actions, Brooks's robots react more directly to local sensors and represent ongoing interactions with the environment, not objects. Figure 5.1 shows one early design for an insect-like robot (developed in collaboration with J. H. Connell).

The robot is built in layers, whose states represent what the robot is currently doing, such as "sensing something to the left side," "moving forward," or "turning." These layers are programmed to combine with and activate each other, according to Brooks's intended operation for the robot. For example, if the robot is moving forward and stops sensing something on

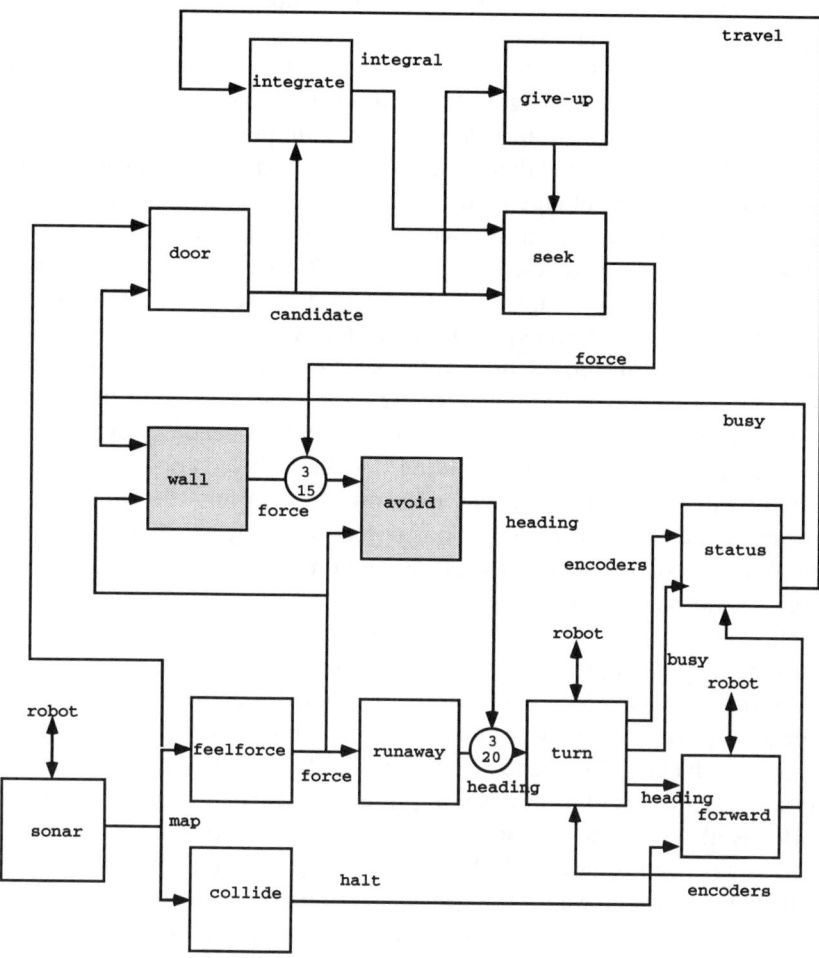

Figure 5.1. Brooks's design for a parallel, layered machine. Stippled boxes in the center correspond to the "wall hugger" layer; above is the "enter doorway" layer; below is the "avoid obstacles" layer. (Reprinted with permission from Brooks, 1991, p. 232.)

the left, this activates a turning behavior. When this behavior is combined with continued moving forward and maintenance of a constant force on one side, we observe that the robot follows walls, turns corners, and enters open doorways. Brooks explains that these are only "partial models of the world . . . individual layers extract only those aspects of the world which they find relevant – projections of a representation into a simple subspace" (Brooks, 1995, p. 68). Brooks views these prewired networks as a sensorimotor mechanism, to be contrasted with the internal maps and models that Mycin and Aaron construct and inspect.

From an observer's point of view, the states of the robot represent what the robot has just been doing and what it is sensing now. Put another way, the notations of Figure 5.1 are *referential* from our point of view because we can read the diagram – and this involves *conceiving a relation* between robot components and our independent categorization of the world. Drawing a contrast with the idea of knowledge as maps, Brooks emphasizes that the robots just interact with the world directly, "using the world as its own representation." There is no map of the world inside (corresponding to a *general model* in an expert system); instead, physical states are historically related to the robot's interactions with its environment. One can argue that these states function as symbols in Newell's sense by providing "access" to a world. For example, the line in Figure 5.1 labeled "heading" encodes the direction in which the robot is pointing. The box labeled "door" represents that the robot may be adjacent to a door. However, the representing process is part of the mechanism; it is not a separately existing *description*. The states encode changes to sensory relations in time such as forces and headings, not named places or events.

The robot's states are *indexical relations* between the robot and its inter-active activity. An indexical relation is always relative to the robot's frame of reference: "facing forward" "on the left side" "heading 90 degrees." In contrast, *descriptive representations* are statements or procedures that refer to specific objects, places, and so on in the world. In the wiring diagram, we can see that an active layer doesn't represent a particular door or wall in the world. Rather, the activation of a layer represents that a *sensorimotor relation* has been established: A force is on the left side, and the robot is following a wall. The wall is not a specific wall but "the wall I am following now." Similarly, a door is not described as a prototypical object with certain expected attributes, but rather as "the door candidate I am encountering now."

Indexical representations are quite different from labels such as "Patient-412" in Mycin: The meaning of an indexical, sensorimotor state is not part of an objective, eagle's-eye map of the world, but *a relation between the agent and the world formed within an ongoing activity*. Nor are internal states stored pointers to things (in the way Mycin's labels give access to internal datastructures). Rather, these designators are ongoing *historical relations between sensor data and motions*, which exist only while the robot is moving. Thus, the mechanism bears some relation to the sensorimotor maps in the owl monkey (Chapter 3). When Brooks says that the robot "uses the world as its own representation," he means that changing interac-tions in time trigger state changes rather than inspecting an internal map. In contrast, the robots of the 1960s and 1970s parsed a video image of the world into objects, constructed an internal situation-specific model, and then planned a path. Brooks's robot *just keeps moving*, sensing and maintaining relations between itself and its environment.

In Maturana's terms, Brooks's robots accomplish and sustain a structural coupling between the robot and walls. For example, wall hugging is continuously enabled by ongoing obstacle avoidance and forward movement, and ongoing wall hugging, in turn, enables doorway entering. Sensations and movements can add, cancel, and inhibit one another. This is not done by rules specifying situations and actions; instead, coordinated movement is accomplished efficiently and directly by layered automata, whose states relate what the program has just been doing and what it is sensing now. In Brooks's design, the layers are activated in parallel. As Brooks points out, the lower levels aren't "invoked" but continue doing their work, sensitive to but not defined by the states of the higher level. Thus, there are *simultaneous processes*, layered so that higher-order controlling processes (which we associate with goals) subsume the operation of more primitive processes. Just as there is no central place in memory where the world is represented, there is no executive program deciding what to do. Thus, we can attribute goals and desires to the program without there being stored plans or descriptions of experience.

Valentino Braitenberg's thought experiments, published in 1984, are one inspiration for this synthetic approach to robot design:

[I]t is sometimes possible to explain astonishingly complex behavior, such as that of a fly navigating through a room and landing on a hanging lamp, by invoking nothing but a set of almost identical, rather simple movement detectors whose output, weighted for position, converges on a few motoneurons. (p. 105)[2]

Braitenberg describes 14 "vehicles" that subsume processes in the manner implemented by Brooks. Braitenberg describes a sequence of vehicles that incorporate layers of detectors: thresholds + inhibition → line → movement → boundary → symmetry → periodicity → frequency. In thought experiments, he shows us in an entertaining way that activity based on such detectors would be ascribed psychological traits such as aversion, decision, and aggression.

People familiar with previous AI research in robotics and vision were astounded by the films of Brooks's robots in 1988, as the machines quickly navigated around a room and avoided obstacles without expensive visual imaging or mapping to internal representations. To cite Braitenberg (1984) again:

A psychological consequence of this is the following: when we analyze a mechanism, we tend to overestimate its complexity. In this uphill process of analysis, a given degree of complexity offers more resistance to the workings of our mind than it would if we encountered it downhill, in the process of invention. . . . The patterns of behavior described in vehicles (just illustrated) . . . undoubtedly suggest much more complicated machinery than that which was actually used in designing them. (p. 21)

Similar points were made by Herb Simon (1969) in his well-known story of the ant on the beach:

Complexity, correctly viewed, is only a mask for simplicity. . . . (p. 1)

Viewed as a geometric figure, the ant's path is irregular, complex, hard to describe. But its complexity is really a complexity in the surface of the beach, not a complexity in the ant. . . . (p. 64)

Simon, like the situated roboticists of today, hypothesized that the apparent complexity of the behavior of an ant is "largely a reflection of the complexity of the environment in which it finds itself." Applying this to "thinking man," Simon wished to emphasize the malleability of the "inner environment" of thought processes: "I would like to view this information-packed memory less as part of the organism than as part of the environment to which it adapts" (p. 65). Ironically, even when considering local reactive behavior and the environment, Simon's interpretation of the ant parable views cognition as an operation occurring in the head. The choice of metaphor is telling: Stored away in memory is "a great furniture of information."

But situated robotics has a different emphasis: Complexity is viewed as a product of an ongoing interaction between the robot and the environment, not *located* either temporally or spatially. Further, complexity is partially in the eye of the beholder, dependent on some categorization of simplicity or regularity, based on some *interest* in kinds of temporal or spatial patterns. As we proceed through the examples of situated robots, we will be considering different designs for the robot's "brain," as well as different designs for an environment. As subsequent examples suggest, situated roboticists are part of a *total system* consisting of robot plus environment plus an observer wanting to see certain kinds of behaviors.

Cooperating, self-organizing robots

Luc Steels adopted Brooks's architecture to the design of a society of robots cooperating to collect ore samples. The robots cooperate by dropping electronic bread crumbs, according to what they are sensing and doing (Figure 5.2). In contrast to the central control, maps, and message passing of descriptive models, there is no point-to-point communication of information; nevertheless, a path builds up between the best places to find ore and the mother ship to which the robots carry back samples. By dropping markers that meaningfully change the later behavior of the system, the robots are

```
OBSTACLE AVOIDANCE
-- if sense obstacle, make random turn.

PATH ATTRACTION
-- if carrying_sample, drop two crumbs.
-- if not carrying_sample & sense crumbs,
move in that direction & pick one up.

EXPLORATION MOVEMENT
-- if returning & at vehicle, explore.
-- if turning, choose lowest gradient.

RETURN MOVEMENT
-- if exploring & no force sensed, return.
-- if have sample, return.
-- if turning, choose highest gradient.

RANDOM MOVEMENT
-- choose random direction and move.

SAMPLE HANDLING MOVEMENT
-- if sense sample & don't have, pick up.
-- if sense vehicle & have sample, drop it.
```

Figure 5.2. Robot situation-action rules. (Adapted from Steels, 1990b.)

using objects in the world to represent their interactive experience and hence bias future activity, related to how people arrange work in different piles on a desk or floor . . . or wherever it might be dropped.

Each robot has the layers shown in Figure 5.2. The mother robot station emits a constant radar signal, whose gradient is detected and used to orient robot movements. This station is itself moving; but again, for the purpose of the present design, the robots needn't represent this movement, only follow it. Rather than specifying how his goals as a robot designer will be accomplished, Steels (1990b) designs behaviors whose interactions will produce behavior with properties he desires:

The strengthening of a path . . . is due to the non-linear interaction of the behaviors: Robots not carrying samples are attracted by the path which increases the chances that they will arrive at a sample and on return contribute to the establishment of the path. (p. 194)

Steels summarizes the advantages of such a design:

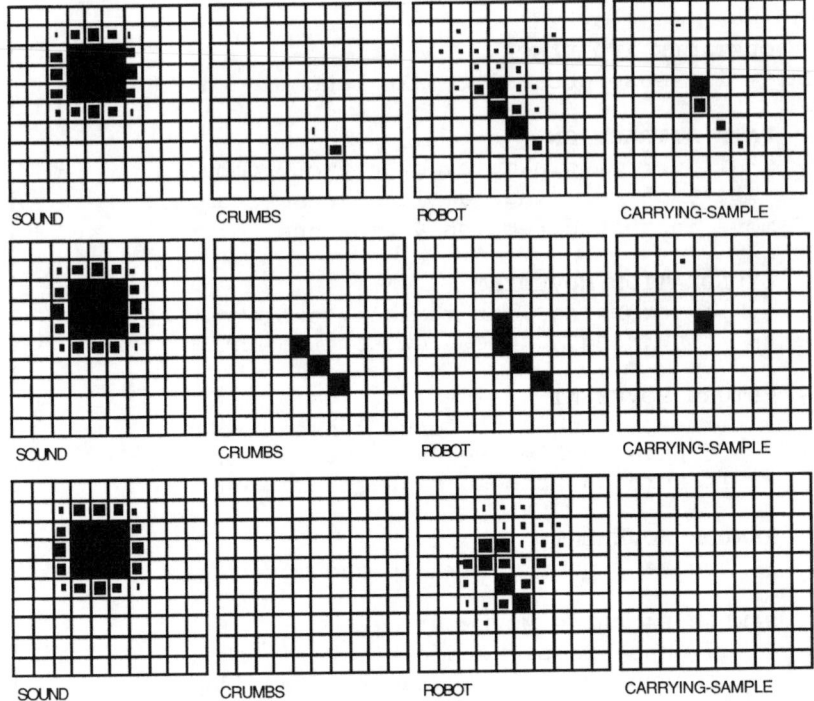

Figure 5.3. Different snapshots of a simulation in progress. The top row indicates the formation of a path of crumbs. In the middle, the path is well established and the robots are cooperating by moving along this path. At the bottom, the ore samples have been exhausted and the system has returned to its original, equilibrium state. (Reprinted with permission from Steels, 1989, Figure 12, pp. 190–192)

- *Fault tolerance:* A few sensors can malfunction, robots can fall into holes and get lost, or a sample might be dropped. The system is loosely coupled and parallel, designed to converge on the desired behavior by many interactions over time.
- *Cognitive and communicative economy:* There are only two states (looking for a sample and carrying it back to the mother station), no maps to interpret, and no knowledge of other aspects of the world.
- *Flexibility:* The robot system can deal with an unpredictable, changing environment, with obstacles, and with varying amounts of ore. The success of the system doesn't depend on the accuracy of models of the world built in by the designer.

Steels has formulated this model mathematically and tested it in a simulation (Figure 5.3). His analysis showed that increasing the number of robots improves the probability that some robot will locate any given ore sample. However, to reduce the time needed to get back to the mother robot, a gradient field emanating from the mother robot was introduced.[3] To improve the probability of identifying a sample-rich area, some kind of cooperation is required. The self-organizing aspect of the group of robots is introduced by the use of crumbs and rules for picking ore samples up and putting them down. Experimental data show that optimal behavior is reached through the subsumption mechanism specified in Figure 5.2 (Steels, 1990b, p. 195).

Steels's self-organization design is based on the conception of *dissipative structures*, which are organizations of components that emerge from the interaction of many elements. Citing the theory of complex systems pioneered by Ilya Prigogine and his colleagues, Steels (1990b) summarizes the properties required for dissipative structures to form (pp. 181–182; Prigogine, 1984):

1. An underlying dynamical system must keep evolving until it reaches equilibrium, a state with internal changes but macroscopically unchanging properties.[4]
2. The system must be open, so that when exposed to an external process, it is disturbed.
3. The dissipative structure must form itself in response to this disturbance, feeding on itself, so the dynamics are nonlinear.

Structures will grow dynamically and then decay again until an equilibrium state is reached. Steels relates the principles of dissipative structures to the ore sampling task:

We will design a system of interacting robots whose equilibrium behavior consists in exploring the terrain around the vehicle. The presence of rock samples constitutes a disturbance. The desired dissipative structure consists of spatial structure (i.e., a path) formed by the robots between the samples and the vehicle. This structure should spontaneously emerge when rock samples are present, it should enforce itself to maximize performance and should disappear when all samples have been collected. (p. 182)

The central idea is that *descriptions of the path* are not built into the robot mechanism. Although the robots are designed to create a path, the nature of the path is not represented as a plan inside the robots. The robots simply behave as individuals, reacting locally and following their hierarchy of rules. Steels, like Brooks, clearly demonstrates that *first-person models* of the world aren't always required for complex activity: Their robots do not create or use maps. These robots naturally make us wonder how ants, bees, and beavers manage in a similar way without descriptive models of their world and plans for acting together. As William James pointed out, the mere fact of recurrence or pattern does not mean that memory is involved. In the case of the ore-collecting robots, the memory is only in the world as a trail. The collective functions through a coupling between the individual robots' mechanisms and how the group changes the world over time. After presenting more examples, I summarize how the mechanisms of emergent structuring and learning are related (Chapter 8). On reconsidering human cognition, situated robot experiments lead us to consider whether similar mechanisms operate in human society, accounting in some part for our intelligence (Hutchins, 1995b).

Toto: Recognizing landmarks, learning paths

Brooks's robots can follow walls, and Steels's robots can follow each other. In these robots, navigation involves merely reactive, moment-to-moment sensorimotor coordination. The crumb-dropping method establishes trails. In contrast, a *particular path* requires recognizing *interactions ordered in time.* How could a robot recognize different places (landmarks) and thus construct a particular path? Learning a sequence of behaviors is central in animal behavior. Can we build an electronic rat that can learn to navigate a maze?

Rather than a rat, Maja Mataric began by building a cat, Toto (Mataric, 1991a, 1991b, 1992; Mataric and Brooks, 1990), that learns the relative locations of landmarks in an environment such as the corridors of an office building. The robot uses a compass to differentiate between obstacles it encounters and an internal data structure to store information about the sequence of interactions it has with its environment:

Toto consists of a three-wheeled circular base, 30 cm in diameter. . . . The base can move in a continuous trajectory with discontinuous velocity. . . . Position and velocity are controllable. . . . The body of the robot consists of a 12-inch high cylinder mounted on the base supporting a ring of 12 Polaroid ultrasonic ranging sensors . . . [which] covers the entire 360-degree area around the robot. . . . The only other sensor on the robot is a flux-gate compass supplying four bits of bearing. (Mataric and Brooks, 1990, p. 2)

How are such internal data structures different from situation-specific models in an expert system? How is Toto's landmark learning and recognition different from the way a person recognizes a boulder on a path or a gas station on a corner? Is Toto a good model of a cat?

How Toto creates and uses maps

Toto integrates three levels of representation and processing:

- Basic navigation: obstacle avoidance and boundary tracing.
- Landmark detection.
- Map-related computation: map construction, map update, and path planning (Mataric, 1992).

Figure 5.4 illustrates a typical office environment that Toto can navigate.

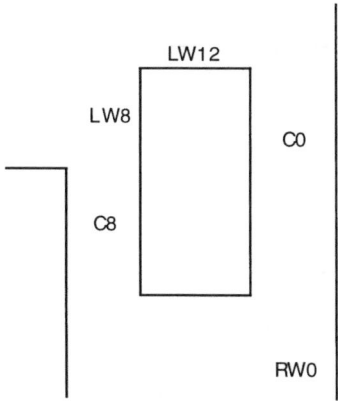

Figure 5.4. Office environment navigated by Toto showing two corridors and labeled landmarks. (Reprinted with permission from Mataric and Brooks, 1990, Figure 10, p. 504.)

The labels in Figure 5.4 correspond to landmarks identified by Toto. The abbreviations indicate a wall on the right (RW), a wall on the left (LW), and corridors (C). A landmark is therefore not a thing, but a *region*. The relative descriptions (right versus left) indicate that landmarks are identified within a sequence of movement; in this example, Toto moved counterclockwise. A sequence of landmarks therefore represents a path with a starting place and an orientation.

Toto's lowest-level tendency is to follow boundaries of objects, such as walls, corridors, and edges of tables. But after a map is built up enough for Toto to traverse the same boundary areas repeatedly, it ventures out into open areas (away from boundaries) on a random but recorded heading (Mataric, private communication).

Figure 5.5 shows a learned sequence of landmarks. This list, represented as a data structure in Toto's program, is the robot's representation of a path starting at the lower left corner of the office shown in Figure 5.4. The numbers indicate the average compass bearing in this region. The compass information allows disambiguating of areas with the same description. For example, the two corridors in Figure 5.4, C0 and C8, are parallel and would be perceived as identical without the compass-bearing information. Similarly, a wall reencountered while moving in the opposite direction can be related to a prior landmark, to indicate a loop in the path, as will be described.

Toto constructs a "map" that is very different from a coordinate system description of a place, such as the map of the Stanford campus (Chapter 2).

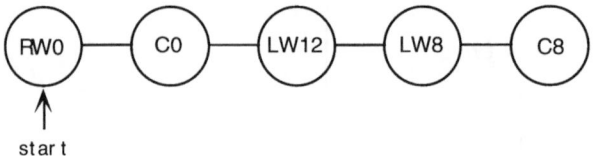

start

Figure 5.5. Learned path corresponding to the office navigated by Toto (Figure 5.4); numbers indicate average compass bearing. (Reprinted with permission from Mataric and Brooks, 1990, Figure 12, p. 504.)

Toto's maps are *part of the robot's mechanism,* embedded in the robot's memory of its coordinated physical movements in space. If Toto could speak, it could not say, "Here is my map of the office – and here is me." Toto does not have a first-person relation to its map; the map is inseparable from Toto's machinery.

To understand how Toto works, we must first emphasize that landmarks are not fixed *places,* but regions – categorizations with physical extensions detectable over time, specifically, left and right *walls* and *corridors.* For example, the label LW8 in Figure 5.5 doesn't denote what we see as the entire segment extending from one corner to another. LW8 represents a *shift in Toto's categorization* of its sensory information from an open space (corridor) to detection of a regular boundary on its left side in the region marked on the diagram. The category "LW8" extends in Toto's experience until its sensory classification leads it to detect a wall on the right side as well; so it records that it is now in a corridor (C8). By default, an area is classified as a "long, irregular boundary" when Toto can't identify it as either a wall or a corridor.

Thus, Toto *continuously* classifies the environment into one of four categories (LW, RW, C, "irregular"), which can then be referenced to find its way about. A person can inspect the recorded path and indicate that a certain landmark is a goal, a place to return to:

The robot's top-level task is to map the structure of the environment based on the spatial relationships of the landmarks, and to use this map to find paths to any previously visited landmark which the user chooses as the goal. (Mataric, 1992, pp. 307–308)

Landmarks are defined in terms of a *combination of sensory features,* such as "moving straight" or "consistent boundary on one or both sides." A landmark is therefore a *perceptual categorization:* "a sufficiently long straight boundary on each side of the robot is eventually detected as a corridor" (Mataric, 1991b, p. 1). The term *eventually* indicates that threshold functions are used to define transitions; for example, the robot continues to categorize a region as LW8 even after detecting something on the right side. But after this detection persists long enough as the robot moves forward (a period of time defined by the threshold), the categorization shifts to C8.

Claiming that Toto creates its own maps is one thing; claiming that the maps are part of Toto's mechanism and not a separate data structure is quite a different claim. Mataric (1991b) describes Toto's learning process:

> Learning . . . consists of constructing and updating a topological map of the environment. Instead of concentrating the learning in a specialised module, a set of learning rules is distributed over the map itself. The map is a topological network of processes, each of which corresponds to a specific landmark in the environment. A process itself is a collection of real-time rules. (p. 131)

Thus, Toto's map is not merely a list of identifiers, but a *network of procedures* (consisting of rules), which together constitute a sensorimotor mechanism. Each "landmark" is a separately running program for categorizing sensory information and exchanging information with other landmark processes:

> The topology of the map is maintained isomorphic to that of the explored physical space. When a landmark is detected, it is broadcast to all the processes in the map. If none recognized it, it is added to the map as new. (Ibid.)

That is, Toto has a separate process for categorizing regions (as LW, RW, C, or irregular) as possible landmarks. Once placed in the map, a landmark has the additional information of its relation to other landmarks:

> A landmark is described by its type, provided by the landmark detector, and the compass heading, provided directly by the sensors. It is also defined by its topological position. This use of context helps disambiguate otherwise identical landmarks. The landmark descriptor is stored inside a new process, and connected to its physical neighbors via communication links. If a landmark is recognized by a process in the map, it becomes the agent's current position within the map. (Ibid.)

Figure 5.6 shows Toto's architecture. Compass and sonar sensor information is broadcast to each previously stored landmark procedure, as well as to the Landmark Detector, a separate module that categorizes sensor information into the four types of regions. Toto is continuously attempting to categorize its sensory data in two ways: by *general type*, determined by the Landmark Detector, and by *specific place*, determined by the procedures in the constructed network. The procedures distributed in the map update "confidence" that a given landmark has been reencountered. The Landmark Detector recognizes the general type of landmark, which is essential for recording new landmark descriptions.

Jumper links allow the paths to be graphs. A restriction on the number of connections for each mode makes connectivity linear in the number of graph nodes; a fan-out of four was demonstrated to be sufficient for office environments (Mataric and Brooks, 1990, p. 502).

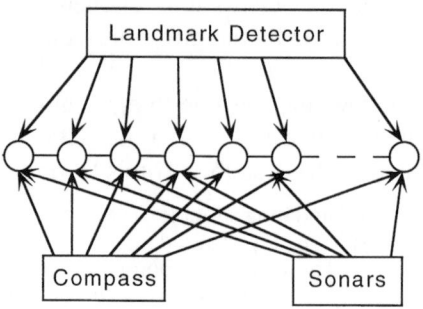

Figure 5.6. Toto's architecture. Circles in the center represent a path, correspond-ing to Figure 5.5. (Reprinted with permission from Mataric and Brooks, 1990, Figure 2, p. 501.)

To disambiguate landmarks, Toto integrates compass-bearing data over time, assuming a constant velocity. Landmarks of the same type (e.g., two left walls) with the same compass bearing are assumed to be separated by some space and hence separated by a predictable time. When a match occurs that was not expected (by activation from the currently established location), the integrated compass bearing (positional estimate) enables Toto to infer that a loop has occurred. (The landmark-matching algorithm accounts for directional symmetries. For example, "left wall heading north" also matches "right wall heading south." This duality is built into the land-mark procedures [Mataric, private communication].)

Toto also stores the number of times a landmark is matched consecu-tively during movement. Again assuming constant velocity, this represents the landmark's length. Taken together, information about compass bearing integrated over time and the number of matches over time makes Toto's path network a representation of *areas* that it sequentially encounters. Using such a constructed representation, Toto can find its way from its current location to a *goal* specified by a person. A goal is a landmark specified in Toto's language for describing space: LW, RW, or C. This information is spread throughout the network by an activation function; strength of activation decreases with the encoded distance (derived from the number of matches in time), enabling the robot to find the minimal path from the current location to the goal.

Toto's design is partially inspired by studies of navigation by bees. When moved away from their hive, bees are observed to fly directly to a previ-ously established feeding site. The bees evidently knew that they were in a different place because they didn't fly off on the bearing from the hive to the flowers. They also had some means of relating spaces so that they could go directly to the flowers because they didn't have to return to the hive first (Gould and Marler, 1987). Toto models this behavior by representing strings of landmarks whose extent (distance) is encoded in terms of how long a landmark is encountered. That is, motion, orientation, and time are integrated with combinations of sensory data in memory. The memory is not a list of objects or places per se and is certainly not named things (such as "Pecos Avenue"). Rather, the memory relates experience over time; it is a temporal record of changing encounters integrated into the sensorimotor system.[5]

Appraisal of Toto

Even though Toto creates its own maps, how is its ability determined by the path-definition data structures designed by Mataric? Mataric claims that Toto's representation of the world consists "entirely of behaviors," not descriptions of "how to" accomplish goals, either as procedures or facts. This is true in the sense that the map directly couples Toto's sensory and motor systems, rather than being a separate set of instructions or descriptions of the world.

But although Toto doesn't have a built-in map, it does have an implicit map construction and navigation procedure that is bound by the three ways of describing the world defined by Mataric: RW, LW, and C. Toto uses the descriptive modeling approach of comparing the current landmark to a stored description of type, bearing, and position. This matching process uses a predefined calculus for manipulating the representation, just as in rule-based systems. For example, the calculus represents the equivalence of a left wall heading south and a right wall heading north (Mataric and Brooks, 1990). Furthermore, Toto doesn't learn with every interaction; for example, it doesn't update its graph if an obstacle isn't a known landmark.

Mataric and Brooks (1990) recognize how Toto's design embodies their own conception of the world:

The primary concern in designing a landmark detecting algorithm is the selection of landmarks which can be robustly and repeatedly detected with the given sensors. This led us to choose walls and corridors as frequent landmarks in our environments (office buildings) which are large enough to be reliably detected dynamically, as well as static and unlikely to disappear while the robot is wandering. (p. 501)

Obviously, Toto is engineered for a certain kind of environment. It would not work as well in a forest or an open meadow. Similarly, the design is tied to a limited purpose – "to explore and learn the large-scale structure of its environment" – and a limited capability – to go to a specified location. As we explore other architectures for perception and memory, we will realize other limitations in Toto's design. It is too soon to discuss these in detail now, but I do want to use this example to introduce some design alternatives.

Instead of unique names of things (e.g., "Hallway 4") and a coordinate system (e.g., "fourth corridor on your left"), Toto's descriptions of the world are *indexical*, as in both Brooks's and Steels's robots. Internal representations are relative to the robot's movement direction and velocity ("LW8 encountered three times"). Nevertheless, Toto does store *descriptions* in a data structure memory. Toto's memory is a static network in the sense that all the nodes in the map are always present for the robot; the map has a *physical existence that persists over time*, even though the various parameters indicating activation and current location are continuously changing. Mataric refers to the nodes as *processes*, but unlike neurological processes in a bee or a cat, these are programs written in a language that Mataric invented and can read.

Subsequent chapters present alternative models of animal memory in which maps are not persistent physical structures – as if the nodes (and procedures) in Toto's map (Figure 5.5) were being re-created over time as the robot moves into recognized locations. These other architectures move away from the idea that processes need to be encoded internally in a descriptive language. Sensory and motor systems can be directly coordinated, without storing descriptions like "LW8." Consider, for example, how the Landmark Detector operates independently of the nodes in the constructed map. Might the specific places be tied to the types of landmarks so that the recognition of a type and a specific place are occurring together?

In summary, Toto's design adheres to classical views of memory as description storage and of learning as controlled comparison and combination of descriptions. On the other hand, the design is consistent with and indeed motivated by the view that the observer's descriptions of behavior (e.g., wall following) needn't be encoded in the mechanism as a map of the environment with an interpreter. Toto's map represents information as constructed, indexical relations, not as given and objective facts about the world.

The fact that Toto constructs a map is not novel. What is new and especially interesting is how map building and navigation are coordinated with primitive behaviors of sensing and moving. In particular, the map is not globally available. Stored information is accessible only in the context of moving through the environment, when the history of interactions activates the nodes in the landmark graph. Each landmark recognition activates the next landmark detection process. This effectively replicates the next-next-next nature of human memory, what Jeanne Bamberger (1991) calls the *felt path*.

But as it stands, the separation of the map from the motion and sensing behaviors violates Brooks's own principle that perception is not an input to action. Mataric and Brooks have simply moved the serial, left-to-right precedence of sense-plan-act (cf. Figure 3.2) to a serial, bottom-to-top precedence in the activation of fixed layers. Other researchers strive for an architecture in which a sense of similarity to past categorizations (bottom-up processes) arises together with the high-level conceptual coordination of behavior. That is, categorizing "what is out there" might arise together with the process of categorizing "what I am doing now" (Chapter 9).

Pengi: Indexical representations

As AI graduate students at MIT in the mid-1980s, Phil Agre and David Chapman broke with the emphasis on planning – describing the world and describing courses of action – as the core aspect of all human behavior. They were especially influenced by Winograd and Flores's (1986) critique and sought to investigate further the indexical aspects of representation. To this end, they developed a simulated robot to play a video game. The architecture of their system and their analysis place situated robotics on a more theoretical foundation, while at the same time illustrating the difficulty of articulating new ideas with old words.

How Pengi uses labels

Agre and Chapman (1987) describe their robot and its task:

> Pengi . . . plays a commercial arcade video game called Pengo. Pengo is played on a 2-d maze made of unit-sized ice blocks [Figure 5.7]. The player navigates a penguin around in this field with a joystick. Bees chase the penguin and kill him if they get close enough. The penguin and bees can modify the maze by kicking ice blocks to make them slide. If a block slides into a bee or penguin, it dies. (p. 272)

Visual processing is based on models of human vision; the emphasis is on rapid, reactive play:

> Pengi has a network of several hundred gates and a VRP (Visual Routines Processor) with about thirty operators. It plays Pengo badly, in near real time. It can maneuver behind blocks to use as projectiles and kick them at bees and can run from bees which are chasing it. (Ibid.)

Like the other situated robots I have described, Pengi operates without a global, bird's-eye view of its world. The robot dynamically names things it encounters using identifiers such as "the-ice-cube-that-the-ice-cube-I-just-kicked-will-collide-with." Again, such a description is indexical in the sense that its reference is implicit in the robot's current location and actions. The

Figure 5.7. On the left: "Finding the-block-that-the-block-I-just-kicked-will-collide-with" using ray tracing and dropping a marker. The two circle-crosses are distinct visual markers, the one on the left marking the-block-that-I-just-kicked and the one on the right marking the-block-that-the-block-I-just-kicked-will-collide-with. On the right: "Finding the-block-to-kick-at-the-bee when lurking behind a wall" (from Agre and Chapman, 1987, p. 271). Copyright © 1987, American Association for Artificial Intelligence.

description is also *functional* because it is couched in terms of the robot's actions and goals (one role of ice cubes is for destroying bees). The program's naming and tracking of objects is based on Shimon Ullman's model of low-level visual processing. Rather than creating internal maps, as in Toto, Pengi works more locally by temporarily associating "markers" with visual "aspects" (Figure 5.7).

Such a mechanism cannot anticipate encounters in the world in the way Steels's robots can find their way back to the home base or Toto can go back to a particular corridor. The machinery interacts directly with the visually recognized objects, which are described in terms of previous or possible actions. Agre and Chapman describe this by saying, "The world is there to be consulted." They refer to indexical-functional labeling and alignment of objects as "using the world as its own model." In describing how Pengi implements their theory of representation, Agre and Chapman say, "The machinery itself does not directly manipulate names for these entities." The key terms here are *machinery*, *manipulate*, and *names for*.

To begin, an object is not represented as a particular thing having status independent of Pengi's actions with it. For example, Mycin's approach would be to number the blocks, "Block-213," and relate them on a temporal-spatial grid, "(NEXT-TO BLOCK-213 BEE-23)". (In this way, the general model of an expert system serves a coordinate system for describing particular situations.) Nor does Pengi attempt to uniquely identify objects experientially, as Toto does (e.g., "the third block I encountered when moving on compass bearing 8"). Rather, like the states of Brooks's robot, an indexical-functional description locates an entity with respect to what the robot is doing now: the-block-I'm-pushing, the-bee-that-is-heading-along-the-wall-that-I'm-on-the-other-side-of. Further, such descriptions are not manipulated in the sense of being used to project future states of the world and construct plans; rather, they are directly "invoked" within a situation–action statement: "I'm-adjacent-to-my-chosen-projectile (so kick it)." These statements are of the form "situation (action)." In Pengi's world, individuality doesn't matter, nor does reasoning about things you can't see. The bee Pengi runs away from may be the same bee it attempts to hit a minute later. When "Pengi needs to know where something is, it doesn't look in a database, it looks at the screen" (Agre and Chapman, 1987, p. 270).

To understand the theory of representation Agre and Chapman are developing, we must first realize that they aren't arguing that everything people do can be done without symbolic reasoning. Rather, they are exploring *what other mechanisms are possible* and what they can accomplish. Obviously, Pengi represents aspects of its world. From Pengi's perspective these are not descriptions, for Pengi cannot read text or understand language. From the designer's perspective, components in Pengi's mechanism, such as the encoded text "the-block-I'm-going-to-kick-at-a-bee-is-behind-me," are descriptions (hyphenated phrases in English). But functionally, in the machinery of Pengi, such tokens are part of a combinatorial network coupling perceptual and motor systems.

It may at first appear that, in terms of functionality within the computer, the situation(action) statements in Pengi have the same status as the rules in Mycin. But Mycin *does treat its rules as text*: It breaks each situation statement (rule precondition) into objects and relations, identifies objects uniquely in a model of the world (e.g., "Organism-1 in Culture-3 of Patient-538"), refers to its database to determine what is true (or asks a question), matches qualified descriptions of classes (e.g., "an organism in the shape of rods") to descriptions of instances, and ultimately, in designed actions, *prints descriptions* (diagnosis and therapy recommendations). Treating the rules as *statements* is essential to Mycin's internal operation: All of its work consists of parsing and assembling *descriptions* of the patient, diseases, and therapies in a situation-specific model. Mycin has no other functions but to input, match, assemble, and explain text.

In contrast, Pengi does not break the internal situation(action) statements into syntactic components; it does not treat the expressions as statements at all. Pengi, like Brooks's robots, could be constructed by compiling such statements into logic networks and executing the networks directly as a perception-action machine. Mycin cannot operate that way because all of its operation depends on recognizing and manipulating *text*. This comes as no surprise, for obviously Mycin is intended to model symbolic reasoning; Pengi is intended to model interactive, visual-motor coordination. Pengi, like the other situated robots we have considered, models navigation, tracking, aiming, alignment, and so on in physical activity. Mycin and other expert systems model the descriptive modeling involved in design, prediction, control, and repair of (biological, mechanical, chemical, etc.) systems in the world. As is readily apparent, diagnosing or designing requires a lot of *talk* and written text manipulation.

A paradox remains: Aren't Mycin and Pengi both *descriptive models*, one modeling reasoning and the other sensorimotor coordination? Aren't they both based on the same kind of computational mechanism – text manipulation? Are we just interpreting the mechanisms differently? The answer is both "yes and no."

Although both mechanisms represent their encounters, what is represented and how it is described are quite different. Mycin's situation-specific model represents a particular *configuration* of objects and events, which it distinguishes and stores as *cases*. A case called "Patient-538" is not just "the-patient-I-am-currently-diagnosing." Mycin stores descriptions for each of the patients it has diagnosed in a library; Patient-538 is not just the patient of the moment, but a different entity from Patient-450. Furthermore, Mycin's situation-specific model sorts out and maintains distinctions and relations between each of the cultures, organisms, and drugs. The program does not flit about viewing the cultures interchangeably, but keeps track of them and orders them. Furthermore, Mycin only represents what it is *told* about, not sensorimotor interactions.

In contrast, Pengi's mechanism is continuously reregistering what is nearby (as bees, walls, etc.) and reacting impetuously to everything that moves into its sensory field. Furthermore, the descriptions are not treated *as representations* to be compared, combined, stored, and so on. In situated robots, the state of the machinery and the representation of experience interpenetrate; we do not have here "Pengi's representation of the world" and there "Pengi's physical coordination network." The network embodies Pengi's sensorimotor interaction with the world.

A lingering question remains: Because Pengi is *built out of descriptions*, isn't it the same kind of mechanism as Mycin in terms of how the designer's descriptions define the space of possible behaviors the program can exhibit? That is, Pengi – like Mycin, Aaron, Toto, and the other situated robots – is ontologically bound by the distinctions made by the designer. This is obviously true in an important sense. Pengi is designed to operate in a world of blocks and bees, just as Mycin is designed to operate in a world of cultures and organisms; Toto in a world of walls and corridors; Brooks's robot in a world of walls and doors; and Steels's robots in a world of crumbs, ore, and a mother ship. An important aspect of these robots' boundedness is that they have no mechanism for detecting false classifications. As observers with another point of view, we can study the programs' behavior and say things like, "Mycin treats encephalitis as if it were viral meningitis," "Pengi treated a die as if it were an ice cube," and "Toto treated a fallen log as if it were a wall."[6] The representational space is fixed by the designers in both cases. None of the programs can construct new categories of any kind. Mechanisms that can do this are considered in Chapters 6 and 7.

Talking about representations

The difficulty of explaining how Pengi works and how it is different from other symbolic systems illustrates some of the conceptual hurdles the AI community has experienced in developing the theory of situated cognition. For example, I have found that by using the idea of *describing* instead of *representing*, it is possible to clarify Agre and Chapman's (A&C) sometimes confusing choice of terminology. To elaborate my points, I will here further unpack A&C's terminology.

To begin, A&C (1987) call the "relevant properties of the immediate situation" that guide the program *aspects* and *entities*. They avoid calling these elements in Pengi *representations* because representations in the AI and cognitive science communities at that time (as illustrated throughout my discussion of Mycin) were synonymous with descriptions. For example, they say:

Registering and acting on aspects is an alternative to representing and reasoning about complex domains, and avoids combinatorial explosions. A traditional problem solver for the Pengo domain would represent each situation with hundreds or thousands of such representations as (AT BLOCK-213 427 991). (p. 269)

Notice the use of the terms *represents* and *representations* in describing traditional problem solvers. By using the term *aspect*, A&C wish to distinguish Pengi's mechanism from a traditional problem solver. But we can analyze and appraise their work better by recognizing that they are arguing for a kind of *indexical representation*. They are not saying that representations are unnecessary, for clearly aspects are representations. But because the word *representation* was used so restrictively, they had to use other terms. Brooks intends the same distinction in the motto "intelligence without representation."

To clarify the distinction, A&C say, "Routines are patterns of interaction between an agent and its world. A routine is not a plan or a procedure; typically it is not represented by the agent" (p. 269). "Not represented by the agent" means that the description of the pattern of activity (the routine) is created by an observer (or learned), not produced as text by the robot. In saying that these descriptions are not procedures, A&C mean that they are not rules or recipes for action examined by the robot. Of course, these remarks refer to certain kinds of sensorimotor routines, not office procedures.

These points illustrate the difficulty of breaking new ground in a field where all the words available seem to mean the same thing: knowledge, representation, description, rule, procedure, strategy, plan. Clearly, when A&C say that Pengi's network "registers aspects using Boolean combinations of inputs from the VRP," they are describing how Pengi internally represents objects in the world. But the choice of the term *register* and the emphasis on a "combinatorial network" are meant to emphasize that Pengi is not receiving *text* as input. Pengi does not interpret the meaning of text, store and retrieve text in its memory, match text descriptions, maintain a short-term memory buffer containing text, or assemble text as output. Pengi is not a text processor, but it *is* an information processing system.

Striving to make their point, A&C move to the extreme of purity in distinguishing Pengi's mechanism from traditional programs: "Aspects, like routines, are not datastructures. They do not involve variables bound to symbols that represent objects" (p. 270). Instead of variables, there is a logic situation(action) network, called the *central system*, that directly couples vision to action. State changes in the central system depend directly on the peripheral, perceptual (visual) system. The coupling between the visual and central systems can be described (by the observer) as *visual routines*, such as "coloring in regions, tracing curves, keeping track of locations usual visual markers (pointers into the image), indexing interesting features, and detecting and tracking moving objects."

By insisting that aspects are not datastructures, A&C are emphasizing that internal states are transient. The central system is *dynamic*, with no static (stored) elements. In contrast, an essential characteristic of variables in computer programs (and, more generally, datastructures) is that they persist over time, independent of the current input. As a computer program, Pengi could be implemented in different ways using ordinary datastructures. But to make their point that Pengi's representations are indexical, functional, and not manipulated as text, A&C require that no values for variables persist between clock cycles. All internal representations (which they call *aspects*) must be propagated dynamically through interactions with the perceptual system (a process they call *registering*).

Although states are not stored and compared in the manner of Toto's map, feedback between the previous representation of the situation and subsequent visual processing is crucial (Figure 5.8):

The visual routine processor (VRP) is guided in what operations it applies to what images by outputs of the central network, and outputs of the VRP are inputs to the network. A visual routine, then, is a process whereby the VRP, *guided by the*

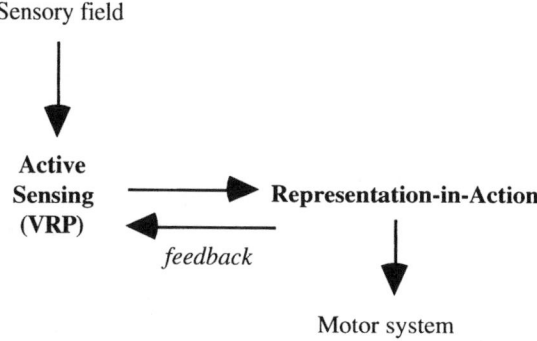

Figure 5.8. Feedback in Pengi between indexical-functional representation-in-action (central network) and visual processing (VRP).

network, finds entities and registers aspects of the situation, and finally injects them into the inputs of the network. (p. 271, emphasis added)

That is, the perceptual system isn't entirely peripheral; its behavior is coupled to the previous state of the situation(action) central network. Of course, most real-time monitoring and control systems use feedback to relate sensory interpretation to ongoing operations. For example, a patient monitoring system categorizes respiratory data as normal or high, depending on the breathing assistance equipment currently in use. But Pengi isn't comparing descriptions of expectations and instantiating plans; rather, it attends, predicts, attends, follows, and aims dynamically, in a tight loop of sensing, representing, and moving (Figure 5.8).

Just as the use of the term *representation* is intended in A&C's writing to contrast with descriptions – which A&C don't articulate very well – the term *planning* is intended to contrast with descriptive modeling. A&C chose the Pengo game to show what mechanisms are important when "events move so quickly that little or no planning is possible . . . in which human experts can do very well" (p. 272). They state their theoretical position as follows:

Rather than relying on reasoning to intervene between perception and action, we believe activity mostly derives from very simple sorts of machinery interacting with the immediate situation. This machinery exploits regularities in its interaction with the world to engage in complex, apparently planful activity without requiring explicit models of the world. . . .
    Before and beneath any activity of plan following, life is a continual improvisation, a matter of deciding what to do *now* based on how the world is *now*. (p. 268)

Here the word *deciding* is used loosely to mean "fixing," not choosing a course of action by manipulating descriptions (symbolic reasoning).

Frederic C. Bartlett (1932) provided a similar argument, emphasizing how the environment presents its own emergent structures and patterns of interaction, which orient human behavior. Bartlett uses the example of a game like rugby football:

Nine-tenths of a swift game is as far as possible from the exploitation of a definite, thought-out plan, hatched beforehand, and carried out exactly as was intended. The members of the team go rapidly into positions which they did not foresee, plan, or even immediately envisage, any more than the bits of a glass in a kaleidoscope think out their relative positions in the patterns which they combine to make. (p. 277)

Bartlett goes on to say that if individuals have to think about what another player is going to do, the team will be in disarray. Of course, we don't want to carry the analogy too far: People are not like bits of glass. People obviously do generate causal theories and plans – even during a "swift game" – which subsequently change behavior. Instead, Bartlett wishes to emphasize that behavior is often possible, indeed required, without planning. The stronger hypothesis, which is intended by A&C, is that not only do we not plan or envisage in certain circumstances, the basic mechanism of physical coordination doesn't involve consulting stored descriptions at all.

But aren't Pengi's indexical-functional representations (the-bee-that-is-heading-along-the-wall-that-I'm-on-the-other-side-of) explicit models of the world? Again, to understand A&C we must view the architecture as a whole:

- Indexical-functional representations are not treated as text by the robot during its internal processing (hence they are called *aspects*, not *representations*).
- Indexical-functional representations are not stored as variables but are transient signals in the central system (hence their activation is called *invoking* and *registering*, not *describing*).

Thus, A&C say that the indexical-functional representations are not *explicit* because they are not distinct from the central system and persistent over cycles of activity. Put another way, they are not *models* because they are not retained, accessed, and modified as separate datastructures in the manner of a situation-specific model in an expert system or a library of cases. In most descriptive models, the term *explicit* refers to text that is accessible to the program such that it can be compared, combined, stored, mapped onto actions, and so on.

Continuing their point about planning, A&C say: "Life is fired at you point blank: when the rock you step on pivots unexpectedly, you have only milliseconds to react. Proving theorems is out of the question." Again, the chosen contrast – "proving theorems" – refers to the argument about the role and nature of reasoning in people. But again, the issue is only superficially stated and explored. First, proving theorems does not mean establishing new kinds of general truths, such as doing a scientific study of the friability of the rock you are stepping on. Theorem proving in robots and expert systems refers to the process of instantiating (applying) previously stored rules about the world and plans for behavior. We can find many examples of such instantiation in Pengi's operation.

For example, Pengi determines what block to kick at a bee that is behind a wall "by extending a ray along the path of the bee indefinitely, drawing a line along the wall, and dropping a marker at their intersection" (A&C, 1987, p. 271). This procedure *models* a visual-motor anticipation coordination. A&C aren't claiming that the robot literally uses written notation ("drawing a line along the wall"). But from the observer's and designer's point of view, the process certainly looks like applying a theorem in geometry. Again, the theorem is implicit in the robot's mechanism; the theorem isn't manipulated *as text*.

Relating how Pengi works to how a bird or mammal aims projectiles requires subtle discussion of neural mechanisms, including the status of markers in nondescriptive physical coordination; Chapman (1992) pursued some of these issues in his dissertation. For example, Pengi must sometimes choose between possible actions. Should the penguin run away from an approaching bee or kick a nearby block towards the bee? A&C describe the "action arbitration" process of selecting among conflicting actions as making "counter-proposals" and "overruling." But again, Pengi doesn't internally post and compare the pros and cons of different actions, as in the manner of a "blackboard" planning system. The levels and preferences are hardwired by Pengi's designers into a network of what to consider in what order, producing a conditional procedure involving "sequencing, nonlinear lookahead to resolve goal interactions, and hierarchical action selection." Similarly, when they say, "State is less necessary and less important than is often assumed" (p. 272), A&C mean that state isn't *stored*; specifically, state isn't stored and manipulated as *descriptions* of the world or of the robot's interactions.

Pengi illustrates that inventing and then describing a new kind of architecture is not easy. Claiming that Pengi doesn't have representations confused everything A&C tried to convey. Attacking the planning and theorem-proving approach, introducing new terms like *registering*, and then lapsing into a descriptive perspective (*counter-proposals*) demonstrate how people can conceive of distinctions without having words to express them. This supports the idea that human creativity and scientific discovery proceed by a mechanism that consists of more than manipulating text. (Examples in Part III consider further the nonlinguistic aspects of conceptualization. The Conclusions chapter considers more broadly what the situated cognition debate itself reveals about cognition.)

I have tried to show that if we view Pengi (and other systems) in terms of *descriptions*, distinguishing between an observer-designer's point of view and what the robot *does* with descriptions, many confusions are resolved. The focus shifts to understanding the mechanism that couples sensory and motor systems. Rather than a central reasoning system that only stores and manipulates descriptions (Figure 3.2), the central machinery must include and be influenced by sensorimotor feedback. That is, the mechanism of physical coordination must be related to the *conception* of goals and beliefs. I explain further what A&C meant by not "relying on reasoning to intervene between perception and action" in the discussion of Gibson's idea of direct perception (Chapters 11 and 12) and then characterize the varieties of symbol systems in programs and animals (Chapter 13).

Classical conditioning architecture

The systems we have considered so far are all based on prewired designs. These robots cannot learn new behaviors; they can only learn about their environment and then interact with it in fixed ways. Paul Verschure, Ben Kröse, and Rolf Pfeifer (1992) have studied the subsumption architecture and criticized its limitations:

Every task-achieving module is implemented as a kind of finite state machine (called an augmented finite state machine) and is capable of generating behavioral output without being instructed by some higher-level planning module. The relations among modules are prewired and expressed in inhibiting/suppressing relations between them. . . .
    Control is founded on predefined knowledge structures implemented in every layer of the subsumption architecture and their interconnections. The performance of the system stays within the limits set by the way these sense–act relations are defined. . . . Also in this approach the success of the system depends on how completely the task domain can be described beforehand by the programmer. When the environment changes in an unexpected way or sensors get uncalibrated some reprogramming has to be done to get the system back on the road again. (p. 183)

Verschure et al. suggested that situated robotics could be based on the basic psychology of *conditioned learning*. They summarize the central tenets of classical conditioning:

Classical conditioning assumes that an organism is capable of perceiving a basic set of stimuli (unconditioned stimuli, US) which will automatically trigger a response to the autonomous nervous system (unconditioned response, UR). We could say that this US–UR reflex is a genetically predefined 'value' for the system since it enhances survival. Classical conditioning allows a system to develop associations between the USs and other stimuli which have no genetically preassigned values (conditioned stimuli, CS). In a basic learning experiment a CS (for instance, the ringing of a bell) will be followed by a US (food). The presentation of the US will trigger a UR (salivation). After a number of trials the presentation of the CS will suffice to trigger a response similar to the UR (the conditioned response, CR). The simple association of a CS with a US is called primary conditioning. . . . CS's which are conditioned to trigger a specific response can in turn act as reinforcers of other stimuli, a process called secondary conditioning. (p. 184)

To replicate the mechanism of classical conditioning, Verschure developed a neural network architecture:

The UR-field consists of a number of so-called *command neurons* which code specific motor responses. Whenever a specific command neuron is activated a specific motor response is automatically executed. The connections between the US-fields and the UR-field are prewired and not modifiable. The command neurons can be considered as part of the value system since they are used to implement the basic reflexes. (p. 185)

The command neurons in the UR layer code the [robot's reflex] actions . . . : "advance", "retract", "turn left 9°", "turn left 1°", "turn right 9°", "turn right 1°". In addition, the system is equipped with a basic motor characteristic, namely to keep on moving until the target is touched with the front end of the system. (p. 187)

Evidence for such a repertoire of command neurons can be found, for example, in the behavior of the orb-web spiders (family Araneidae). The prewired nature of web making is manifested in the ability of young spiders to build species-specific webs on their first try. Variations from adult webs can be explained in terms of body size, such as the length of legs. On the other hand, spiders exhibit forms of classical conditioning in their ability to associate the web's vibration frequency with the taste of captured flies (Foelix, 1982, p. 107).

Verschure et al. (1992) emphasize that what is needed is not just a direct stimulus – response system of primary conditioning – but the associative learning of secondary conditioning, by which built-in reflexes become associated with other environmental interactions:

The association mechanism that we use allows the system to couple all kinds of sensory input to the more primitive US–UR, the sense–act reflexes. . . . (pp. 190–191)

This model allows a system to integrate multiple sensors into its reflexive actions which are triggered by interaction with its environment. All actions of the system are initially only triggered by predefined US–UR reflexes. Through learning, however, CSs are associated with specific USs and on the basis of this association they can start to trigger the actions that were initially related to these USs. (p. 184)

Hence conditioned associative learning relates a CS to US–UR; the relation is not just S–R. There is always an existing S–R that is modified; the existence of US–UR allows for species-specific programs, as is evident in the varied design of orb webs. The learned associations constitute sense–act equivalence classes, created by partitioning the sensory input into regions with equivalent actions:

The properties of the CS sensors limit the sensory domain that the system has available to pick up information from the environment. How the state space bounded by these properties will be integrated into the action repertoire depends on the actual system environment interaction. The association mechanism separates this sensory domain into regions that relate to specific actions. The only precondition on the properties of the sensors is that there be a systematic relation between sensory states and environmental events, i.e., a stable transducer function. (p. 191)

Verschure's robot is programmed as a simulation program; sensor data are simulated by predefined fields. Experiments show that "the robot starts 'anticipating' obstacles and thus starts turning earlier with increasing number of steps." This anticipation emerges from the classical conditioning architecture:

If the robot approaches an obstacle from a certain direction and collides with it, the CS pattern related with this collision will be learned by modifying the weights between the CS-field and the US- [the collision detector]. When on a later occasion an obstacle is approached from approximately the same direction, a similar CS pattern will start to develop. At a certain point, this CS pattern will lead to activation in US- because of the connecting weights, eventually triggering an 'anticipatory' response. As long as the weights increase, this CS pattern will be able to trigger the appropriate response with lower activity. . . . It is important to note that the robot develops a behavior which might be called anticipation, but there is no component in the system to do anticipation per se. In this sense this behavior is *emergent*. (p. 191)

Verschure's work provides another way of approaching the representation debate. By viewing navigation in terms of classical conditioning, he builds on decades of work in studies of animal behavior, moving from talk about symbols to talk about behaviors, the history of encounters, and emergent patterns of interaction. The mechanism is concisely described in terms of activation, reflexes, conditioned stimuli, and so on; there is no place for talk about reasoning and beliefs. Again, the scientific purpose of the work is to understand what kinds of representing enable what kinds of behaviors, starting with basic forms of navigating in an unknown, changing environment.

Computational neuroethology

Brooks's robots are cars that move around without purpose. Even Pengi resembles more the typical AI program of the descriptive modeling school, which attempts to do something clever but is not very much like an animal living in the world. Much of the subsequent work in situated robotics has examined the navigation problem in what J. A. Effken and R. E. Shaw (1972) call "modeling simple whole animals in the environment" (p. 252). A "whole animal" is one that gains sustenance from the environment, avoids toxins, shuns predators, and so on.

Randall Beer followed Braitenberg's synthetic approach to robot–animal psychology. He developed an artificial cockroach with a fixed repertoire of behaviors that cannot be assembled, substituted, or adapted except by varying their speed (Beer, Chiel, and Sterling, 1990; see the discussion in Effken and Shaw, 1992, pp. 253–255). Like Verschure's design, Beer's architecture is based on the idea of command neurons and prewired reflexes, which are direct connections between sensory and motor neurons. Like the visual processing module in Pengi, mechanisms of the model are based on what is known about biological processes. For example, Beer's model builds on the ideas of reflexes, taxes (orientation and movement with respect to the environment), stereotypic action patterns (e.g., web spinning, courtship, evasive maneuvers), and motivated behaviors (e.g., actions caused by hunger).

Beer's simulated cockroach is "capable of locomotion, wandering, edge-following, and feeding, as well as properly managing the interactions between these behaviors in order to survive within its environment for an extended period of time" (Beer et al., 1990, p. 175). Furthermore, like Verschure's simulation, the robot's wiring is intended to explicitly model neural connections and firing. Beer indicates that his model omits other typical insect behavior: "fleeing, fighting, nest building, foraging, grooming, mating, and communication"; the neural circuitry information for these behaviors is not currently available (p. 184).

Comparison and assessment of minimalist robots

Table 5.1 compares the situated robot designs we have considered. We find many differences in whether the robot is actual or simulated, what kind of learning occurs, and research goals. The main commonality is a commitment to the synthetic approach with minimalist designs, focusing on the behavior of simple animals.

As we discussed in the analysis of Pengi, the design of these situated robots resembles rule-based systems with sensorimotor feedback loops. Ironically, the hardwired situation–action mechanisms of expert systems finds new application for understanding how spiders build their webs or cockroaches find a scrap of food. These programs start to develop our understanding of *kinds of representations*. We can now contrast indexical, local-to-the-moment representations (Brooks, Steels, Pengi), local maps of places (Toto), and situation-specific models instantiated from general process models (Mycin). We can contrast reactive mechanisms (Brooks and Steels) with local selection (Pengi, Toto, Aaron), and planning (Toto and Mycin). And we can contrast representations embedded in a "central situation-action network" (Pengi, etc.), subsumed control layers

Table 5.1. *Comparison of situated robots in terms of architecture, relation to animal behavior, and learning*

	Brooks	Steels	Mataric (Toto)	Agre/Chapman (Pengi)	Verschure	Beer
Metaphor	Insect	Ants	Cat	Agent playing a video game	Invertebrate	Cockroach
Nature of robot	Actual device, interacts with arbitrary world	Simulated	Actual device, designed for office environment	Simulated	Simulated, arbitrary world	Simulated world of a cockroach
Nature of behavior links	Prewired	Prewired	Prewired; constructs spatial-temporal maps	Prewired	Prewired reflexes; neural model; primary and secondary conditioning based on "values"	Prewired reflexes; neural model; top levels control appetite and feeding
Function	Follows walls, open doors	Constructs paths and collects "food"	Develops topological map; can return in minimal distance	Plays game	Avoids obstacles	Seeks food
Sensed internal state	Operation of behaviors on different levels	Operation of behaviors	Topological map relations by activation in constructed network	Feedback	Conditioned stimulus affects activation level for other sensors	Senses internal "energy level"
Grouping and sequencing of behaviors	Subsumption architecture enforces preconditions	Subsumption architecture combined with paths created in world	Topological representation of encounters	"Central system" encodes ordering and preference logic	Conditioning; learns to anticipate stimuli	Subsumption architecture

representing interactive states (Brooks), and representations treated as text (Mycin).

But the stored program mechanisms in the situated robots I have described reveal very little about how *new coordinated sequences* of behavior are learned. Only Verschure's work makes modifications to the behavior network (by classical conditioning) integral to the architecture. Toto creates a representation of its experience, but landmark detecting and map creating are not integrated in a principled way with basic physical coordination; it's just a different level, operating in an entirely different way from the obstacle avoidance levels below.

These architectures raise two important questions: How are new *kinds of behaviors* learned? How are new *categorizations* learned? To a certain extent, a prewired architecture may suffice for replicating the behaviors of ants and simple insects, but it surely won't do for modeling mammals such as cats. Even the classical conditioning work of Verschure says little about how simple *sequences of behavior – habits –* might be constructed. Strikingly, Toto's sequences are just movements in space, not coordinations of primitive behaviors in more complex routines (such as stalking a prey, playing with it, and then eating it). Pengi has several complex routines (such as lining up blocks of ice and kicking them), but these are all hardwired (although flexibly invoked) procedures.

Further, the only attempts to go beyond the simple goals of obstacle avoidance and food detection required encoding category recognizers (e.g., "left wall" in Toto and "the bee" in Pengi) as hardwired networks for combining sensory features. Although it is reasonable that the contrast detectors and similar categorizers in the visual response unit of Pengi are hardwired and inflexible, the identification of kinds of objects in the world and their relations is apparently learned by birds and mammals (Griffith, 1992), not defined at birth and fixed. Designers' decisions at the level of sensory categorization fundamentally constrain what behaviors are possible, even if routines could be modified.

By focusing on the behaviors that result from interacting with the world, rather than building in maps and map-following routines to control behavior, the first situated robot designers demonstrated flexible, robust mechanisms with emergent functionality. Perhaps the most striking example is the construction of paths from "food" to the mother station in Steels's robots – paths that change over time as the mother station moves and inherently require a collection of robots behaving in similar ways. Throughout, this research reconsiders the relation of knowledge attributions in terms of *descriptions of behavior* (an observer's descriptions of pattern associations in what robots do over time in some environment) and the *mechanisms* that coordinate sensation and action (such as the subsumption architecture).

The initial efforts, summarized in Table 5.1, are encouraging for several reasons: They demonstrate what simple mechanisms can do; they begin to define an engineering methodology based on incremental, bottom-up synthesis; and they begin to ground the study of intelligence more broadly in observations of animal behavior. In sum, these efforts bring cognitive science and AI back to the broader view of cognition and feedback mechanism found in earlier psychology and cybernetics. Robot designs in subsequent chapters focus on feature learning and build further on biological studies.

6 Perceiving without describing

Until the advent of content addressible parallel-distributed processing networks, information processing was conceived solely in terms of symbol processing. Symbol processing failed to achieve facility in pattern recognition. Whenever figural processing is critical, it appears that signals are better conceived in terms of Gaborlike elementary functions – quanta rather than bits of information. The full impact of this additional "dimensionality" with which to characterize information is still to be felt.

> Karl. H. Pribram, *Brain and perception: Holonomy and structure in*
> *figural processing*, 1991, p. 271

What kind of mechanism can categorize sensory data without mapping stimuli to a fixed set of features by which categories are defined? In this chapter I present two recent computational models of learning that address the limitations of situated robots with predefined ontologies (Chapter 5) by building on biological insights (Chapter 4). These programs learn new features by differentiating sensory interactions over time. *Configurations of features* constitute repeated or distinguishable *categorizations* of prior states. Hence, the ability to learn new features enables programs to adapt the categories they learn to the distribution of stimuli they actually encounter. In effect, these programs detect variations in stimuli that contrast or correlate along different dimensions (space, time, frequency, etc.) and thus construct features to fit these variations. By showing that perception can be more than *mapping* sensory data to presupplied category descriptions, these programs illustrate how *information is not given* to animals, but *created* as transformations of stimuli (Reeke and Edelman, 1988, p. 66). In turn, this demonstration provides a basis for understanding how symbols are not provided to animals in an input stream, but are categorical constructions of a certain type functioning in a special way (Chapters 11–13).

What mediates behavior?

We saw in Chapter 5 that Toto, which models the perception–action coordination of a cat, works by storing descriptions of past encounters, such as "left-wall compass-bearing 8." This appears paradoxical: How could a cat, which clearly has no language ability of this sort, have developed a data structure in which the name of a place and a compass reading are stored? A cat has no ability to classify the world using words; how can it categorize and recognize places? How in general do animals navigate and become oriented to places and things without *describing* their experiences? In comparing and disambiguating descriptions – "the landmark I am sensing now" and "the landmark description I stored in my graph" – Toto simulates human reasoning, which is a strange foundation on which to build a model of a cat. We must assume that such built-in names and decision processes are placeholders for learned or innate mechanisms, which require further explanation as a developmental and evolutionary theory.

As I discussed in Chapter 5, the situated robot experiments focusing on navigation begin to clarify the difference between representations used by people (road maps, knowledge bases, journal papers) – which are all descriptions in some language – and indexical-functional registration in the brain. For example, we saw in the analysis of Pengi that a distinction can be drawn between a feedback signal in a sensorimotor network and Mycin's process of parsing a rule and mapping it onto a globally accessible, situation-specific model. The processes of constructing and interpreting descriptions, which occur in people in cycles of perceiving and commenting (speaking, writing) over time, are different from activation and comparison of signals in a feedback network.

Distinguishing the perception-deliberative-motor aspects of cognition, Zenon Pylyshyn (1984) characterizes perceptual processes as "cognitively impenetrable," but this doesn't prevent descriptive modelers from supposing that perception operates by a mechanism analogous to conscious decision making. By this assumption, recognizing letters of the alphabet or recognizing that something is an envelope operates subconsciously, just like reading addresses and sorting the mail. Subconscious processes supposedly operate on an internal cache of symbols and descriptions by a mechanism of comparing, posting, and assembling that directly parallels what people consciously accomplish in their interactive, manipulative behavior over time. In contrast, starting with the assumption that perceived structures like Mycin's rules and unperceivable neural structures are different kinds of representations, situated roboticists formulated the mechanism of behavior networks, in which components are not treated as text. The lingering problem is that the networks still *look like text* and couldn't be designed by people if the components weren't named to correspond to the observer's point of view (cf. Figure 5.1). An appropriate developmental and evolutionary story of how such networks came to exist in animals will require a different level of explanation and probably a different kind of coordination mechanism.

As we have seen, when situated cognition theories suggest that descriptions don't mediate human behavior within each cycle of perceiving and acting, they mean that we don't necessarily – and at some level must not – create or consult *descriptive models* of the world or how behavior should appear. The essential components of such a modeling language can be formulated in different ways. For example, referring to systems like Mycin, a language for representing situation-specific models requires distinctions such as subject-action-object, type-instance, instance-property, tense and modality (e.g., uncertainty), and qualifiers (adjectives, adverbs). We have little or no evidence that nonhuman animals have developed or evolved such languages.

But we have more than the intelligent behavior of animals to suggest that coordination without descriptive modeling is possible. We can readily detect our own abilities to categorize and coordinate behavior that appear to have a nondescriptive, noninferential basis. For example, we have the remarkable ability to walk across a darkened room and, within an inch or so, reach under a lamp shade for a familiar switch. Some of us can hear a song or a foreign accent and, like a parrot, quickly mimic the rhythm and accent, as if it were grasped internally in one stretch. Indeed, these examples illustrate how perceptual learning and coordination may be inseparable.

As we press the hypothesis that a descriptive language cannot be the foundation of memory – which all the animals about us and the facts of evolution make obvious – we are left with some striking puzzles. For example, how could a cat be *motivated to go somewhere* without a descriptive language? Does a cat learn indexical-functional categories that operate like those in Pengi – the-bird-I-could-eat-in-the-tree? My cat doesn't jump at every bird it sees, avoiding in particular the blue jays, even as they are eating out of his food dish. He distinguishes among bird-stalking situations. But having a goal has been equated with *having a description* of a desired state ("catch the bird"); we must therefore consider that the study of cognition has fundamentally failed to understand goal-directed animal behavior. In order to distinguish properly between how a Boy Scout uses a compass bearing, what it means for Toto to store descriptions of landmarks, how birds might migrate by interacting with a magnetic field, and so on, we will need to distinguish more clearly how perceiving and acting might be related through *different mechanisms for coordinating interactive behavior in time* (including emergent changes to the environment, as in Steels's robots or a beaver's constructions). Reference, conceptualization, and goal directedness are intimately related in ways we do not yet understand. Understanding perceptual categorization as a noninferential process is the foundation for a new theory of intentionality.

As we will see by the examples in this chapter, the modeling methods required to build perceptual systems are quite different from the knowledge representation languages of descriptive cognitive models. A different mathematical, biological, and engineering background is required to formulate and understand these models. The opening quote of this chapter hints at the complexity involved. To take this one example, the Gaborlike functions mentioned by Karl Pribram (1991) characterize *microprocesses* in the cortical receptive field in terms of a Fourier transform:

> The Fourier transform opposes two different orders, two different ways in which signals become organized . . . characterizing the input to and output from a lens that performs a Fourier transform. On one side of the transform lies the space-time order we ordinarily perceive. On the other side lies a distributed enfolded holographic-like order referred to as the frequency or spectral domain. (p. 70)

Pribram's holographic theory is controversial, but his adherence to *sensorimotor reciprocity* is based on Gibson's analysis and is fully consistent with the situated robot approach. In particular, Pribram indicates that "operations performed on cortical activity patterns," enabling construction of macro-space-time features, occur *by virtue of* and *within* a sensorimotor circuit:

> The motor apparatus of the organism provides a scan over the sensed environment. With respect to this first stage of perception, oscillatory movements of receptor surfaces are critical: tremors for touch, respiration in olfaction, the movement of cochlear hair cells in hearing, nystagmoid displacements of the retina in vision. (p. 89)

Pribram emphasizes that this transformational mechanism is quite different from the *cascading stages* postulated by previous descriptive models of vision:

> This approach differs from that taken by some others interested in computational modeling (e.g., Marr . . .) in that the full measure of sensory input (generated by the retinal process) reaches the cortical level. No sketch pad image-processing stage is demanded. . . . (p. 92)

I mention Pribram's work here chiefly to remind the reader that there is a vast literature and a large community of research with which situated cognition makes contact. The methods, data, and especially biological grounding of this community are now transforming the practice of robot design. The two programs described in this chapter provide some of the first computational methods for replicating biological processes of categorizing, with mechanisms involving sensorimotor reciprocity and oscillation. These programs show how perceptual learning without presupplied feature descriptions and memory without storing descriptions of objects or events are possible.

A feature-learning robot

David Pierce and Benjamin Kuipers (1994) describe a simulated robot that "can learn sets of features and behaviors adequate to explore a continuous environment and abstract it to a finite-state automaton" (p. 1264). Unlike the robots described in Chapter 5, their system doesn't begin with precoded categories such as "wall" or "corridor" or even sensory features such as "constant force on the right." Like Toto, the program creates a topological network of its environment, but effectively *develops* "behaviors" that are like the human-designed layers of Toto's design. That is, this robot develops a finite state automaton (FSA) that becomes the machinery of the robot, as opposed to constructing a data structure on which a preexisting FSA operates.

An FSA provides a powerful target abstraction for modeling the structure of the world by integrating movement, changing sensory data, sequences, and location into a single, connected network of sensory data, features, and primitive actions. *Primitive actions* are *learned* ways of controlling the motor apparatus of the robot with respect to the given (two) degrees of freedom (translation and rotation). *Features* are functions over time of the *raw sense vector*. The program's design specifies what *kinds* of features may be learned from the sense vectors. These include the vector itself, a component of the vector, the average value of components, and derivatives over time of components. In contrast, the robots described in Chapter 5 can only use built-in features for recognizing built-in categories.

Pierce and Kuipers's program uses a relatively complex mechanism of generating and testing features by searching for local minima in the sensory input and tracking positions and orientations of local minima over time. Thus an unstructured, uninterpreted sense vector is organized into a dynamic field of intersensor (e.g., sonar, distance) correlations over time. By this approach, the robot senses objects ("blob image features") but doesn't segment or recognize types of objects. The approach is essentially what Gibson and ecological psychologists have described and modeled in the past three decades.

The robot begins by exploring the environment randomly and gathering information about "when an action has an effect on a feature . . . and how large that effect is" (a search process called *hill climbing*). This produces a *static action model* of first-order effects that guides further learning. The static action model makes predictions based on context. For example, the orientation of the robot with respect to a wall will affect a minimum-distance feature's value; moving forward will decrease the feature's value if the robot is facing away from the wall or leave it invariant if the robot is facing parallel to the wall. The robot detects and discriminates *regions* as combinations of objects by encoding the context in which an object (blob) is found; specifically, the program "encodes the angle of the object whose distance is given by the feature's value." Such conditions and consequences are encoded into the FSA.

The robot's ability to learn new features is based on two principles of interaction between the robot and its environment: the idea of feature invariance and the nature of active exploration. *Invariance with respect to an action* means that some "action leaves a feature's value invariant." By finding such correlations between features and actions, it is possible to define path-following behaviors. That is, the abstraction program examines correlations detected over time to develop a control program for keeping the robot on a path (i.e., keeping a feature y, such as force at an angle, at a desired value). This produces a *dynamic action model* that enables coordination of movement with respect to sensory data over time. By searching for and incorporating information about "which derivative of the feature is influenced by the action" being controlled, such as wall following, the program can derive an error-correcting version of its navigating behavior. After creating a dynamic action model, the robot is designed to prefer a learned path-following behavior over a learned hill-climbing behavior. Otherwise, it "randomly wanders until another behavior becomes applicable."

The second principle enabling learning of new features is *active learning*. Pierce and Kuipers claim that learning an FSA that "captures the input–output behavior of the environment" is tractable when the agent actively chooses its actions. In contrast, other approaches, such as the fixed subsumption architecture used in Toto, build in a "predefined set of local control strategies such as hall following"; the active learning approach allows the robot to "discover and learn path-following behaviors on its own."

Of course, Pierce and Kuipers's robot's architecture is not a biological model: The learning algorithm operates on and creates numeric vectors and formulas, which can be viewed only as a very coarse abstraction of neural processes. Instead, Pierce and Kuipers's work examines the information processing possible when operating on raw sensory data with respect to movement over time. The method presupposes methods of correlating sensory data by grouping and structuring features two-dimensionally, finding local minima, tracking orientations, and so on. The mechanism shows the computational possibility of learning features and path following *within the dynamics of controlled movement itself*. This is a great advance from the engineered networks of the situated robots that operate on a built-in ontology of features and categories.

A chaotic model of perception

Walter J. Freeman is a neurobiologist who uses computer modeling to understand how the brain "transforms sensory messages into conscious perceptions." Freeman's work illustrates the nature of nondescriptive perceptual recognition. In contrast to Pierce and Kuipers's design, Freeman and his colleagues have investigated how features might emerge from *chaotic interactions* in neural networks. This work advances situated cognition in two ways: first, by relating computational mechanisms more directly to biological evidence and, second, by demonstrating a form of memory and recognition based on emergent properties of networks as wholes, not by storage of already encoded categories (as in simple connectionism; Chapter 3). The rapidity and certainty of recognition experience motivate modeling how features are learned and flexibly adapted and how categories are so quickly discriminated:

Within a fraction of a second after the eyes, nose, ears, tongue, or skin is stimulated, one knows the object is familiar and whether it is desirable or dangerous. How does such recognition, which psychologists call preattentive perception, happen so accurately and quickly, even when the stimuli are complex and the context in which they arise varies? (1991, p. 78)

How a rabbit discriminates odors

Freeman describes perception as involving entire neural systems acting in unison, not as local transmission, storage, and matching of already meaningful signals. He sketches a theory of self-organized, chaotic activity:

We have found that perception depends on the simultaneous, cooperative activity of millions of neurons spread throughout expanses of the cortex. Such global activity can be identified, measured, and explained only if one adopts a macroscopic view alongside the microscopic one....

Chaos is evident in the tendency of vast collections of neurons to shift abruptly and simultaneously from one complex activity pattern to another in response to the smallest of inputs....

The number of activated receptors indicates the intensity of the stimulus, and their location in the nose conveys the nature of the scent ... [in the] entorhinal cortex, where signals are combined with those from other sensory systems. The result is a meaning-laden perception, a gestalt, that is unique to each individual.

Every neuron in the bulb participates.... In other words, the salient information about the stimulus is carried in some distinction pattern of bulbwide activity, not in some small set of feature-detecting neurons that are excited only by, say, foxlike scents....

Bulbar functioning is self-organized ... not determined solely by the stimulus. (pp. 78–79)

Strikingly, there is little evidence of discrete structures corresponding to symbols, as electroencephalograph (EEG) experiments show:

The wave changes every time an animal inhales, even when the same odorant is repeatedly sniffed. The identity of an odorant is reliably discernible only in the bulbwide spatial pattern of the carrier-wave amplitude. (p. 80)

The bulb's activity changes with every stimulation. A memory effect is involved, involving an "assembly of neurons" (also called a *neural map*):

We believe that something we call the nerve cell assembly is both a crucial repository of past associations and an essential participant in the formation of the collective bulbar burst. The hypothetical assembly consists of neurons that have simultaneously been excited by other neurons during learning. . . . (p. 81)

The strengthening occurs not between the receptor in the nose and the bulbar neuron, "but in the synapse between connected neurons that are simultaneously excited by input neurons during learning":

Such strengthening is predicted by the widely accepted Hebb rule, which holds that synapses between neurons that fire together become stronger, as long as the synchronous firing is accompanied by a reward. . . .
     We infer from our data that a nerve cell assembly, consisting of neurons joined by Hebbian synapses, forms a particular scent as an individual is reinforced for learning to identify that odorant. Thereafter, when any subset of neurons in the assembly receives a familiar input, the entire assembly can rapidly become stimulated. . . . The assembly, in turn, directs the rest of the bulb into a distinct pattern of activity. (pp. 81–82)

     Freeman goes on to describe how this mechanism explains the preference for stimuli strongly reinforced in the past, generalization-over-equivalent receptors, and an increase in gain (output response for a given input) during excitation:

First, excitatory input to one part of the assembly during a sniff excites the other parts, via Hebbian synapses. Then those parts reexcite the first, increasing the gain, and so forth, so that the input rapidly ignites an explosion of collective activity throughout the assembly. The activity of the assembly, in turn, spreads to the entire bulb, igniting a full-blown burst. (p. 83)

Reexcitation by a feedback loop corresponds to what Edelman calls *reentry*. In particular, nerve cell assemblies in the cortex (having their own distinctive carrier wave and a spatial amplitude pattern) are coupled reentrantly to the olfactory bulb.

     One of the clearest signs of self-organization is the presence of this continuous wave:

[There is] an aperiodic (nonrepeating) common carrier wave everywhere in the bulb . . . even when there was no extrabulbar stimulus driving the collective activity. The lack of external driving meant that the activity was self-generated by the bulb. (Ibid.)

Freeman compares chaotic activity to a crowd of commuters in a train station. In contrast to random activity, the flow is ordered, as we can

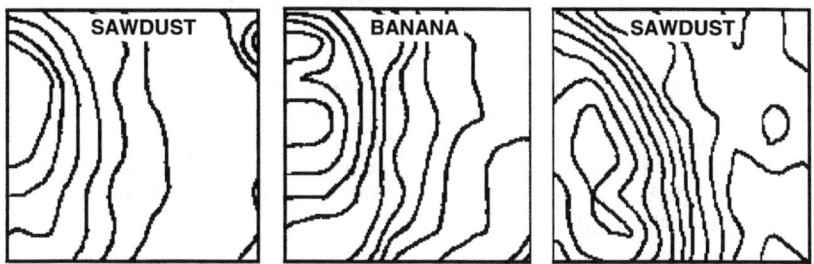

Figure 6.1. Rabbit's EEG response to a sequence of odorants. (Reprinted with permission from Freeman, 1991, p. 84.)

observe when a track change is announced: "No single announcement would make a large mob become cooperative."

To test the hypothesis that the self-organization of the olfactory bulb is chaotic, Freeman developed a computer model based on "ordinary differential equations that describe the dynamics of local pools of neurons." Experiments demonstrated that the model resembled the EEG data, including the production of learned amplitude maps. When new simulated odorants were tried, the maps associated with other odors changed, as the EEG shows (Figure 6.1):

After the animal learned to recognize the smell of banana (middle) . . . reexposure to sawdust led to the emergence of a new sawdust plot (right). The change shows that bulbar activity is dominated more by experience than by stimuli; otherwise, sawdust would always give rise to the same plot. (p. 84)

The model was manipulated to produce phase transitions, that is, bursts of simulated EEG activity, demonstrating "dramatic changes in response to weak input," a distinguishing characteristic of chaotic systems. Plots of amplitude changes over time show coherent shapes, such as a spiral or torus:

The shapes we found represent chaotic attractors. Each attractor is the behavior the system settles into when it is held under the influence of a particular input, such as a familiar odorant. The images suggest that an act of perception consists of an explosive leap of the dynamic system from the "basin" of one chaotic attractor to another. . . . In our experiments, the basin for each attractor would be defined by the receptor neurons that were activated during training to form the nerve cell assembly.

We think the olfactory bulb and cortex maintain many chaotic attractors, one for each odorant an animal or human being can discriminate. Whenever an odorant becomes meaningful in some way, another attractor is added, and all the others undergo slight modification. (p. 85)

But what reinforces a new recognition pattern? Freeman argues that the reentrant link between the bulb and the cortex constitutes a coupled system, so the activity of the bulb is modulated by the activity of the cortex:

We suspect chaos in the brain arises when two or more areas of the brain, such as the bulb and the olfactory cortex, meet at least two conditions: they excite one another strongly enough to prevent any single part from settling down, and, at the same time, they are unable to agree on a common frequency of oscillation. Competition between the parts would increase the sensitivity and instability of the system, contributing to chaos. (p. 85)

In fact, separating the bulb and cortex causes the two parts to "become abnormally stable and quiet."

In summary, Freeman views neural systems as dynamical. The chaotic properties of the olfactory bulb were detected by plotting changing values of EEG amplitudes. Possible changes over time constitute the phase space of the phenomenon. A few remarks about dynamical modeling may be helpful to understanding the kind of patterning involved here.

Phase space diagrams are often introduced in teaching thermodynamics as graphs that relate the pressure, volume, and temperature of gases, showing transitions between liquid, solid, and gaseous states. Chaotic coupling provides a way of explaining state changes in a system that doesn't depend on storing and comparing values. To understand how chaotic mechanisms differ from classical force action, consider the different causal processes by which "trajectories of change"[1] may occur:

1. *Classical mechanics*: In Newtonian mechanics, force (energy) is imposed from outside, is additive with respect to the existing energy (e.g., velocity), and is viewed as imposed at a point. Energy is conserved in the system as a whole. The "trajectory of change" is viewed as something external influencing internal states in the system.

2. *Deterministic chaos*: Deterministic chaos is illustrated by the now familiar diagram of two spiraling circles forming an S-shape. The attractors in the system are preexisting. Signals perturb this internal state; the system may shift abruptly to a different attractor. An observer may say that the *attractors* represent the signal, but the state is not a description of the outside world. The operation of such a system is not described in terms of symbols, input–output information, and storage, but in terms of transitions in a space of phases.

3. *Nondeterministic chaos*: Nondeterministic chaos occurs in Freeman's model; the attractors are not preexisting but change over time. In the details of activation, every state within a subsystem is new.

The kinds of causal systems might also be expressed in terms of kinds of interactions (Van Gelder, 1991, p. 500):

1. In classical mechanics, we describe interactions between parts of the system. Often, this is in terms of the physical location or changes in the form

of a system's component over time. We call this the system's *state* (e.g., whether a valve is open or closed, a switch is on or off). Patterns of interaction are characterized in terms of the appearance of the system over time, that is, changes in its internal structure or its observed behavior.

2. In dynamical systems, we describe interactions between *parametrized values of states*. The pattern is in the trajectory of change of the state, that is, the *appearance of the graph* as a function of time. Such descriptions are inherently relational or, more specifically, relations of relations, such as the concept of acceleration.

These kinds of interactions and ways of modeling trajectories of change are not different types of physics, but rather *kinds of descriptions within a physics*. We could use classical mechanics to describe a pendulum in terms of changing parts or describe it instead as a dynamical system. Such descriptions are not incompatible; a dynamical analysis can be based on the componential breakdown of the structural–behavioral analysis.[2]

Implications for a theory of perception

Freeman (1991) uses his experiment to draw general conclusions about the nature of perception and memory:

> Our evidence suggests that the controlled chaos of the brain is more than an accidental by-product. Indeed, it may be the chief property that makes the brain different from an artificial intelligence machine. . . .
> Chaotic systems continually produce novel activity patterns. We propose that such patterns are crucial to the development of nerve cell assemblies. More generally, the ability to create activity patterns may underlie the brain's ability to generate insight and the "trials" of trial-and-error problem solving. (p. 85)

Although the model and data relate only to one sensory system, Freeman believes that chaotic activity underlies all perception:

> I predict that when people examine drawings in which foreground and background are ambiguous, so that perception alternates between two images, the amplitude maps will be found to alternate as well. (p. 85)

Freeman argues for a structural coupling between perception and motion, referring to recursive, "reafferent messages" between the system. However, he speaks loosely when he says, "the brain seeks information" and the limbic system "funnels a command to the motor system" – phrases associated with the serial, local view he seeks to refute. In contrast, his conclusion fits the situated cognition perspective:

> An act of perception is not the copying of an incoming stimulus. It is a step in a trajectory by which brains grow, reorganize themselves and reach into their environment to change to their own advantage. (p. 85)

Of course, a fuller discussion of "advantage" needs to be couched in terms of conceptualized social activity, not neural activations. Freeman (1995) has begun this exploration in subsequent work.

We might also quibble whether *brains* can "reach" anywhere. Indeed, Freeman's olfactory model is limited precisely by not showing how odor recognition is tied to movement. Perhaps this is appropriate for olfaction, which has apparent differences from vision. For example, odors generally cannot be *imagined* by people, suggesting a lack of feedback links and self-activation that is present in visual imagination. Also, visual features appear to have *form constants* that may correspond to hardwired recognizers (Cytowic, 1993, p. 125).

Instead of a feedback coupling to movement, Freeman's model incorporates something like the "energy level" in Beer's model of the cockroach (Chapter 5). In particular, the priming effect of "modulatory chemicals" increases general arousal, enhancing the responsiveness of nerve cell assemblies (and hence partially accounting for rapid, massive responses to weak signals). In contrast, the sensorimotor models we consider in Chapter 7 explain the varying nature of map activations in terms of what other maps are active. Freeman's models are more local, explaining in lower-level detail the variability of patterning within cell assemblies.

Beyond perceptual categorization, other work suggests that chaos may play a role in rhythmic, sequential processes. For example, Freeman's observation that the olfactory cortex in the rest state is moving around in the phase space of previous transitions suggests a mechanism for controlling serial behavior. In particular, chaos theories reveal that self-similarity of structure in the heart enables finer-grained timing coordination between muscle fibers (Gleick, 1987, p. 109). Also via apparently fractal structure, "the lungs pack in a surface area of a tennis court" (ibid., p. 108). To make a perhaps superficial analogy, could the surfaces of neural maps be fractal in character, like the branching of aorta in the lungs? Might such an infinity of embedded surfaces, hierarchical and self-similar on different scales, play a role in the self-organizing and coordination properties of the brain? If so, this is a kind of mechanism we have not until now even dreamed of building.

Mark Bickhard and Loren Terveen (1995) advocate the study of oscillatory and topological mechanisms in their summary of *interactivism*:

Interactivism forces an architecture with natural timing and natural topologies. This dynamic system architecture offers forms of control and computation more powerful than Turing machines. It also offers natural approaches to problems of binding across parallel processes. There is no message hang-up with the oscillatory modulations of this architecture. It also offers a natural framework within which representation can emerge, and, thus, in which learning and development can occur. In this view, it is no contingent accident of evolution that the brain functions in terms of modulations among oscillatory processes. (p. 330)

The coupling between the olfactory bulb and cortex, hypothesized by Freeman, is a kind of "binding" occurring in categorization that doesn't require descriptions or messages. Bickhard and Terveen argue that an oscillatory mechanism, as in the nondeterministic, chaotic model of Freeman, may provide a means by which *representing emerges in the mechanism.* Of special interest is the distributed nature of the recognizer: We cannot say that the olfactory bulb has representations within it because when the bulb and cortex are separated, the behavior of the bulb becomes stable and quiet. Representing is a characteristic of the combined interaction of these modules during stimulation itself. Thus Freeman's chaotic model demonstrates how, by a certain form of simultaneous co-organization, memory could be nonlocal and yet brain components become "modular" (cf. the discussion of localization in Chapter 3).

The discussion of indexical-functional representation in Chapter 5 and the examples of feature learning presented here provide an empirical basis for understanding theoretical issues about symbols (Part III). But I have more situated robots to describe, with even more unusual, productive designs for relating cognition to neural processes. The robots I present in the next chapter learn by a mechanism called *selectionism.* Along with the ideas of structural coupling and nondeterministic, time-dependent systems, selectionism shows how the descriptive modeling languages take for granted processes of sequencing, binding, and recoordinating that neural processes accomplish more efficiently and flexibly.

7   Remembering without matching

Learning is not a process of accumulation of representations of the environment; it is a continuous process of transformation of behavior through continuous change in the capacity of the nervous system to synthesize it. Recall does not depend on the indefinite retention of a structural invariant that represents an entity (an idea, image, or symbol), but on the functional ability of the system to create, when certain recurrent conditions are given, a behavior that satisfies the recurrent demands or that the observer would class as a reenacting of a previous one.

> Humberto Maturana, Biology of cognition, 1970; reprinted in Maturana and Varela, 1980; cited by Winograd and Flores, 1986, p. 45

Avoiding obstacles and even creating features say little about how organisms *coordinate sequences* of behavior over time. None of the robots we have considered so far can develop habits or routines that are not directly coupled to topological features or built in by their designers. In contrast, most descriptive cognitive modeling has focused on the "knowledge" of associations, conceptualizations, and procedural skills. Situated cognition research seeks to understand these abilities as dynamically reconstructed and adapted processes, which heretofore have been described only as fixed, stored routines. In terms of robot design, we must consider not just moving through corridors or recognizing regions but *remembering ways of interacting*, such that actions are not merely reactively triggered, but themselves categorized and sequenced. In the large, this moves us to the nature of multimodal conceptualization (playing the harmonica while pounding on the drums), which no robot today can learn and improvise in the manner of a person.

Accomplishments to date are more modest: I present here two robots that model remembering as a *categorized coupling* of sensory and motor systems. Going a step beyond feature learning, they develop new categories by feedback within movement. I present these robots in some detail, for they show how complete architectures for coordinating perception-categorization-action are possible without descriptive, inferential processes (cf. Figure 3.2). They replace the decision-making "post alternatives and compare" method by a selectional-coupling mechanism. The next chapter relates the methods of the situated-robotic approach. Then, in Part III, I reconsider the nature of symbolic mechanisms, which these robot experiments are intended to reformulate.

146

Neural Darwinism: An alternative to the encoding view of learning

Gerald Edelman's model of learning is based on his earlier model of the immune system, for which he received the Nobel Prize in 1972. In the earlier work, he showed that recognition of bacteria is based on competitive selection in a population of antibodies. This process has several intriguing properties (1992, p. 78):

- There is more than one way to recognize successfully any particular shape.
- No two people have identical antibodies.
- The system exhibits a form of memory at the cellular level (facilitating antibody reproduction).

In his theory of neuronal group selection (TNGS), Edelman extends this theory to a more general *science of recognition*:

By "recognition," I mean the continual adaptive matching or fitting of elements in one physical domain to novelty occurring in elements of another, more or less independent physical domain, a matching that occurs without prior instruction. . . . There is no explicit information transfer between the environment and organisms that causes the population to change and increase its fitness. (p. 74)[1]

Here Edelman follows von Foerster's usage (Chapter 4), suggesting that the term *information* be reserved for categories constructed by an organism in segmenting and classifying signals.

By analogy, mental categories, coordinations, and conceptualizations are like a population of neural maps constituting a "species." There is a common *selectional mechanism* by which the organism "recognizes" offending bacteria, as well as a previous interaction:[2]

Memory is a process that emerged only when life and evolution occurred and gave rise to the systems described by the sciences of recognition. . . . It describes aspects of heredity, immune responses, reflex learning, true learning following perceptual categorization, and the various forms of consciousness. . . . What they have in common is relative stability of structure under selective mapping events. (pp. 203–204)

The species concept arising from . . . population thinking is central to all ideas of categorization. Species are not 'natural kinds'; their definition is relative, they are not homogeneous, they have no prior necessary condition for their establishment, and they have no clear boundaries. (p. 239)

As we will see, in relating neuronal populations to species, Edelman is viewing neural structures as competitively selected groups that are doing something together as part of a larger system.

TNGS explains "how multiple maps lead to integrated responses, and how they lead to generalizations of perceptual responses, *even in the absence of language*" (p. 82; emphasis added). Like Maturana and others,

Edelman is reacting against the descriptive cognitive modeling approach, which assumes that learning occurs by being told or being given an already categorized world and a description of correct responses. Edelman characterizes this approach as *instructionism*, and seeks instead a theory that explains the development of language rather than presupposing it. This means explaining how categorization occurs at the neural level, without making the assumptions of simple connectionism (Chapter 3).

TNGS has three components:

1. How the structure of the brain develops in the embryo and during early life (topobiology[3]).
2. A theory of recognition and memory rooted in *population thinking* (Darwinism).
3. A detailed model of classification and neural map selection (neural Darwinism).

Population thinking is a characteristically biological mode of thought, emphasizing the importance of diversity – not merely evolutionary change, but selection from a wide variety of options. Applied to populations of neuronal groups, there are three tenets:

- *Developmental selection*, by which neural circuits are selectively strengthened and die out during early sensorimotor learning.[4]
- *Experiential selection*, the creation of a secondary level repertoire, called *neuronal groups*, through selective strengthening and weakening of the neural connections.
- *Reentry*, which links two maps bidirectionally through "parallel selection and correlation of the maps' neuronal groups" (p. 84).

The levels of nested components involved in categorization are neural cells, neuronal groups, neural maps, classification couples, and global maps. I summarize these components in the following two subsections.

Neuronal groups and classification

Neuronal groups are collections of neural cells that fire and oscillate together (Edelman, 1992, p. 95). Neuronal groups are the units of selection in the development of new functioning circuits (pp. 85–86). By analogy to organisms in a species and lymphocytes, neuronal groups are individuals (Table 7.1). Reactivation of a neuronal group corresponds to selection of individuals in a species.[5] Although one might suppose individual synapses or neurons to correspond to individuals in a population, individual neurons are in general always selected within a group and influence other neurons only through groups: Each neural cell "receives inputs from cells in its own group, from cells in other groups, and from extrinsic sources" (p. 88).[6] The existence of neuronal groups is controversial, but has been experimentally demonstrated (pp. 94–95).

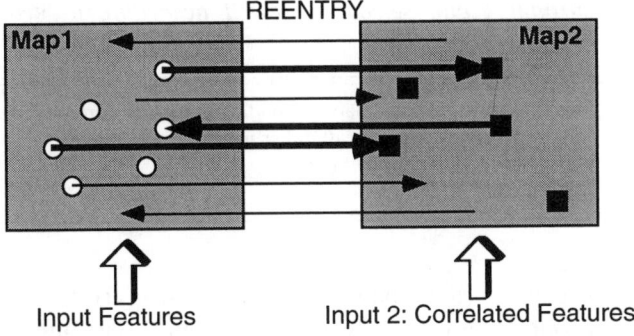

Figure 7.1. A classification couple. "Reentry. Two maps of neuronal groups receive independent inputs (1 and 2). Each map is functionally segregated; that is, map 1 responds to local features (for example, visually directed angles) that are different from those to which map 2 responds (for example, an object's overall movement). The two maps are connected by nerve fibers that carry reentrant signals between them. These fibers are numerous and dense and serve to 'map the maps' to each other. If within some time period the groups indicated by the circles in map 1 are reentrantly connected to the groups indicated by the squares in map 2, these connections may be strengthened. As a result of reentrant signaling, and by means of synaptic change, patterns in responses in map 1 are associated with patterns of responses in map 2 in a 'classification couple.' Because of synaptic change, responses to present inputs are also linked to previous patterns of responses" (Edelman, 1992, Figure 9–4, p. 90). Copyright © 1992 by BasicBooks, Inc. Reprinted by permission of BasicBooks, a division of HarperCollins Publishers, Inc.

The fundamental hypothesis of TNGS is that categorization is a process of establishing a relation between different neural structures, called *neural maps*. A neural map is composed of neuronal groups. Categorization is a process of physically relating two functionally different neural maps by reentrant connections in what is called a *classification couple*:

Each map independently receives signals from other brain maps or from the world. . . . Functions and activities in one map are connected and correlated with those in another map. . . . One set of inputs could be, for example, from vision, and the other from touch. (p. 87)

The emphasis is on physical activation of structures, not storage and retrieval. Hence, we talk of *categorization*, not categories per se. Furthermore, maps aren't merely isolated classifications of features, but always *relations* of classifications. Figure 7.1 (with Edelman's caption) summarizes these ideas.

Each circle and square in Figure 7.1 represents a *neuronal group*, an intrinsically connected array of 50 to 10,000 neurons. Individual groups develop as the brain develops, but membership of neurons in a group develops through early sensorimotor coordination learning (called *developmental selection*), rather than being genetically preordained or merely cir-

Table 7.1. *Neuronal group selection viewed according to evolutionary Darwinism*

Species	Functionally segregated map, responding to local features and participating in classification couples with other maps
Population	Map composed of neuronal groups
Individual	Neuronal group

cumstantial correlations (like a palm print). Neural maps (referring again to Figure 7.1), in contrast, are entirely constructed and constitute the fundamental units of memory (called *experiential selection*). That is, a map is a set of neuronal groups locally related by sensory or motor signals (e.g., a visual system may have several dozen different maps, functionally specialized by color, movement, etc. [p. 85]).

The formation of a map depends on the physical connections that grow when the brain develops, including, of course, physical links to sensory organs and muscles, and the relation to other mapping processes. In particular, functional segregation arises through local connections, as well as through categorization learning (a process of differentiation between maps). Indeed, the point of Figure 7.1 is to show that activation of neuronal groups within a map is dependent on signals from correlated maps, not just on sensory or motor signals. In a simple way, this model addresses Dewey's criticism of serial, stimulus–response theories: Each activation is part of a circuit, a coordination (Chapter 4). We do not have temporally first the stimulus and then the motor response, but a single circuit of activations arising temporally together. As Edelman puts it, "memory is a property of the entire system" (p. 103), not a place where stuff is stored.

Edelman doesn't relate neuronal selection as clearly to species evolution as we might expect, given his explicit reference to Darwinism. Table 7.1 is an attempt to explicate the analogy.

First, a significant number of nonidentical neuronal groups can function similarly within maps (responding to the same inputs), a fundamental property of TNGS called *degeneracy* (Edelman, 1987, p. 6). This roughly corresponds to different individuals in a species having different genotypes but selected within an environment for similar functional characteristics. Apparently, a population of neuronal groups becomes a "species" when it becomes functionally distinct from other populations. This occurs when maps interact during the organism's behavior. In effect, the "environment" for a map consists of other active maps.

Excitatory and inhibitory interactions between maps correspond to interspecies interactions at the level of competitive and symbiotic relations in the environment. Neural maps effectively define each other's populations by activation relations between their neuronal groups.

Reentry (bidirectional activation between *populations* of neuronal groups)[7] provides the means for map interaction and reactivation during organism behavior. Reentry explains how "brain areas that emerge in evolution coordinate with each other to yield new functions" (Edelman, 1992, p. 85) during an individual organism's lifetime. Specifically, local maps can be *reused without copying* by selection of additional reentry links to form new classification couples (with specialized interactions between their neuronal groups). Edelman concludes that reentry thus provides "the main basis for a bridge between physiology and psychology."

Putting the pieces together, Edelman emphasizes that learning coordinated motion occurs through feedback-in-motion from different senses, including effectors:

Perceptual categorization occurs only when, after disjunctive sampling of signals in several modalities (vision, touch, joint sense) . . . [the program] activates an output through its reentrant maps. . . . For example, as a result of explorations with its "hand-arm" and "eye" it "decides" that something is an object, that the object is striped, and that the object is bumpy. Given . . . [the] higher-order value system for output on such a categorical decision, it then activates a neural circuit that flails its arm. (p. 93)[8]

Coordinating categorizations by global maps:
Sequences and concepts

Another level of organization, corresponding to what psychologists typically call *conceptualization*, is required to coordinate categorizations dynamically with ongoing sensorimotor behavior. We also refer to this as *prelinguistic* conceptualization to emphasize that the neural structures do not map strictly onto words and definitions; and of course, such organizations exist in animals without language.

Conceptualization, as hypothesized by Edelman, involves a composition of categorizations – the process by which perceptual categorization occurs again at a higher level in coordinating perceptual categorizations, both in simultaneous multimodal relations and sequentially, over time. Thus, the compositional process has two dimensions: first, laterally in coupling diverse sensorimotor categorizations and, second, temporally, as a nesting of network activations (so a currently active network is included within or *subsumed by* the network that is activated next). Edelman doesn't emphasize the idea of subsumption of networks in time, but it appears to be essential for sequence learning. Further categorization of sequences would then correspond to procedural chunks.[9]

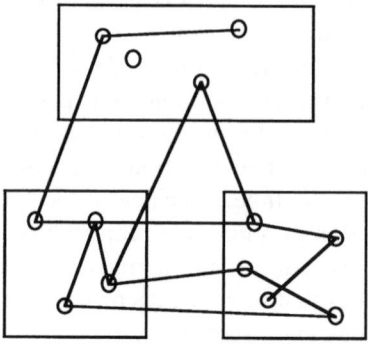

Figure 7.2. A map of maps (Edelman, 1992, p. 103). Copyright © 1992 by BasicBooks, Inc. Reprinted by permission of BasicBooks, a division of HarperCollins Publishers, Inc.

Continuing with Edelman's presentation, we consider the neurological underpinnings of conceptualization:

What brain operations give rise to these properties? The TNGS suggests that in forming concepts, *the brain constructs maps of its own activities*, not just of external stimuli, as in perception. According to the theory, the brain areas responsible for concept formation contain structures that categorize, discriminate, and recombine the various brain activities *occurring in different kinds of global mappings*. Such structures in the brain, instead of categorizing outside inputs from sensory modalities, *categorize parts of past global mappings* according to modality, the presence or absence of movement, and the presence or absence of relationships between perceptual categorizations. . . .

Structures able to perform these activities are likely to be found in the frontal, temporal, and parietal cortices of the brain. They must represent *a mapping of types of maps*. Indeed, they must be able to activate or reconstruct portions of *past* activities of global mappings of different types – for example, those *involving different sensory modalities*. They must also be able to recombine or compare them. (p. 109, emphasis added)

A *global mapping* involves categorization of maps; that is, a global map is a map of types of maps. "A global mapping is a dynamic structure containing multiple reentrant local maps (both motor and sensory) that are able to interact with non-mapped parts of the brain" (p. 89). This idea is illustrated in a highly abstract way by Figure 7.2.

"The brain categorizes its own activity" means that signals in a map of maps come from other maps, including ultimately perceptual and motor classifications. *A global mapping* is a dynamic complex of such maps of maps, involving both sensory and motor maps, plus parts of the brain that are not mapped, such as the hippocampus, cerebellum, and basal ganglia, which are responsible for timing and sequencing (p. 105). A global mapping is thus a sensorimotor circuit. To be clear, a global mapping consists of many maps of maps like that shown in Figure 7.2.

Conceptualization is the process of *categorizing global maps*. As with all neural activation, conceptualization occurs – to put it quite simply – while everything else is happening. That is, conceptualization occurs *as part of an ongoing sequence of sensorimotor coordination. Here we find, in neuropsychological terms, the idea of situated cognition at the structural level (cf. Table 1.1): Perceiving, meaning, and acting arise together as structural couplings. Perception is not an isolated peripheral device that feeds input to a pattern matcher that selects descriptions and procedures from memory, to be subconsciously assembled into motor sequences (cf. Figure 3.2). In terms of computational jargon, animal memory is highly proceduralized, but *remembering is acting*, not an internal module or an independent subprocess. Functional modularization occurs, but all differentiations are with respect to other functional categorizations as relations (see the discussion of Maturana in Chapter 4 and of Freeman in Chapter 6). (Chapter 9 develops these ideas further and shows their origins in Dewey's transactional philosophy.)

Selection continually occurs within local maps of a global map, making connections to motor behavior, new sensory samplings, and successive reentry events, allowing new categorizations to emerge:

Categorization does not occur according to a computerlike program in a sensory area which then executes a program to give a particular motor output. Instead, sensorimotor activity over the whole mapping *selects* neuronal groups that give appropriate output or behavior, resulting in categorization. (pp. 89–90)

"Appropriateness" is determined by internal criteria of value that constrain the domains in which categorization occurs, exhibited most fundamentally in regulation of bodily functions (respiratory, feeding, sex, etc.):

The thalamocortical system ... evolved to receive signals from sensory receptor sheets and to give signals to voluntary muscles. ... Its main structure, the cerebral cortex is arranged in a set of maps ... as highly connected, layered local structures with massively reentrant connections. ... The cortex is concerned with the categorization of the world and the limbic-brain system is concerned with value. ... Learning may be seen as the means by which categorization occurs on a background of value. ... (pp. 117–118)

Categorization is therefore relational, occurring within, and in some sense bound to, an active, *ongoing coordinated sequence* of sensory and motor behavior: "The physical movements of an animal drive its perceptual categorization" (p. 167). Crucially, global maps themselves rearrange, collapse, or are replaced by perturbations at different levels (p. 91).

Memory "results from a process of continual *recategorization*. By its nature, memory is procedural and involves continual motor activity" (p.

102). Hence, memory is not a place or identified with the low-level mechanisms of synaptic reactivation; and certainly neural memory is not a coded representation of objects in the world (p. 238). Rather, as we saw in Freeman's model of odor recognition, "memory is a system property" (p. 102). More generally, memory involves not only categorization of sensorimotor activations, but categorizations of *sequences* of neural activations:

> The brain contains structures such as the cerebellum, the basal ganglia, and the hippocampus that are concerned with timing, succession in movement, and the establishment of memory. They are closely connected with the cerebral cortex as it carries out categorization and correlation of the kind performed by global mappings.... (p. 105)

> The brain ... has no replicative memory. It is historical and value driven. It forms categories by internal criteria and by constraints acting at many scales. (p. 152)

Building on Lakoff's analysis of language and meaning (Chapter 3), Edelman distinguishes between concepts and linguistic symbols:

> The word "concept" is generally used in connection with language, and is used in contexts in which one may talk of truth or falsehood. I have used the word concept, however, to refer to a capability that appears in evolution prior to the acquisition of linguistic primitives.... (p. 108)

Conceptualization is a kind of categorization, operating as part of a recognition system:

> This recognition must be relational: It must be able to connect one perceptual categorization to another, apparently unrelated one, even in the absence of the stimuli that triggered those categorizations. The relations that are captured must allow responses to general properties – "object," "up–down," "inside," and so on. (Ibid.)

Verbal conceptualization certainly dominates intellectual problem solving. But in general, concepts may develop in other modalities, prior to speech, both in the evolution of the species and in our personal experience in articulating an idea:

> Unlike elements of speech, however, concepts are *not* conventional or arbitrary, do *not* require linkage to a speech community to develop, and do *not* depend on sequential presentation. Conceptual capabilities develop in evolution well before speech. Although they depend on perception and memory, they are *constructed* by the brain from elements that contribute to both these functions. (Ibid.)

Rather than operating on stimuli directly, conceptual categorization operates on internal categorizing: "This means that special reentrant connections from these higher-order cortical areas to other cortical areas and to the hippocampus and basal ganglia must exist to carry out concepts" (p. 109). In particular, *intentional behavior* involves sensorimotor sequencing influenced in a top-down manner by conceptual reactivation and construction: "because concept formation is based on the central triad of perceptual categorization, memory, and learning, it is, by its very nature, intentional" (p. 110). I discuss the relation between conceptualization as higher-order categorization and intention in Chapters 12 and 13.

Design of Darwin III: Synthetic neural systems

Edelman's theories are being tested by development of computer models in projects led by George Reeke. Darwin III is a "recognition automaton that performs as a global mapping" (Edelman, 1992, p. 92) that coordinates vision with a simulated tactile arm in a simulated environment.[10] It is capable of "correlating a scene" by reentry between value-category memory and perceptual categorizations. Values are built in (e.g., light is better than darkness, tactile stimulation at the center of vision is "favored over stimulation at the periphery" [p. 93]), but the resulting features and perceptual categorizations are all internally developed. The system consists of 50 maps containing 50,000 cells and over 620,000 synaptic junctions (Reeke et al., 1990a, p. 608). This system rests on the model of reentrant cortical integration (RCI) which has been tested with much larger networks (129 maps, 220,000 cells, and 8.5 million connections) that simulate visual illusions and the detection of structure from motion in the monkey's visual cortex.[11]

The statistical, stochastic nature of selection is common to many connectionism models. It was mentioned by Bateson (1972) in his own discussion of parallels between the evolution of biological phenotypes and the development of ideas. Edelman's model probes deeper by specifying how neural nets are *grown*, not merely selected, and how learning is based on internal value. Neural Darwinism can be contrasted with other neural network approaches in these aspects:

- The influence of epigenetic and infant development as the source of variability.
- Degenerate (redundant) populations of preferred maps for recognition.
- Selection that is not merely eliminative (the rich get richer), but also maintains variability.
- Details concerning global mapping, reentrancy, sensorimotor maps, generalization, and classification couples.

We can also apply Pagels's (1988) criteria for comparing models (pp. 140–141). First, like connectionist models, Darwin III is not *realistic at the neural level* and arguably lacks massive parallelism. But unlike most connectionist models, Darwin III is *not constructed by building in words* referring to concepts and things in the world that it will learn about (recall the discussion of Pengi in Chapter 5). Finally, Darwin III is *based on a series of principles* involving evolution, selectionism, development, the

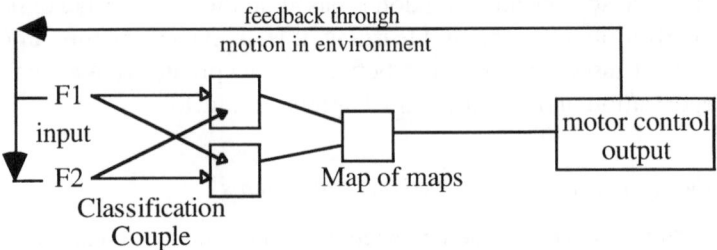

Figure 7.3. Darwin III shown as a system with environmental feedback (the motor system is autonomous, outputting gestures; other versions model the fine-grained motor tracking and smoothing by the cerebellum via internal feedback of motor signals). Tracing objects in the environment leads to internal coactivation of neural maps in a *classification couple* (i.e., categorization). Higher-order maps correlate the responses of multiple sensory channels (tactile, touch and kinesthesia) to produce an output gesture. (Reprinted with permission from Reeke et al., 1990b, pp. 1513, 1515, and 1522.)

nonencoding nature of representations, and a distinction between concepts and names. Figure 7.3 provides another way of contrasting connectionist models with a robot based on TNGS.

Connectionist networks can adapt by error correction, but the feedback in Darwin III (and some other situated robots) is under the control of the robot itself: Categorizations lead to actions that then modify the categorization process. Connectionist systems often skip the *perceptual categorization* (words are input) or they have no activity (categorizing is not part of a sensorimotor circuit). In situated robots, feedback occurs in action as *encounters with the world* or by correlating sensory and motor signals. This highlights the fact that most connectionist models are not circuits: Designed signals go in and categories come out. Indeed, in NETtalk (Chapter 3), both input and output are expressions in a language. The idea of built-in value ensures that some kinds of categorizations will have an inherent interest, thus "motivating" looking, searching, and so on. Feedback can thus involve functional differentiation of world, not merely a classification or description force-fed by the human operator.

NOMAD is a robotic implementation of Darwin III, claimed to be "the first nonliving thing capable of 'learning' in the biological sense of the word" (Edelman, 1992, p. 193). But Edelman demurs of replicating the capabilities of the brain. Building a device capable of primary consciousness (as may occur in birds and mammals) will require simulating "a brain system capable of concepts and thus of the *reconstruction* of portions of global mappings":

Artifacts with higher-order consciousness would have to have language and the equivalent of behavior in a speech community. . . . The practical problems . . . are

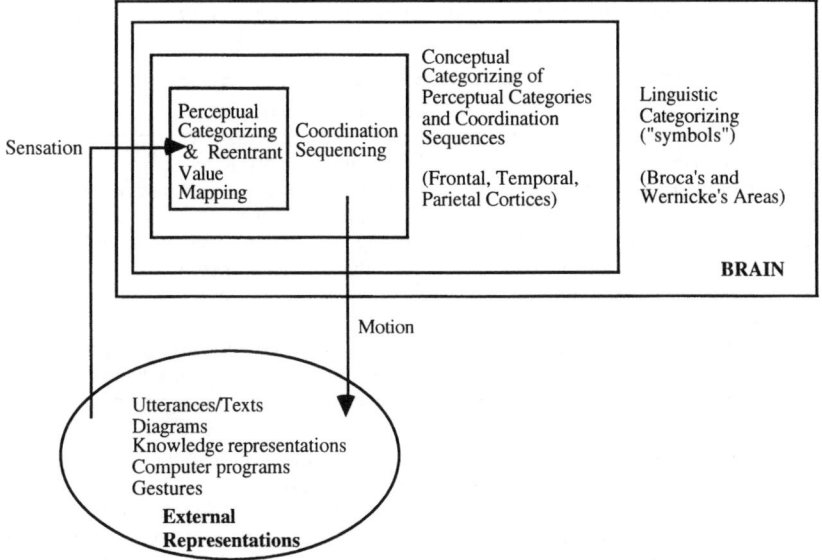

Figure 7.4. Situated cognition view of sensorimotor coordination. Placement of the "motion" line is arbitrary.

so far out of reach that we needn't concern ourselves with them now. (1992, p. 194)[12]

A situated cognition interpretation of neural Darwinism

Figure 7.4 shows a highly simplified, schematic view of how different organizations in the brain are composed (in my interpretation and extension of Edelman's theory). In contrast to the classical, descriptive modeling architecture, *neural processors coconfigure each other* (through reactivation, competitive selection, and composition). All action is embodied because perception (what we believe is in the world) and action (what we say and do) arise together: Learning is inherently situated because every new activation is part of an ongoing perception–action coordination. Situated activity is not a kind of action, but rather the nature of animal interaction at all times, in contrast to most machines. This is not merely a claim that context is important: What constitutes the context, how animals categorize the world and conceptualize activity, arises together with processes that are coordinating physical movement.

Figure 7.4 emphasizes the different *roles* categorizing can play through composition and relation of different parts of the brain:

Table 7.2. *Composition of categorization into levels, with associated common names*

Level of categorization	Cognitive interpretation
Coupling of maps	Perceptual categorization
Sequence of map activations	Coordinated behavior sequence in time (e.g., path learning)
Categorization of sequences of maps (procedural skill) or categorization of simultaneous maps in different modalities (gestalt)	Conceptualization of interactions and situations (routines, images, rhythms)
Categorization of conceptualization	Names and named relations for object classes, situations, goals, problem-solving strategies

- Perceptual categorization is always occurring with respect to ongoing conceptual and sequential movement coordination.
- Habitual coordination involves a process of reactivation and recomposition of classification couples, both at different levels of organization and over time. (The diagram emphasizes organizational levels but doesn't depict temporal relations.)
- Impasses (discoordinations) are resolved by developing a higher level of organization.
- Maps and their recurrent relations may be viewed as representations, but they are not encoded *descriptions*.
- Active maps are always part of complete sensorimotor circuits; areas of the brain do not form and operate independently, in the sense of computer modules providing input and output structures for processing by other modules at another time.
- Descriptions of the world and our behavior are created in our activity, placed physically in the world as pictures, utterances, and so on or experienced in our imagination as speaking or visualizing.

The levels of Figure 7.4 correspond to levels of composition of maps, what Edelman calls "categorization of the brain's own activities" occurring over time. Table 7.2 gives my interpretation of these levels.

The compositional diagram (Figure 7.4) should not be interpreted as implying a controlling relationship, localization, or serial sequencing. Because the architecture involves structural coupling, organizations at different levels are forming at the same time. However, over time a person may "put an experience into words" or "follow instructions about where to look." Organizations at perceptual or verbal levels may be willfully held active, allowing causal influences to move up or down through the composition of categorizations. For example, we may hold on to a perceptual detail and try to relate it to a larger conception or we may seek to categorize causally conceptions of different situations (Chapter 9). Furthermore, claiming that organizations are always occurring and influencing each other at different levels doesn't mean that we can't move silently or think with our eyes closed: Different modalities of sensing and moving can be coordinated in different ways. And we must often focus our attention selectively, as when we ask someone to stop talking so that we can relate and describe our own conceptions.

The diagram's boxes shouldn't be interpreted as places where things are stored. We can't draw a line inside the brain and say "Here are concepts and here are the relations" in the same sense that we can examine a computer model and say "Here are the nodes and here are the links." It is better to view all categorizations as relations, and it is best to say "*categorizing* process" than to speak of a categorization thing. Conceptualizing and meaning, exemplified by Dewey's example of "light-that-means-pain-when-touching-occurs," arises holistically in the sense of being a sensorimotor circuit.

Specifically, locating a kind of categorization at some level does not entail "presentation" there as a kind of input to be examined by another categorizing process. Neural categorizations are not perceived representations or sensed signals.[13] The network arises together as a *circuit*. The diagram depicts functional relations between maps, not places where things happen. Michael Arbib (1981) contrasts the viewpoint of serial programming with the control theorist's view of structurally coupled systems:

> In the flow diagram of a conventional serial computer program, each box corresponds to a single activation of a subsystem, only one system is activated at any time, and the lines joining the various boxes correspond to transfers of activation. . . . On the other hand, in the block diagram of the control theorist, each box represents a physically distinct system, *each such system is to be imagined active at the same time*, and the lines joining the different boxes correspond to the transfer of actual data, as in the pathways conveying the control signals and the feedback signals in a conventional feedback system. . . . (pp. 35–36; emphasis added)

Neural maps are obviously located physically, but the global mappings that coordinate sequences of sensorimotor activation, including conceptualization and speaking, are distributed networks, which activate together. The activation relations between global mappings are not stored somewhere, but constitute a memory for sequencing of categorizing.[14] The habits of human behavior, and what is known about the practice effect in learning skills, suggest that some activation relations are stable and become the components of new organizations. In this way, our experience, stories, and ways of talking accumulate into more complex, self-consistent ways of understanding and behaving.

The term *value* in Figure 7.4 emphasizes that every categorization is with respect to our interests and ongoing activities. Some values are built in, corresponding to survival and reproductive concerns. Value is inherent in a perceptual categorization. Value makes *something present* for the person. Every categorization (perceiving, understanding, speaking) is with respect to the person's history – previous ways of coordinating experience. In people, conceptual categorization of role and identity within a community are overarching; hence experience is subjective.

The categorizations, sequencing, and coordinations depicted in Figure 7.4 correspond to what we call a person's *knowledge*. Obviously, this greatly exceeds whatever someone says that he or she knows. People can describe experience by reciting facts, causal relations, and the like, but such models are *representations of knowledge*. Conceptualization doesn't strictly map onto words, definitions, and rules because many conceptualizations are nonverbal and because the meaning of even verbal conceptualizations is coupled to nonverbal categorizing.[15] Consequently, we can't create a descriptive inventory of what a person knows. Nevertheless, because language plays such a pivotal, organizing role in human life, there is an important coupling between conceptualizations and how we model the world in our speech and diagrams.

Understanding TNGS as a *mechanism* involves changing our linear, modular view of machines. In a dynamic reconfiguration, components are causally coupled, but the components are not fixed parts; they come into being as physical entities and then disappear. Unlike the procedures of computer programs that move and create structures, the "programs" of the brain are created at runtime, inseparable from the structures they are organizing.

To understand this in more detail, contrast selectionism with the familiar "generate and test" approach of heuristic programs. In a generate and test program, descriptions of the world and plans for behavior are selected and composed from a presupplied set or generated from a parametrized description of primitive components. For example, Mycin constructs a therapy plan for the patient by composing a set of drugs from a map associating bacteria and antibiotics, which was built in by the knowledge engineers and physicians. In contrast, in a selectionist architecture, evaluation of alternatives is operating on all the elements of a population in parallel. That is, all the members of a species are implicitly tested at once. Testing alternative categorizations occurs not as matching or scoring of feature descriptions, but as functioning processes competing to be part of an ongoing coordination.

TNGS, as I have extended it here, begins to explain how patterning of behavior is possible without requiring an initial ontology and without *reasoning* about a categorized world. That is, TNGS addresses the ability of animals in general to learn, navigate, improvise, and socialize without words for describing what they are doing. To be clear, my analysis (especially Figure 7.4) goes somewhat beyond Edelman's claims. I emphasize the recompositional, transformational, and coupling aspects of categorization operating on itself over time. Furthermore, I hypothesize that the brain is *accomplishing* what descriptive models claim. For example, I assume that the brain accomplishes what transformational grammar suggests: It takes previous coordination processes (e.g., sentences) and recomposes them to create new behaviors. The idea of structural coupling, and specifically Edelman's theory of selectionism, shows how such patterns may arise "in line" without having to be categorized as being patterns, as consciously occurs when we create grammar descriptions. Much more can be said about the relation of descriptive models to neural mechanisms. I consider this topic after presenting an additional example of a selectionist architecture, which shows how there might be principles for relating modules in a sensorimotor architecture.

Prometheus: Coupled recognition–action machines

Philippe Gaussier and Stephane Zrehen (1994b) describe a robot called Prometheus that can recognize objects like cubes in a landscape and learn to navigate to prescribed targets.[16] They propose a kind of sensorimotor architecture that is not based on engineered categories or a subsumption network (Chapter 5), but instead provides the possibility for hierarchical control by learned categories. One of their main goals was to overcome the limitation of ad hoc design: They believe that the perception–action coordination mechanism should be applicable to other cognitive problems. Therefore, they focused on finding the smallest number of processing elements that can be used in many applications. They demonstrate what can be done with one model of neural networks, incorporating topological maps and three types of links: probabilistic projection (unsupervised learning), product combination and cascading (reinforcement learning), and unconditional reflexes (implemented with a product rule). Thus, their approach proposes generic mechanisms for organizing neural processes into functional systems.

To begin, Gaussier and Zrehen repeat the now-familiar principle that directs situated robotics research:

"Knowledge" is built and transformed while interacting in the world. Our main claim is that acting in the world is necessary to the interpretation of perceived signals, i.e., to the emergence of "cognition".... (p. 2)

The key idea is a feedback process by which acting modifies what is perceived, in the service of categorization and action selection:

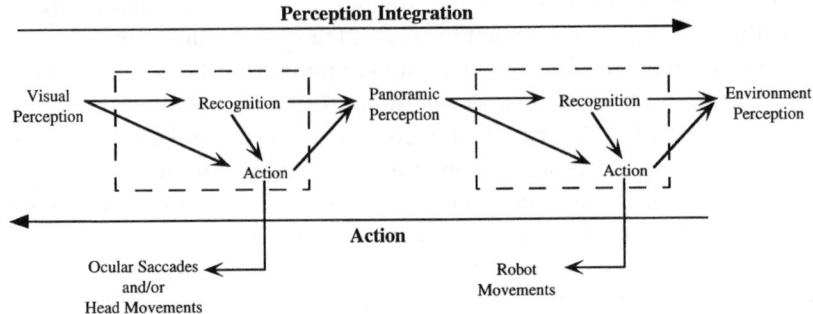

Figure 7.5. Prometheus architecture. "The global neural network for visual scene recognition and navigation: made of two PerAc blocks [designated by the dashed rectangles], the first for vision and the second for navigation." (Reprinted with permission from Gaussier and Zrehen, 1994a, Figure 14, p. 287.)

Performing an action modifies the subsequent perceptions, thus reducing the complexity of the recognizable scenes.

Action helps remove the ambiguities from perceived signals.

Choosing an action avoids exploring all the interpretation possibilities. (Ibid.)

Ironically, Gaussier and Zrehen use a real robot

to simplify the simulation phase and to avoid problems linked to toy universes. Moreover, it helps to take advantage of the possible emergent behavior of our robot due to its interaction with the world in unforeseen circumstances. (p. 14)

The program uses a neural network that locates an interesting potential feature in the picture; a second stage uses a sequential and temporal analysis to determine what the feature is.

Ocular movements in Prometheus are activated by a combination of a local recognition group of neurons and a proposed eye movement group. Similarly, robot movements are activated by a combination of a global recognition group of neurons and a proposed movement of the robot in space. Each stage is called a *PerAc block* (Figure 7.5).

The motor neuron group codes the directions of movement. Such an internal coding should be contrasted with describing movement with respect to a coordinate system in the world. Further, proceeding from experiments involving rats' hippocampal place fields, the "motor information is used to find the object size and the angle between two objects." The response of given cells is a "function of the distance to a given location relative to landmarks." Again, representation is not a *description* of places and measure of distances in the world, but a direct coding of control integrated over time. The representation is fully internal, constructed via feedback during actual motion.

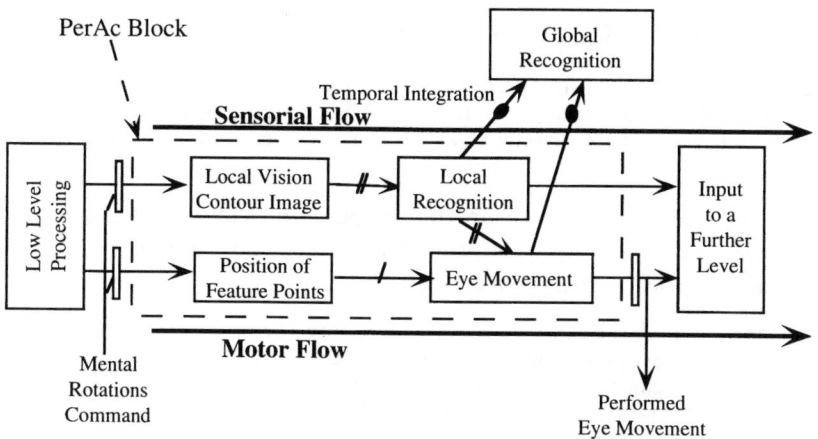

Figure 7.6. "The PerAc architecture for visual scene interpretation. Each block is a group of neurons. There is topology preservation in Local Vision, feature points, and Eye Movement groups. Local recognition and Eye movement are WTA." (Reprinted with permission from Gaussier and Zrehen, 1994a, Figure 8, p. 283.)

In the second stage, "the neural network that allows target retrieval is simply grafted on the unit block that allows visual scene recognition" (p. 14). As Figure 7.5 shows, there are "two data streams," sensory and motor; sensory flows forward to affect "higher" levels of action, action feeds backward to affect "lower" levels of perception. In this way, perceptual categories develop strictly by the actions associated with them (p. 15) (to be contrasted with Freeman's model of perceptual categorization without movement).

Examining a PerAc block in more detail (Figure 7.6), we see that "perception" feeds topological-preserving information to recognition and action maps. The recognition neural network level is winner-take-all (abbreviated WTA); the motor map is preceded by a motor proposal.

Links in a PerAc block occur as follows:

Each arrow represents a link between two groups of neurons. The arrows crossed by one short line represent one-to-one neuron links whereas the arrows crossed by two short lines represent one-to-all neurons links. Commonly, the one-to-one links are reflex pathways and are considered as unmodifiables as in classical Pavlovian conditioning. (1994a, p. 283)

Developing weights in each PerAc block involves two phases of local and global learning, as in Darwin III, including a built-in value system and interactions with the world. As in Darwin III, the number of cells in each group, as well as the types of links between the groups, are hardwired. Specific connections between neurons of two groups develop as a function of the interactions.

Figure 7.6 further shows how eye movement flows forward as input to further levels – a form of internal feedback:

The eye movement group is a topological map with a WTA, with input in the perceptive and motor flow: the position-of-feature-points group proposes movement, and the local recognition group is associated to a given movement. (Ibid.)

For example, focusing on a characteristic point of a cube (such as a corner), the robot performs invariant transformations and mental rotations to recognize vertices. At the same time,

to complete an interpretation or remove ambiguity, the robot focuses on the other [previously learned] characteristic points . . . according to learned saccadic movements. Objects can thus be recognized in a real scene even if they are partially occluded or rotated or if there is noise. (p. 282)

A mental rotation is a process of matching a presented image to a learned representation. Integration over time is used to simulate short-term memory; hence a previous interpretation will directly affect current processing.

The key point is that proposed eye movements are activated directly from those that occurred under similar circumstances. In this way, performed saccades correspond to those learned when exploring the cube's vertex *for the first time*. Notice that the entire architecture is based on what movement to make: Local recognition feeds (one to all) into eye movement, which itself feeds forward to global navigation.

Gaussier and Zrehen summarize the advantages of the PerAc block architecture. They are a kind of

basic building block and a systematic tool to combine motor and perceptive information. In addition, the PerAc architecture takes into account the dynamical aspect of the robot's behavior and solves robot control problems in which "autonomy" is needed. Indeed, PerAc architecture relies on the postulate that the recognition of any cue can be simplified if the system can act on it. (p. 287)

In many robotic architectures, there is one level for each step of processing (e.g., sensation, feature, category, object, distance, movement) yielding a pyramid of maps, "classifying local features before taking the results as inputs to higher levels." But Prometheus integrates control using just two levels: a local one coupling seeing and looking and a global one coupling recognition and navigation. Gaussier and Zrehen claim that this model "agrees with the motor theory of speech recognition which postulates we recognize speech signals by trying to imitate the heard sound" (p. 15). The main achievement of the PerAc approach is thus to solve apparently very different problems with the same architecture.

Probabilistic topological maps

Advancing Prometheus's design requires good models of neural groups. Gaussier and Zrehen's use of probabilistic topological maps illustrates one approach (Zrehen and Gaussier, 1994). Their model is clearly consistent with Edelman's emphasis on competitive selection, but it explores more precisely how sensory and motor systems might be coupled in *levels of internal control*. Freeman's chaotic spaces might therefore be viewed as single-level models of the input space, which are probabilistic and feed into the topological maps (corresponding to a single vision input to recognition mapping). Gaussier and Zrehen's topological maps are in effect a generalization of a WTA recognition mechanism, but the internal representation preserves the topology of the input.

In the model's landmark-based retrieval, "motor information is used to find the object size and the angle between two objects." Relative placement of landmarks is learned by circling around a target (a process in bee navigation studied by Tinbergen and others). In this phase of "local exploration . . . it learns the association between given neurons in the localization groups and other neurons in the motor group." Then, in search mode, it "makes one step in the direction associated with the closest place field." Viewing the target at the center, the landmarks therefore induce a set of pie wedges around the target. A vector associated with each landmark points at the target. By observing which landmark is closest and moving in the vector of that *place field*, the robot quickly hones in on the target. *Forbidden zones* may also be introduced that inhibit movement. Combining information, a probabilistic mechanism smoothes the trajectories. Further use of *topological arrays* allows learning with fewer trials by generalizing the response with respect to proximity (similar to the *activation wells* of de Bono[17]).

Gaussier and Zrehen (1994b) describe the learning process as follows (Figure 7.7):

Each neuron in the secondary map receives afferences from all cells in the primary topological map; Input I is presented and P is the winner in the primary map. Only the weight between P and the maximally responding cell in the secondary map is modified by reinforcement learning. Input J is presented and Q is the winner in the primary map. The activity in the secondary map cell decreases with the distance between P and Q. (p. 14)

The concentric rings around Q represent the "activity bubble" induced by the single (later) presentation of Q within the topological map. P is not activated from the sensory map because of the WTA process that selects Q instead. But P is activated within the *topological map* because it is close to

Secondary
Map

Primary
Topological
Map

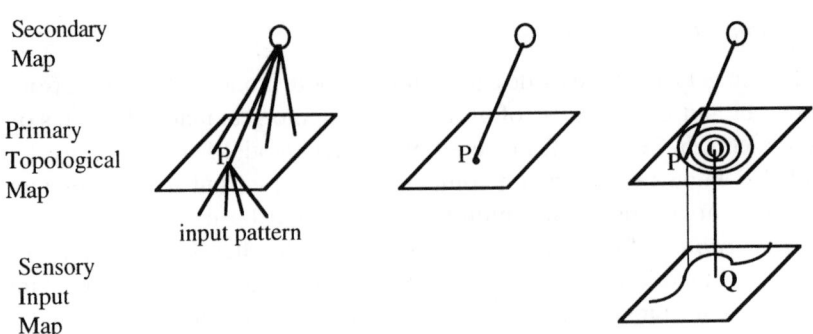

input pattern

Sensory
Input
Map

Figure 7.7. "Probabilistic topological maps allow generalized associations between a secondary map and a primary topology. Learning from instance P is generalized so response to subsequent input Q depends probabilistically on distance from P." (Reprinted with permission from Gaussier and Zrehen, 1994b, Figure 17, p. 14.)

P. The effect is that "all links to a further group [the secondary map] need not be learned." In this example, the previously learned association between P will be sufficient to activate the secondary map when Q is selected from the input. This kind of generalization explains in part the plasticity and systematicity discovered in the owl monkey's sematosensory map (Chapter 4).

Gaussier and Zrehen (1994b) summarize the general mechanism their method illustrates:

Topology preservation is possible only relatively as one projects high-dimensional spaces onto a two-dimensional discrete space. However, locally, it is possible if small movements correspond to changes of a little number of variables. This is the case with the coding . . . for Khepera's infrared sensors, and it is the case with any optical flow (Gibson, 1979): a small movement can be identified by important changes of a limited number of variables in the flow. If the input are of that nature, then local topology preservation is possible and can be used for identification of subjective categories on the robot's part. (p. 240)

Coupling of perception and action

How are perception and action codeveloped in Prometheus's architecture? Not in a direct coupling of recognition and movement – this architecture is one-directional, with recognition causing movement – but in a *proposal of movement* based on feature points. The feedback from movement to recognition occurs over time in actual movement. Possible or learned movements affect *looking*, which affects what is recognized. For example, eye movement proposals are activated by current sensory information to affect eye movements. Eye movement doesn't feed directly into what is recognized.

Combining the two architectures of Darwin III and Prometheus, we have movements (affect what's seen), proposals (affect where to look), and motion detections (affect seeing invariants). In the words of Reeke et al. (1990b), "changes in sensory inputs can be correlated with self-produced movements" (p. 675). This is accomplished in two ways: *over time* by feedback from looking (as in conditioned associative learning) and by learning movements associated with features through internal feedback ("features . . . detected by kinesthetic responses to tracing movements of the arm" [p. 690]; also the first PerAc block). Coupling movement *proposals* to what is currently recognized does not occur in these architectures.

The Prometheus architecture suggests how architectural levels create useful boundaries; we don't want navigation to drive saccades directly. In animals, looking for an *object* might prime interest in features. This kind of attention is not modeled by the neural networks we have considered because it suggests holding a pattern of categorizations active, a kind of coordination within a sequence of *looking for something*. In situated robot architectures, built-in values provide the weakest form of goal (e.g., "food," "energy," "protection," "interesting shape").[18] Through conditioned learning, categorized things or details in the world, such as food sources, can be recognized and pursued in behaviors observers call *goal driven*. Of course, robots with fixed programs such as Steels's ore-finding robots (Chapter 5) may produce apparently goal-driven sequences, too. Modeling how animals carry out protracted activities with different stages, such as a bird's seasonal nest building with a lifelong mate or a beaver's creating a flume for floating cut logs, requires a theory of coordination that more carefully teases apart emergent effects, reflexes, and conditioned learning from conceptual control (Chapter 8).

Summary of neuropsychological claims

Table 7.3 outlines the shift in perspective from the descriptive models of memory based on indexing and matching of labels to a situated cognition model of memory based on selective activation within a sensorimotor circuit.

The basic aspects of selectionism as a recognition mechanism are as follows:

- Physical structures that coordinate sensorimotor activity are reconstituted from previously active neural maps and are constructed in the activity itself.
- Neurological processes are not stored and retrieved by a language of indices, and no *matching* is required.

Table 7.3. *Descriptive, indexing model of memory compared to TNGS and related models*

	Descriptive approach: Indexing and matching tokens	Situated cognition: Selective activation of circuits in place
Memory	Stored rules or schema structures in a descriptive modeling language, recording experience, behaviors, how the world appears	Neural nets reactivated and recomposed in-line via selection
Representation	Meaningful forms internally manipulated subconsciously or consciously	Consciously created and interpreted in our activity (first person) as artifacts and experiences or internal couplings; don't refer but functionally differentiate External representation artifacts not to be equated with representing to self in imagination, which is not to be equated with neural structures
Internal processes	Modularly independent; can perceive and reason without acting	Codetermined; always adapted (generalized from past coordinations); related as simultaneous or sequential configuration
Immediate behavior	Selected from prepared possibilities (preexisting actions) (Newell, 1990, p. 146)	Adapted, composed, coordinated; a sensorimotor circuit

- Categorizations are not necessarily categorized as referential (also known as *tokens* or *symbols*); they are adapted relations within a coordination, not things with a fixed structure.

Shifting to our deliberate cognitive experience, situated cognition further suggests that a fundamental distinction should be drawn between internal processing and activity over time in the person's behavior (Table 7.4). For example, the "working memory" of decision-making models (Figure 3.2) describes our *experience* of saying something to ourselves or imagining something. Multiple experiences may remain quiescent, so they may be reactivated quickly and consciously related. Consider how, in planning an order for running errands, we can think of the various interactions we need to do and project a sequence in our imagination. This ability to hold conceptions active is to be contrasted with a buffer of registers in programs where descriptions are subconsciously written down and stored.

Table 7.4. *Shift in how deliberate cognitive experience is explained*

	Descriptive approach	Situated cognition
Reasoning	Supplants immediate behavior; goes on subconsciously to relate perception and action	Occurs in sequences of behavior over time
Speaking	Meaning of the utterance is described before speaking occurs	Speaking and conceiving are co-organized; describing meaning is a process of commenting on (interpreting) previously created descriptions
Learning	Secondary effect (chunking) (Newell and Simon, 1972, p. 7)	Primary learning is always occurring with every thought, perception, and action; chunking occurs as categorization of sequences
		Secondary (reflective) learning occurs in sequences of behavior over time; requires perception and language to model the world and behavior; conceptualization of the self's activity is higher-order consciousness

Table 7.5. *Shift in how descriptive (symbolic) models are viewed*

	Descriptive approach	Situated cognition
Knowledge representation (descriptive cognitive model)	Corresponds to physical structures stored in human's brain (e.g., Mycin's rules correspond to expert physician's memory)	A model of some system in the world and operators for manipulating the model; abstracts agent's behavior, explaining interaction in some environment over time
Concepts	Labeled structures, corresponding to linguistic terms, with associated descriptions of properties and relations to other concepts, i.e., *meanings are described and stored*	Multimodal categorizations of perceptual categorizations; ways of coordinating perception and action; have no inherent descriptive structure; cannot be inventoried; meaning and activity are inseparable
Analogy	Feature mapping of concept descriptions	Process of constructing a present experience by recomposing a previous coordination (e.g., "seeing as")

A buffer model may have some functional characteristics similar to those of human experience; but equating the two hinders our understanding of the nature of envisioning, multimodal coordination, and the categorizing of reference. For example, Bartlett's reconstructive theory of memory suggests that imagining a complex coordination (as in hitting a tennis ball or skiing off a ramp) is actually constructing projective physical coordinations that are later enacted (Gallwey, 1974). Thus, the limitations of a descriptive cognitive model go well beyond what terms like *symbol grounding* suggest.

Finally, Table 7.5 summarizes how we might now view knowledge bases and cognitive models. On the one hand, we view descriptive models such as Mycin quite starkly, as artifacts created by people, expressed in some notation that can be read and interpreted. On the other hand, we are confronted with an unknown landscape: How do neural processes of conceptualization in mammals differ from physical coordination in insects? How do perceptual processes of recognition relate to conceptual similarity? How do we *simultaneously* coordinate the meaning of what we are saying while we construct a well-formed utterance within an ongoing conversation? What role does emotional experience play in categorization? These are just some of the aspects of coordinated action that a full-blown selectionist-descriptive theory must address. Parts III and IV, particularly Chapter 13, address how the perspectives may be united by redefining what a symbol is and showing how conscious deliberation differs from the classification coupling aspects of reasoning going on behind the scenes.

8 Engineering transactional systems

If we desire to explain or understand the mental aspect of any biological event, we must take into account the system – that is, the network of closed circuits within which that biological event is determined. But when we seek to explain the behavior of a man or any other organism, this "system" will usually not have the same limits as the "self" – as this term is commonly (and variously) understood . . . mind is immanent in the larger system, man plus environment.

Gregory Bateson, *Steps to an ecology of mind*, 1972, p. 307

In the spring of 1988, Allen Newell and Kurt van Lehn organized the 22nd Carnegie Symposium on Cognition. A dozen AI researchers were invited to present their "architectures for intelligence." Their approaches ranged over a surprisingly broad spectrum: descriptive (symbolic) models, neural networks, and the subsumption architecture. Brooks's "insects" (Chapter 5) were the fresh new entry and couldn't easily be related to programs that automated an intensive care unit, proved beliefs about the weight of blocks, or modeled a student's subtraction methods. In this part of the book, I survey the abilities of situated robots and argue that they demonstrate how perception, navigation, and learning are possible without building in either categories or features of objects.

The shift in perspective from knowledge engineering's professional view of knowledge to situated robotics is also a shift in how we view the causal foundations of intelligence. The combination of the synthetic approach, focusing on simple animal behaviors, a dynamic-interactive perspective, and a selectionist mechanism, has breathed new life into AI research. Instead of equating intelligence with the ability to use descriptive models, we are now examining mechanisms by which a machine can explore, categorize, and survive in an unknown environment. Having arrived at the problems of learning new features and *coordination memory*, the point of view that all knowledge can be captured, packaged, and disseminated, which drove the design of systems like Mycin, appears narrow and arcane – this is progress! On the other hand, we have robots that essentially have only the most rudimentary survival goals, form no habits, and, of course, have no conceptual ability. An appraisal of the architectures and their differences from human ability is necessary if we are to improve on the descriptive cognitive modeling approach.

Conceptualization is, broadly speaking, a means for an agent to coordinate behavior without being bound to reflexes or the history of conditioned learning. In contrast to the descriptive cognitive modeling approach, situated robotics approaches the study of concepts and goal-directed behavior indirectly, first seeking a biologically plausible mechanism for physical coordination. The strategy is clear:

- Do not build in models of the world; don't merely replicate patterns of behavior by instantiating stored descriptions.
- View designed data structures, such as Toto's topological network, as incomplete efforts – models of neural processes we don't understand.
- Use a minimalist, synthetic approach, striving to understand how feedback and emergent interactions are productive for the organism.

The central thesis is that, to develop a broad theory of cognition, engineers must make explicit the different roles, points of view, and causal properties of the *designer*, the *specification* of the internal coordination mechanism, processes in the operational *environment*, and the *observer* who later describes and theorizes about the machine's behavior. The framework highlights the perceptual and interpretive abilities of the designer and observer; contrasts indexical representations and descriptive models; and reveals the role of feedback-in-motion and emergent organization of the environment. As Bateson indicated, the design perspective broadens beyond the idea of an *intelligent agent* to study the agent–environment system in terms of mutually determined effects.

One result of this analysis is viewing knowledge as a capacity attributed by an observer, not as a static "body" stored in the robot's memory. As quoted at the beginning of Chapter 2, Newell's knowledge-level analysis took a significant step in this direction. By considering the space of descriptions that a given mechanism could learn, Newell called our attention to how a designed architecture is ontologically bound. We now need to reorient this study in terms of a sensorimotor coordination architecture. To do this, we need a way of relating different kinds of mechanisms, feedback, and emergent organization. In this chapter I discuss several ways of characterizing what a robot knows, what it can do, and how it learns. The best approach at this stage in the history of robot design is to explore broad ways of describing complex systems, usually starting with taxonomies of methods. Here I elaborate on the frame of reference perspective; introduce the idea of a transactional system; contrast the different means of representing in situated robots; and present ways of characterizing behavior systems, emergence, and adaptation. I end by briefly characterizing contrasting situated robot mechanisms with conceptual processes, which will be the focus of Part III.

Frames of reference for describing knowledge

In focusing on the role of descriptive models of the world and behavior, situated robot research reconsiders the *nature of planning* in cognition. Precommitments made by the designer of a stored plan are characterized as *ontological*; that is, they concern the designer's view of the kinds of objects and events and their properties that can occur in the robot's world. Historical objections to the idea that action occurs by following plans may be summarized according to the three levels of the situated cognition framework (cf. Table 1.1):

- *Structure:* Bartlett argued that skill schemas (e.g., postures), perceptual categories, and concepts are always adapted in action.
- *Function:* Contextualists (following Dewey) argued that interactions with artifacts and other people are improvised transactions, constrained by the totality of how one conceives the present situation and one's role.
- *Behavior:* Anthropologists argued that instructions are interpreted and policies adapted within a socially created world of tools and facilities, settings with which we interact and shape into resources (e.g., there is someone you can ask, and materials can be arranged to perform a computation) (Lave, 1988; Suchman, 1987; Wynn, 1991).

Proceeding experimentally, as engineers, situated roboticists arrived at their understanding of plans from more pragmatic considerations and objectives:

- Agre, Chapman, and others emphasized the *resource and information limitations of real-time behavior.* Deliberation between alternatives must be extremely limited, and many details about the world can't be anticipated by the designer or by the robot (e.g., will the next closed door I approach open from the left or the right?).
- Knowledge engineers and robot designers found that *formal analyses of knowledge bases are problematic*: How can structures in a computer program be related in a principled way to the world, that is, interpreted as being *the program's knowledge*, when their reference depends on the designer's changing interpretations of what the representations mean (Rosenschein, 1985)?
- Harold Cohen was wedged in *the creator's conundrum*: Because Aaron was supposed to produce new drawings of people standing in a garden, how could Cohen build in *any* representation of these drawings before they were made?

If ontological commitments are inevitable for designed artifacts, how can the specification process be accomplished in a principled way? Situated robot designers have adopted four basic perspectives:

1. *Classical planning – knowledge is the model in the robot's memory.* In the classical approach, descriptions of regularities in the world and regularities in the robot's behavior are called knowledge and located in the robot's

memory. This approach is illustrated especially well by natural language programs, which incorporate in memory a model of the domain of discourse, script descriptions of activities, grammars, prose configuration plans, conversational patterns, and so on. To cope with the computational limits of combinatoric and real-time constraints, some researchers are reengineering their programs to use parallel processing, partial compilation, failure and alternative route anticipation, and so on. These approaches might incorporate further ontological distinctions (e.g., preconceptions of what can go wrong), but they adhere to the classical view of planning.

2. *Knowledge is the competence described by the designer's specification of the total system.* In contrast to the classical view, which focuses on the memory of the robot, Stan Rosenschein and his associates (Rosenschein, 1985, p. 12) view the full sensorimotor system as a designed artifact. Their method is to compile programs into digital circuits from a formal specification of robotic behavior in terms of world objects, machine states, and input–output relations between them. Thus, the robot's knowledge is viewed as a theoretical construct specified by the designer in terms of the properties of a circuit's interactive coupling with its environment.

3. *Knowledge is the capacity to maintain dynamic relationships.* Pengi's descriptions of entities *specify interactions* with the world – combining the robot's functional viewpoint (what it is doing now) and the interactive role of environmental entities (e.g., an ice cube for hitting the bee). Pengi's design demonstrates that an internal representation of the world needn't be global and objective, in the form of a map, but – for controlling reflexes at least – can be restricted to ontological primitives that relate the robot's perceptual categories to its activity. Similarly, emergent path creation in Steels's robots, feature construction in Pierce and Kuipers's robot, and the feedback architecture of Prometheus demonstrate how properties of *dynamics* – sensation within a coordinated movement – as opposed to properties of objects can be used to construct an *interactive ontology*.

4. *Knowledge is attributed by the observer.* Harold Cohen's (1988) work nicely articulates the distinction between designer, robot, behavioral dynamics, and observer's perception:

Aaron draws, as the human artist does, in feedback mode. No line is ever fully planned in advance: it is generated through the process of matching its current state to a desired end state. . . . All higher-level decisions are made in terms of the state of the drawing, so that the use and availability of space in particular are highly sensitive to the history of the program's decisions. (p. 190)

Aaron's internal, general representation of objects is sparse; it doesn't plan the details of its drawings; and it maintains no "mental photograph" of the drawing it is producing. There is no grammar of aesthetics; rather, three-dimensional properties, *as attributed by an observer*, emerge from following

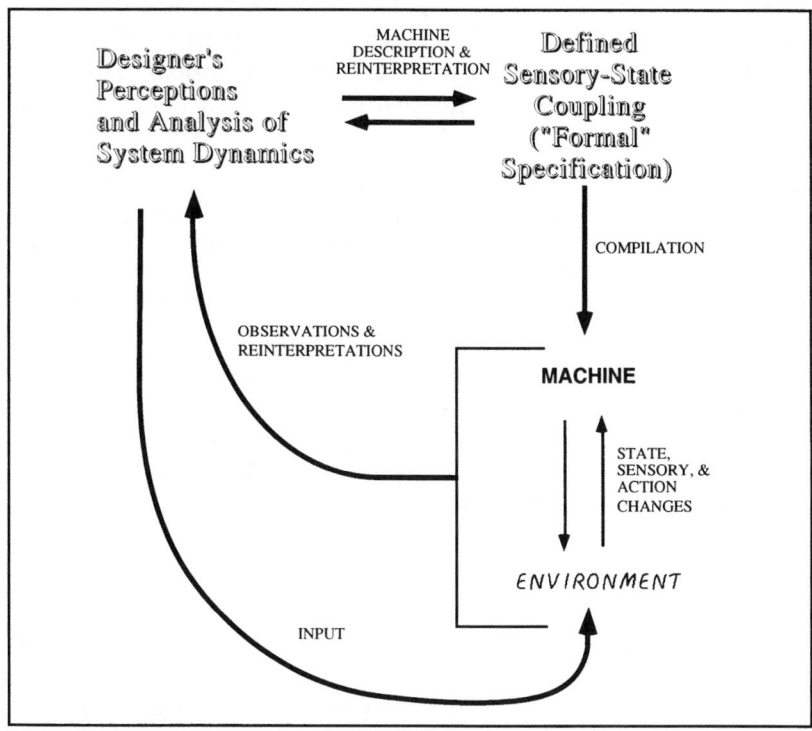

Figure 8.1. Relation of the designer's theory to the machine and coupling. A machine specification is a description derived from the designer's interpretation of the machine's interaction with its environment.

simple two-dimensional constraints like "find enough space." This point is made by Agre (1980), who says that the purpose of the robot's internal (indexical) representation is "not to express states of affairs, but to maintain causal relationships to them" (p. 190).

The transactional perspective

Situated robotics demonstrates the usefulness of viewing intelligent machine construction (and cognitive modeling in general, as indicated by Bateson in the opening quote of this chapter) as a problem of designing an *interactive system-in-its-environment*. That is to say, we don't simply ask "What knowledge structures should be placed in the head of the robot?" but rather, "What sensory–state coupling is desired, and what machine specification brings this about?" Figure 8.1 summarizes this perspective.

No objective descriptions are imputed – how the machine's behavior is described is a matter of the observer's selective perception, biased by expectations and purposes. The recurrent behavior attributed to the machine by the observer-designer is a matter of how people talk about and make sense of the world, as stated by Verschure (1992):

> The chunk of action that an observer can call wall following is related to a set of actions that become a connected whole in the frame of reference of the observer. To explain this behavior it should be viewed from the perspective of the system. . . . What is wall following from the observer's perspective can only be explained from the system's perspective as a sequence of approach or avoid actions given the immediate sensory and the internal states. (p. 657)

Furthermore, the specification – usually a description in the form of equations, logic propositions, and networks – is itself prone to reinterpretation: What the specification means (its semantics) cannot be described once and for all. The validity of the specification lies in the overall coherence of the designer's goals, the machine's behavior, and what the designer observes.

Figure 8.1 summarizes a shift in cognitive modeling. Rather than simply describing what an expert perceives (an ontology of objects and events), we split the system into agent plus environment and inquire: What are the problems (and resources) presented by the environment?[1] What interaction between agent and environment produces the observed effects? What feedback enables detecting errors and sustaining a desired relation? Such questions produced the wall-following and navigation architectures we described in earlier chapters. These questions lead computational ethologists (Chapter 5) to reconsider previous assumptions about animal behavior: Do birds migrate by a *cognitive map* or by more local perception (like Steels's robots)? Does the dance of the bees *show* a direction or *entrain* their comrades to a certain kind of effortful, oriented flight? Might the observed "return" of salmon to their native stream be explained by a random walk (Jamon, 1991)? My scientific bet is that understanding the mechanisms at work here – the effect of structural coupling, feedback, topological projection, and emergent structures – will provide a basis for understanding how human conceptualization and intentionality are possible.

The analytical shift in frame of reference is essentially the *transactional* perspective of ecological psychology, which Dewey pioneered. Irwin Altman and Barbara Rogoff (1987) summarize the basic idea:

> Transactional approaches treat "events" as the fundamental unit of study. Events are composed of psychological, temporal, and environmental aspects and therefore require methodologies that tap these facets of the unity. . . . The researcher must always treat the process as embedded in a context, and no context can be assumed

to be widely generalizable. . . . And the field benefits from attempts to sample settings broadly. . . . The location, attitudes, and behavior of the observer are aspects of the phenomenon. . . . (p. 34)

Transactional dynamics concerns the flow of events from the agent's perspective, considering self-regulation (error correction and homeostasis) and oscillation (integrating change over time). In psychological studies, concepts such as motivation, recurrence, intention, and equilibrium are described within this holistic framework:

Persons, processes, and contexts mutually define one another and serve as aspects of the whole, not as separate elements. These aspects do not combine to yield the whole; they are the whole and are defined by and define one another. (p. 32)

The transactional point of view has played a central role in methodological analyses in fields as diverse as anthropology and physics. Applied to human psychology, dialectic descriptions of persons and contexts may be at first puzzling. Until the 1980s, AI and cognitive science research was not driven by such metatheoretical analyses. Most researchers simply assumed that the world can be exhaustively and uniquely described as theories (in terms of ontologies and causal processes) and that learning itself involves manipulating these descriptions – a correspondence view of reality (Chapter 3). That is, theories (in a representation language) correspond to a reality *that can be objectively known* (especially by the scientist observer), and real knowledge consists of scientific theories.

The objectivist-correspondence view, qualified by the limits of relativity and quantum mechanics, is, of course, highly productive in the physical sciences. But as a means of understanding how *designs and policies* are socially constructed and applied, objectivism falls flat (Schön, 1987; Wynn, 1991). The objectivist view of scientific reasoning – applying general theories to produce situation-specific models – is incomplete for understanding how design and policy descriptions are *constructed* and *interpreted* and how social action is choreographed. According to the functional view of situated cognition (cf. Table 1.1), the *developing practice* of a group changes the ontologies of social discourse, producing new conceptualizations as well as new descriptive models (new plans, designs, and procedures). Such changes are inevitably poorly characterized as *manipulations within* a descriptive model, as assumed by the view that knowledge consists exclusively of descriptions stored in memory (or equivalently, that concepts can be reduced to words). Put another way, the causal theories of change and reorganization assumed by descriptive models of learning (including scientific discovery) are too limited. As we have seen (especially in Chapters 4 and 7), biologists and cyberneticists argue that there are different ways to view causality, the relation between structures and processes, and how an entity and the environment influence each other.[2]

From the perspective of situated robotics, the transactional perspective should be contrasted with what Altman and Rogoff (1987) call the *trait*, *organismic*, and *interactional* perspectives. Each adopts a different view of causality.

- The *trait* approach accounts for events in terms of inherent properties (traits) of objects or agents. For example, the trait perspective would say that one robot is aggressive and the other is afraid to explore. Change is explained in terms of preprogrammed sequences.
- The *interactional* approach "treat[s] psychological phenomena like Newtonian particles or billiard balls" (p. 15).[3] The particles exist separately but have cause–effect relations to each other's properties. Change is explained in terms of the interactions of variables (such as force and energy). Direction, events, and functioning are discretized and attributed to individual parts in snapshots of time, which additively combine through interactions (p. 17).
- The *organismic* approach subordinates the parts of a system to "the principles and laws that govern the whole, and the parts exist in a relation of dependency to one another and to the whole" (p. 11). For example, the paths in Steels's robots are parts whose existence and form change dynamically, dependent on the overall operation of the collection of robots and mother station. The system is an "organized whole"; "system relationships are mutual and reciprocal." Change is explained in terms of positive feedback or deviation-amplifying processes that affect stability. The system is viewed as having an "equilibrium point," with purpose viewed in terms of an *end state*.

The transactional perspective fundamentally breaks with the others by moving beyond the assumption that a system is a collection of interacting components. The units of analysis are instead *events*, which are not separable objects but a *confluence* of changing relationships. Referring to Figure 8.1, the transactional approach involves defining (and explaining) each of the aspects – coupling specification, the robot's mechanism, environmental influences, and the observer's perception of patterns – in terms of each other. Rather than breaking each aspect into parametrized parts and explaining change in terms of the causal effects of variables, the transactional approach claims that "the different aspects of wholes coexist as intrinsic and inseparable qualities of wholes." That is, the system is constituted (formed) as a whole, such that the presence of qualities of the machine, the environment, and the observer supplying input are not only mutually influencing each other, but their qualities are *ongoing relations* of interactive processes.

To be sure, each of these perspectives is useful; probably no researcher or school of thought has exclusively adopted and pursued any approach in a pure form. Instead, the distinctions are drawn sharply by Altman and Rogoff to call our attention to these strategies of analysis and (indeed, adopting the transactional view) to suggest that we more deliberately consider how our chosen scientific perspective affects our theories and what we build. Their bias, and the bias of situated cognition as I interpret it, is "to encourage greater use of organismic and especially transactional world views. Psychology and environmental psychology have thus far neglected or misunderstood these approaches" (p. 11).

David Marr's (1981) claim that there are two kinds of information processing theories can be related to the different views of Altman and Rogoff:

> *Type 1 (interactional) theory:* Algorithmic description, such as a grammar for composing actions or search procedures in game playing. This is a "clean theory" formulation like a law in physics.
>
> *Type 2 (organismic) theory:* Mechanism consisting of "simultaneous action of a considerable number of processes, whose interaction is its own simplest description" (p. 131). It is exemplified by many biological processes, such as protein folding and olfactory discrimination. This is a "brute force," "set of processes" theory.

Marr emphasized that scientific models may combine theories of both types. For example, his model of vision combined a "Type 1 theory for the basic grouping processes that operate on the primal sketch" with "a procedural representation of many facts about images . . . to help separate figure from ground" (p. 133). Marr's insights about biological processes appear to be correct, but his view of procedural representation was confused. He made the essential distinction between mechanisms driven by descriptions of the product (Type 1) and mechanisms whose products are emergent (Type 2). But he viewed information processing mechanisms exclusively in terms of processes operating on descriptions. Consequently, applications of Marr's analysis tend to characterize a Type 2 theory superficially as being an "implementation" of an algorithmic description. Unless the effects in the implementation fit the *organismic perspective*, the so-called Type 2 implementation is just another algorithmic description – not a different kind of mechanism. Furthermore, Marr's view of Type 2 theories was only organismic, lacking the transactional perspective of confluences. In effect, Altman and Rogoff add *Type 3 (transactional) theory* to Marr's framework.

Given the complexities and benefits of shifting from trait-interactional theories, it is no surprise that biological theories often settle on an organismic view. The transactional perspective in situated cognition goes further, shifting the focus from the robots to the people designing them. Such research is the province of the anthropologist, not the robotic engineer. For the purpose of building insectlike robots, it may be sufficient to view Figure 8.1 as an interactional framework describing serial, incremental refinement of designs: description, specification, machine operation, and redescription. Once engineers have understood the role of the observer and the nature of indexical representation, they can shift their perspective back to the organismic level of analysis. The transactional view reminds us that situated roboticists have rigged environments and imaginatively interpreted robot interactions; but for the most part, these considerations are not important in designing a robot that can only follow walls or find its way home.

The transactional perspective is important when one system is the environment for another, as within an individual's conceptual system and within social systems. For example, the transactional interpretation of Figure 8.1 becomes important when we try to build groups of robots that instrumentally modify the environment. Contrast Steels's robots in this respect, whose life history affects future behavior, with Brooks's insects. More generally, when animals learn *routines that become coupled to a modified environment,* expectations cannot be explained only in terms of feedback of sensory signals, and error correction cannot be explained only in terms of motor controls. So again we go back to the anthropologists who have been watching the robot experiments: One way to understand human conceptual coordination in a social system is to study how *engineers* create new designs and interpretations, especially the serendipity involved in manipulating materials in perceptual space (Chapter 9).

An organismic perspective is important for understanding why expert systems work. We go beyond the idea of users as suppliers of information to consider how user and program depend on and constrain each other. Most notably, when a person provides input by responding to the program's queries, he or she is effectively interpreting internal structures and changing the coupling between machine and environment. The observer's interpretation is an inherently subjective, perceptual process that incorporates an understanding of the machine's role and abilities. When Mycin asks, "Did the patient respond to treatment with Drug-2?" the observer implicitly considers whether this drug should be continued or whether the corresponding diagnosis is correct. By telling Mycin, "Yes, the patient responded," one can bias it to continue the drug and believe the implied diagnosis. Such coupling may occur without a moment's thought by the user of how an answer steers the program.

In designing Mycin's questions, we were often confronted with a contradiction in our trait view of knowledge: We motivated the consultation dialogue approach by assuming that users had no medical knowledge; we conceived of the program as advice giving. But we could not phrase questions to ensure accuracy without assuming that users were competent observers: Are the bacteria shaped like rods or are they short chains of balls? Later programs reconfigured the relation between program and person, allowing the user to enter a diagnosis or therapy recommendation to be critiqued. But here again, the terminology belies the designers' perspective of one-sided authority and control. To build systems that respect social roles and human experience, the interactional perspective is not enough (Greenbaum and Kyng, 1991).

Perhaps the most radical implication of the organismic and transactional perspectives for the design of intelligent machines is the demise of the centrality of knowledge as an organizing concept: Situated roboticists design *interactions* rather than structures in memory. When knowledge was equated with structures in the robot's memory, it was clear enough that making behavior more intelligent required storing more factual and procedural statements and devising more appropriate languages for efficiently modeling the robot's world and controlling behavior. But adopting at least the interactional view requires that we step back and attribute knowledge to the designer and the observer or users of the program. This is obvious in the case of expert systems; it becomes a kind of trick in the design of Aaron (although the internal two-dimensional plan may accurately model the artist's imagination). It becomes a warning about overattribution when we consider how bees navigate or whether interactions between Steels's robots constitute a social activity.

Perhaps even more disconcerting, the organismic view means that information itself is not a trait or even an interactive product, but is dynamically constructed within a coordinating process. The work of Pierce and Kuipers – illustrating the ecological approach pioneered by Dewey, Bateson, von Foerster, and Gibson – demonstrates how features should be viewed as *emergent properties of sensory fields*, not static things in the environment that are merely detected, selected, or *picked up* (Chapters 4 and 11).

In summary, the situated study and design of intelligence focuses on behaviors as interactive relations between internal processes and between organism and environment. As in many engineering disciplines, robots are designed by building increasingly complex architectures on top of *already functioning subsystems*, such as the composition of maps in TNGS and the chaining of PerAc blocks in Prometheus. But this is very different from how knowledge engineers build expert systems, or indeed, how many psychologists have built descriptive cognitive models of their subjects. By locating all knowledge in the descriptive store, the already existing skills for perceiving and coordinating action are inadequately characterized. Similarly, a situated analysis of cognition does not begin with an inventory of "all the information" in a situation; analysis focuses on the robot-subject's developmental process of constructing features and categories. In short, instead of talking about the knowledge of the organism, we focus on the *representing processes* that sustain *productive relations* between the machine and its environment.

Table 8.1. *Kinds of representing demonstrated by situated robots*

	Representing associations	Coordinating motion on paths
Sensation only	Classical conditioning (Verschure)	Emergent structures (Steels)
Plus features	Abstracted via subsumption (Brooks)	Learned FSA (Pierce and Kuipers)
Plus categories	TNGS (Edelman) Prometheus (Gaussier and Zrehen)	Dynamic landmarks (Mataric)

Note: Some robots learn or sustain only associations between sensations, features, or categories. Others construct or recognize paths. A *sensation* is a raw signal generated over time by the robot's sensors, such as infrared detectors. A *feature* is a stable signature in this signal, that is, an invariance with respect to multiple channels, such as amplitude and time. A *category* is a classification or typology of encountered objects, regions, or events, such as a left-wall/compass bearing.

Situated cognition research has much further to go before reaching up from this nether world of cockroaches to the medical world of Mycin or Cohen's aesthetic intentions. It will serve us well at this point to review in more detail what we have learned about mechanisms from the various situated robotics approaches. Specifically, can we provide a useful, engineering definition of *emergence* and *adaptation*? How can we move from the idea of built-in values to the idea of changing goals? Can the ideas of dynamic, categorical learning be related to analogical reasoning, language, and deductive argumentation?

Comparison of mechanisms for representing and coordinating motions

Table 8.1 summarizes the kinds of representing in situated robots in terms of the means of representing associations[4] and coordinating motion on paths. To recap: Verschure models classical conditioning associations between *sensations*.[5] Brooks's networks abstract sensations into *features* (such as a constant force on the left side) and associate them. Edelman's TNGS associates features (such as shapes) as *categories* (thus establishing via selection an ontology of features). Creating and sustaining motion on paths is possible by sensing just a simple signal (e.g., the food grains and chips of Steels's robots). Creating a map of a space and navigating through it to avoid obstacles is enabled by encoding features in the environment within an FSA. Finding a minimal path back to a place is enabled by dynamically creating landmarks (e.g., Toto's categories of regions, which qualify the results of presupplied wall and corridor recognizers with direction-time features).

The principles of representation used by these architectures include:

- A distinction is drawn between sensations and features, and their combination into categories of regions, objects, and events.
- Change in the motor subsystem may be internally sensed and incorporated in categorizations.[6]
- Sensory fields are dynamically affected by a perception–action loop (i.e., what is sensed is affected by the movement of the sensors), producing sensory invariances (i.e., features).
- Sequences of events and actions may be represented by FSA, such that feature representations of the environment are indexical-functional.
- Emergent structures (object invariances) may develop through the interaction of agents and their environment over time when changes to the environment are incorporated in the perception–action loop.
- Categorizing is possible by a selection mechanism operating on populations of *neural networks*; stable associations may develop as interacting modules select and reinforce chaotic attractors; probabilistic networks allow generalization of topological associations.

Taken together, these architectures begin to show how we can incorporate neurological structures such as *command neurons* and *reflexes*, as well as psychological processes such as reinforcement learning, in robot design. The subsumption architecture demonstrates how coordination might be modeled as a composition of *continuously running processes*. Selectionist models demonstrate how categorizing with respect to internal value primes the learning of associations.

The contrast between structural coupling and inference (*deliberation*) will turn out to be pivotal in understanding cognition. At first glance, it appears plausible that perceptual categorization involves a mechanism quite different from a production system (Figure 3.2). Perceptual categorization occurs much earlier in mental processing and is found in much simpler animals than humans. In Part III, I show how some forms of conceptualization apparently occur as structural coupling, too. On that basis, it is possible to discriminate between categories that function referentially as symbols in inferential processes and categories that are directly coupled and hence not functioning referentially. In the context of situated robots, we can begin this analysis by considering how sensation and categorization are integrated in these architectures (Table 8.2). Aaron, Pengi, and Brooks's and Steels's robots are not included in this table because they don't learn.

The kinds of categories in Toto require special discussion. For example, compass bearing is a feature and "left" is a perceptual category (a relation between compass bearings); conceptual categories include "wall" and regions such as "left wall." Toto's actions, of course, affect the features recorded, but not dynamically in the way motion affects the sensory field in other robots. In Darwin III, there is no tactile sensation without arm-hand

Table 8.2. *Coupling, inference, and feedback in situated robots that learn*

Architecture	Examples	Characterization
S ⇔ PF	Freeman's model of rabbit olfaction	Perceptual features learned as chaotic attractors
S ⇔ PF -> Action	Pierce and Kuipers's robot	Perceptual features constructed as feedback relations between action and sensory field
S ⇔ PF ⇔ PC -> Action S ⇔ PF ⇔ PC ⇔ Action	Darwin III Prometheus	Both features and categories are learned; actions tied to categories by built-in values; external feedback dynamically couples action and sensation
CS ⇔ US -> Action (UR)	Verschure's conditional learning	Conditional stimulus (CS) (e.g., obstacle detector) becomes coupled to unconditional stimulus–unconditional response (US–UR) reflex (stimulus is a fixed pattern associated with an object)
PF → PC → CC → Action	Toto	Features are built in, and new categories are *inferred* from them; the world is modeled as regions and paths; feedback in motion not integrated in the mechanism

Abbreviations and symbols: S = sensory stimuli; PF = perceptual features; PC = perceptual categorizations; CC = conceptual categorizations; Action = movement of arm, eye, wheels, and so on; ⇔ indicates structural coupling; → indicates steps of symbolic inference or calculation; -> indicates command-neuron triggering.

motion. Edelman (1992) describes this relation as the "alteration of sensory sampling by movement" (p. 91). Hence, the creation of features and categories through structural coupling is a *temporal relation* – feedback occurs during motion, not as reflection afterward. The *relation* of action and sensation is what is being categorized.

In contrast, Toto's relations are all inferential: Encoded representations (of the world or the robot's relation to world structures) are compared and combined in calculations. Some of these representations are indexical and constructed in the course of interactive movement, as in Pengi (Figure 5.7). Feedback in sampling does occur, but it only affects sensation on the next cycle. That is, we have perceiving → acting → change in world or orientation → perceiving something new. In such feedback over perception-action cycles, a robot may correct its path or look at the world in a different way (as Pengi uses visual processing to apply a motion operator). Aaron's operation is similar in relating local effects of what it has drawn to its overall plan.

Feedback over cycles (Toto, Pengi, Aaron) adapts behavior to *categorized circumstances*, in contrast to *feedback in motion* (Pierce and Kuipers, Darwin III, Prometheus, Verschure), which adapts categorizations to how sensory stimuli are *created by motion*. Both forms of feedback lead to situated action, but a dynamic architecture (structural coupling) provides a developmental account of how *what is represented* arises interactively and is inherently a functional differentiator. This functionality is from the organism's perspective of how the world is changing *such that potential actions are distinguished*, not the designer's conception of the robot's *purpose* or regularities that appear over time. Of course, in these situated robot designs, the designer's conception of what the robot is supposed to do is pervasive, even when indirectly encoded as built-in values.[7]

In considering function and values, it is obvious that the work on path learning is radically incomplete. Efforts to make navigation fully learned (as in Darwin III, Prometheus, and Pierce and Kuipers's system) produce robots that have *nowhere to go*. Efforts to make navigation goal directed (as in Toto, Steels, and Beer's cockroach) involve engineering the environment and the robot for extremely limited objectives, such as gathering food and going to some place. Designing robots in this way to perform specific tasks may be appropriate for insects and simple animals. Certainly, we want the basic architecture to ensure survival of the organism and other self-maintenance activities. How can we understand self-regulation from a systemic, organism-in-an-environment perspective?[8] "Survival of the fittest" is a descriptive theory referring to populations. How do we characterize the value system of an individual organism?

Situated robotics has made some progress in getting beyond the ontological bounds of the designer, but we have hardly begun to tackle the central concern of symbolic AI, namely, goal-directed behavior. The only sequencing demonstrated by these robots is topologically constrained. This is an entirely appropriate first step. But what about the sequencing by which a cat stalks a mouse in the grass? Or a bird builds a nest and woos a suitor? Or by which a monkey pretends not to notice a banana until his friend leaves the scene (Barresi and Moore, 1996)?

Behavior systems, development, and emergence

To go forward, we must consider the learning mechanisms we understand so far and how they might be involved in learning sequences. Here I consider Steels's analysis of behavior systems and emergence. In the next section I consider adaptation from the perspective of what is known about evolution.

Steels (1994) characterizes situated robots as *behavior systems*:

We call a sequence of events a behavior if a certain regularity becomes apparent. This regularity is expressed in certain observational categories, for example, speed, distance to walls, changes in energy level. A behavior is emergent if new categories are needed to describe this underlying regularity which are not needed to describe the behaviors (i.e., the regularities) generated by the underlying behavior systems on their own. (p. 89)

Notice that the ideas of regularity and emergence are defined with respect to the descriptive categories of the observer. According to the framework presented earlier in this chapter, Steels adopts an organismic perspective:

A *behavior system* is the set of all mechanisms which play a role in establishing a particular behavior. The structures of a behavior system that can undergo a change due to learning are usually called behavior programs. Often the name of the behavior system indicates the functionality to which it contributes. But strictly speaking, we should be more careful. For example, there could be a "homing in" functionality achieved by a "zig zag behavior" toward a goal that is the result of a "phototaxis mechanism." Phototaxis means that the goal has a light source acting as a beacon and that the robot uses light sensors to minimize the distance between itself and the beacon. . . .

A behavior system is a theoretical unit. There is not a simple one-to-one relation between a functionality, a behavior, and a set of mechanisms achieving the behavior. The only thing that has physical existence are the components. (p. 80)

A *behavior system* is thus an interacting set of components, not just a program. We are cautioned to distinguish between the *attributed functionality* (characterizing the organism's goals within its environment), the *behaviors of the organism* (such as kinds of movements relative to the environment), and the *mechanism* (coupling perception-action systems).

Steels incisively lays out the architectures of situated robots and the promising directions for further developing the sensorimotor coordination techniques. His analysis clarifies, for example, the difference between different kinds of *activation*:

- One behavior system activates another through a *control* (*command neuron*) link (as in Brooks's subsumption architecture).
- Behaviors are *always active*, but vary in strength, as in a dynamical architecture (as PerAc blocks affect each other in Prometheus).
- Behaviors are *selected* to become part of the functioning of the system (as in TNGS).

Steels also provides a framework for formalizing emergence. First, he describes three kinds of variables for describing a system (p. 90):

- *Controlled variable*: directly influenced by the system, such as forward speed.

- *Uncontrolled variable*: "changes due to the actions of the system" but can be affected only "through a side effect of its actions, such as distance from a wall." For example, a robot might directly change "direction of movement, which will then indirectly change the distance."
- *Visible variable*: "characteristic of the environment which, through a sensor, has a causal impact on the internal structures and processes and thus on behavior." For example, infrared sensor may allow measuring distance directly.
- *Invisible variable*: characteristic of the environment that observers can measure, but that the system has no way to sense and that does not play a role in the physical "components implicated in emergent behavior," such as the length of a path in Steels's robots.

An *emergent behavior* is then defined:

For a behavior to be emergent, we expect at least that the regularity involves an uncontrolled variable. A stricter requirement is that the behavior (i.e., the regularity) involves only invisible variables. So, when a behavior is emergent, we should find that none of the components is directly sensitive to the regularities exhibited by the behavior and that no component is able to control its appearance directly.

A further distinction can be made between emergent behavior upon which the system does not build further, and semantic emergence (Cariani, 1991) . . . in which the system is able to detect, amplify, and build upon emergent behavior. The latter can only happen by operating on the behavior programs that causally influence behavior. . . . (p. 90)

Two examples of emergent effects in situated robots are wall following (a side effect) and path formation (a transient spatiotemporal structure). A Brooks insect can follow a wall, without a single component of the robot being specifically designed to recognize or control this state. Similarly, Steels's robots don't *recognize* paths, but sense and respond only locally to their presence. Such feedback in Bateson's terms is "news of a difference."[9] Notice also that two kinds of side effects emerge in these robots:

- The combination of obstacle avoidance and wall seeking plus a wall yields a side effect of *dynamic stability of motion* (process).
- Changing the environment can produce *dynamic stability of a new structural form* (substance).

Possibly in neural systems, both processes and structures (such as sheets, columns, or nested hierarchical cones [Edelman, 1987, p. 168]), with emergent and stable forms, are being constructed internally. Table 8.3 shows how emergent internal processes and structures might be understood in terms of external patterns we can observe. My point is that we have just begun to understand the formation of self-organized, modular systems (such as the brain). It is far from clear how to relate such diverse theories as Pribram's holographic theory, Freeman's chaotic attractors, Stuart A. Kauffman's (1993) "soup of strings," and what we know about other organ systems in the body. To address these questions (and restate them from this

Table 8.3. *Types of emergent stability in neural structures and processes, with external analogs*

Emergent stability	Internal to agent	External analog in the environment
Dynamic process	"Coordination"; multimodal sequencing of sensorimotor circuits	Wall following
Dynamic structure	Chaotic patterns of Freeman? Prometheus's PerAc blocks?	Path formation

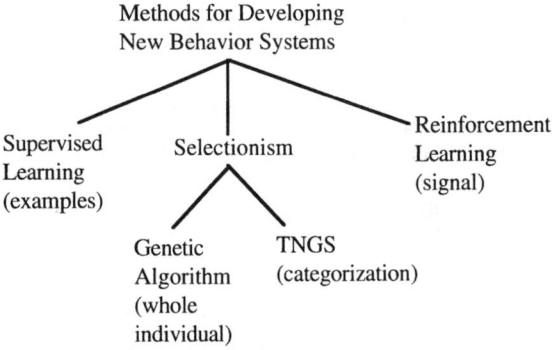

Figure 8.2. Methods for developing new behavior systems: Change may occur by a teacher's intervention, by interactive selection of new behaviors, or by reinforcement of associations in a repertoire.

probably very naive form), many scientists suggest a developmental and evolutionary perspective, to which we now turn.

Methods for developing new behaviors

Applying Steels's behavior system perspective, the abilities of the situated robots summarized in Table 8.1 can be characterized by how behaviors are configured or adapted. To begin, we draw a distinction between fixed behavior systems, such as Brooks's insects, and an architecture that develops a new behavior system. Figure 8.2 summarizes the different learning methods we have considered. The genetic algorithm, a means of recombining phenotypic properties of whole organisms, is explored in artificial life research; like TNGS, it is a form of selectionism following the principles of Darwinism. Most descriptive models and many connectionist systems learn from examples, generally with a human supervisor to indicate good per-

Table 8.4. *Development of new behaviors, depending on different sources of information*

Learning method	Information source	Weaknesses of method
Supervised learning	Deliberate training: information defined by input–output examples	Begs question of how complex systems (like the human supervisor) develop; generalization process may be difficult if network is too complex
Selectionism	Alternative internal structures compete; individuals with higher fitness are activated more often	Does not explain how behaviors become composed into coordinated sequences
Reinforcement learning	Reward (punishment) signal provides feedback	Credit assignment problem: rewards results that may be emergent; best for simple sensory association

Note: Both as explanations and as mechanisms, learning methods have different limitations.

formance. On the other end of the spectrum, reinforcement learning occurs by direct feedback from some signal detected in action.

Methods for developing new behaviors may be combined; for example, supervised learning is used to train Darwin III's oculomotor system to focus on objects. What varies in these methods is the information source for changing the system's behavior (Table 8.4).

Summarizing, to understand how changing behavior is possible, we must investigate the "sources of the delta" – the origin of information about variability that feeds back to modify the system. In selectionism, alternative relations may compete operationally to see which structure will be activated (as in TNGS) or a set of systems may be activated that then compete for reproduction (as in a population of individuals). In TNGS and PerAc blocks the fitness function pertains to internal, predefined (built-in) values; in population genetics competition between organisms is also important.[10] In short, we must understand the interactions between organisms and within organisms:

Emergent functionality is not due to one single mechanism but to a variety of factors, some of them related to internal structures in the agent, some of them related to the properties of certain sensors and actuators, and some of them related to the interaction dynamics of the environment. (Steels, 1994, p. 101)

In effect, we are drawn to a model of learning that emphasizes competitive dynamics both between *internal behavior systems* and between *agents in the environment*. This approach deemphasizes the instructive view of learning that depends on crossing system boundaries (providing a signal in the environment or an output that must be related to internal mechanisms). Rather, we emphasize associations *at the same system level,* such as between agents constructing something they all can sense in the environment or between sensorimotor relations competing for activation.

An evolutionary perspective on adaptation

So far, we have considered adaptation as change occurring to a single behavior system during its lifetime. But if we are to understand organism–environment dynamics, we must consider populations of organisms and how they change over time. Specifically, this larger perspective provides means for evolution of better sensorimotor systems, not merely the adaptation of a fixed phenotype. Working within the framework of artificial life research, Peter Cariani suggests that we focus on the *adaptive characteristics of sensory systems.* He claims that the problem of ontological boundness cannot be surmounted by designing robots per se. We must address the questions of how such systems *evolve,* especially how sensory systems emerged.

Cariani (1991) begins by categorizing robot adaptivity:

- *Nonadaptive robotic devices* (fixed sensorimotor systems and associations).
- *Computationally adaptive* (e.g., supervised and reinforcement learning); may add features within a sensory repertoire, as in Pierce and Kuipers's robot.
- *Semantically adaptive* ("construct and select their sensing and effecting elements contingent on performance" [p. 778]); examples are the spider's web (a prosthetic sensor) in evolution and the development of the immune system in individuals.

Cariani claims that sensory evolution must be considered by artificial life research:

Physical construction processes are necessary for the augmentation of the functional capabilities of real devices. We cannot create more absolute memory in a machine by solely performing computations on the device (although we frequently can make better use of the limited memory that we have by designing more elaborate computations). Similarly, we cannot create new sensors or effectors simply by performing computations on the data that comes out of existing ones. . . . (Unpublished manuscript, p. 2)

Cariani provides a thorough analysis of the historical development of these ideas in the work of Gordon Pask, W. R. Ashby, and others in the 1950s and 1960s. In this early work on self-organization, key issues of *organizational closure* (cf. the discussion of Maturana in Chapter 4), the relation of the observer to the system, and networks of *observer-participants* were explored and formalized. These systems theorists explored how an *assemblage* can develop *distinctions* (perceptual features) to create a *reference frame* (in Ashby's terms, "a system of observable distinctions"). These ideas were later reformulated by Maturana in the theory of autopoiesis.

For example, in these terms Ashby would say that the robots we have investigated "fail to achieve epistemic autonomy relative to their designers because all possibilities [of the state space of observables] have been prespecified by their designers; they have no structural autonomy" (Cariani, 1993, p. 30). On this basis, Cariani insists that we must build devices that can "defy the designer's categories" in their behavior by developing their own physical *sensors* and *effectors*. At least, this is required if one wishes to realize "self-constructing, conscious, autonomous agents capable of open-ended learning" (p. 31), as artificial life research advocates.

How should we straddle the distinction between evolving and developing? Does artificial life research now inherit AI's goals of developing an artificial intelligence? Must artificial life start with one-celled creatures or is it fair to build in complex, evolved structures such as regulator genes? Why doesn't more artificial life research start with plants rather than emphasizing animals?

Does AI need artificial life first?

Recent studies of animal behavior suggest that an evolutionary approach may help us relate aspects of cognition to parts of the brain. Scientists have been intrigued by the manner in which the reptilian complex, limbic system, and neocortex (called the *triune brain*) developed. Richard Ctyowic (1993) warns that this idea must be taken metaphorically but agrees that "specific categories of behavior could be assigned to different types of brain tissue, each of which had a unique evolutionary history":

Subcortical tissue [is] not enormously important to behaviors that could not be dismissed as merely "instinctive" (reproduction, feeding, and fight-or-flight situations, for example). In general terms, the behaviors in question include grooming, routines, rituals, hoarding, protection of territory, deception, courtship, submission, aggression, socialization, imitation. . . . (p. 155)

Does this provide clues for designing behavior systems? Should engineers begin by replicating instincts?

Stephen Jay Gould's (1987) studies of evolution suggest many reasons why a "designed evolution" approach will be fraught with error. First, even if we replicated insects using the behavior-based approach of situated robotics, we might be far from understanding human cognition:

Ants behave, in many essential respects, as automata, but human beings do not and the same methods of study will not suffice. We cannot usefully reduce the human behavioral repertoire to a series of unitary traits and hope to reconstruct the totality by analyzing the adaptive purpose of each individual item. (p. 119)

Especially, Gould warns that without better understanding mechanisms, we cannot understand evolutionary adaptation:

Historical origin and current function are different aspects of behavior with no necessary connection.
    We have to grasp the "hows" of structure before we can even ask whether or not a direct "why" exists. (p. 123)

This is especially true with respect to the structure of dynamic-emergent systems.

    Gould's insights suggest that artificial life researchers may have a simplistic understanding of adaptation, which fails to distinguish between competitive improvement and circumstantial use of functions in a changed situation:

Pandas are "adapted" – they are getting by. But this sense of adaptation has no meaning – for all animals must do well enough to hang in there, or else they are no longer with us. Simple existence as testimony to this empty use of adaptation is a tautology. Meaningful adaptation must be defined as actively evolved design for local circumstances . . . the primary theme of panda life must be read as a shift of function poorly accommodated by a minimally altered digestive apparatus. (p. 23)

The idea of competitive selection and evolution presupposed by artificial life research suggests a simple, idealistic, linear view of progress that Gould presses us to avoid. Instead, to understand the development of intelligence, for example, we should start with the idea of conflict and compromise in balance. Ideas of steady progress, levels, and accumulating parts do not fit the haphazard nature of evolution. Again, histories (our descriptions) linearize what is multiply determined and codetermined in nature:

Strict adaptationism, ironically, degrades history to insignificance by viewing the organism's relation to the environment as an isolated problem of current optimality. (p. 24)

Strict adaptationism assumes that a need existed, changes occurred, and eventually a solution existed. An historical approach describes how the species survived along the way (with backaches, headaches, diseases, wars, etc.).

    These observations are relevant for understanding both how cognition developed and how it functions every day. The view that every behavior or process "fits" and exists because it evolved to play the role it plays today misconstrues the nature of selection:

I am willing to admit that harmful structures will be eliminated by natural selection if they cause enough distress. But the other flank of the argument is not symmetrical – it is not true that helpful structures must be built by natural selection. Many shapes and behaviors are fit for other reasons. . . . [C]ontinued success of flying fishes . . . absolutely depends upon their propensity for falling back into the water after they emerge. But no one in his right mind would argue that mass was constructed by natural selection to ensure a timely tumble. (p. 49)

In short, existing abilities and dispositions may be functional for new behaviors. We should view biological processes as a "set of tools, each individually honed to benefit organisms in their immediate ecologies" (p. 31). Again, in Gould's view of species, we hear by analogy echoes of Dewey's active view of learning and Bateson's total-system perspective – mental process not as container, but as constructor of order:

Cardboard Darwinism . . . is a theory of pure functionalism that denies history and views organic structure as neutral before a molding environment. It is a reductionist, one-way theory about the grafting of information from environment upon organism through natural selection of good designs. We need a richer theory, a structural biology, that views evolution as an interaction of outside and inside, of environment and structural rules for genetic and developmental architecture – rules set by the contingencies of history and the physiochemical laws of the stuff itself. (p. 50)

Hence, Gould says that the idea of "information in the environment," which was found to be misleading for understanding perception and memory, is also inadequate for understanding evolution.

As an example of how theories of animal behavior might combine emergent interaction, cognition, and evolution, consider Boekhorst and Hogeweg's (1994) analysis of travel band formation in orangutans. Their model describes how individuals choose to scan for fruit, walk, rest, and so on, as members of groups. A self-organizing process yields travel bands (between small fruit trees) and aggregation (in large fig trees). These emergent colocations could then be the basis of selective advantages and further evolution of socialization. We can't necessarily conclude that observed grouping behavior developed *directly* because of adaptive value – it is contingent on the season and on fruit in the trees. Just as we have realized that not all behavior patterns are planned (predescribed), we now see that not all patterns are *adapted*. This is obvious in the case of crystal structure but less clear when studying cognition or social behavior in animals.

Indeed, artificial life research has fundamental riddles in ecological patterning to unravel. Paraphrasing Haldane, Gould asks, "Why are there so many kinds of beetles?" Of the million species on earth, *more than a third are beetles*. Similarly, proponents of an evolutionary strategy for developing artificial life should consider the following questions:

Why are there more species in tropical than temperate zones? Why so many more small animals than large? Why do food chains tend to be longer in the sea than on land? Why are reefs so diversely and sea shores so sparsely populated with species? (Gould, 1987, p. 181)

Gould complains that the science of ecology is too lost in descriptive explanation and blind to the bigger picture of spatial and temporal diversity:

As an explanatory science, ecology traffics in differential equations, complex statistics, mathematical modeling, and computer simulation. I haven't seen a picture of an animal in the leading journal of evolutionary ecology in years. (Ibid.)

The parallels are clear in the stored description view of knowledge, which has yet to come to terms with the diversity of conceptual modes, individual differences (Gardner, 1985a), and the oddities of neurological dysfunctions (Sacks, 1987).

On the other hand, researchers who toss around metaphors about "social" agents must beware of making sociobiology's mistake – trivializing the nature and affect of mechanisms on robot capability: "The issue is . . . the degree, intensity, and nature of the constraint exerted by biology upon the possible forms of social organization" (Gould, 1987, p. 113). Steels's "society" of robots is not a culture; there are no enduring artifacts, tools, or conventions for making things. Without a better understanding of structural relations of reflex, instinct, and consciousness we cannot understand how cognition evolved or its accomplishments.

Furthermore, even discounting the long time periods nature required, Gould suggests that the path humans and artificial life have taken are so contingent on historical circumstance that we cannot presume progress over even long time spans or that what develops would resemble life and cognition as we know it today (although this is highly controversial). We are unlikely to transition from situated robotics to even rudimentary mammalian cognition anytime soon via artificial life experiments alone.

But for many engineers, the relevant aspect of a design will be its functionality within a mechanism, not whether it was built or evolved (Morris, 1991, p. 45). Why should an artificial life researcher wait for controller genes to evolve in an experiment? Why not just build them into the mechanism (Stone, 1994, p. 400)? Similarly, once we understand the mechanics of neural coordination, can't we just build a silicon engine to replicate it? Possibly. We might build much better robots and "intelligent agents" by even replicating just a few principles of self-organizing processes from the brain. But Gould would suggest that only then would we be posed to understand the *transactional functions* of such capabilities in the organism's everyday life in a local niche. Cognitive science would then embrace a whole range of robot engineering, with behaviors ranging from the navigation of ants and beaver dam building to the territory protection of a crow. Research emphasis would shift from the chronicling of novice-expert capabilities and problem-solving methods to include the dynamics of social change, innovation, and resistance. With such a transformation, cognitive science would be necessarily biological and social, helping the social scientists, too, to develop a total-system view of individual and group development.

The conceptualization problem

To recapitulate what we have found in this part of the book: Situated robotics are contrasted with architectures based on stored descriptive models. The input–output view of information and interaction has ignored, first, the observer's role in abstracting behavior patterns and, second, the dynamic-emergent effects of feedback both within a perception–action cycle and over time as the environment is modified by action. Situated robot research focuses on mechanisms that enable a robot to develop its own features, categories, and sensorimotor maps. Models that explain how a frog, for example, flips his tongue out for a passing fly, without having a "fly concept,"[11] are a fundamental contribution to our understanding of cognition.

There have been some quick wins in building situated robots, but moving from a cockroach to a bird or a cat is incredibly difficult. To start, methods of perceptual categorization alone do not enable robots to learn sequences of behaviors; instead, the designers rely on hardwired associations (as in Pengi) or stored grammars (as in Aaron). Even replicating the control mechanism of a motor system is still rudimentary. For example, Darwin III has no way to select from or relate multiple gestures.

What mechanisms would procedurally organize behavior without relying on a descriptive store of maps and plans? To start, we might try to create a robot with simple, *temporally organized habits*. For example, the bee experiments that partially inspired Toto's design revealed that bees fly out to the same field of flowers every morning at 10:30 a.m. How could we get Toto to wait on the steps for Mataric return to her office every morning? The combination of conditional learning, values, and Toto's landmark-based actions provides one way of understanding how habits develop.

We need to understand how methods for developing behavior systems (Table 8.2) interact so that we can systematically relate the different aspects of interaction: emergent sequences like wall following, practiced skills, conceptualized coordinations, named goals, and programmatic plans. As a first pass, we might begin by trying to understand protracted, organized behavior in animals that cannot describe to themselves or us what they are doing, who do not know the world as labeled places, things, and qualities. The commonality between our linguistically organized behavior and the deliberate actions of, say, a dog looking for a ball under a chair appears to be *conceptualization*. Descriptive modeling implies conceptualization, but conceptualizing is possible without it.

Conceptualization goes beyond habit formation to include an aspect of attention that orders behavior, so a behavior system is actively organized and sustained over cycles of perception–action in coordinated action. Such action is conventionally described in terms of goals and focus of attention. Habits, by contrast, are assumed to be a necessary precursor, involving the simpler formation of temporally ordered patterns of behavior (corresponding to *chunking* in descriptive models). Building on the compositional relation between sensations, features, and perceptual categories, it appears reasonable to hypothesize that concepts are *categorizations of coordinations*, that is, categorizations of multimodal perceiving and acting over time. In particular, many goals described in problem-solving models, such as "diagnose the patient" or "check the therapy for contraindications," are *categorizations of sequences of behavior*. Of special interest are nondescriptive organizers such as categorizations that allow coordinating the motion of three objects when learning to juggle, mimicking an accent, and mentally rotating an image.

Although Toto forms habits of a certain kind, none of the situated robots categorize how their behaviors are coordinated in time. Put another way, none of the robots constructs *new ways of coordinating* their behavior in time. For example, what mechanism could learn Pengi's coordinated action of lining up a block with a bee and kicking it? What robot mechanism could replicate a sea otter's learned behavior of breaking open clams with a rock while floating on his back? Chimpanzees have been observed to show their children how to use tools (Boesch, 1991, p. 532). How is that done without descriptive instruction? At the very least, mimicry must be added to the explanatory combination of learning mechanisms (it has played almost no part in cognitive theories of instruction).

As Braitenberg has warned, our challenge is to distinguish between a local reactive pattern (perhaps explaining why a blue jay throws acorns down on us) and a multiple-step, ordered sequence (perhaps illustrated by a raven standing on and pulling on a thread to bring up food to his perch) (Griffin, 1992, pp. 104–105; Heinrich, 1993). On the one hand, we have a one-shot behavior (so to speak); on the other, we have a deliberately coordinated procedure, which must be discovered and attentively carried through. In between, we have a habit, a sequence biased to recur, but not *controlled in time* as a sequence. Again, the nature of feedback is essential. According to models of problem solving, the most important feedback occurs in cycles of perceiving and acting over time; thus, different methods are substituted and compared. Nevertheless, tactile and visual feedback-in-the-moment are essential for inventive recoordination, which is part of everyday reasoning (Chapter 9).

In terms of a neural architecture, we are asking how neural processes form that are composed and *coordinated over time*. The subsumption architecture suggests that composition may occur as *inclusion* of previously learned coordinations, just as perceptual details are included within a remembered sequence (cf. Bartlett's account of story remembering in Chapter 3). To distinguish between mere *physical coordination* – as in a sea otter balancing a clam on its chest – and *conceptual coordination* – as in deliberately seeking a good rock and holding both a rock and a clam at the same time – we must account for substituting different objects of attention on repetition. The very notion of searching for a certain kind of object suggests holding a perceptual categorization active as the *object* of an inquiry (in Dewey's sense). From here it is one more step to the notion of *having an idea*, such that one categorization *refers* to another. From this perspective, reasoning involves *coordinating ideas* in the physical, behavioral sense of holding categorizations active and categorizing their relations.

Strikingly, the architectures of the situated robots lack the ability to *segment and compose behaviors* – the very ability descriptive cognitive modeling has emphasized. Turned around, the problem may be stated as follows: Architectures based on stored descriptions have limited ability to interpret, improvise, analogize, or adapt because the understanding of conceptual models in people is based on and consists of the experience of physical coordination. Part III examines how conceptualization is related to perceptual categorization and, more broadly, how inference relates to structural coupling. On this basis, although we cannot yet build it, we will be able to better characterize the mechanism by which people think.

Part III

Ecological theories

9   Transactional experience

What if "Truth" in some very large, and for us, overriding sense is information not about what we perceive (the green leaves, the stones, that voice, that face) but about the process of perception?

> Gregory Bateson, Epistemology and ecology, *A sacred unity*,
> 1991, p. 227

Perception and action are of the same logical kind, symmetric, cyclic, and mutually constraining.

> Robert Shaw and M. T. Turvey, Methodological realism, 1980[1]

He shapes the situation, but in conversation with it, so that his own methods and appreciations are also shaped by the situation. The phenomena that he seeks to understand are partly of his own making; he is in the situation that he seeks to understand.

> Donald Schön, *Educating the reflective practitioner*, 1987, p. 73

The transactional perspective (Chapter 8) not only covers sensorimotor reflexes, as in Dewey's critique of stimulus–response theories (Chapter 4), but is also applicable to the relation between perceiving and conceiving in intentional activity. One form of conceptual coordination apparently occurs by the coupling mechanism found in simpler sensorimotor systems (in Maturana's sense; Chapter 4). Distinguishing this coupling mechanism from inferential processes operating on symbols is my objective in Parts III and IV.

To show how a conceptual categorization (in Edelman's sense; Chapter 7) comes to function as a referential symbol, I first provide examples of *how conceiving can be structurally coupled to perceiving* (this chapter). I then discuss how concepts can be structurally coupled to each other in type-instance hierarchies (following Wilden; Chapter 10). I argue that conceptual "islands" (Calvin, 1991) are related by inference through *referential categorizations* (treating categorizations *as ideas*). On the basis of this coupling–inference distinction, I reformulate Gibson's notion of *affordances* (Chapter 11) and restate his controversial claim about *direct perception* (Chapter 12). Finally, I reformulate the notions of *symbol* and *symbolic* in terms of the transactional perspective, showing how insights in descriptive cognitive modeling can be recovered and what it will take to

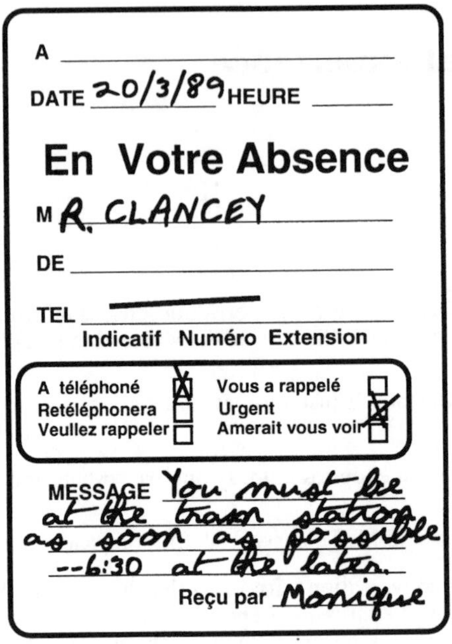

Figure 9.1. A phone message received in Nice.

build a machine that constructs and operates on symbols in the manner of the human brain (Chapters 13 and 14).

The chapters in Part III constitute a theoretical treatment I characterize as *ecological* because this concept provides a broad, systems perspective for understanding the nature of context and change. This chapter begins with two examples of how perception and conception of meaning may arise together. Subsequent discussion builds on these examples: I elucidate the contextualist view of experience as *transactional events* and how subconscious coordinating and conscious describing are recursively related (Figures 9.3, 9.4, and 9.6). My central point is that the conscious activity of inquiry (in describing and manipulating materials) has been superficially equated with what descriptive models do; hence the other aspect of human reasoning, the subconscious coordination of perceiving and conceiving, has been misrepresented and inadequately understood (Figure 9.5).

A message in Nice

Here is a phone message I received at my hotel in Nice on a rainy day (Figure 9.1). My friends and I had just come in from dinner and maybe had had a few drinks too many. "En Votre Absence: R. Clancey." Rosemary

Clancey? Why did my mother call me? "You must be at the train station as soon as possible." What? (Paranoid thought: Somebody is forcing me to leave town!) "6:30 at the later." Tomorrow morning? Why?

Actually, this message was supposed to be read to me over the phone, before dinner, while I was still in Antibes. It nicely illustrates the *indexical* nature of representations: How we interpret a representation *as a description* – how we perceive its form and conceive its meaning – depends on our ongoing *activity*, including in this case the time of day, the city I was in, and whether I had been drinking. If I had received this message before dinner, I would have known to go to the Antibes train station and wait for my ride to take me to the restaurant.

This example illustrates how, in the most general case, perceiving and conceiving meaning may be structurally coupled. Not only is meaning contextually determined, but what constitutes *a situation* to the observer – the context – is itself partially constructed within the interpretation process. The meaning of a representation is not inherent, partially because the *representational form* itself is not inherent. Both the perceptual form of the representation and its meaning can arise *together* – not serial, not parallel-independent, but *coupled and mutually constraining*, like the relation between olfactory bulb and cortex in Freeman's chaotic model (Chapter 6) and the classification couples in Edelman's TNGS (Chapter 7). In particular, reading and comprehension are not merely processes of *indexing* labels and associated meaning from memory (as descriptive theories suggest), but constructing a coupled *perception–interpretation* on the spot. Not only is the person perceiving the representation determining what it means (as theories of semantics have long established), the perceiver is determining what forms should be treated *as being a representation*. As contextualists discovered (Chapter 3), this process of situation construction by the comprehender is missed if experiments supply tidy puzzles with one carefully designed, self-consistent configuration (as in speech recognition for chess playing).

In this example, perceiving involves, at the very least, segmenting the written squiggles of the message. I saw "R. Clancey" as the name of the person who left the message. In practice, symbol structures like "R. Clancey" are not merely *given* as objective and unambiguous tokens (though typeset text certainly minimizes the reader's work). In the general case in everyday life, materials are reperceived and hence reconstructed as objects by the perceiver. *What I saw* on the page (what I believed needed to be understood) is partly determined by *what I understood* the message to be about. The conventional descriptive modeling approach suggests a process of receiving input symbols, comprehending meaning, and acting on the basis of the interpretation (Figure 3.2). As described in cognitive models, the reading and comprehension process is iterative, so we may return to the environment for more information in order to bolster an evolving understanding. But this approach still assumes that the symbols needing to be understood are given on the page, and looking is just a matter of *selecting* from what is there.

The Nice message illustrates that *what constitutes information* to the observer – *what needs to be understood* – is simultaneously determined by interpretations *as they are conceived*. This should not be surprising in view of the analysis of sensorimotor coordination (Chapter 4 and Part II): An agent's ongoing interactions – an organized process of movement, interpretation, and orientation – partially determines how the world is categorized into objects and events. In situated robots, the categorization process constructs boundaries, defining what constitutes a form, such as a region. Going one (big) step further, in people this perceptual construction process is *dynamically* influenced by possible meanings: Data are construed as present *while* understanding is developing. In contrast, the hypothesis-testing view of comprehension postulates a bottom-up or top-down (or mixed) relation in which hypothesis and evidence exist independently and need only be linked together.

Certainly, there can be repeated cycles of going back to look again, redescribe, and recomprehend what is there. But at a basic level of organization, segmenting the world and interpreting what is there may be inseparable. In our example, "R. Clancey" was seen, rather than "MR. Clancey." Obviously, visual categorizing is constrained by what is on the paper; the segmentation is an interaction of visual stimuli resulting from physical stuff in the world. But the conceiver has some leeway in saying what the stuff on the paper is. For example, my segmenting ignored that the space between the M and the R is quite narrow compared to the space between R. and "Clancey." The common unit "Mr." was indeed not present because the "r" was capitalized. Visibly, "R. Clancey" was a more familiar unit. And being in France, being continuously jarred by unusual conventions, perhaps I tacitly could view "M" as meaning both "Monsieur" and "Madame." None of these considerations was consciously entertained.

In short, the simple information processing view that symbols are given as input, in the manner of a stream of numbers or letters in a book, doesn't hold up when we examine everyday examples in which people *perceptually configure* representations. In particular, the separation into a *perceptual problem* and a *comprehension problem* is especially inadequate for understanding how children create their own notations (wonderfully illustrated by Jeanne Bamberger's (1991) study of how novices segment and represent music). On the other hand, Hofstadter (1995b) points out that the *blackboard approach* to modeling comprehension, as in the Hearsay II speech-

$$S <=> PF <=> \quad PC \quad\quad <=> \quad\quad CC$$

Salutation: S <=> "R." <=> "R.Clancey" <=> "Mother called"

Body: "Must be at ..." => "run out of town"

Figure 9.2. Nice message interpretation modeled as structural coupling: Perceptual Features (binding of "R" to period), Perceptual Categorization (name), and Conceptual Categorization (mother called) arise together as a mutually constrained construction when reading the salutation. But the meaning of the message body is inferred (cf. Table 8.3).

understanding program, begins to capture the *parallel terraced scan* of perceptual grouping and composition in people (pp. 91, 111). However, as he indicates, the parallel construction of *multiple top-level interpretations* is implausible; experience suggests that the brain does not multiply assign perceptual components to high-level conceptualizations of a situation. We can flip back and forth, but we do not see or hear in two ways at once. As I have emphasized, descriptive cognitive modeling does indeed capture the comprehension process in general form, but the retrieval-matching-assembly, "post in a buffer and then output" mechanisms do not strictly fit all cognitive experiences. In my example, inference to alternative interpretations takes place only *after perception–conception coupling has occurred.* Applying the notation used to compare situated robots (Table 8.3), the categorizing in the Nice example is summarized in Figure 9.2.

Conceptualization via coupling is a form of recognition, like perceptual categorization. As a coordination, my conceptualization of who called partially reflects my emotional attitude and how I was already conceiving my role and my relation to what was happening in the environment (indeed, I was probably mired in an argument about symbols and feeling a bit on the run). As my story shows, the interpretation of the body of the message occurred secondarily, "on a different cycle." My conception of the message body (a stern order: "Must be at the train station . . . at the later") and inquiry (Why did my mother call me?) are combined to *infer* that the message is a warning. This conception ("paranoid thought") arises *after* the earlier categorizations of the sender and the message tone. The relation is not another coupling, but a deduction operating on these held-in-place categorizations. Referring to Figure 9.2, PC ("R. Clancey") and CC arise together, but forming the conception of being run out of town involved holding CC (Mother called) and the categorization of the message's superficial content (involving where to go and when) active at the same time and then relating them to a third idea ("this message is a warning").

My concern here is not with the particular descriptions given to the various categorizations I made in the story, or how often or under what circumstances the kind of ambiguity in this example actually arises. Instead, my point is that there are two kinds of mechanisms for temporally relating categorizations: *structural coupling*, in which categorizations arise together, and *inference,* in which categorizations are held active in awareness and related. As I will explain in subsequent chapters, this latter form of conceptualization corresponds to *symbolic reasoning.* The thesis for the moment is that different categorizing mechanisms are operating. Showing that the first, structural coupling, is not sequentially chaining referential categorizations (the symbols in a descriptive cognitive model, such as PA-TIENT-512 in Mycin) – but is indeed occurring in symbolic reasoning – will take some explanation over the course of the next few chapters, but that's where I'm headed.

I want to emphasize that the perceptual-conceptual construction in interpreting the Nice message is not merely fitting a context to a message. The way in which the context is conceived *and changed* by the interpretation process itself is important. This is the central notion of a *transactional experience* (cf. the quote by Schön at the start of this chapter). In particular, as social scientists stress in their analyses of situated action (Lave and Wenger, 1991; Wenger, in preparation), the understanding I am constructing and affirming in interpreting the Nice message is my *conception of my self:* who I am and what is happening to me. That is, for a human being, the primary notion of *context* or *situation* is with respect to the person as a social actor, as being someone who is right now constrained by social norms and right now playing an interactive role in some persona (even when alone). This is the functional aspect of the situated cognition framework (Table 1.1). (The reader may wish to review my depiction of Harold Cohen as an artist in this perspective; see Figure 1.2.)

In reading the telephone message, what I am already doing, how I am viewing myself and conceiving that other people are viewing me, and the plausibility of actions the message appears to entail will constrain my interpretations. When reading the message, going to the train station was not part of my current activity, suggesting that maybe something nefarious was afoot. Had I received the message at the phone booth of the train station itself, when I was already waiting for instructions, I might have read the salutation as "Mr. Clancey." Meaning is contextual, but my process of interpreting occurs *within* – as part of – my ongoing process of *constructing what my current activities are.* That is, my context is – in its most general but always present aspect – the meaning of *who I am as an actor:* Am I being run out of town or being picked up for dinner? Thus, the conventional view of context as being information in the environment or a problem-solving task is flawed in two ways: Neither information nor task is strictly supplied, and both are conceived within the agent's larger, developing conception of social role and sense of place.

In conclusion, reading comprehension in everyday life – a paradigmatic example of symbol processing – does not strictly fit the perceive-reason-act model of descriptive cognitive models (Figure 3.2). The next example sharpens this point by showing how perception–conception coupling may be embedded in a larger activity of causal reasoning and invention.

Inventing a synthetic paintbrush

In his critique of descriptive cognitive models of analogical reasoning, Donald Schön analyzes an example of a group of people inventing a synthetic paintbrush.[2] At first, the brushes created by the design team don't spread paint properly. Perceiving gloppiness in the painted surface produced by the synthetic brush, the inventors use a natural hair brush again and again, looking for new ways of "seeing how it works." Suddenly, a new contrast comes to their attention: They see that paint is *flowing* between the bristles. Perceiving the spaces as *channels*, someone proclaims, "A paintbrush is a kind of pump!" With this new orientation, they look again at *painting*: In what ways is this way of viewing the brush appropriate? They look again at their well-practiced use of a brush and observe that they *vibrate* a brush when they paint, causing the paint to flow. Finally, they develop a theory of "pumpoids" (how is a rag a kind of pump, too?) and relate their observations in a causal model of how flexible bristles allow vibrating, even flow, and hence smooth painting.

Schön argues that the invention of the synthetic paintbrush proceeded through several representational stages:

1. *A similarity is conceived* in terms of the flowing of a liquid substance: "A paintbrush is a kind of pump." The old idea of a pump is used metaphorically to represent what a paintbrush is. Painting is put in the context of pumping.
2. *New details are now perceived and described:* "Notions familiarly associated with pumping . . . project onto the painting situation, transforming their perception of pumping." Spaces are seen between the bristles (channels); *bending* the brush forces paint to flow between the channels (paint is not merely scraped off the bristles).
3. *An explicit account of the similarity is articulated* as a general theory of pumpoids, by which examples of pumps known previously are understood in a different way.

This development process occurs during "the concrete, sensory experience of using the brushes and feeling how the brushes worked with paint":

At first they had only an unarticulated perception of similarity which they could express by doing the painting and inviting others to see it as they did, or by using terms like "squeezing" or "forcing" to convey the pumplike quality of the action. Only later, and in an effort to account for their earlier perception of similarity, did they develop an explicit account of the similarity, an account which later still became part of a general theory of "pumpoid," according to which they could regard paintbrushes and pumps, along with washcloths and mops, as instances of a single technological category.

The contrast to description-driven models of invention is stark:

- *Features of paintbrushes were not supplied as data to be reasoned about or retrieved from previously constructed descriptions.* New properties were attributed to paintbrushes in the process of invention. For example, spaces between the bristles weren't even seen as *things* to be described until the pump metaphor developed. Similarity wasn't based on searching and matching descriptions, as in inductive models of discovery, but on perceptually recategorizing the visual field (cf. Table 8.1). As in the Nice example, the data about the system to be understood were created as descriptions from perceptual forms.
- *The pump metaphor was not previously known by a fixed set of features* (e.g., channels, flowing). New properties were attributed to pumps after the metaphor was conceived. More fundamentally, a pump is reconceived with respect to this example; it is not a general category that is just instantiated or matched against the situation. Knowing what the situation is and categorizing it develop together; they are not source and target or givens and goals.
- *Viewing the paintbrush as a pump is a coupled perceptual–conceptual process.* The categorization of similarity provides a basis for new descriptions to be created. In Dewey's terms, the descriptions are artifacts, *instruments* for carrying out their inquiry in a coordinated activity of looking, manipulating stuff, and modeling descriptively what they experience.

Rather than being merely retrieved, matched, or assembled in some subconscious way, descriptions of the paintbrush and pump develop incrementally within their inquiry: "The making of generative metaphor involves a developmental process. . . . To read the later model back into the beginning of the process would be to engage in a kind of historical revisionism." This is another way of saying that the *conditions* of the painting situation are not given but represented – categorically and in descriptions – by the participants themselves as part of the inquiry process. The painters' work of recognizing and relating is not well captured by the idea of "parsing perceptions in terms of theories" (a common way of describing scientific understanding) because knowledge of pumping and painting, as perceptual-motor coordinations, consists of more than descriptions.

Crucially, the idea of what a pump is develops during the invention process: "both their perception of the phenomenon and the previous description of pumping were transformed." This is an essential property of *metaphorical descriptions*: In perceiving and saying that one thing, the paintbrush, is an example of something else, a pump, we change both how we view paintbrushes and how we view pumps. Thus, the metaphorical conception is *generative* of both perceptual features and descriptions. Indeed, the painters' experience indicates that the previously articulated features of these objects are incommensurate at first; all they have is a sense of similarity (in the seeing) and a sense of discord (in the saying). The new way of seeing and the tentative way of talking arose together, but the painters don't yet have a descriptive model to explain this relation.

To paraphrase Schön's analysis, *experience of similarity is not description based*. Knowing that a similarity *exists* (a paintbrush is like a pump) precedes and forms the basis for *describing what the similarity* is (the spaces between bristles are channels). Seeing-as *and knowing that you are seeing-as* precede the interactive process of descriptive theorizing. You conceive relationships before you can articulate a model. But the effect also goes the other way over time: Describing relationships is a coordinated way of creating new conceptions (you cannot speak without conceiving unless you want to mimic one of today's robots). We do not speak by *translating* internal descriptions of what we are going to say.

At this point, the reader may be thinking, "Well, not all symbols need be linguistic; what is this argument saying about symbol systems?" As I mentioned in the discussion of the owl monkey (Chapter 4) and elaborate in Chapters 12 and 13, perceptual categories may be viewed as symbols in the broad sense intended by the physical symbol system hypothesis. At issue is how the internal constructs, which may be broadly called symbols, are created, change, and function. The idea of structural coupling suggests that not all neural categorizations are like terms in a language (an alphabet or a vocabulary of labels to be recombined), but are *relations* that are activated and reconfigured in use.

Thus, I seek to explicate the causal interaction of category formation and what kinds of categories are involved. In particular, my analysis of the paintbrush inventors hypothesizes that viewing painting as pumping generalizes previous processes that were active in the experiences of talking about, seeing, and using pumps. As the painters talk, where do the descriptions of vibrating, pumps, and channels come from? In part, the physical, sensorimotor processes involved in describing, perceiving, and using pumps and paintbrushes are reactivated and recoordinated. Categories are generalized (*channel* is applied to the almost invisible, flexible space between bristles), and new properties are tentatively claimed (the bristles are vibrating). This process bears some discussion to understand how it is different from the strict retrieval-indexing and matching model of most explanations of analogical reasoning.

To begin, the sense of similarity is an example of what is often called *tacit knowledge* (Polanyi, 1966), but this term is misleading. On the one hand, we have descriptions of knowledge (e.g., statements of belief, theories about pumps). On the other hand, we have active neural processes coordinating what we are doing and how we are perceiving the situation (what Schön calls *knowing in action*). In this respect, knowledge as a capability to coordinate perception and action is *always tacit* or implicit. Descriptions are *always explicit* because they are consciously created and perceived. How interpreting descriptions reorganizes ways of seeing and talking is precisely what we now need to understand.

The painters are not (only) looking for prelabeled features; they are not merely searching the world. They are also *seeking a new way of seeing*, which involves *recoordinating* what they are seeing and how they talk about paintbrushes. They do not know in descriptive terms what they are looking for; the properties they need in creating an explanatory story have not yet been articulated and (in this case) will be new to the objects being investigated. In this deliberate process of reperception, the familiar becomes strange as "new particulars are brought in." For example, *vibrating* was not a description that was part of the professional procedure of "how to paint," just as *channels* was plausibly never part of their description of properties of brushes. *Vibrating* and *channels* are in the general vocabulary of the painters, but were only conceived in this context as they were looking at and manipulating brushes in a special way – in order to explain *how particular effects* (now noticed as aspects of smooth delivery) *are physically produced*. Again, perceptual categorization is not an infinite regress of feature description and pattern matching (cf. Chapter 6); the way of talking (e.g., *vibrating*) was *coupled* to the way of seeing. We might describe the looking as being directed by a conception of "How, other than the conventional ways, might I see what the brush is doing?" In this respect, as in the Nice example, tacit conceptualization provides a complex *contextual constraint* for organizing perception (cf. Jackendoff, 1987).

More generally, over time perceptual details that are noticed are given meaning by describing what is happening (e.g., "vibrating the brush is pumping" subsumes the detail that bristles are curved).[3] Thus the meaning of the perceptual experience is a *relation* between details, metaphoric conceptions, and verbal explanations. In some sense, the verbalizing process *holds active* disparate experiences originally associated by only a superficial perceiving-as coupling (of image, sound, gesture, odor, etc.), allowing a more abstract conceptualization to be constructed (a theory of pumpoids).

Dewey (1938) describes how perceptions and theoretical concepts are intricately linked in time:

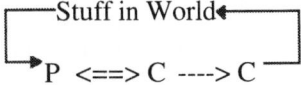

Figure 9.3. Coupling, inference, and feedback in transactional processes. Changing stuff in the world during inquiry to see its properties and looking in new ways change what we perceive; perceived similarity shifts to a different domain (P ⇔ C); general ways of coordinating the inquiry may lead to hypotheses about causal relations or decisions about things to try next (C → C).

Perceptual and conceptual materials are instituted in functional correlativity with each other, in such a manner that the former locates and describes the problem while the latter represents a possible method of solution. Both are determinations in and by inquiry of the original problematic situation whose pervasive quality controls their institution and their contents. . . . As distinctions they represent logical divisions of labor. . . . The idea or meaning when developed in discourse directs the activities which, when executed, provide needed evidential material. (pp. 111–112)

The "original problematic situation" is the sense of discord (and despondency) on seeing gloppy paint on the wall. The *breakdown in prior coordinations* of seeing and doing (how paint should flow as the brush moves along the wall) drives the painters' looking, conceptualizing, and subsequent theorizing. New ways of seeing and describing, "developed in discourse," direct subsequent physical experiments and talk. Now, in feedback (or what Schön calls *back talk*), the new stuff on the wall stimulates further ways of seeing and talking about experience, provoking commentary about the meaning of what is seen and heard ("needed evidential material"). Figure 9.3 illustrates this feedback relation. This diagram represents the effortful experience of acting, hearing-seeing-smelling, and doing that occurs when making bread, drawing something, playing music, writing, and so on.

Working with the new particulars (the spaces, the flow, the vibration), the painters develop the metaphor of a pump. That is, the painters describe what the paintbrush does *in terms of* a pump. As Schön argues, the relations are perceptual and activity based: The painters *recoordinate* their seeing, doing, and talking so that the *process of painting* is like the *process of pumping*. Certainly, saying things like "flow" and "forcing the liquid" is part of this correlation of activities. But again, the description-matching model of analogy comprehension is incomplete. Remembering is itself a transformation of previous experience, such that pumping is seen through present details and the overarching inquiry. The currently active details thus transform and generalize what pumping means.

Schön summarizes why the reconstruction and generalization of past *experience* are inadequately modeled by a mechanism based on manipulation of descriptions alone:

[T]he two descriptions resisted mapping. It was only after elements and relations of the brush and the painting had been regrouped and renamed (spaces between bristles made into foreground elements and called "channels," for example) that the paintbrush could be seen as a pump.

This regrouping involves a *perceptual recategorization* (a figure–ground shift in seeing channels) and a *conceptual recoordination* that subsumes and hence transforms painting, as well as the old way of seeing pumps. The old way of seeing pumps influenced what the painters were seeing and how they were talking *before* anyone thought to talk about pumps ("the researchers were able to see painting as similar to pumping before they were able to say 'similar to what'"). This is the essential shortcoming of descriptive cognitive models: "Knowledge in action may often be that which an individual knows how to do but cannot yet say" (Bamberger and Schön, 1983, p. 690).

Put another way, the painters experience similarity but don't at first notice *similarities*. This experience of similarity might be explained in descriptive models in terms of a subconscious discovery of a match, which is later translated into speech. My claim is that this match is sometimes *a perceptual reconfiguration a*nd may involve relating *new, generalized conceptual categorizations* not previously attributed to the objects in question. The coupling categorization is experienced as similarity.

Characterizing the invention process as relating descriptions of data and explanatory hypotheses that are independently preexisting and need only be linked via a mapping process fails to capture or explain a wide variety of phenomena in human reasoning:

- How and why new perceptual features are constructed and new properties attributed to materials.
- How physical coordinations are coupled to ways of perceiving and talking.
- How subsequent theorizing requires realizing (conceiving) that you are seeing something *as* something else; that is, categorizing categorizations as "events I experience" objectifies experience by constructing an I-world–subject-object higher-order relation.
- How theorizing requires categorizing talk as being about something; that is, categorizing a conceptualization as *referring to* other categorizations, as "being about" them, makes the talk a description of experience: "My talk is about *that*."
- How the brain holds disparate conceptualizations active so that non-coupled aspects can be related; that is, the categorizations I am holding active ("*that*" I have experienced and am referring to) function as symbols in inferential associations ("*vibrating* forces the *liquid* to . . .").
- How inferential, verbal categorization in descriptive modeling (such as causal talk about pumpoids) constructs a unifying conception that itself remains tacit.

Of course, the invention process can be informally described (as I have talked about it here) or modeled in computer programs (what Douglas Hofstadter (1995a) calls the *frozen caricatures* of *structure-mapping* engines). But naturally occurring human invention involves feedback and coupling on different levels of neural, physical, and social interaction (cf. Table 1.1). In particular, we have only the vaguest understanding of the ongoing, multitracked, multimodal neural process that is reactivating and recomposing the painters' previous perceptions and actions as they paint, look, listen, and speak.

Contextualism revisited: No elementary properties

To this point, my thesis in this chapter has been that perception and conception may be coupled, which means that they arise and develop together. Of course, over time, a perceptual categorization may proceed a later conceptualization, and indeed, a strong perceptual detail may strike us independently of its present relevance (as a flash of light or strong smell may get our attention); often in inquiry, the causality runs the other way, as partial understanding shapes the looking and manipulating process. The constructive process is therefore neither top-down from concepts nor bottom-up from perceptions. It is a kind of mixed architecture that we have not replicated in descriptive models, such that some features and some concepts do not have independent temporal existence apart from each other: Their relation is neither serial, in the sense of Figure 3.2 in which features are sitting in a buffer before they are processed, nor parallel, in the sense of an *independent creation* that is later matched or combined.

Dynamic simultaneity in coupling of perception and conception (as illustrated by both the Nice and painters examples, which I represent as P ⇔ C) implies that there are different ways of characterizing the world as objects, properties, and events. What is perceived depends on how stuff in the world and observer interact, as well as what is of interest. Within inquiry, different professional disciplines will bring different tools, languages, and analytic methods to the problem situation, and hence people will claim that different sets of facts are relevant or that different features count as evidence (Schön, 1987). This is not an idealist position that the world doesn't exist apart from our ideas; rather, the *experience* of attending to features and their significance is subjective.

For my purposes, even though I find a transactional physics appealing, it only suffices to argue that some of the features we construct arise within movement (as in situated robots) and that other features are alternative, mutually incompatible ways of grouping stuff in the world (such as binding "R." to "Clancey" instead of "M" and the figure–ground shift of perceiving channels instead of bristles). In general, features are not given, objective things or properties, but *relations*. Indeed, this was Bateson's point: "'Information' and 'form' resemble contrast, frequency, symmetry, correspondence, congruence, conformity and the like in being of zero dimensions and therefore are not to be located" (Chapter 4). Interactive relations, such as flux and trajectories, are not states or things, but changes over time. For most purposes, the only physics we need to adopt in cognitive science is not Aristotelian (the trait view; Chapter 8), but Newtonian (the relational view). The transactional perspective – as developed by Bohr and Heisenberg's philosophy – may be especially important for describing change when *independently created systems* interact (Gregory, 1988; Heisenberg, 1962; Petersen, 1985).

Recalling the discussion of contextualism (Chapter 3), perceptual experience arises as *events* within (as part of) transactions, not as isolated detection of properties per se. Robert Hoffman and James Nead (1983) provide a broad historic overview of contextualism and its implications for psychology:

The version of experimental psychology known in the early 1900s as functionalism can be taken as an example of a contextualist scientific theory. In contrast with the elementaristic early behaviorists, the functionalists emphasized the place of specific stimuli and response in their global contexts. . . . In contrast with mentalistic and mechanistic structuralists such as Wundt and Titchenener, the functionalists focused on mental "operations" rather than associative memory structures. . . . Functionalists concentrated on the analysis of the evolutionary, functional, and practical significance of consciousness, and the notion that perceptions and thoughts are of events rather than of elementary sensations, stimuli or responses. (p. 520)

The contextualist idea that people dynamically construct an ontology of objects and properties "places an emphasis on the 'perceptual learning' which the theorist must undergo in order to specify the relevant events for the domain." (Here a "theorist" is the subject, such as an expert television sports commentator evaluating diving performances.) As illustrated by Schön's analysis, a contextualist studies what's perceived, the sensory fields and other physical interactions, and activity as one system. In contrast to an exclusively inferential model of problem solving, as in Mycin, this analysis allows for coconstruction of perceptions and interpretations: "The inferences the expert makes may appear to be made in a serial order (e.g., where to put the stethoscope), but the actions are governed interactively and dynamically by past experience and present information" (Hoffman and Nead, 1983, p. 521). Again, "past experience" is not a set of descriptions, but previous ways of coordinating perception, interpretation, talk, and physical examination.

In descriptive cognitive models, such as the formulation of reading comprehension, operators map the features of the linguistic utterance level to the features of situation-specific models of what is being discussed. At every level, productions (situation-action rules) control the retrieval, comparison, and assembly of features and their descriptions. How does this bottom out? The NL-Soar research team acknowledges that perhaps the most fundamental learning problem remains to be addressed: "We have not solved the genesis problem (*Where does the knowledge in the lower problem spaces come from?*)" (Lehman, Lewis, and Newell, 1991, p. 39; emphasis in original text). The hypothesis I am presenting here is that NL-Soar's lower problem space describes *concepts that are coupled to nonverbal categorizations*. Below the level of domain terms, features, and relations, NL-Soar requires a conceptualization ability that Edelman labels "prelinguistic." But the mechanism will not be mapping (for you cannot map onto what does not yet exist), but rather a coupling coformation process, like the formation of attractors in different subsystems in Freeman's model (Chapter 6).

I conclude this discussion of contextualism by returning to Dewey's description, which highlights that *situations are conceptual* first and foremost, not descriptions, objects, or data:

What is designated by the word situation is not a single object or event or set of objects and events. For we never experience nor form judgments about objects and events in isolation, but only in connection with a contextual whole. (1938, p. 66)

An experience is always what it is because of a transaction taking place between an individual and what, at the time, constitutes his environment, whether the latter consists of persons with whom he is talking about some topic or event, the subject talked about being also a part of the situation; or the toys with which he is playing; the book he is reading (in which his environing conditions at the time may be England or ancient Greece or an imaginary region); or the materials of an experiment he is performing. The environment, in other words, is whatever conditions interact with personal needs, desires, purposes, and capacities to create the experience which is had. Even when a person builds a castle in the air he is interacting with the objects which he constructs in his fancy. (1902, p. 519)

The context in which problem solving occurs – what constitutes the *situation* for the agent – is arising in activity itself. Viewing the brain as a system itself, this means that the perceptual, conceptual, linguistic, and motor processes in the brain don't strictly control each other, but arise together: Conception is the context for perception and vice versa. Perhaps now we can understand Dewey's description of aesthetic experience, which I quoted at the start of Chapter 1: "The doing or making is artistic when the perceived result is of such a nature that *its* qualities *as perceived* have controlled the question of production." That is, the conception of what the drawing was to be ("the question of production") is partially shaped by the qualities of what is produced.

In the remainder of this chapter, I elaborate on the relation of what happens "within a perceptual-motor cycle," and in cycles over time, to bring out the relation between subconscious coupling and the conscious behavior of descriptive inference.

Conceptual composition over time: Consciousness, feedback, and error

In contrast to a single utterance, or phrase, such as saying "Glad to meet you," conversational speaking, as in the inquiry activity of the painters, involves multiple, iterative steps of speaking and listening. A related process occurs in an individual's reading and thinking, as in my inquiry in reading the Nice message. In general, inquiry involves language in *cycles* of perceiving discord or similarity, describing, and comprehending. Donald Schön (1979, 1990) clarifies these levels of behavior in his analysis of the logic of inquiry (with Schön's terms given parenthetically):

- *Doing (knowing-in-action):* Attentive action occurs automatically, including both physical manipulation (as in painting) and talking (generating descriptions).
- *Adapting (reflection-in-action):* We are caught short momentarily, but easily continue. We "glitch" on something unexpected but respond immediately, proceeding from another conceptual coordination (e.g., paint is running down the wall, but the problem is familiar and the recovery maneuver is practiced).
- *Framing (conversations with the situation [back talk]):* What are we talking about? What categorization fits our activity of speaking? We are transforming the conversation (deliberately attempting to generate appropriate descriptions of the situation). (The paint is all gloppy: What is going on? What is happening? Is it me or the brush or the wall or the paint or the humidity or . . .)
- *History telling (reflection on knowing-and-reflection-in-action):* We are articulating new theories, relating images to words, describing how we feel, and reviewing what has been said so far (reflecting on a sequence of behavior and prior descriptions, composing past perceptions into a new way of seeing). ("It's almost like using a brush that wasn't properly cleaned – the bristles are too stiff.")
- *Designing (reflective conversation with the situation):* We are deliberately guiding the conversation so that it becomes an inquiry-project, resolving a problematic situation (defining what models should be about; creating and carrying out an activity involving the preceding four components to some end; representing what we intend to compose and then managing that composition process). (A paintbrush is a kind of pump. Is a rag a pump, too?)

This framework suggests how descriptions in a modeling process build on one another. For example, one form of reflection, which I call *history telling* (Schön's reflection on knowing-and-reflection-in-action), involves commenting on a *sequence* of prior perceptions and descriptions. The stages suggest that descriptions play a different *role* in organizing behavior; they function differently in the activity: as part of acts, segues, frames, stories, and theories. Through our coordinated inquiry, we compose a story and a conceptual web that relates our observations (perceptions and descriptions) to our individual roles and concept of our activity.

Schön's framework requires a shift in perspective: We view descriptions as *created in conscious behavior* – in imagining, speaking, writing, drawing, not manipulated in a hidden, cognitively impenetrable way inside the brain. In its primary manifestation, human memory is the capacity for automatically composing processes of perceiving and behaving, including creating representations (doing, adapting). In cycles of such behavior, what James called the *secondary* aspect of remembering, we *model* what we have said and done before (framing, history telling) and engage in a meta-activity of modifying our language, tools, facilities, and social organizations (designing).

Talking about all intelligent behavior as "reasoning" or "symbolic information processing," or saying that we are "using representations" when we perceive, act, reflect, theorize, and so on is far too flat a characterization. As I keep emphasizing, arguments about serial versus parallel miss the point. Conceptually coordinated behavior is both serial and parallel and transactionally coupled. Such a system doesn't consist of descriptions, top to bottom. The system we are describing is the-person-in-the-environment, a person who constructs descriptions by subconsciously adapting old ways of perceiving and talking, by putting models out into the world as artifacts to manipulate and rearrange (diagrams, drawings, piles on a desk, gestures, knowledge bases, messages), and by perceiving and recomprehending personal descriptions over time, relating them in imagination to past experiences or future consequences.

Thus, I separate human *symbolic processing* into two aspects: a subconscious aspect by which conceptualization occurs and the conscious awareness of conceiving of and commenting on situations. As I have said, conceiving involves different modalities; two of the most important conceptual organizers are scene visualization and descriptive modeling (a form of sequential coordination in verbal language). Among animals, descriptive modeling occurs only in humans; the stages of framing, history telling, and design constitute the higher-order consciousness of self-activity (Edelman, 1992). In Bartlett's (1932) terms:

An organism has somehow to acquire the capacity to turn round upon its own 'schemata' and to construct them afresh. . . . It is where and why consciousness comes in.

A new incoming impulse must become not merely a cue setting up a series of reactions all carried out in a fixed temporal order, but a stimulus which enables us to go direct to that portion of the organised setting of past responses which is most relevant to the needs of the moment. . . .

To break away from this the 'schema' must become, not merely something that works the organism, but something with which the organism can work. . . .

It would be the case that the organism would say, if it were able to express itself: "This and this and this must have occurred, in order that my present state should be what it is." And, in fact, I believe this is precisely and accurately just what does happen in by far the greatest number of instances of remembering. . . . (p. 202)

The process by which by people create models in computer programs is a special form of verbalizing or *describing*. Two aspects of descriptive modeling may be distinguished:

- The process by which people articulate their experience, including especially interpreting previously created descriptions (in books, conversations, knowledge bases, etc.).
- The process by which programs, such as expert systems, retrieve, match, and assemble descriptions people have created (as in Aaron and Mycin).

Descriptive cognitive modeling, as a research approach to understanding the nature of intelligence, equates these processes: human perceiving-conceiving-articulating, on the one hand, and mechanically manipulating descriptions in a calculus, on the other (Chapter 2). Consequently, the stored-description architecture neither adequately models *human conceptualization* nor replicates the ways in which people create and use models. What such machines do, and do well, is automate symbolic calculating.

We may find it useful to call expert systems intelligent, but they lack the *mechanism* of human conceptualization. This is the essential distinction between human knowledge and computer representations. Symbol calculators not only lack the creativity of people but, once "fully loaded" with a knowledge base and shoved out into the world of shopping malls, doctors' offices, and our living rooms, they will appear to be dysfunctional morons (or idiot savants) because of their one-dimensional, verbal mode of coordination. Indeed, studies of neural dysfunction by Oliver Sacks (1987) reveal that multimodal coordination (verbal, visual, gestural, melodic) is important not only for invention, but for dressing oneself, organizing the day, and developing an historical persona.

Figure 9.4 shows another way of depicting the transactional perspective: Speaking, visualizing, and transforming things in the world occur *over time, in protracted activities, coordinated by cycles* of neural categorization and composition. Creating, manipulating, and interpreting descriptions (again, broadly including diagrams, speech, and gestures) involve *a sequence of experiences*. Having an idea – even saying something to oneself – occurs in

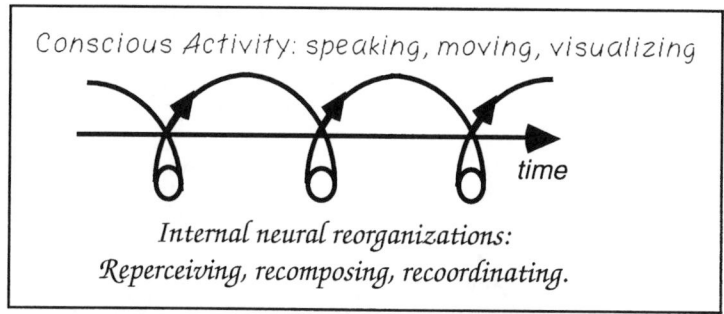

Figure 9.4. Deliberating and representing are activities, protracted over time, and coordinated conceptually, by neural reactivations and recompositions.

activity as an experience. (In more technical terms, referential categorizing is a *behavior*; cf. Chapter 8.) This contrasts with the folk psychology distinction between thinking and acting in the sense of first deliberating and then carrying out a plan. *Deliberating is itself an activity*, constrained by time, space, conception of one's role and the values of the community, and so on. Dewey's term *inquiry* is more appropriate than *deliberating* or *reasoning* because it doesn't separate thinking and doing. Complex neural reorganizations and adaptations occur throughout our effortful attention but subconsciously, in the manner of any physical skill.

An observer watching a person's behavior over time will detect patterns and an overarching organization, such as language syntax and logic in reasoning (e.g., how a physician forms and tests diagnostic hypotheses). However, an observer's pattern descriptions – expressed as rules, schemas, and scripts – are not prestored inside and *driving* the subject's individual statements. Supposing otherwise is what Schön calls *historical revisionism*. To view words or descriptions or even verbal conceptualizations as *controlling* behavior is to misconstrue the coupling relation between perception and conception, as well as to ignore the coordinating role of other modalities (visualization, rhythm, etc.).

How does the brain as a transactional system categorize, sequence, and compose in physical coordination over time? What we take for granted in computational models, and indeed receive for free in our programming languages – composition, substitution, reordering, negation, identity, and holding active multiple categorizations in registers – is *what the brain must accomplish*. And the brain does this more flexibly and adaptively on the fly than our descriptive cognitive models because it builds new categorizations and sequences by reactivating old ones rather than by storing, indexing, and matching. The brain's coordinating generalizes, detects novelty, and co-

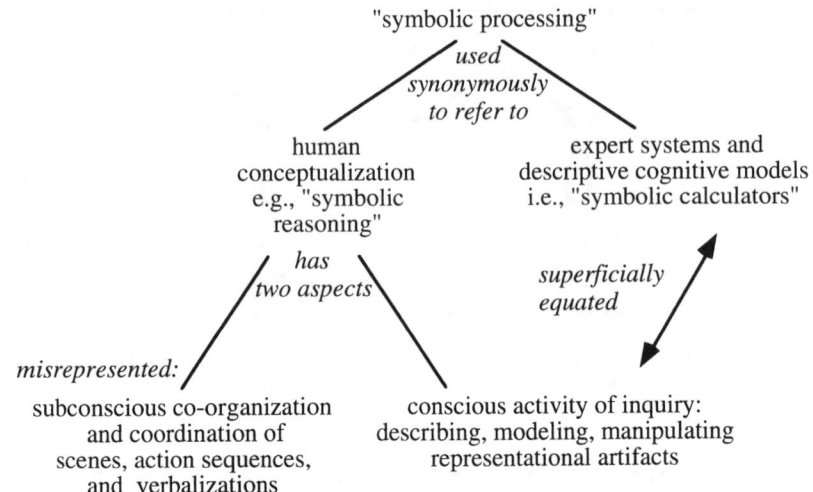

Figure 9.5. Conventionally, the term *symbolic processing* is used to refer to what people and expert systems do, misrepresenting the subconscious aspect of conceptualization and thus superficially equating reasoning with the calculus of descriptive cognitive models.

organizes processes without needing buffers describing expectations or monitoring systems to model and compare alternative behaviors. Instead, the operations of noting, comparing, and describing are occurring in conscious activity of *the person* over time (Figure 9.4) as higher-level cognition, involving language and other forms of representational manipulations in the environment we call *symbolic information processing*.

Figure 9.5 summarizes how I relate human knowledge to computer representations. Breaking *symbolic processing* into two components, a subconscious aspect of conceptualization and a conscious activity of inquiry, leads to two basic conclusions. First, verbal conceptualizing has a discrete, composed aspect that at a macro level resembles the operation of description manipulation in cognitive models. Specifically, verbal conceptualizing, in logical reasoning especially but also in the recurrent use of everyday phrases, resembles the way in which descriptive systems model speech by word definitions, grammars, and stored phrases. Second, consciousness plays a necessary role in the flexibility and novelty of human processes of creating and using descriptions.[4] In short, revealing the role of consciousness reveals why stored-description mechanisms inadequately replicate human abilities. Put another way, by ignoring consciousness, researchers have swept under the carpet those aspects of intelligence that descriptive cognitive modeling fails to explain.

Reasoning is inherently a conscious activity; what occurs within cycles, subconsciously, is not more description manipulation, but a process of a distinctively different character, involving different modalities, not just verbal, which allows describing to occur and gives it the power it has to change our behavior. In effect, equating symbolic calculators with the outward activity of symbol manipulation in human reasoning (Figure 9.5, right bottom), misconstrues the subconscious aspect of physical coordination that occurs in perception, conceptualization, and movement sequencing (left bottom). The actual subconscious aspect is omitted.

The distinction emphasized in situated cognition between descriptions and knowledge was originally interpreted by some researchers as claiming that "there are no representations in the head." In part this interpretation reflects how the term *representation* has been used in describing AI programs. Using the terms *knowledge* and *representations* synonymously, early situated cognition publications, including my own, say that "representations are not stored in the brain." A better formulation is that descriptions are not the only form of representation involved in cognition, and storage is the wrong metaphor for memory.

Perhaps most amazing in retrospect is that no distinction was made in descriptive cognitive models between conscious processes of creating and using descriptions and subconscious coordination. According to the descriptive approach, reasoning, as modeled by inferential manipulation of descriptions in Mycin, could just as well be occurring subconsciously as in the person's awareness. Indeed, most researchers building expert systems assumed that the application of rules in Mycin modeled highly practiced steps in a physician's reasoning, so they occurred quickly and without awareness. Or perhaps the rules are "compiled" into another, subconsciously stored form – which, of course, assumes that they had to be explicit descriptions at one time, and gets us back to the question "Where do the primitive terms and relations come from?" Again, perceptual categorization and its coupling relation to conceptualization was ignored.

All the talk about representation in the 1970s and 1980s by and large missed Bartlett's point: Describing the world and behavior is a way to step outside of another mechanism, one that coordinates activity more directly. This stepping out has many aspects (Figure 9.6). Note, first, that the stuff in the world (*task materials*) may consist of substances being used (e.g., paint, mud, rocks), arranged materials serving indirectly as a kind of memory (e.g., tools, trails, piles), and materials serving to represent some situation or activity (i.e., descriptive arrangements, such as drawings, notated music, a phone message, directional signs). As far as we know, descriptive arrangements are created only by people. A special form of descriptive arrange-

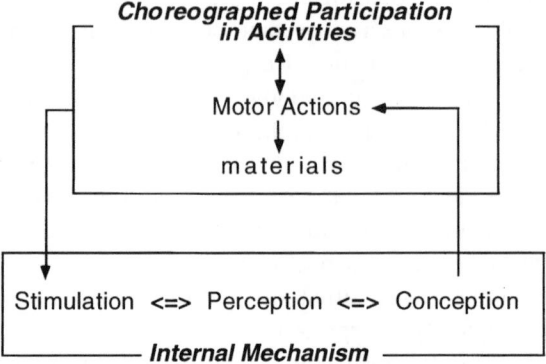

Figure 9.6. Forms of feedback within neural-person-social interaction. Perceptions and conceptions (internal experiences) are coupled. Motor actions change materials (including models) and occur as transactions within a socially choreographed time-place-role. Inferential chaining of conceptions is not shown.

ment is a model, which broadly includes designs, policies, cognitive models, and expert systems.

Comparing programs to people is essentially taking just the material stuff of a model, something we have put out into the world, and comparing it to the entire system depicted in Figure 9.6, which in normal use *includes* the expert system (for example). This is a category error. The model is held at arm's length and viewed as if it had an existence apart from the human inquiry that created and incorporates it – the very maneuver by which we start talking about Aaron as an artist (cf. Figure 1.2) or ignore how answering Mycin's questions causally relates those descriptions to our perceptions and understandings of what is happening to the patient. Of course, some highly regular processes, as in manufacturing, can be routinely handled by mechanical sensing, automated modeling, and control. That is a wonderful achievement, but it is not what people do in creating such devices, in reading text, or in diagnosing a disease.

Human behavior is not determined the way Mycin's reasoning, Aaron's drawing, or even the owl monkey's life is determined. We extend our mental processes out into our experience over time by categorizing an experience as past, by recognizing a perspective as being a perspective, by finding causal relations in stories, and by creating symbolic calculi for modeling. By doing all of this, we are able to predict, plan, and better control our experience. There is much we do not understand about the mental gymnastics required for "turning round upon its own 'schemata'" (Bartlett, 1932, p. 202) in this way. In this chapter, I have illustrated a number of fundamental distinctions necessary for understanding and building such a mental coordinating mechanism:

- Distinction between structural coupling (⇔ in Figure 9.6) and inference (deductive discourse over time).
- The feedback effect of putting descriptions into the environment to be rearranged and reinterpreted is necessarily conscious, different in kind, and operates on a different time scale than neural coordination. Representing occurs in different recursive levels in the total system (Figure 9.6) with different temporal relations and functions.
- The conception of interpersonal activity is ever-present and provides overarching order to what constitutes data, a task, a context, and a solution.

Figure 9.6, in contrast to Figure 3.2, emphasizes the inherent feedback relations of human cognition: between subsystems of the brain, within a socially conceived activity, and between person and stuff in the world over time (Bredo, 1994). In this system, representing is pragmatic, oriented to further action and interaction. The mechanism of internal coupling and feedback-in-action means that categorizations are indexical (not based on *correspondence* with reality), inherently modal (differentiated by actuality, possibility, and necessity), action based (arising within coordinated experience), and adapted reconstructions (Bickhard, in press).[5] Distinguishing internal categorizing from encodings in descriptive models, Mark Bickhard summarizes the nature of *interactive representation*:

Representational correspondences are intrinsically atemporal. . . . Encodings do not require any agent in order to exist; they are not dependent on action. . . .

Interactive representation cannot exist in a passive system – a system with no outputs. . . . Representation and interaction are differing functional aspects of one underlying system organization similarly to the sense in which a circle and a rectangle are differing visual aspects of one underlying cylinder. Action and representation are not, and cannot be, distinct modules. (p. 7)

Bickhard further indicates how the pragmatic orientation of the system enables "the emergence of representational error, thus representational content, out of pragmatic error" (p. 8). For example, Aaron lacks the ability to detect errors or shortcomings in its drawings because its drawings are not constructed as *being representations* or as *being contributions* within a social milieu. Without perceptual–conceptual coupling – either remembered experience or experience of the drawing itself – Aaron's drawings are not about anything and so cannot be *functioning* as representations of experience. Without social feedback – without the pragmatic orientation of a *participant* – Aaron's drawing is not a social-transactional event, putting stuff out into the lived-in world for others to see. There is a relation between Aaron's mechanism and its products, but it is not the conceptual and social coupling of an *agent making* something. As people, we relate to Aaron's drawings because Harold Cohen judges the functionality of the program and conforms its actions to the experience and pragmatic interests of his colleagues and audience in the art and research world. For Cohen, the drawings are configured from experience (albeit indirectly through the drawing mechanism) and are produced *as part of his experience* of being an artist-researcher.

In omitting both conceptual and social-transactional feedback, the *unified theory of cognition* of Newell is relatively flat and linear, viewing biological and social processes as just the implementation and context for descriptive modeling. But there is something fundamentally right about the discreteness of categorizations and sequential, *inferential steps* of descriptive models. For example, some of the structures in Mycin's situation-specific model are descriptions of its interactions. Insofar as these stored descriptions are coupled to a person's beliefs, how is the product of Mycin's model manipulation different from a person's inferences? Are labeled data structures like "TREATINF" functioning differently than concepts in human reasoning? Do subsumption coupling and inferential chaining operate together in human reasoning? What neural mechanism is required for inference to be possible? Is the mechanism for syntactic speech actually the mechanism of reasoning (Polk and Newell, 1995)? To relate inference in descriptive models to human reasoning, we need to consider more carefully how conceptual coupling works, how coupling differs from inference, and how the symbols in computer programs relate to human concepts.

10   Dialectic mechanism

A strictly reductionistic approach to science doesn't work. You can take systems apart. You can find out what the components are and you can find how they work in isolation. But this understanding is not sufficient to enable you to put them back together and to re-create the properties of the whole system.

> Jim Brown, quoted by J. Stites, Ecological complexity takes root,
> *The Bulletin of the Sante Fe Institute*, Spring 1995, p. 12

A new reciprocal form of causal control is invoked that includes downward as well as upward determinism. This bidirectional model applies, not only in the brain to control of emergent *mental* events over *neuronal* activity, but also to the emergent control by holistic properties in general throughout nature. . . . What started as an intradisciplinary revolution within psychology is thus turning into a major revolution for all science.

> Roger W. Sperry, The impact and promise of the cognitive revolution,
> 1995, p. 37

The philosophy of change

In this chapter, I step back to show how the idea of coupling and transaction (Chapters 4, 8, and 9), exemplified by the discussion of sensorimotor and perceptual–conceptual circuits, is part of a broader scientific conception of causality in ecological systems. By further discussion of the generality and value of *dialectic mechanisms* in scientific theories, I hope to give the reader more insight into the nature of human cognition.[1] The examples in this chapter provide another benefit: They illustrate how concepts not only may be related inferentially (C → C; cf. Table 8.2), but may also be *coupled* in subsumption hierarchies (C ⇔ C; cf. Figure 9.6). Hence we find that ecological thinking tells us not only how biological systems in the world develop, but also how conceptual systems develop. In this respect, we are considering an individual person's conceptual structures not only as a deductive or inferential system, but also as an ecology of competing, interacting, mutually determined behavior organizers.

Ecology concerns the complex of relations between an entity and its environment *(Webster's New World Dictionary of the American Language).* Ecological analysis emphasizes how parts of a system are developmentally related to the whole; thus ecology is a "philosophy of change." The causal logic of ecology defines *property, complement,* and *hierarchy* in terms of

225

mutual, ongoing development between the parts. The ecological view is *holistic,* claiming that productive functioning inherently changes the entities in the process of their interacting, such that roles and properties are developed and defined with respect to each other. That is, functions or roles are relational and dynamically sustained, not residing as *traits* of parts.

In contrast, the logic of information processing is based on compartmentalization, flow, and storage, assuming that localized, preexisting parts find each other, exchange something, and work together in interlocking producer and consumer relations. The interactive approach of Newton[2] (Chapter 8) has driven most scientific analysis and engineering of physical systems, especially computer programming (where, indeed, a *function* is a thing stored in memory). But such a reductionistic view is not sufficient for understanding human development, healing dysfunctional behaviors, or creating living systems. In short, a reductionistic view is insufficient for theories of learning, medicine, evolution, and AI.

As we have seen in the discussion of sensorimotor systems (Chapters 4 and 8) and perceptual–conceptual systems (Chapter 9), the transactional view of causal relationship, what we might call *eco-logic,* is based not only on serial or parallel relations in the sense of most computational processes, but on *codependence* – a mutually sustained relation that makes the parts what they are. Such relations are called *dialectic* because each aspect is the developmental context for the other. More generally, a *dialectic relation,* as I use the term here, is any functional, historically developed relation of codependence.

Ecological change occurs not by external control or instruction, but by differentiation of the parts as functions within a self-organized whole. We have seen that this shift in perspective requires a different understanding of the nature of information, heralded by the claim that information is not given but created by an organism (Chapter 4). Understanding this claim requires, as Bateson suggested, a shift from substance, here-and-now views of things to developmental, historical views of *recurrent feedback relations* between emergent forms and events (referred to as the *transactional* perspective; Figure 9.3). As we have seen, the result is a nonsubstance idea of information and hence a noncorrespondence notion of perception. The same conclusions will apply as we move forward to consider conceptual structure and symbolic reasoning (Chapter 13).

In effect, we are asked once again to understand how *the logic of human understanding* differs from the inferential chains of descriptive cognitive models. The temptation will be to codify any description I give here into a formal model and to suppose that such a description is equivalent to the logical development of concepts. In effect, conscious, inferential behavior ($C \rightarrow C$) as a way of thinking – and as a way of doing psychology or AI –

tends to dominate and recast subconscious sources of concept formation ($P \Leftrightarrow C$ and $C \Leftrightarrow C$). The idea that concepts are related by inferences (the production rules of Figure 3.2) applies when concepts develop independently and are related through argumentation (as in the framing, story telling, and theorization of the paintbrush inventors). It has long been known that concepts are also related hierarchically – but the mechanism of this relation has only been *described* in cognitive models, and for the most part viewed, as if it is *just another form of inference*.

To break through the tendency to view all conceptualization as inferential, I begin with Wilden's account of *both-and* relations, which characterizes how conceptual hierarchies are formed and reveals how dualistic (also called *either-or*) reasoning has dominated cognitive theory. To provide another perspective on the same idea, I present Stephen J. Gould's explanation of dialectic relation. After laying this foundation, I show how the ideas are applied in ecological psychology (Chapter 11), especially in Gibson's theory of affordances, as interpreted by Turvey and Shaw. I then show how these ideas have been misinterpreted from an inferential point of view (Chapter 12). Finally, considering what the idea of *symbol systems* adds that Gibson left out, I produce a new synthesis (Chapter 13).

I want to underscore that understanding eco-logic is complicated by the tendency of an either-or perspective to suggest that there is only one kind of scientific theory, and hence situated cognition poses a threat to the descriptive approach. In particular, the reader is cautioned against interpreting the message to be delivered as "analytic logic is bad." The claim, as I will repeat again and again, is that a certain way of describing systems – the ideas of compartmentalized traits, flow, and storage – has obscured the nature of a causal, coupling mechanism (cf. the discussion in Chapter 8 of Altman and Rogoff's work). In effect, descriptive cognitive models reflect an either-or understanding of modules and causal flow, which is inadequate both as a *physical theory* and as a *psychological theory* for understanding how perceptions and concepts are related to each other (cf. the examples in Chapter 9). In contrast, the neurobiological models of Merzenich and Maturana (Chapter 4), Freeman, Edelman, and others (Part II) attempt to replicate codependent modularity, which I call here a *dialectic mechanism*. In short, Wilden's analysis provides a general, philosophical approach to understanding causal processes in ecological systems and hence a better understanding of conceptual systems.

Both-and logic

Anthony Wilden has written a far-reaching book about symbols, knowledge, and information, *The Rules are No Game: The Strategy of Communi-*

cation (1987). With an eclectic drive, similar to Bateson's style, Wilden relates cybernetics, linguistics, and semiotics to produce a theory of communication that applies to cognitive modeling, film theory, and rationality. Indeed, his analysis helps us understand how the conflict between the symbolic approach and situated cognition has arisen in different guises throughout human history. He aims to show that *a combination of approaches, a both-and view, is preferable.*

Provocatively, Wilden argues that the conflict we have experienced in cognitive science is part of an ongoing political struggle for what world view will control human organizations:

> You may rightly ask how a noncontextual, one-dimensional, static, and closed-system logic, based on the principles of the watertight compartment, has continued to dominate our ways of thinking, to the point of ruling contextual and relational views out of court. The answer is that those who presently define what is logical and what is not, have the power to make it so. They have so far had at their command the physical force, the organization, and the means of communication and representation to make this domination real. (p. 62)

Indeed, Francis Bacon's slogan "Knowledge is power," picked up by the proponents of knowledge engineering, claims that codifying all human reasoning into descriptions of the world and rules dictating how to behave is a source of power. Of course, the reasons for the domination Wilden describes are complex: The process of reflecting on conceptual relations in our understanding may itself create figure–ground categorizations that become conceptual dichotomies; the dominant schema for causal reasoning we learn in school breaks complex systems into separately existing components and processes; more general styles of speaking, by which we *articulate* experience in subject–object distinctions, causally order dependent relations into named agents causing sequences of events (Tyler, 1978); and, as Wilden suggests, social relations and communication tools may shape our understanding.

But the rise of new ways of understanding complexity (e.g., Gleick, 1987; Kauffman, 1993; Waldrop, 1992) demonstrates that a combination of world views – admitting different ways of understanding causal relations – is preferable for scientific theorizing. The problem, as I will describe, is that, viewed from the perspective of the traditional analytic, linear way of modeling complex systems, a broader approach is not possible; it appears to involve a contradiction. The solution, as we will find in Wilden's writing, is that a dialectic approach allows world views to be combined without contradiction: We can keep the benefits of the linear, analytic view by embedding it in a broader understanding.

To repeat a key point: This different view of causality involves a different way of reasoning about causal relationships and, hence, is a different kind of logical relation. As a physical theory, it means that subsystems may be modular, yet not separately existing (as in ecological analysis, the environment and the organism depend on each other); as a psychological theory, it means that concepts may have a general–specific relation, such as type–instance, but activate and develop together. Simply put, this is a *both-and* way of viewing system structure and function; specifically, this view (a theory of causality) integrates routine interaction, structure memory, and development.

In the following key passage, Wilden explains how *dialectic logic*, a way of understanding complex systems that fits selectionism and chaos theories of development (Chapters 6 and 7), admits a kind of *causal dependency* that is more general than the *analytic logic* view of separately existing components and linear physical relations. He begins by saying that this broader view of causal dependency will include the more narrow view, rather than making them alternatives that we must choose between:

The dialectic way includes the analytical way as its necessary complement, and neither of them violates the principle of noncontradiction.
    When analytic logic says 'either A or not-A', it means this:
either A *or* not-A

– a choice. When analytic logic says 'both A and not-A' it means this:
both A *and* not-A
– a contradiction.

    When dialectical logic says 'both A and not-A' it means this:

both   ⌐‾‾not-A‾‾¬

and   ⌐‾‾A‾‾¬

– a dependent hierarchy between open system [A] and environment [not-A].

    Analytic logic is a single-level and static logic, outside time and change. It is the symmetrical logic of classical physics.
    Dialectical logic is a many-leveled and dynamic logic, within time – and dependent, like learning, on duration.
    The both-and of analytic logic is a secondary relationship derived by addition from its basic operation of division, either/or. The perspective of analytic logic is thus '*either* either/or *or* both/and.'
    The both-and of dialectical logic is a primary relationship derived by connection from relations between levels, such as the both-and relation between open system and environment. The perspective of dialectical logic is thus '*both* either/or *and* both/and.' (pp. 276–277)

    Wilden's diagram shows that A and not-A coexist as a relation in a dependent hierarchy without *contradiction*. This is not ordinary symbolic (propositional) logic, but a different way of modeling how systems and parts can be *causally related*. The descriptive modeler might assume that dialectic logic is a kind of symbolic logic and provide accordingly a notation and a calculus of derivation rules. The descriptive modeler would then claim to have shown that although there are different kinds of logic (monotonic, first-order, situational, etc.), they are all expressible as a descriptive calculus. This maneuver would seriously miss the point.

Wilden is not saying that we can't represent dialectic, both-and meaning in some kind of notation. Obviously, the diagram Wilden provides is itself a symbolic notation for *presenting* dialectic relations. The issue is how a dialectic causal mechanism (based on codependence) differs from how causality is described in analytic models. The root of the distinction is expressed by the following observation:

> The both-and of analytic logic is a secondary relationship derived by addition from its basic operation of division, either/or.

Analytic logic starts by dividing systems, objectifying into parts and types (this is Lakoff's point; Chapter 3). "Either/or" means that a part is of one type or another. But difficulties arise in modeling the world this way: For example, a penguin has characteristics of a bird and of a fish. Following the analytic approach, the descriptive modeling techniques developed by AI define "both/and" blends in terms of *primary*, "either/or" properties from more general classes (e.g., describing birds and fish). In general, the combination or addition of properties is called *inheritance.* In this way, meaning is compartmentalized and concepts are viewed as nodes (actually islands) in a network. "Both/and" examples of conceptual interactions, as arise in describing penguins and the pope (an unmarried male who is not a bachelor), are viewed as exceptions that must be handled by special mechanisms.[3] Indeed, within these analytic frameworks (referred to as *extensions* to symbolic logic), the kind of inheritance is viewed as a choice – either it is within the standard notation or it is handled by the "both/and" extension:

> The perspective of analytic logic is thus '*either* either/or *or* both/and.'

Descriptive modelers may find themselves continuously drawn back to argue for the value and adequacy of their approach. They may say, "But we can invent a notation; we can handle those cases; look at what the programs can do." As a pragmatic approach for engineering well-defined, nonopen systems, none of this is in dispute. Wilden summarizes very well the accomplishments of the "either/or" perspective:

> You use analytic logic to connect the patterns of stars, measure out the land, aim a siege engine, chart the seas, construct a railway network, discover the malaria parasite, dig a canal, organize communications, find your way to the moon, design an army, build a prison, or structure a corporation. (p. 61)

But analytic logic is just a perspective, one way of describing systems in the world. Its limitations arise in understanding systems whose behavior is driven by *history*, not the current state:

Used alone, analytic logic, static logic, ignores the context of natural and social relationships and fails to recognize the realities of change. It treats every relationship or situation it singles out as a unique, closed, and separate event, as if it is not related to its past and present contexts, and not part of any pattern of events. (p. 61)

Our analysis of Edelman's and Freeman's models of the brain is helpful here. An analytic view suggests that a system is in some state and that its next state is predictable. Both the selectionist and chaotic views of neural organization suggest that the next state is not a simple reconfiguration of parts, like gears turning or bits flowing through a wire. Instead, *subsystems arise together* on a kind of trajectory reflecting past configurations and the functioning of the system in its environment (see Shaw and Todd's formalization of the history function in Chapter 12).

Viewed at this level of abstraction, the dominant cause of physical organization of a dialectic (structurally coupled) system is not substance contact and flow, but *historical relations* between processes. Intuitively, we can view the next state as a selection from a past organization, as if a new system of modules comes into existence, restricted both by *how the system is currently changing* and by *its previous configurations*. Such a system must, of course, still be understandable within our usual views of substance and causality, as illustrated by Edelman's story of the formation of neuronal groups and maps. But understanding the system's operation as developmental – such that learning is inherent in functioning – requires a different kind of analysis, referring to the past configurations of the system within its environment. The claim is not merely that reductionism of the usual sort is scientifically inadequate, but that, as the opening quotes of the chapter attest, scientists must work hard to think about structure – process relationships in a different way. Wilden's analysis is a kind of philosophical thought pump for developing new *kinds* of physical theories.

Fundamentally, the notion of dialectic dependence (eco-logic) is an understanding of *nonlinear causal relations*. Like Bateson and many other theoreticians viewing mental processes from the perspective of biology, Wilden argues that living systems are *open*:

Machines and ordinary physical systems are closed systems; closed or self-contained systems can exist independently of their environments. In contrast, living systems, at the organic level, and social systems, at the person level, are open systems. They depend for their structure and survival on the exchange of matter, energy, and information with their environments. (p. 60)

The key phrase here is "depend for their structure." The structure of a closed system may be causally influenced by the environment. But the existence of parts and their relation to each other in a closed system are understood as existing prior to interaction with the environment. That is to say, *a closed system can have a state without inputs from the environment.* By contrast, an open system has no structure or identity without actively exchanging "matter, energy, and information" with its environment.[4]

This is the notion of *logical dependence* Wilden and other ecological theorists emphasize: The causal relation between system and environment is inherent in the system's *existence*; causality is not merely a matter of the system's operation. The system is dynamically sustained as a functioning unit – indeed, this is what makes it an ecological system. Wilden expresses this (both-and) dependence in terms of the "Extinction Rule": If you delete the environment ("not A"), the system will cease to exist ("A"). In general, this is how functional differentiation may work in the brain, in which one module (A) develops a role *with respect to* the other modules (not A) or one categorization (figure) is constructed with respect to other categorizations (ground).

Wilden describes four causal characteristics of dialectic systems (p. 274):

1. "Unlike oscillating or cyclic systems, the dialectical process is irreversible."
2. "Dialectical change is not a change of motion, but a transformation of organization. Dialectical changes are not matter-energy processes, but semiotic ones. They are changes in levels and types of complexity governed by information."
3. "Dialectical systems . . . depend on their relationships to their (often multiple) environments for sustenance and survival – and often for the origin of certain kinds of change."
4. A dialectical system, unlike a machine or an ordinary physical system, is open to new information and hence capable of the creation of order from disorder, which is "the hallmark of dialectical change."

By this definition, Prigogine's dissipative structures (cf. Steels's robots in Chapter 5 and formalization of emergence in Chapter 8) constitute a dialectic system, as do the chaotic processes in Freeman's model of the brain (Chapter 6) and Edelman's selectionist model of categorization (Chapter 7). In terms of learning, "open to new information" means capable of making new kinds of distinctions. In terms of the concern of descriptive modeling, such a system is capable of developing knowledge (new coordinations and organizers), not just becoming more efficient by compiling or finding new ways to access or assemble what has been categorized and stored by the human designer.

Examples of dialectic relations

Wilden's critique of analytic logic is extremely broad, going well beyond biological processes and focusing especially on human experience and knowledge:

You cannot use analytic logic by itself to understand a feeling, to teach a child, to love a person, to appreciate beauty, to understand history, to enjoy a film, to analyze nature, to explore imagination, to explain society, to recognize individuality, to communicate with others, to create novelty, or to learn the principles of freedom. (p. 61)

With a pluralist perspective, Wilden immediately cautions us to recognize the value of analytic logic and use it appropriately:

We have to be careful at this point not to throw common sense out the window. The 'either/or' of analytic logic is essential to every process of decision; the digital computer could not exist without it. But in the either/or thinking of analytic logic, the 'either' usually excludes the 'or'. Don't let the ingrained pattern of 'all-or-none' thinking lead you to assume that we should try to do without analytic logic or replace it with another one. What I am saying is that we should use analytic logic where it works, and contextual and many-level logics, including both-and logic – dialectic logic – where it doesn't. . . . (Ibid.)

Wilden amply illustrates the value of dialectic analysis throughout his book. He emphasizes that we have many habits of thinking that make it difficult to understand *codependency* between A and not A. Indeed, the dominant view of scientific thinking is so much a particular, analytic view of mechanism, laws, and causality that to suggest that complex systems may develop and operate in a different way may sound at first like an attack on science itself. Ironically, Wilden wouldn't have developed his understanding of dialectic logic without adopting an analytic frame of mind. The trap to avoid, which the descriptive approach has fallen into head first (so to speak), is identifying a descriptive model with the cognitive process being studied. A rational reconstruction or historical revisionism has its place, but it cannot functionally replace the mechanism that made such thinking possible.

To understand how the dialectic and analytic modes of relating might be viewed as coexisting perspectives for understanding living systems, we might begin by considering further Wilden's application of the dialectic analysis to everyday examples. The point of these examples is to reveal how *our understanding* of relationships is not adequately captured by binary oppositions, and such descriptions, once made, confuse our understanding:

The doctrine that binary oppositions are basic to human relationships – they are called the 'unity (or identity) of opposites' – has consistently confused our understanding of the relationships between organisms and environments in nature, be-

tween people and groups in society, and between reality and the domain of images and ideas (whether in verbal, visual, logical, or sensual thought).
    Consider as examples the following pairs of terms:

culture	nature
mind	body
reason	emotion
conscious	unconscious
white	nonwhite
capital	labor

We have only to apply the Extinction Rule to realize that not one of these pairs is a real opposition. They are the symmetrization – the reduction to a single level – of a dependent hierarchy. Only in the imaginary can these categories be seen as symmetrical opposites rather than as relations between levels. The second term in each pair (e.g., emotion) is in fact the environment that the first term (e.g., reason) depends on for sustenance and survival. (Similarly, labor is the source and sustenance of capital.) But by turning each hierarchy upside down like the inverted image of a camera obscura, the first term (e.g., culture) either appears to dominate the second (e.g., nature), or does in fact dominate it (e.g., white and nonwhite). Each term on the left-hand side is an open system apparently free to exploit whatever it defines as its environment. . . . (p. 82)

Strikingly, in Wilden's examples pertaining to cognition, the historically subsequent and organized part views itself as being in control of the whole. But this is an illusion by which the reasoning, conscious person views a descriptive causal story as reality itself.

    Wilden's point, which has been made repeatedly in the philosophical literature, has often been confused with the idea of *binary notation* and *on-off electronic switching*, absurd as this might appear. For example, one will find claims that computers can't handle nonbinary opposition (Rychlak, 1991; discussed in Ford, Hayes, and Adams-Webber, 1993). This is at best a poetic restatement of the problem. The real claim is that the *modeling methods* used by cognitive scientists are inadequate – a shortcoming in the understanding of causal mechanism, not necessarily the computer hardware. Both Darwin III and Mycin can be implemented in the same digital computer, but the formation of parts and their interactions at the level of representational function are quite different. At issue is *our understanding of how systems form and change over time*, not the structure of today's computers or how they operate.

    The binary opposition of inside/outside, agent/environment, knowledge/data, deliberation/action, reasoning/perception, and so on exists *in our descriptions*, our qualitative models of expert systems and human problem solving. This binary opposition *is* related historically (conceptually and culturally) to the binary nature of computers. But saying that the design of computers reflects "a binary way of thinking" confuses the kind of analysis that produced the hardware with the design of the models that run on the machines. It is true that the stored memory architecture of most computers was influenced by an attempt to replicate human calculation using simpler machines (e.g., for calculating missile trajectories in World War II). But it is an open – and *different* – question whether we need to build a different kind of computational substrate to replicate structural coupling and memory as they occur in neural systems.[5]

In summary, Wilden reveals the duality of oppositions we create in analytic descriptions. In contrast, as illustrated by the paintbrush inventors story (Chapter 9), conceptual processes are *contextual, many-dimensional, and open*. This means that a proper both-and view of cognition must relate *both-and conceptualization* to *either-or descriptions*. That is, we need to explain how descriptive analyses relate to conceptual structures and why the either-or perspective takes hold and dominates our attention once it has been constructed, appearing to be the whole story of how cognition works.

To begin, the conceptual change required by a dialectic perspective is not a mere rearrangement of previous ideas. For example, we might simply invert the view by which compartmentalized (descriptively reified) knowledge operates on data:

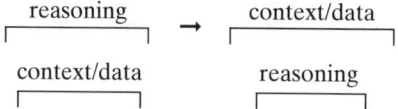

But this is still an either-or view, suggesting priority and control of context over reasoning (e.g., a reactive system). Instead, to invert the dominance of knowledge over the environment, we claim a both-and relationship:

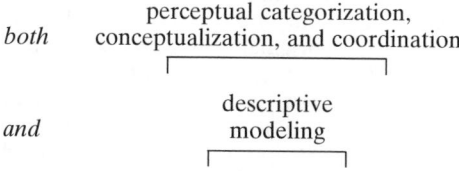

In this diagram, I show that the processes of descriptive modeling are within a dependent hierarchy whose context corresponds to the experiences and capabilities of perceptual categorization, conceptualization, and physical coordination. We saw such a dialectic relation in the interplay of perception, action, and theorizing in the paintbrush example (cf. Figures 9.4 and 9.6). In human society, these aspects of cognition develop together, such that descriptions cannot be viewed as purely derivative from or isomorphic to categorizations, just as coordination is not strictly controlled by instruction and planning. By this view, speaking itself is a kind of coordination that constructs meaningful concepts.

Demonstrating again the power of the dialectic perspective, Wilden applies the concept to the idea of objectivity:

Objectivity in communication is as imaginary as perpetual motion in mechanics. Because communication involves goals, it necessarily involves values. But the critique of objectivity does not imply that all knowledge and communication are subjective (relative to the individual). Taking refuge from "objectivity" in "subjective realism" (or "cultural relativism") is simply a switch between imaginary opposites. Subjectivity is real and unique, but it is not strictly subjective, and it has no opposite.... True subjectivity, like true self-interest, is a "self-and-other" relationship. The so-called "autonomous subject" is another figment of the imaginary. Much of what we believe to be "subjective" or "objective" is really collective, mediated by communication with our environments and other people, conscious or not. (p. 125)

The mutual dependence of subjectivity and objectivity can be understood by changing our understanding of the relation between quantitative and qualitative:

The imaginary opposition between subjectivity and objectivity may be usefully compared with the similar confusion between quality and quantity. In logic as in life quality precedes and constrains quantity. Any decision about quantities is based on prior decisions about (general) framing and the (detailed) punctuation of the subject matter by decisions about qualities, whether these are consciously made or not.

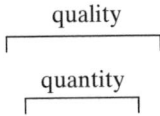

Quality and quantity are not opposites: the second depends on the first. Faced with measuring an object, we have to decide what quality to measure – matter, energy, or information, weight, size, or exchange value, and so on – before making any decisions about quantities. ... Quality and quantity are not of the same level of communication or reality. (In the terminology originally used by Bertrand Russell to distinguish between a class and its members, they are not of the same logical type.) The relationship between quality and quantity is not symmetrical: the one cannot legitimately take the place of the other. (Quantity is a kind of quality, but quality is not a kind of quantity.) Quality and quantity do not exist in an 'either/or' relationship of opposition, but in a 'both-and' relationship between levels. Only in the imaginary do the two appear to be opposites. ... Objectivity is itself a quality, if an imaginary one, as is the assumption that objectivity speaks – or ought to speak – in numbers. (Ibid.)

This passage suggests that *the dialectic notion of relationship underlies all the conceptual shifts* regarding the nature of objectivity, information, context, quality, and so on called for by situated cognition. Furthermore, the passage cautions us once again to avoid lapsing into binary, either-or analysis when we criticize descriptive models. This error of failing to move to a higher level of discussion is recurrent in some situated cognition writing:

It is the community rather than the individual, that defines what a given domain of work is and what it means to accomplish it successfully. (Suchman and Trigg, 1991, p. 73)

The point is not so much that arrangements of knowledge in the head correspond in a complicated way to the social world outside the head, but that they are socially organized in such a way as to be indivisible. (Lave, 1988, p. 1)

As Wilden shows, we cannot understand relationship by trying to extinguish one half of the relation. The limitations of either-or thinking are perpetrated by seeking to make social analyses dominant. It is fine to talk about the social organization of knowledge, but a theory of social change requires talk about arrangements in the head, too.

One may wonder if putting quality over quantity, preconceptual over linguistic, and so on in Wilden's diagrams is not perpetuating the idea of control. To begin, rather than calling the binary oppositions of analytic models *symmetrical opposites*, Wilden might have called them *asymmetrical*, for the binary opposition view presumes that domination is possible over the long run, that one part can be functionally replaced by or redescribed in terms of another. Accordingly, Turvey and Shaw argue for a *symmetrical analysis* (Chapter 11), which recognizes the mutual dependence of the parts or perspectives; this corresponds to Wilden's dialectic logic.

Consistent with Lakoff's (1987) idea that concepts are often grounded in physical postures, we tend to view the higher term in Wilden's diagrams as controlling the lower. Perceptually and conceptually, the upper hand is in control. Redrawing the diagrams from left to right, "NOT A | A," or in concentric circles would only again imply ideas of succession (rightmost gains control) or containment (outermost includes inner), which we don't want. Any spatial layout will tend to be perceived according to the existing conceptual framework we are attempting to change. Probably Wilden drew the diagrams in this way to force us (or to help us) reconceive the relation of the terms. But we should try to view the relation as symmetric in the sense of the Extinction Rule.

Conceptual dependency hierarchies

Wilden intends a dependency diagram to show a *hierarchical* relation. This is clearer when there are more than two levels (Figure 10.1). Recall that the general notion is that the higher level(s) are the environment for the lower levels. The lower, more complex systems come into existence after the environment. But throughout the development process, the functional role of the environment is fundamentally changed by the existence of the developing subsystems. This is clear, for example, in ecological analyses of

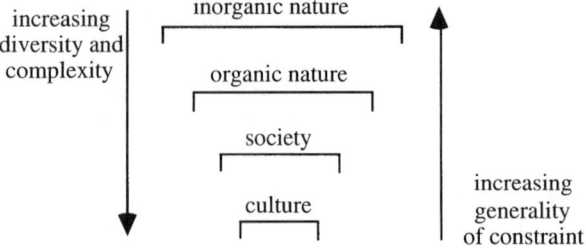

Figure 10.1. "The four major orders of complexity [form] a dependent hierarchy. It is called 'dependent' because the open systems of the lower orders in the diagram depend for their existence on the environment of the higher ones. (Open systems depend on their environments for production, reproduction, and survival.) Complexity increases downwards; the generality of the constraints increases upwards. Note that since the human individual includes all four of these orders of complexity, and the individual organism a complex of two of them, the individual cannot be fitted into this kind of hierarchy." (Reprinted with permission from Wilden, 1987, p. 74.)

predator–prey and symbiotic relationships. As illustrated by the appearance of flowers and visual capabilities of bees, codependence is such that in organic nature it may be difficult to separate the components of the system, even historically, into organism and environment.

Wilden emphasizes that the boundaries represented in Figure 10.1 are open-system boundaries, not separations or barriers. Consider, for example, the relation between the concept of pumping and the practice of painting (Chapter 9). The painters' understanding of pumps changes because of the inquiry about painting. Paintbrushes are seen within the larger context of pumps, but both are changed by this relationship. Now the meaning of a paintbrush – how it operates and what it is supposed to do – is inseparable from the understanding of the complexity of theory and examples of pumps. This conceptual broadening, generalizing the meaning of *pump*, is signified by the inventors' use of the term *pumpoids* as they ask, "Is a rag a kind of pump, too?" The *meaning of these concepts is dialectic* because they developed in relation to each other.

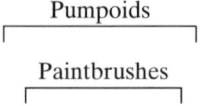

Recalling our analysis of the paintbrush inventors, the relevance of pumping to the present inquiry wasn't inferred by matching descriptions of properties. Rather, *perceptual relations* – seeing the bristles as channels, the paint flowing, and the vibrating – activated the conceptual construct of pumping. Painting, as an activity occurring now, was reconceived within the context of experience about pumps (including perceptions, conceptions, and descriptive theories). Descriptions on different levels of detail were articulated throughout, so it is difficult to order events into a timeline. Indeed, in any individual's experience, the order of thought might have been multiply determined. Undoubtedly, whatever conceptual coupling between paintbrushes and pumping developed prior to the protracted inquiry about the theory of pumpoids was strengthened and elaborated by the story telling and causal reasoning that followed.

To summarize the main points about conceptual dependency from the painting example:

- It is plausible that the conceptualization of pumping became *coupled* to the conceptualization of paintbrushes and painting by virtue of a reactivated perceptual categorization ("I am painting now but suddenly seeing it as pumping right before my eyes."). The previous conceptualization is broadened to encompass the current activity.
- Through descriptive modeling of the painting situation and what was previously said and experienced with pumps, a network develops that includes perceptual categorizations and awareness of differences. This process is descriptively modeled by *structure-mapping* theories of analogy.
- The resulting concepts include a combination of verbal and nonverbal categorizations. But strictly speaking, the instance (paintbrushes) and the type (pumps) are dependent. In some sense, the example "a paintbrush" represents the class; the part stands for the whole (metonymy).

I am hypothesizing that a hierarchical relationship of concepts, which is, of course, well known in cognitive science, may be organized through structural coupling in the brain. Moving up the hierarchy might occur by activation of global maps, such that instances are maps that activate and hence are subsumed by their generalizations (cf. Figure 7.2). This mechanism would be consistent with other observations that descriptive models based on stored properties do not strictly fit analogical "reasoning."[6] Again, I emphasize that both coupling and inference are combined in normal experience; the point is that more than inference is occurring.

A coupling mechanism also fits the way in which experts relate concepts by combining space and causality (e.g., the hyphenated term *brain mass-lesion* combines a location, substance type, and cause). Coupling also explains how previous descriptions are reinterpreted by generalizing (the conceptual broadening of the "SIGNIFICANT" example in Chapter 2). In general, the apparently perceptual or gestalt reorganization of conceptions, as in the paintbrush example, suggests coupling relations, as opposed to inferences. Conceptual coupling also fits our common experience of isolated "islands" of thought (after 6 months of media bombardment, you finally notice that Ron Goldman, who sits in the adjacent cubicle, has the same name as the person on the news every night), as well as the overly rigid, dichotomous views of multiple personalities (Rosenfield, 1992).

A conceptual dependency is an example of a gestalt. In a critique of descriptive cognitive modeling, Wertheimer (1985) summarizes the idea:

> What is a Gestalt? It is an articulated whole, a system, within which the constituent parts are in dynamic interrelation with each other and with the whole, an integrated totality within which each part and subpart has the place, role, and function required for it by the nature of the whole. It is the antithesis of a sum, or of a bundle, or of a tree diagram or of a flow chart whose component parts happen to be arbitrarily or haphazardly connected. The structure of a typical Gestalt is such that alteration of one part almost inevitably also produces changes in other parts or in the whole itself; parts of a Gestalt structure are not isolated components that are indifferent to each other. A slight displacement of a single playing card in a house of cards will make the entire structure come tumbling down. A break in one tiny point in a soap bubble produces an instant and dramatic change in the entire whole. In a Gestalt, the nature of the whole and of its constituent parts are all integrated, such that the characteristics of the whole determine the characteristics of each part and its function in the whole, and the characteristics of various parts are mutually interdependent. (p. 23)

When Wertheimer says that the flow chart is "arbitrarily and haphazardly connected," he does not mean that it is without design or rationale. Instead, flowchart parts do not intrinsically depend on each other, but rather depend on a description of what the parts mean, which, of course, is open to interpretation. Similarly, a structural diagram of an analogy shows only (and is indeed intended to show) how *independently conceived* parts are related.

In a gestalt system, the parts have an identity because they are within a system. Seeing and naming of the parts occurs in a process of insight from the whole to the parts. That is, we view the relationship *as a system* first, and this "top-down determination" allows us to "speak of part–whole relationships" (p. 25). For example, when we are relating pumps and paintbrushes, we view paintbrush-as-a-pumpoid as a conceptual system and speak of pumps and paintbrushes with respect to this relation. Indeed, it is by such reconceiving of a description-within-a-setting that we understand a flowchart, too.

Wertheimer's examples involve physical structures, revealing that gestalt relations are of general value for modeling complex systems. For example, he applies the idea of a gestalt to physics: "The characteristics of a whole determine the attributes of its parts, as for instance, in an electric field" (p. 25).

The ecological approach to epistemology is similar, as in Bateson's characterization of the "ecology of mind" (quoted at the start of Chapter 8): "Mind is immanent in the larger system, man plus environment." By *immanent* Bateson emphasizes that mental processes are developed and manifest in the larger system. The system cognitive scientists and robot builders seek to understand is not a mind or an environment in isolation. For Bateson, a cyberneticist, we must study mind (A) and environment (not-A) together because we are actually studying *circuits*, which do not reside in one part, nor could they exist separately in one side (cf. Figure 9.5). Bateson's historical commentary is illustrative of the conceptual shift required for a dialect theory:

> The word "cybernetics" has become seriously corrupted since it was put into circulation by Norbert Wiener. And Wiener himself is partly to blame for this corruption of the conception in that he associated "cybernetics" with "control." I prefer to use the term "cybernetic" to describe complete circuiting systems. For me, the system is man-and-environment; to introduce the notion of control would draw a boundary between these two, to give a picture of man versus environment.
>
> We used to argue whether a computer can think. The answer is, "No." What thinks is a total circuit, including perhaps a computer, a man, and an environment. Similarly, we may ask whether a brain can think, and again the answer will be, "No." What thinks is a brain inside a man who is part of a system which includes an environment. (1991, p. 202)

Recall that this is the interpretation we give of Mycin's coupling to the environment through the human's interpretation and response to its questions (Chapter 2). This becomes the foundational approach of ecological psychology in the work of Gibson and others who emphasize that our description of the environment as psychologists must be with respect to an agent's actions and categorization capabilities.

Bateson also understands conceptual hierarchies in terms of circuits:

> We shall expect that information (i.e., news of difference) about events in one circuit may be "fed back" to change some parameter within that circuit. It is the use of information about information that is characteristic of multiple-step hierarchies. In a more lineal paradigm, the hierarchies of naming and classification are similar. The ladders – name, name of the name, name of the name of the name; and item, class, class of classes, etc. – are familiar. (Ibid.)

A good part of Bateson's work in diverse fields consisted of diagnosing how conceptual coupling (especially "seeing as") happens transparently, such that contexts, actions, and their classes are frequently used interchangeably in inferential argumentation:

> Less familiar are the errors which people continually and disastrously make in failing to recognize the logical typing of their own ideas. The concept "exploration" provides a typical paradigm. Psychologists are surprised that "exploration" in rats is not extinguished if the rat encounters danger or pain inside boxes which he explores. But "exploration" is not a name of an action. It is the name of a *context* of action, or perhaps a class of actions which class is to be defined by the animal's perception of the context in which he is acting. The "*purpose*" of exploration is to find out which boxes (for example) are safe, where "purpose" is a partial synonym for "name of context." Now if the rat finds an electric shock in the box, his exploration has been

a success. He now knows that that box is unsafe. He obviously will not give up exploring after that success. (pp. 202–203)

In related examples concerning crime, Bateson argues that actions are organized by an agent's "perception of context." This corresponds again to the idea that actions are not merely input–output operations that may be directly rewarded or punished, but that behavior proceeds according to implicit, broader conceptions of role and relationship, which constitute the environment for the actor. Hence, in a conceptual system feedback is construed and evaluated by the actor, not something strictly given by outsiders.

I have presented Bateson's application of dialectic relations to show how it helps us better understand conceptual structure and development. I will conclude this chapter with some more general observations about science that help us understand how levels of analysis are related.

Scientific levels as dialectic

Eco-logic is *a scientific approach*, a strategy for explaining how systems work and develop: What *parts* we will identify and how we will *describe* those parts will be with respect to the whole system. Stephen Jay Gould (1987) provides a useful introduction:

Thus, we cannot factor a complex social situation into so much biology on one side, and so much culture on the other. We must seek to understand the emergent and irreducible properties arising from an inextricable interpenetration of genes and environments. In short, we must use what so many great thinkers call, but American fashion dismisses as political rhetoric from the other side, a dialectical approach. (p. 153)

The idea of dialectic relation is often wrongly equated with one of its applications, *dialectics*:

The Marxian process of change through the conflict of opposing forces, whereby a given contradiction is characterized by a primary and a secondary aspect, the secondary succumbing to the primary, which is then transformed into an aspect of a new contradiction. (*American Heritage Dictionary* online)

Gould believes that dialectics has been "discarded because some nations of the second world have constructed a cardboard version as an official political doctrine." But this is no excuse for failing to understand and use appropriately the more general dialectic philosophy of change:

When presented as guidelines for a philosophy of change, not as dogmatic precepts true by fiat, the three classical laws of dialectic embody a holistic vision that views change as interaction among components of complete systems, and sees the components themselves not as a priori entities, but as both the products of and the inputs to the system. Thus the law of "interpenetrating opposites" records the inextricable interdependence of components; the "transformation of quantity to quality" defends a systems-based view of change that translates incremental inputs into alterations of state; and the "negation of negation" describes the direction given to history because complex systems cannot revert exactly to previous states. (1991, p. 154)

Note that the dialectic view of systems provides an interesting twist to Herb Simon's view of a "nearly decomposable system." In his *Sciences of the Artificial* (1969), Simon argues that such a system is one in which intersystem interactions are considerably less important than intrasystem interactions – as in the intermolecular forces of rare gases:

We can treat the individual particles for many purposes as if they were independent of each other.... As a second approximation we may move to a theory of nearly decomposable systems, in which the interactions among subsystems are weak but not negligible. (p. 211)

But in structurally coupled systems, such as the chaotic attractors of the olfactory bulb and cortex (Chapter 6), short-run behavior is *not independent*; the configuration of a "component" directly depends on the state of another component. Indeed, structural coupling goes to the extreme: The *short-run* behavior of a component appears to "depend on the aggregate behavior of the other components." The analytic framework of near decomposability is useful to predict, for certain kinds of dynamic systems, how subsystems will behave. But studies of neural systems, such as the owl monkey's sensorimotor maps (Chapter 4), suggest that development and memory cannot be viewed by such a localization hypothesis (Chapter 3).

Simon acknowledges that only "very special dynamic systems" will have the property of near decomposability, and he postulates that hierarchical systems, such as social organizations, have this property. The mistake is to assume that an approach that works well for *describing* complexity (decomposition into parts and interactions) is an explanation of how the system's operations came to be what they are. Not every causal story is a developmental story. In particular, systems with memory, whose configurations are reconstructions of historical interactions, may have systemwide, relational origins. Again, the notion of *interaction* is inadequate, for it views operation in terms of fixed parts. What is needed is a transactional, developmental view.

Most descriptive cognitive models are based on the approach of near decomposability. Modelers name parts and assembly rules for the flow of information and construction of outputs. All they have done is to mechanize analytic descriptions. The relation of the data and model to the initial description is circular. How the system came to be in the wild is not explained.

The shortcoming of near decomposability is also important in relating the sciences to each other. The relevant factors to be related on different levels of analysis depend on the context of inquiry. Hence, in studying cognition (as opposed to genetic reproduction, for example), biological and social perspectives interpenetrate. Again, this is the contextualist position (Chapter 3): "The claim of contextualism is that the interpretation of 'basic units' at any one level of description will necessarily rely upon contextual factors at another level" (Hoffman and Nead, 1983, p. 523).

Gould (1987) reminds us again that an either-or approach to science has made the dialectic view appear threatening, as if rejection of reductionism is the antithesis of science:

Our struggle is to figure out how biology affects us, not whether it does. The first level of more sophisticated argument that goes beyond crude nature–nurture dichotomies is "interactionism" – the idea that everything we do is influenced by both biology and culture. . . . (p. 152)

But the extreme form of this, advocated by "biological determinists,"

separates biology and culture; it still views genes as primary, deep, and real, and culture as superficial and imposed. . . . The chief fallacy . . . is reductionism – the style of thinking associated with Descartes and the bourgeois revolution, with its emphasis on individuality and the analysis of wholes in terms of underlying properties of their parts. . . . (p. 153)

Hence, we see the real fallacy of arguments about realism: Arguing whether the parts are "really" there or not misses the point that an explanation based on underlying parts won't work anyway. Such explanations aren't wrong because relativism is right, but because reductionism is inappropriate:

We must . . . go beyond reductionism to a holistic recognition that biology and culture interpenetrate in an inextricable manner. One is not given, the other built upon it. Although stomping dinosaurs cannot make continents drift, organisms do create and shape their environment. . . . Individuals are not real and primary, with collectivities (including societies and cultures) merely constructed from their accumulated properties. Cultures make individuals too; neither comes first, neither is more basic. . . . (Ibid.)

Now in the sense that each level has its own emergent relations, we can view the system hierarchically – not in Simon's reductionistic sense of separately operating parts whose products flow up and down – but as a system whose levels constitute each other (a dependency hierarchy):

[T]he notion of hierarchical levels that cannot be reduced, one to the next below is no appeal to mysticism. A claim for the independence of human culture is not an argument for fundamental ineffability (like a soul), but only for the necessity of explaining culture with principles different from the laws of evolutionary biology. New levels require an addition of principles; they neither deny nor contradict the explanations appropriate for lower levels. . . . In this sense, the notion of partially independent hierarchical levels of explanation strikes me as a statement of common sense, not mystery or philosophical mumbo-jumbo. (p. 69)

Thus "near decomposability" works for descriptive explanation of structures and operation over the short run. But because it is based on compartments, flow, and storage, such a framework is inadequate for *developmental* explanations. In particular, the view of knowledge as individually conceived and transmitted through a culture fails to show how an individual's self-conception is inherently social, such that interest, values, and contributions are formed as *social transactions* (Figure 1.2).

The idea that theories of context and organism interpenetrate is perhaps most developed in ecological psychology. The idea of a *niche* in particular relates an organism's evolution, behavior, and even the physics of interactions. Gould defines a niche as "an expression of the location and function of a species in a habitat" (pp. 183–184). But is a niche "an organism's address or its profession"? Isn't a niche fixed relative to plasticity of behaviors? "Organisms do create ecospace through their activities, but the nature of physical space and resources sets important limits." In the next chapter, I round out the discussion of ecological theory by elaborating the ideas of a niche and affordance, which helps us understand further the nature of coupling and feedback in biological systems.

11 The ecological approach to perception

The invariance of perception with varying samples of overlapping stimulation may be accounted for by invariant information and by an attunement of the whole retino-neuro-muscular system to invariant information. The development of this attunement, or the education of attention, depends on past experience, but not on the storage of past experiences.

> James G. Gibson, *The senses considered as perceptual systems*, 1966, p. 262

My hypothesis is that there has to be an awareness of the world before it can be put into words. You have to see it before you can say it. Perceiving precedes predicating. . . . The parts of it he can name are called concepts, but they are not all of what he can see.

> James G. Gibson, *The ecological approach to visual perception*, 1979, pp. 260–261

Toward the reconciliation of the situated and symbolic views

In the study of knowledge that I have broadly described as situated cognition, a few ideas stand out:

- Neurobiological systems have a form of *self-organization with memory* that is different in kind from the mechanism of storage and retrieval systems (e.g., Merzenich's model of sensorimotor maps in Chapter 4; Freeman's model of rabbit olfaction in Chapter 6; Edelman's model of perceptual categorization in Chapter 7).
- Construction of simple animal-like robots is facilitated by *designing the robot-in-its-environment as one system* (e.g., Steels's analysis of emergence in Chapter 8).
- The relation between internal structure and changes to the environment is *transactional*; that is, events are symmetric – "processes and contexts mutually define one another and function as aspects of a whole" (the analysis of Altman and Rogoff in Chapter 8).

I summarized these ideas in the previous chapter under the broad rubric of *dialectic mechanism*, emphasizing for cognitive scientists and robot builders alike that we are talking about *a kind of causal mechanism* – new to engineers but common to biological systems – that needs to be understood if we are to replicate the flexibility of human conceptualization, memory, and coordination. I suggested that just as we understand the environment to be an ecological system, we could view the internal, neural activation,

246

development, and interactions of categories as an ecological system. By Bateson's and Maturana's analyses, the representational relations of such a system are tautological; the system is *structure determined* (Chapter 4). Thus, I highlighted in Wilden's analysis how conceptual relations develop such that they arise together and are codependent. I illustrated this idea by two examples in Chapter 9:

1. The codependence of perceiving *representational forms* in the Nice message and the *conception of a situation* (perceptual categories, linguistic meanings, and context are coconstructed, rather than context being strictly prior to interpretation in time).
2. The codependence of *visual perception of new features* (bristles seen as channels) and *articulated analogies* ("a paintbrush is a kind of pump") in the invention of a synthetic paintbrush (again, perceptual categories and conceptualization arise together).

In both examples, the idea of dialectic relation is described as a kind of *coupling* mechanism, which I contrasted with the sequential causal relations of *inferences*, in which categories are chained (cf. Table 8.2). Specifically, perceptual categories may be coupled to conceptual categories, and conceptual categories may be coupled to each other. This claim is supported by how the categories develop in time (simultaneous versus sequential) and by the process of feature construction in perceptual systems (e.g., new visual groupings, figure–ground shifts; cf. the summary of situated robot learning in Table 8.1). The remainder of this book further develops the hypothesis that categories may form in two ways: by coupling and by inference. In effect, the analysis of knowledge representations (Part I) and new robots (Part II) has moved us to the point of reconciling the situated and what I have called the descriptive modeling (symbolic) perspectives. The seeds of this reconciliation are to be found in the work of James G. Gibson and his ecological theory of perception.

Unfortunately, as is perhaps apparent in the first chapter-opening quote, Gibson's work is often no more comprehensible or useful to AI researchers than the early situated cognition rails against representation. Indeed, Gibson's work can be viewed as a form of contextualism (Chapter 3), and as such it anticipates the 1980s arguments of Lakoff, Winograd, Brooks, Agre, and others. Gibson's remarks about storage (in 1966!) were hardly greeted enthusiastically by a community that was only then inventing semantic net models of memory – and doing so with considerable success. Stopping the descriptive (symbolic) approach then would have indeed been throwing out the baby with the bathwater.

What makes Gibson's work more germane today is that the descriptive approach to cognitive modeling has matured, and its limitations are now of interest to many cognitive scientists – especially the relation of perception to inference, the subtext of connectionism research. Gibson addressed in careful detail the mechanism of perception and sought to contrast it with the mechanism of inference by calling it "direct." But his examples and terminology are more easily understood if you know (and agree with) what he is already trying to say. And his insights are sometimes overstated – referring to the quote previously referenced and recalling the experience of the paintbrush inventors attempting to understand their partners' talk about pumping – in the creation of a generative metaphor, some people may "say it" before others can "see it" (though the claim may hold for the first person who saw the bristles as channels).

Thus, this chapter serves as a bridge to introduce the reader to the debate about *direct perception*, which I elaborate in Part IV in terms of the distinction between coupling and inference. My approach here is to introduce Gibson's theory by way of its specialization in the *ecological psychology* of Turvey and Shaw. Indeed, my entire presentation of situated robots and neurobiology in Part II is just a setup for explaining ecological theories – thus proceeding from engineering designs and new scientific models backward to the philosophy and intuitions that inspired them. With the philosophy more credible, we can go forward again to reexamine what ecological theorists were saying and finally understand how their ideas complement the descriptive modeling approach (Chapters 13 and 14).

Turvey and Shaw's interpretation of ecological psychology directly applies to the design of situated robots; indeed, they cite that work and draw the relations for us. Like some of the situated robot research, Turvey and Shaw's analysis focuses on the navigation of insects, using the concepts of *information* and *dialectic relation* already presented (Chapters 4 and 10). The example of a dragonfly's navigation is especially useful for understanding the ideas of affordance and direct perception. I believe these ideas to be central for understanding what conceptualization adds to perceptual categorization, and thus pivotal for moving from today's situated robot designs to human capabilities.

To further explain the ideas of affordance and direct perception and to show why they have been difficult to understand, I survey the different meanings of *information* in the literature and show how they can be arranged on a spectrum that addresses different aspects of cognition: sensing, perceiving, and conceiving. That is, the same word is used for different concepts. In effect, the tension between Gibson and cognitive scientists of the 1980s is really a conflict between the study of animal cognition in the large and the study of people. The analytic notion of *knowledge* is fundamentally different in the two domains of animal survival-navigation and symbolic reasoning; one emphasizes *perceptual coordination*, the other *conceptual coordination*. Both are required for the study of human cognition

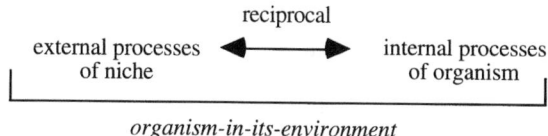

Figure 11.1. Dialectic view of the organism-in-its-environment as the system to be studied.

(cf. my breakdown of symbolic reasoning into subconscious and descriptive-manipulative aspects in Figure 9.5).

All of this is a prelude to the next chapter, where I review in detail the debate about direct perception. I show how the debate can be resolved by distinguishing between "direct" categorization occurring as *structural coupling* and second-order, "semantic" *categorization of reference* occurring when people make inferences. Thus, I show that both the situated and descriptive points of view are complementary; and in effect, acknowledging their relative contributions provides the basis for understanding the nature of consciousness and its manifestations in different animal species.

The reciprocal view of knowledge

The ecological approach to perception strives for a functional description of coordination as a sustained perceptual-motor relation of the organism to the environment (Turvey and Shaw, 1995, p. 165). To analyze coordinated behavior, ecological psychologists characterize the organism-in-its-environment as a dialectic, *reciprocal relation* (Figure 11.1).

This idea, expounded by Bateson, von Foerster, and Wilden, inspired the analysis and neurobiological modeling of Merzenich (Chapter 4), Freeman (Chapter 6), and Edelman (Chapter 7), the reactive approach to robot design (Chapter 5), and Schön's theory of generative metaphor (Chapter 9).

Information processing theory has been based on a substance view of information; thus perceiving is sampling (Figure 11.2). Sampling operates either directly on the input stream (words) or on symbols created from "transducers" operating on more primitive stimuli (sounds, pixels). In either case, perceiving is a kind of mapping process onto stored descriptions and is not inherently a learning process; reasoning coordinates action. Even simple connectionism, which limits the role of inference, assumes that inputs (and outputs) are supplied (Chapter 3).

Gibson, the central figure in the ecological psychology of perception, repeatedly criticized the descriptive perspective as equating all physical aspects of information processing with conscious deliberation or inference

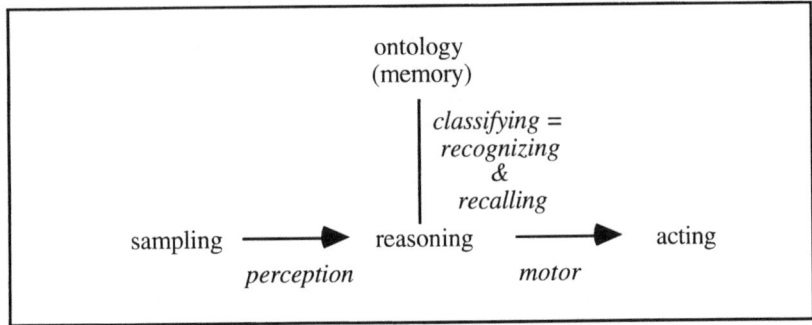

Figure 11.2. Descriptive (information processing) view of perception as sampling information in the environment.

(Figure 3.2). Today, Turvey and Shaw, two prominent ecological psychologists trying to reform cognitive science, express their nemesis as follows:

> The disembodying of cognition is consonant with organism–environment dualism and reinforced by the choice of what counts as a paradigmatic cognitive phenomenon. Popular choices are the human capabilities of syntax, problem solving, remembering, expert knowledge, and the like. These phenomena seem to be so focused *at* or *in* the individual, and so trivially dependent on the current environment and ongoing behavior, that they invite analysis in purely formal, abstract terms and the modeling of the environment and behavior (conceived as inputs and outputs, respectively) in the same abstract terms. (1995, p. 154)

From the ecological perspective, the descriptive approach ignores the nature of perception "in the wild." In particular, all cognitive processing must not be viewed as relying on inference:

> The presumed logical independence [of the knower and the known] has sponsored theories of "knowing about" in which organisms are continually in the business of figuring out the world in which they act, much like detectives facing the scene of a crime with only vague clues as to the perpetrator. (p. 148)[1]

As I will show, the controversy between the symbolic and ecological views can be resolved if both sides acknowledge the other's perspective. There are two coordination mechanisms – coupling and inference – whose functional and developmental relations must be theoretically elaborated.

Turvey and Shaw aspire to cognitive theories like the laws of physics, which abstract from actual situations to general laws. In contrast, they claim that problem-solving studies are based on *concrete descriptions*, referring directly to objects, events, and operations of the domain itself. If physics were like this, it would describe the colors of apples rather than the properties and components of light. What is wanted, according to Turvey and Shaw, is a more abstract account of "knowing about," more generic than any of its manifestations and less complex than a problem-solving account. Specifically, how researchers describe the mechanism of knowing in an insect must be integrally related to how they describe the known environment.

In short, the ecological approach to perception adopts the gestalt perspective (Chapter 10) in viewing the organism-in-its-environment as a cognitive system and viewing psychology inherently as a study of an ecology. This follows from Bateson's claim that epistemology is a part of biology, what he called "the science of knowing." This approach emphasizes the relational, *dynamic* aspect of knowledge (Bateson, 1991, p. 232; idea credited to McCulloch, p. 216). Rather than beginning with a preconceived anatomy of the organism, an ecological approach identifies the parts and attributes of the parts *with respect to the functioning of the whole*. This turns the analysis inside out: One views the environment as *functioning for* the organism (as *being fit* for the species' evolution and fit for knowing about) and the organism as being fit for knowing, learning, surviving, and reproducing in this environment.[2]

Knowing about as a disposition

In ecological psychology, as formulated by Turvey and Shaw (1995), knowledge is a relation between the knower and the known. Organisms are physical systems with a capacity to know:

> The disposition to know is a natural property of a certain class of material systems called organisms. Historically, all attempts to understand this property have been shaped by the metaphysical stance of dualism. Psychologists and philosophers have long referred to the dualism of mind and body, identifying the need for two noninterconvertible languages (mentalese and physicalese) to describe what appear to be two radically contrasting aspects of nature. Close relatives of the dualism of mind and body are symbol–matter dualism, subjective–objective dualism, and perception–action dualism. To adopt dualism in any of the preceding forms is to cleave to a particular methodology in which the two things referred to are defined independently of each other, and interpreted through independent scientific accounts. (p. 147)

In contrast, the dualism of descriptive theories begins by breaking cognitive behavior into world and idea and then seeks to bring them together in the subject's mind. The result is, as Dewey said (Chapter 3), a collection of pieces that now need to coordinate and flow. These "conceptual divisions in science give rise to mysteries . . . that become apparent as soon as questions are raised about how the states or processes in question are connected" (Turvey and Shaw, 1995, p. 148).

To avoid a dualist account, Turvey and Shaw build on Gibson's idea of *direct perception* or *direct apprehension*. The idea of *directness* means without intermediate categorizations, such as beliefs involved in inference, and without a memory involving retrieval and matching of descriptive representations (pp. 156, 165).[3] The theory of direct perception fundamentally acknowledges the presence of physical constraints in the environment by defining information with respect to the environment and perception with respect to information:

Very importantly, direct perception does not create the epistemological paradoxes that would be expressed by phrases such as "the dragonfly's visual system invents its surroundings," "the thicket and the prey are illusions of the dragonfly's brain," "the dragonfly has foreknowledge of space," "the dragonfly has foreknowledge of the basic concepts needed to interpret the signals from its sensory organs," and so on. For Gibson, perception is specific to the environment and to self-movements because (a) information is specific to the environment and to self-movements, and (b) perception is specific to information. (p. 165)

Turvey and Shaw are realists, but they seek to avoid at the same time requiring innate categories by which the environment is known. Instead, they describe the environment as it is physically knowable and *knowing as a physical interaction.*

For Turvey and Shaw, a theory of categorization is to be based on a *biologically relevant information theory*, whose top priority must be an understanding of *specificity*: "of how one thing can specify another and how specificity can be preserved over different and time-varying components of an organism–environment system." In effect, specificity plays the role in their theory of representation that correspondence plays in an objectivist theory. But rather than sampling, perception establishes a reciprocal relation in the physical coordination of the organism: The category specifies an interactive potential, and the environment and self-movements specify the category. This is what Maturana called a *structural coupling*. The reciprocal relation is an *invariance* within time-varying sensory changes within a movement coordination (cf. the Pierce–Kuipers robot in Chapter 6 and Prometheus in Chapter 7). Specificity is with respect to the organism's self-motion; therefore, what counts as information is temporally bound to activity. Grounding "knowing about" in the interactional dynamics of perceiving and moving will help us understand "the persistence of intention over perception–action cycles," another reciprocal relation (p. 166).

Niches, affordances, and invariants

Let's step through Turvey and Shaw's analysis to understand the ideas of invariance and knowing about. We begin with a distinction between a habitat and a niche:

The term habitat refers to where an organism lives, the term niche refers to how it lives.

One principal goal of evolutionary ecology is descriptions of the surfaces and substances surrounding an organism that capture uniquely the fit of that organism to its surroundings and clarify the partitioning of any given habitat into distinct niches. (p. 151)

Here is the beginning of the process of defining the organism's behavior and the environment in a symmetric way. The environment for the organism is effectively a partitioning of the habitat (where the organism lives) into interactional surfaces and substances (how it lives). That is, what constitutes a surface and a substance *for the organism* is what the ecological psychologist must study, both as a description of what is out there and how it is partitioned categorically within coordinated behavior.

This partitioned environment, the niches, can be described in terms of a space of *affordances*:

Gibson . . . coined the term affordance to provide a description of the environment that was directly relevant to the conducting of behavior. (p. 152)

Turvey and Shaw give the example of an animal standing by a creek that is too wide to jump across. But an animal running, approaching the creek, perceives that it "affords" jumping:

A change of pace or a change of location can mean that a brink in the ground now affords leaping over whereas at an earlier pace or location it did not. . . .
The environment-for-the-organism is dynamic and action-oriented while the environment-in-itself, that which has been the target of most modeling in the latter decades of the present century, is fixed and neutral with respect to the organism and its actions. . . . (Ibid.)

The example of a running animal highlights the essential characteristics of affordances: They are relative to coordinated action, and they are perceived by the organism-in-action. This means that perception of the opportunity for action (such as jumping the river) is also within the activity itself, as opposed to being a "view from nowhere" that objectively describes the environment. "What is (perceptually) the case" for a dragonfly, a horse, and a human alike depends on what the organism is doing, and, as we will see, for some animals this includes how it is *conceiving what it is doing.*

In short, an affordance is *a scientist's description* of the environment relevant to some organism's coordinated action:

An affordance of layout is an invariant combination of properties of substance and surface taken with reference to an organism and specific to an action performable by the organism. (Ibid.)

Layout, as used here, refers to a relation between the environment and the organism. Layout is a way of describing the organism's perception of the environment as *being* a niche, a configuration enabling possible actions:

Affordances are opportunities for action and perception of them is the basis by which an organism can control its behavior in a forward-looking manner, that is prospectively. To assume this essential role, however, the term affordance cannot refer to states of affairs that depend on perception or conception for their existence but must refer to real opportunities. From our perspective, this relatively innocuous identification of a niche as a space of real opportunities for action promises to revolutionize the study of cognition. (Ibid.)

Affordances are relations between space, time, and action that work for the organism ("real opportunities"). Perception-in-action is revealing the possibilities for action ("prospectively" but *within* a coordination) – what Maturana calls "bringing forth a world of actions" (Chapter 4). This is the mutuality: What the world *is* to the organism depends on what the organism is doing and might do next. An affordance is therefore a physical disposition but not a static or inherent property of the environment. As a *dynamic*, relational property, an affordance exists *within* a coordination as part of a circuit (Figures 7.4 and 9.6).

Conception may also be coupled to action, as we saw in the stories of the message from Nice and the paintbrush inventors (Chapter 9), but inferential action (reasoning) provides a way of separating conceptualization from direct perception (Chapters 12 and 13). For the moment, we are only concerned with perception and coupled conceptualization, not with inference. In the case of the dragonfly, all affordances are by assumption perceptual; in humans jumping over creeks, the categorization can be assumed to always be conceptual, too. In horses and dogs, the distinction is less clear. For the moment, whether conceptualization is occurring is irrelevant; we are concerned with the nature of perceptual categorization.

As another example, consider the perceptual categorization of an object's *heft*. Heft is detected by moving an object, such as by moving a milk carton up and down to determine how full it is. Heft is not weight per se but the perceived resistance of the object in motion. Heft is a relation between the mover, the object, and physical interactions involving gravity and atmosphere. Given such a combination, we say that the object *affords moving in a certain manner*. In contrast, *mass* is a property of the object and *weight* is a relation between the object and gravity. Heft is relative to an organism's perception–action coordination, which is characteristic of an affordance relation.

An affordance is an *invariance* in the sense of being a recurrent, *generalized* relation between the environment and the agent's activity (pp. 153, 161). The invariance is a dynamic relation, a disposition whose characteristics are prone to change over time. For example, the relation of "a space that affords jumping" is an invariance because this *categorization* of the environment is more general than the particular creek and many other aspects of the runner's current experience. The same organism–environment–activity relation will recur in many physically different circumstances, such as puddles at crosswalks, crevices in the snow, and so forth. To repeat: The relation is not inherent in the creek or the organism, but is a property of the creek with respect to the organism's ongoing activity (such as running perpendicular to the creek). The term *affordance* emphasizes that this is a *property with respect to action*. That is, its existence is real, but only with respect to this *dynamic frame of reference*.

Turvey and Shaw emphasize that an affordance is a special kind of dispositional property, one that "is reciprocated or complemented by another dispositional property" (p. 152). That is, we define the informational properties of the environment (what is known about the niche) with respect to the properties of the organism to act:

An affordance is a particular kind of physical disposition, one whose complement is a property of an organism. . . . The upshot is that, from the perspective of "knowing about," an organism and its niche constitute two structures that relate in a special way such that an understanding of one is, simultaneously, an understanding of the other. (pp. 152–153)

As we saw in Chapter 10, this is the essence of a dialectic model of causality. By this maneuver – attributing properties to the environment and organism that are grounded in how they influence each other – we attain scientific objectivity without dualism: "They act and react in reciprocal but distinct ways that nevertheless fulfill one another."

Defining physical properties with respect to "an opportunity for action" is an attempt to ensure that the observer-scientist does not adopt a language of description that inherently has no bearing on organism behavior, leading to paradoxes of correspondence, mapping, transduction, and so on: "There must be reciprocal expressions of the organism as knower and the environment as known." That is, how we describe the environment *requires* a physical theory of *how it is knowable*.[4]

Energy and information

To understand what is meant by an "opportunity for action," we need to elaborate on the idea of *detection*. When we say that the dragonfly's "maneuvering through a thicket to nab a gnat" consists of an operation of "detecting information" (Turvey and Shaw, 1995, pp. 155–160), we are relating a description of the environment to a description of action. This detection operation is not a process of matching descriptions. It does not mean that the information in the environment is encoded or represented in the sense of being independently characterized in some structures. Indeed, it is unnecessary to talk about encodings in the dragonfly because the concepts of reference and meaning are irrelevant in an organism that doesn't *make inferences about* its world. (This distinction is so important and has been so roundly missed in the debates that I devote an entire chapter to it, Chapter 13.)

An ecological, symmetric analysis focuses on the processes occurring in the dragonfly in-the-thicket *system*. This system is always changing. Processes transition to other processes because of an energy exchange. The objective of Turvey and Shaw's analysis of the dragonfly's flight is to describe information in terms of energy exchange.

How are energy and information related? For an organism to detect anything, there must be some "pattern of variety" in the physical environment, as explained by Wilden (1987):

> Information in the simplest sense is a pattern of variety (such as the number of this chapter) carried by a matter-energy marker or medium (in this case ink and paper). . . . (p. 72)[5]

What makes variety information is the observer's categorizing:

> Information is in no intrinsic way distinguishable from any other form of variety (W. Ross Ashby). Information is not inherently distinct from noise. In and for a given observer and a given system–environment relation, variety recognized as information is *coded* variety, and variety not so recognized is noise, i.e., *uncoded* variety. . . . (p. 183)

By *coded* Ashby meant "perceived as ordered," not necessarily a description in some conventional language:

> Information is a relationship, not a thing. . . . The relationship between order and disorder is relative to its context – physical, biological, human, historical. Disorder does not necessarily mean randomness or chaos, only that it is not perceived or not perceivable as order. (Ibid.)

The essential idea is that information is a different *logical type* than matter-energy. When we talk about the reality of matter-energy and the reality of information, we are referring to different realms of existence:

> Matter-energy is real and does not depend for its existence on being perceived by living creatures or human minds or senses. Information may be symbolic, imaginary, or real and does depend for its existence on being perceived by living creatures or human minds or senses.[6]

> Matter-energy and information are distinct from each other both in kind and level of reality. There is no causal relation between the marks on this page and the information they communicate. (p. 72)

How can we give an account of information in terms of energy if there is "no causal relation" between substance in the world and information? Here Wilden is referring specifically to information in the conceptual sense, using the example of written marks and communication. There is no causal relation in the sense of a necessary correspondence between particular marks and particular meanings. A conceptual relation between marks and meaning is cultural, historical, and categorical.

In weaving our way through this thicket of information, energy, and meaning, we must be careful of this distinction between information in the most general sense, as *coded variety*, and information as a conceptualization. Coming from the side of insects, Turvey and Shaw are ignoring conceptualization; Wilden appears to straddle the two meanings. The conflation of the two ideas is responsible for a great deal of the controversy over Gibson's ideas, which I summarize later in this chapter.

Turvey and Shaw (1995) proceed to establish the mutuality between agent and environment by expressing information about the environment in terms of energy: "The actions by which 'knowing about' is expressed require that information about environmental facts be referential to the energy for behaving with respect to those facts" (p. 158).[7] For example, descriptions of information in the environment of the dragonfly must refer, through physical laws, to concepts of *work, force,* and *torque* inherent in controlled locomotion through the thicket. To answer the question "How does the dragonfly physically control locomotion through the thicket of reeds to catch a mosquito?" we must make reference to the time-to-contact, impulses, and directions determinable by the dragonfly (p. 158).

Following Gibson, Turvey and Shaw summarize how information is an invariant relation between affordances and "properties of ambient energy distributions." What we call *gaps* in the dragonfly's thicket and *edible objects* must be modeled with respect to the dragonfly in terms of dynamic transformations of *optical fields*:

An ecological conception of information is founded on the assertion that invariant relations exist between layout properties of general significance to the governing of activity (affordances) and macroscopic, noninertial properties of structured ambient (optical, mechanical, chemical) energy distributions (Gibson, 1966; 1979/1986). The latter, therefore, can specify the former. In the case of the dragonfly . . . the structured light available during flight consists of transformations of different intensities, spectral contrasts, and specular highlights in different directions. The mathematics and physics of fields are needed to reveal, for example, the optical properties lawfully generated by gaps that are pass-throughable and by edible objects that are interceptible. (p. 159)

Turvey and Shaw strive for "laws of information" that would help us understand the construction of perceptual systems, just as laws of mechanics and thermodynamics are required to understand metabolic processes (p. 161). As an example relating animal behavior to physics, Turvey and Shaw cite the law that "animals different in form and locomotory style but of the same mass require the same amount of energy to move the same given distance" (p. 162). The research program to formulate such laws is still in its infancy, but the philosophical direction is clear enough.

In summary, different theorists have provided pieces of a complex, circuitous argument: Dewey viewed perception and action as functionally disjoint but mutually constrained, occurring always as part of a circuit. Cyberneticists like Bateson and von Foerster emphasized that information was relational, not a substance or a correspondence. The ecological psychologists brought perception back to physics, pursuing a competence theory of knowing that relates energy and physiology. Biologists, such as Maturana, saw the organism and niche as a structural coupling, a reciprocal, symmetric system. And finally, the neurobiologists found structural coupling between neural subsystems, providing our first glimpse of how subsystems develop as functional differentiators within a perception-motor circuit.

But we are far from done! The ideas of information, perception, categorization, and knowing about require substantial reworking before we can even talk straight about the different aspects of cognition in insects and animals, and especially the nature of concepts. To this end, I now present Gibson's claims so that we can see what he was trying to articulate. I then discuss more carefully the different meanings of *information* we have encountered. In essence, we have a case where the descriptive approach said "A is the same as B," and some of the insights from the detractors are telling us about A, some are telling us about B, and the rest are telling us about how A and B are related. Until we map out this spectrum, the debate is just a muddle.

Gibson on information and perception

I have deferred a direct presentation of Gibson's statements until I showed how the ideas were elaborated, both by subsequent theory and by the model building of situated robotics. But now I would like to give a quick tour in Gibson's own words. This provides background for the presentation of the debate in the next chapter.

To begin, Gibson was clearly a realist, acknowledging that the world has properties and complex structure, existing independently of how we interact with it. This is important because the first step in moving toward a dialectic account of cognition is to throw out a correspondence view that all representing is grounded in a relation of veracity between the map and the territory. As we have seen, the descriptive view imposes the perspective of the scientific investigator on the entire cognitive system (knowledge is a model of the world, and knowing is forming and testing hypotheses). But others have taken equally extreme positions, such as the apparent stand by Maturana that structure is only an ephemeral, dynamic relation. Gibson's entire theory can be viewed as an attempt to locate some structure in the stimuli and not require everything to be constructed by the organism:

Environmental stimulation always *has* structure. The Gestalt theorists failed to realize that even dot patterns or inkblots cannot be wholly 'unstructured.' Hence their emphasis had to be on a hypothetical process that *imposed* structure on stimulus inputs. (1966, p. 274)

Now, the crucial step is to avoid identifying information (perceptual categorizing) with stimuli structure. The relation is not merely a mapping or a sampling. For example, in contrasting his theory of a *resonance* circuit (tuning) with Hebb's (also influenced by Lashley), Gibson emphasizes that we "detect" or differentiate "variables of form" in optical information; the resonance between optical structure and cortical processes is not "an isomorphism between visual form and cortical form," a kind of objective *reproduction* (p. 275).

Echoing Bartlett (Chapter 3), Gibson views information as a relation between past and present:

Information does not exist exclusively in the present as distinguished from either the past or the future. What is exclusively confined to the present is the momentary sensation. . . . Resonance to information, that is, contact with the environment, has nothing to do with the present. (p. 276)

Gibson's either-or style ("has nothing to do") is not helpful. Fortunately, he elaborates what he means:

The ordinary assumption that memory applies to the past, perception to the present, and expectation to the future is therefore based on analytic introspection. . . . The simple fact is that perceiving is not focused down to the present item in a temporal series. Animals and men perceive motions, events, episodes, and whole sequences. The doctrine of sensation-based perception requires the assumption that a succession of items can be grasped only if the earlier ones are held over so as to be combined with later ones in a single composite. From this comes the theory of traces, requiring that every percept lay down a trace, that they accumulate, and that every trace be theoretically able to reinstate its proper percept. This can be pushed into absurdity. It is better to assume that a succession of items can be grasped *without* having to convert all of them into a simultaneous composite. (Ibid.)

In particular, space and time are categorized in coordinated motion with respect to adjacency and succession (cf. Toto's maps in Chapter 5), not as perceived place and remembered place:

The idea that "space" is perceived whereas "time" is remembered lurks at the back of our thinking. But these abstractions borrowed from physics are not appropriate for psychology. Adjacent order and successive order are better abstractions, and these are not found separate. (Ibid.)

Consistent with Bateson's view (Chapter 4), information should be viewed in terms of difference or, more specifically, direction of change:

Natural stimulation consists of successions as truly as it consists of adjacencies. . . . The information in either case is in the direction of difference: *on* or *off, skyward* or *earthward*. The visual system in fact contains receptive units for detecting both kinds of information. It is absurd to suppose that these sequence detectors have to make a comparison of intensity *now* with the memory of intensity *then*. (pp. 276–277)

Perceptual recognition of novelty suggests a more direct process than a failure to match:

Recognition does not have to be the successful matching of a new percept with the trace of an old one. If it did, novelty would have to be the failure to match a new percept with any trace of an old one after an exhaustive search of the memory store, and that is absurd. (p. 278)

In contrast, notice how the term *meta-cognition* (Flavell, 1979) was coined to explain what Gibson calls *primary memory* – knowing without a search that you don't know something. From Gibson's perspective, being able to say immediately that you don't know the president's phone number is inherent in how the memory mechanism works; it doesn't require *meta* or special knowledge. "Tell me who sat in front of you in first grade" can be immediately answered because "nothing happens" when we try to remember. If anything, *meta-knowledge* is knowing that you are unlikely to remember such things.

Of course, Gibson's argument that exhaustive search is "absurd" will not satisfy everyone. Perhaps a parallel search might be exhaustive and fast enough. As we will see, Gibson objects to identifying subconscious search with mental operations, such as forming hypotheses that direct your remembering (e.g., "Let's see, in first grade I was in New Brunswick . . ."). He views deliberation as special, not the same as perception. Thus, Gibson follows Bartlett in viewing remembering as inherently a conscious experience and banishing talk about recording and comparing from a theory of how remembering itself occurs. *Subconscious remembering* is hence an oxymoron; as Bartlett says, such an identification provides no explanation of how consciousness is possible or what function it provides.

In summary, Gibson's position can be expressed as follows. Sensory stimuli (S) are structured in accord with environmental relations between objects and events, such as the layout of light. Perceiving categorizes stimuli (S $\Rightarrow$ P) via a process of *tuning* and *resonance* with respect to invariances (e.g., direction of difference in space-time). Perceiving is active because stimuli are changing through self-motion. Perceiving is "direct" because it doesn't involve storing and making inferences about categorizations or descriptions of past experience.[8] The detected relations between stimuli are best expressed in terms of transformations:

The classical theory of memory . . . presupposes that the observer gets only a series of *stimuli*. But in active perception for the sake of information a series of transformations and transitions has been produced. The series is a product of activity and, since the perceptual system is propriosensitive, the changes merely specify exploratory responses. (p. 264)

This requires a kind of memory "to explain *repeated* apprehension over time" (p. 265). But ultimately Gibson doesn't explain how categorizing depends on past categorizing, and hence doesn't deliver a mechanistic theory, something that could be built with the properties he describes.[9] The situated roboticists are effectively realizing this research program.

Different views of *construction* and *contained* in

Before proceeding to examine how Gibson's work was debated in the 1980s (Chapter 12), I'd like to tie together how different critics have described information. The best approach is to understand what position they are arguing against. To begin, here are the representative statements we find in the literature:

- Bateson: "Information has zero dimensions." Information is a relation, not located.
- Maturana: There is no information in the environment.
- Reeke: The organism is the creator, not the receiver, of information.
- Neisser: *Construction* sounds arbitrary and indirect, too much like *reasoning*:
    If percepts are constructed, why are they usually accurate? . . . The answer must lie in the kind and quality of optical information available to the perceiver. But if this is admitted the notion of "construction" seems almost superfluous. (1976, p. 18)
- Gibson: Information is directly picked up. Perception reveals, not creates, information.
- Wilden: "no causal relation between the marks on this page and the information they communicate."
- Throughout the descriptive cognitive modeling literature: The information is there, and we can get better at accessing it. For example: "The visual system does not make full use of the information available to it" (Ullman, 1980, p. 377).

In these quotes, *information* is either undefined or its meaning varies across researchers from "stimulus structure" to "symbol structure" to categorization relation. To Neisser and Maturana, perception is not information processing because it is not descriptive modeling. To many others, perception involves information and processing, so it is "information processing."

The contain–create spectrum is especially interesting (Figure 11.3). At one extreme, the traditional view is that information is contained in the environment; at the opposite extreme, it exists only as mental categories. Gibson tries to relate these positions by saying that perceptual categories

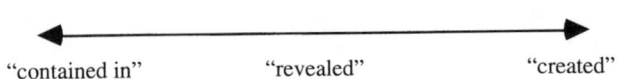

"contained in"   "revealed"   "created"

Figure 11.3. Spectrum: What is the relation of information to the environment?

are learned from stimuli via a resonance or tuning mechanism. Thus, his notion of *picked up* is not sampling from a container or extracting input from outside, but a detection made possible by (1) the relation of stimuli to environmental structures and properties and (2) invariance over space-time during action. Hence, picking up is learning relations.

Notice that the very metaphor of a container suggests that the operation performed is search, matching, and retrieval on *contents*. This requires in the descriptive approach intervening variables to hold candidate or accumulating results (such as a buffer). In contrast, a coupling mechanism forms categorizations through "direct" *selectional activation* (e.g., a classification couple in TNGS in Figure 7.1).

On the other hand, the purely created or constructed metaphor suggests that there are no environmental constraints, which is clearly at odds with the ecological view that the environment must be somehow fit for the organism's functioning. In general, environmental processes have structure in many different dimensions. Which structures are revealed (functionally significant, picked up, detected, *selected*) depends on the organism's sensors (e.g., an insect might detect the polarization of light) and the organism's movements. (As illustrated in Chapter 9, in people conceptual purposes and ways of framing a situation provide additional constraints on perception.)

To capture the reciprocality of perception, environment, and action, Gibson (1966) introduced the idea of an affordance. Features are constructed, but they are neither arbitrary nor in the environment. Categories are relational, interactive distinctions constructed within sensorimotor and perceptual–conceptual couplings: "The acts of picking up and reaching will reveal certain facts about objects; they do not create them" (p. 274). These "facts" are not properties of the world in some independent sense, but the product of interaction. At the lowest level, these facts are known only as feedback within interaction, such as the invariance of a stimulus with respect to a certain motion.

Stepping back, Gibson emphasizes that affordances are not created but may be objectively described by a scientist who relates the properties of the world to the properties of the organism. This is Turvey and Shaw's idea of characterizing the niche as a mutual relation. As Gibson put it: "The stick's invitation to be used as a rake does not emerge in the perception of a primate until he has differentiated the physical properties of a stick, but they exist independently of his perceiving them" (p. 274). Further, Gibson argues that the "invitation qualities" of gestalt theory is not just in the world as a "phenomenal field." Rather, affordance is a categorization that *emerges* in the action of an organism, through differentiating operations that transform light–form relations that exist independently of his interest.

In short, affordances and differentiated properties are categorizations. They may be described as relations in an ecological theory independent of particular experiences of the organism; but they are emergent phenomena, not residing in one place or another. Categorizations exist in the organism, but affordances are an observer's characterization of the coupling relation. Hence, when Gibson talks about "information in the layout," he is describing a dispositional property, the *possibility* of categorization tuning by perceptual processes. The idea of *contacting information* refers to constructing a coupling (S ⇔ P).

Relating perception and conception

The analysis of the dragonfly is relatively simple compared to understanding how conceptual processes and inference construct information. For example, one may construct information by an inference, as in Bateson's example that the failure of the IRS to send a letter is information about the tax return. *Contacting* emphasizes that *sensory fields* are dynamic, in motion; features are motion dependent. *Creating* emphasizes that *perceptual categorizations* are *constructs* that record events with respect to *differences* from past *experience*. Hence the idea of creating information builds on the idea that detecting is an event, an experience in time. *Constructing* (by one interpretation) goes a step further to *conceptually relate categorizations* and form a story or causal argument (cf. Schön's framework in Chapter 9). Hence, the different views of information being contained or created reflect the spectrum from automatic, reactive systems to inferential, conscious systems.

In the domain of insects, we can adequately characterize *knowing about* in terms of mutuality, logical types, feedback, dissipative structure, and so on. We find little place for talk about stored knowledge, deliberation, and memory structures. But Turvey and Shaw are describing insects and frogs, not diplomats. Their analysis is useful for perceptual categorization, in the case of insects, and may very well form the basis of all animal perceptual categorization; such a reciprocal theory does fit the situated robots developed to date (Part II). But for organisms that can conceptualize (agents), perception is influenced by ongoing conceptualization. Thus, what is a "real opportunity," an affordance for a person, is conceived and often named. An affordance is not merely a physical state of affairs, but a *conceptual state of*

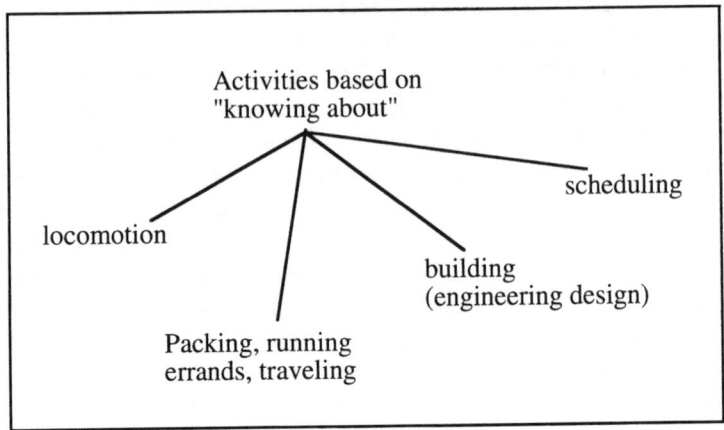

Figure 11.4. Activities of knowing about: From physical to descriptive coordination.

affairs. People are interacting with their own constructions, not merely with the ambient light array.

Turvey and Shaw's analysis of the dragonfly, like Maturana's view of the frog and robotic models of insects, needs to be complemented by a notion of information that information processing theory has focused on, namely, information as *conceptual*, a categorical relation of categories, not merely stimuli. If the flaw of information processing is to view all information as conceptual ("patterns that denote"), the flaw of a strict ecological approach to perception is to view all information as only patterns of signals.

Once conceptual and linguistic processing becomes part of the brain's organization, perceptual organization will become biased by the prior conceptual and linguistic organizations in which it has participated. This is quite different from the view that descriptions *mediate* perception or that goals *control* perception. The relation may also be a dialectic coupling, with conceptual and linguistic categorization serving as higher-order constraints. In the conscious human, perception is *both* signal processing *and* information processing, operating at different temporal and spatial scales of system organization. In Bateson's terms, the mental processes of perceiving and conceiving are of different logical types, dialectic levels within a dependent hierarchy. Gibson also said that perceiving and conceiving are "different in degree, but not in kind" (1979, p. 258). But he said very little about *inference* (or inquiry), which I take to be different in kind because of its sequential, transactional nature (cf. cycles in Figure 9.4 and feedback from manipulation of materials in Figure 9.6).

Figure 11.4 shows how the environment of an organism – what information can be about – ranges from the physical clutter of the dragonfly's reed thicket to the conceptual clutter of the workplace. Significantly, the categorized objects and relations are increasingly *artifacts*, things that people create, order, and name. People move within a physical and conceptual space of their own making (and not necessarily designed). For the most part, this space is so overwhelmingly more complex and ordered than the natural scale out of which it is constructed that *our world* of buildings, lawns, chairs, tools, and documents is the *recognizable* structure of our culture's making. We are coupled not merely to the ambient light array of Turvey and Shaw's analysis, but also to the shapes, names, and processes named and related in descriptive models.

We need a theory of information that does justice to the physical and descriptive accounts, and this apparently requires an account of consciousness. Ecological analysis of the dragonfly's navigation will help immensely, for now we know *what kind of theory* to look for, and we know about structural coupling as a categorizing mechanism. But an account of human information and coordination must relate to inference and, more generally, *design*. In this manner, a theory of information will be inseparable from the idea of inquiry, and hence a theory of situated action will be fundamentally related to language, story telling, and descriptive models.

Part IV

Symbols reconsidered

12   Coupling versus inference

The inputs are described in terms of information theory, but the processes are described in terms of old-fashioned mental acts: recognition, interpretation, inference, concepts, ideas and storage and retrieval of ideas. These are still the operations of the mind upon the deliverances of the senses. . . . What sort of theory, then, will explain perception? Nothing less than one based on the pickup of information.

J. Gibson, *The ecological approach to visual perception*, 1979, p. 238

If, as we have argued, perception is an inferential process, then what goes on in perception is the construction of certain kinds of "arguments" – viz., from the premises that transducers make available to conclusions which express perceptual beliefs.

J. A. Fodor and Z. W. Pylyshyn, How direct is visual perception?
1981, p. 183

If one thinks of perceptions as descriptions, like predictive hypotheses of science, as I do, then direct theories seem deeply misleading. . . .

R. L. Gregory, The future of psychology, 1995, p. 142

Putting inference in its place

Although perception is not an investigative process, scientific theorizing is, and we are now at the closing scene, with all the participants in one room and the murderer about to be revealed. What has been "murdered," of course, is the idea of direct perception or, more broadly, the idea of structural coupling. The idea that scientific thought is the paradigmatic form of cognition and that inference is the basis of all knowing has run roughshod through our house. Now is the time for the culprit and the offended to be reconciled. In this part of the book, I show how the "structural" aspect of situated cognition (Table 1.1) may be understood in terms of a coupling mechanism, on which the inferential processes described in studies of symbolic reasoning depend. Subsequent chapters then reformulate the discussion about symbols in these terms.

In one of the chapter-opening quotes, Gregory makes the typical mistake of thinking that perceiving is describing. This is not a straw man position, but is probably the dominant view, appearing in new articles even as I write. Fodor and Pylyshyn's (1981) analysis is more subtle, for they understand

269

that certain neural processes are "cognitively impenetrable, and hence unmediated by a certain kind of deliberate deduction (e.g., the sort of deduction that enters into explicit question answering)" (p. 187). To an extent, they recognize that information processing theory is circular: Inference requires perception first, but perception is explained in terms of inferential processes operating on categories, indeed, operating on symbols representing the sensed world. Where did these representations come from? That's partly what a theory of perception has to explain.

But any theory has unanswered questions, and Fodor and Pylyshyn are reluctant to give up the advantages of the symbolic inference point of view.[1] They refuse to accept Gibson's view that *subconscious deliberation* is an oxymoron, that cognitively impenetrable processing is by definition not inference. Indeed, it is Gibson who appears to ignore the facts: Why do descriptive models of perception and memory (Figure 3.2), based on inferential processes of storage and retrieval of ideas, fit human cognitive behavior so well? Yes, it is irksome that in these models there is no necessary distinction between subconscious and conscious inference. Yes, it is irksome that consciousness may then be viewed as "epiphenomenal" or just a form of awareness or just the part of reasoning that involves input and output. But to say that perception is not mediated appears like rank behaviorism to the descriptive modeling theorist, a disavowal of any internal processes at all, a reduction of what is apparently complex to something immediate or direct. How could that be?

For Fodor and Pylyshyn (1981), inference – mental operations of comparison and deduction on internal representations called *beliefs* – is fundamental and always operating: "Perception depends on ambient stimulation *together with inference*" (p. 174; their emphasis). The relation between stimuli and perceptual categories requires intervening variables and associative steps: "The notion of 'invariant' and 'pickup' can be appropriately constrained only on the assumption that perception is inferentially mediated" (p. 141). Thus, to Fodor and Pylyshyn, perception is not direct because there must be something happening between the stimulus event and the formation of perceptual categories (defined in Part II; see Table 8.1). There must be a mechanism, a mechanism that *mediates* because it constructs something.

Fodor and Pylyshyn have no sense of a *noninferential mechanism,* and Gibson didn't provide any. Both parties appear to agree that the distinction is direct versus inference, but direct perception is absurd to Fodor and Pylyshyn because it suggests that there is no mechanism, no process occurring at all. Today, thanks to the work of the neuroscientists and situated roboticists I have surveyed, we do have an alternative, noninferential mechanism: direct (structural) coupling. Unlike Fodor and Pylyshyn's transducers, coupling is a mechanism of categorical *learning* – a means of representing that *creates* features.

As we have seen in the discussion of connectionism (Chapter 3) and Dewey's struggle with stimulus-response theory (Chapter 4), the arguments about perceptual representing are profound: Why is an organism *noticing* anything at all? Why are inputs (given to subjects in information processing experiments) of *interest*? Attending and looking must be part of the theory of perception. A broader biological view, starting with the birds and the bees, suggests that perceiving is not sampling or accessing, but *detecting*, picking up information of interest. Information *in-forms* because it functions as part of an overarching activity, such as feeding or building a nest. The best theoretic models (such as Freeman's, Edelman's, and Pierce-Kuipers's in Part II) suggest that perceiving is not detecting stimuli, but selecting features – in Bateson's terms, "differences that make a difference." Such features are not inherent properties, but dynamic relations, lifted or picked up from the sensory array. Information processing theory chops up the dialectic relation of the circuit, S $\Leftrightarrow$ P $\Leftrightarrow$ M, serializing it (Figure 3.2) or postulating parallel-independent operations. Instead, the mechanism of physical coordination (which may include conceptualization, as defined by Edelman in Chapter 7) is a *coupling* – not a flow, but a mutual organization, a formative dependency.

Without the alternative mechanism of structural coupling in hand, Gibson may appear like an idiot: "According to Gibson, perception is not mediated by memory, nor by inference, nor by any other psychological processes in which mental representations are deployed." We have similar statements in the late 1980s, such as "situated cognition claims there are no representations in the brain at all." The arguments get quite heated because in a land where pivotal terms mean the same thing, it is difficult to make distinctions. To Fodor and Pylyshyn, *mental* means everything going on in the brain. To Gibson, it means conscious, deliberative processing. To others, it means "symbolic." If we agree that *inferential* implies *symbolic processing* (as in argumentation), then the useful distinction is between direct coupling and inference. The word *mental* is like *mind* and should just be dropped in this discussion. Even Gibson got confused. As Bickhard says, "Gibson's arguments are telling, but the conclusions are overdrawn: They are stated as applying against all mental-processing models, but they apply only to encoding models, not to interactive models" (Bickhard and Richie, 1983, p. xi).[2]

At issue is what *kind* of representing is possible, sufficient, and occurs biologically? What kind of representing mechanism is adequate for a frog to catch a fly? Coming the other way, others ask, "Why should these processes be needed in man?" (Johansson, von Hofsten, and Jansson, 1980, p. 388).

The ecological psychologists have shown that models of dragonflies and frogs do not require "the mental" to be identified with "the symbolic." But how does Gibson's talk about "directly detected properties" relate to *beliefs* about properties of objects, as in inference? How can an organism detect *properties* without having beliefs?

Despite missing Gibson's point, Fodor and Pylyshyn have something fundamental to defend that Gibson misunderstood or ignored. As I indicated in the conclusions of Chapters 8 and 11, an adequate theory of human perception must relate perceiving to conceiving. This is ultimately what Fodor and Pylyshyn are struggling with. To move us in this direction, I elaborate here on the distinction between direct coupling and inference. Here is my plan for this chapter:

- Present the evidence that direct perception exists in human cognition.
- Review Ullman's analysis of direct perception, showing in summary form how and why descriptive modelers misunderstand Gibson.
- Survey Gibson's interpreters, who effectively elaborate on the evidence for and ramifications of his theory.
- Return to Fodor and Pylyshyn, arguing that their notions of correlation and picking up concern reference and intentionality, not perception alone.

Fodor and Pylyshyn's distinctions allow us to articulate how a neurological structural coupling mechanism, such as TNGS, needs to be augmented for categories to function as referential symbols. On this basis, I return to Mycin and Aaron in the next chapter to better explain the difference between the signal processing of situated robots, the information processing of descriptive models, and the conceptual processes in human cognition.

Examples of direct perception in people

One might summarize the debate over Gibson's theory as "only" concerning What's direct? What's detection? And what's a property? Examples of affordances in the previous chapter (the "jumpability" of a creek and the heft of a milk carton) emphasize how perception involves and is in the service of action. Here I present two examples that emphasize the distinction between directness and inference in human experience.

Imagine that you are blindfolded, given an object, and asked to identify it. You can directly – without posing and testing hypotheses – perceive by feeling the shape and texture that the object is an apple. But counting the bumps on the bottom (opposite the stem), you *infer* that it is a Delicious apple. Characteristic of inferences, the mental process is cognitively penetrable – there are steps we can answer questions about ("I noticed this, and then this; then I checked such and such"). The thoughts are contextual ("It is an apple; what kind of apple?") and associative (five bumps on the bottom is a property of a Delicious apple).

Fodor and Pylyshyn (1981) do not acknowledge the distinction we experience between direct perception ("I felt it and knew") and inference ("I noted, checked, and confirmed"). Instead, they say, "Object recognition, for example, is a perceptual process par excellence, and it appears to be cognitively penetrable through and through" (p. 188). But object recognition is not a unitary phenomenon: The categorizing of the frog recognizing the fly (feature detection within a circuit), the person recognizing a Delicious apple (perception and inferential deduction), and the paintbrush inventors recognizing that a paintbrush is a kind of pump (perception and inferential induction) are not the same. The elevation of *recognition* to a primary phenomenon in psychology, existing independently of purposes and action, highlights the mistake: Perceiving is not primarily *identification* but functional differentiation, part of an activity (and in the laboratory, this activity is "participating in a psychological experiment").

A second example distinguishing between direct coupling and inference is provided by Geoffrey Hinton (1980):

People can describe a sequence of steps that they went through in performing a complex addition, but they cannot generally give any decomposition of the step of recalling that 3 plus 4 makes 7. It just does. Similarly, they cannot say how they saw the digit 3. This is an unanalysable single step *in everyday psychology.* One thing that Gibson means by saying perception is direct is that unlike doing arithmetic or following an argument, it does not involve a sequence of mental operations of the kind that we can introspect upon or instruct others to perform. (p. 387)[3]

Descriptive accounts fit serial, inferential operations very well. But the stark contrast between the inefficiency and errors of descriptive models of perception versus human experience is telling:

Digital computers have influenced theories about human perception and cognition in two rather different ways. By providing a medium for building working models, they have forced theorists to be explicit, and they have drawn attention to the extreme difficulty of tasks which people perform effortlessly, like the segmentation of a natural scene into objects. However, in addition to forcing theories to be explicit and to address the real problems, computer programs have provided an information-processing metaphor in which computation is performed by the sequential application of explicit stored rules to explicit symbolic expressions. . . . It is the metaphor which Gibson so disliked. It is quite a good metaphor for what happens when people do arithmetic computations, but perception isn't like that. I think that is what Gibson meant when he asserted that perception does not involve computation. . . . A person performing arithmetic computations or making inferences is a very bad model for perception. (pp. 387–388)

This is not an argument that neural processing isn't *computational*; rather, stimuli and categories are not related by a process like calculation, involving an intermediate language of variables that *descriptively model* objects and properties:

There is a different computational metaphor which does not fit so naturally with current machine architectures or programming languages, but which is more compatible with Gibson's approach. Perception is seen as a parallel, distributed computation in which a large network settles into a particular state under the influence of the retinal input.... This kind of computation can be simulated on a conventional computer, but it does not fit the standard symbolic information processing metaphor.... It does not, for example, involve decisions about which rule to apply next. (p. 387)

Descriptive cognitive modeling requires intermediate descriptions, which are then manipulated instead of the stimuli:

Early computer vision researchers tried to reduce the input data to a much sparser, more manageable symbolic representation. They believed that they could overcome the inadequacies of this representation by using complex control structures to facilitate clever inference, often based on knowledge of particular objects. (p. 388)

In contrast, the new approach considers "the detailed structure of the intensity image. For example, gradual intensity changes that were previously regarded as noise for an edge-finder are now seen to provide the basis for shape from shading" (p. 388). Thus, connectionist models, despite their limitations as mechanisms for multimodal physical coordination, demonstrate that coupling mechanisms can do something efficiently that inferential mechanisms can only do badly.

The debate: What theorists misunderstood or poorly explained

In the early 1980s a community of scientists debated what Gibson meant. The pros and cons were especially well articulated in commentary on Ullman's article "Against Direct Perception," appearing in *The Behavioral and Brain Sciences*. Ullman (1980) defends the idea that perception involves "processes operating on internal representations" (p. 379). The commentators generally agreed that the key issues are:

- what *kinds* of operations (local activation propagation versus inference on propositions),
- what *kinds* of representations (features and categories versus beliefs), and
- the relation between mental operations and the *formation* of representations.

In reviewing the debate, I am highlighting *both* what Ullman missed *and* what Gibson didn't explain adequately. I describe five points on which miscommunication occurred: what *direct* means; the idea of *information*, the idea that a mechanism must be an algorithmic description, the identification of the mental with the symbolic, and the identification of perceptual categories with concepts. I have discussed each of these already (mostly in Chapter 11). So I will be brief, just to set the scene for the more elaborate discussion of the responses to Ullman. (Section headings are Gibson's claims.)

Direct = without inference, not without processing at all

Ullman (1980) wrongly interpreted *direct* to mean that there is "no processing of any sort on the part of the perceiver" (p. 380). Or if there is processing, it is "trivial" and therefore "one is led to search for 'immediately registerable' information" such that the process is "essentially equivalent to a basic table lookup operation" (p. 375). Ullman called this *direct registration*.

Crucially, Ullman notes that his analysis does not consider the related controversy of "the role of past experience in perception" (p. 381). But at issue is the nature of memory, how categorization involves generalization over time. To Ullman, the only mechanism of memory imaginable involves storing something, and recognition (processing) is retrieval and matching (table lookup). Perception is thus broken into something direct (sensation) and something inferential (perception proper). In this second phase, categorization learning occurs. Falling back on stimulus–response theory, Ullman acknowledges that there may be a "direct coupling of input–output pairs" – in which inputs and outputs are presupplied and need only be associated – the sort of argument Dewey refuted in 1896 in his analysis of the "reflex arc" (Chapter 4), which not a single person in this debate cited.

Information = invariant (stable) dynamic relation, not an isolated representation

Because Ullman (wrongly) views a perceptual category as an isolated property, he views invariance not as a dynamic relation but as a kind of description: "The perceived structure is, of course, an invariance. But the registration of *this* invariant is simply equivalent to the original problem." To Gibson, information *is* the invariant relation. Strictly speaking, the invariance is a perceptual categorizing process functioning in the same relation to motor actions.

Ullman's rephrasing uses the container metaphor: "reliable information exists in the light array" (p. 380). Admittedly, Gibson's phrasing – "the perception system simply extracts the invariants from the flowing array" – does suggest that information resides in the array. But elsewhere he says,

"The retinal mosaic is sensitive to transformations," meaning that invariances such as unchanging shape are categorizations in time, as an object moves, not something that could "reside" in a buffer. *Existing in* and *extracted from* must be understood as dynamic, temporally determined aspects of a sensory-perceptual system. Gibson means *picking up* in the same sense in which we "grasp" an idea (which is why he says perceiving and conceiving are different in degree but not kind).

Algorithmic theory = description, not a mechanism

Ullman applies David Marr's framework to perceptual theory: A *functional description* characterizes what perception must accomplish; an *algorithm* describes how perceptual processes work; and a *mechanism* implements the algorithm (in silicon or neurochemistry). In Chapter 8 I argued that this is a superficial interpretation of Marr's distinction between Type 1 (algorithmic-interactional) and Type 2 (organismic) theories, caused by Marr's own bias that the only kind of cognitive mechanism is one operating on descriptions (whether graphic or verbal). Hence Ullman, like most descriptive modelers, takes a descriptive model (an algorithm) to be part of the mechanism itself (the software) and the mechanism proper to be the interpreter or machine on which the program operates.[4] Ullman is right to say that "understanding the function of the system as performing arithmetic operations would facilitate the study of the mechanism" (p. 380), but this does not mean that a mechanism performing computations of this sort is the only kind that exists.

Indeed, the algorithm–mechanism distinction, also characterized as representation versus implementation, is a false dichotomy; an alternative exists. Consider, for example, Brian Smith's characterization:

Here is an informal test to distinguish implementation from representation. Suppose that x either implements or represents y. Blow x up. If y is destroyed, the relation was one of implementation; if not, representation. (Now pepper that characterization with the appropriate modals.) ... Distance and disconnection are exactly what implementation lacks. If x implements y, then, in an important (if not especially clear) sense, x *is* y. (Smith, in preparation, Chapter 2 of Volume 1)

Now suppose that X = S and Y = P; then the coupling S ⇔ P (⇔ M) is such that "blowing up x" will destroy y, even though as a categorization it is only a representation. This is because the relation between S and P is dynamic, not static; it is mutual, not physically independent (distant and disconnected) in the sense of a place (x) and a photograph of it (y) or independent in the way descriptions of perceptions, ideas, and actions are parametrized in descriptive models. In short, in coupled systems a categorization (x) may be *both* an implementation (because it is a physical mechanism) *and* a representation. Crucially, such a representation is not descriptive; it doesn't refer to or stand for something; rather, it is a dynamic *relation*, a distinction generated with respect to a functional role.

The rejection of the representation–implementation distinction, manifest in Gibson's objection to a perceptual theory in terms of mental operations, gets translated by descriptive modelers as meaning that "there is no interesting level of description between everyday psychology and neurophysiology" (Hinton, 1980, p. 388). From Ullman's perspective, Gibson was violating Marr's framework by ruling out a "middle level which includes processes, representations, and the integration of information" (Ullman, 1980, p. 380). Gibson's argument that such descriptions "consist[ed] of immaterial 'intervening variables'" appears, then, to mean that no processing is occurring at all. For the descriptive modeler, there is no other way to "relate the level of function to the level of physical mechanisms" aside from a stored program operating on data structures. Hence, the usual interpretation of Marr's framework is indeed a tacit hypothesis that the only kinds of mechanisms that are possible are those that implement programs of the sort positing variables, comparisons, storage, and so on. Marr did suggest this, but his examples of Type 2 theories are precisely those kinds of phenomena – such as topological molecular immunology – that coupling mechanisms, and not inferential processes, explain.

Gibson: Perception = resonance ≠ mental = symbolic;
Ullman: Perception = symbolic ≠ mental = subjective

In contrast to the traditional descriptive modeling perspective, Ullman (1980) views subjective human experience as something more than descriptive models capture:

While Neff, Gibson, and others view symbolic events as mental, others have committed the opposite error, reducing subjective experiences to symbolic processes. . . . More generally, I do not wish to claim that the computational/representational theory is likely to encompass all aspects of perceptual phenomena, certainly not all aspects of the mind. The claim, however, is that it provides a more satisfactory psychological theory of perception than the DVP [direct visual perception] theory. (Ullman, 1980, p. 381; see Ullman's footnote 13)

Here again, a *psychological theory* to Ullman is by definition a descriptive model, one in terms of objects, properties, and associations (rules, frames, etc.). Hence, he wants a symbolic account of perception. In contrast, Gibson explains perception in terms of a causal mechanism of resonance, which is to be contrasted with the symbolic reasoning of mental operations.

Ironically, Ullman's criticism of Gibson becomes a criticism of descriptive cognitive modeling:

Gibson dismisses perceptual processes as "old-fashioned mental acts".... But a distinction has to be drawn between "symbolic" and "mental." The mediating processes in the computational/representational theory do not operate on subjective experiences, nor are they intended to account for their origin. (p. 377)

But, of course, Ullman's view is not the *Establishment* position (as Fodor and Pylyshyn call it). For example, descriptive cognitive models of reminding make no distinction between subconscious and conscious comparing and inferring (Chapter 3).

Perceptual = categorical but not conceptual

The arguments given by Ullman (and later by Fodor and Pylyshyn) suggest that they have difficulty understanding the idea of coupling because they do not always distinguish between perceptual and conceptual categorization. For example, Ullman (1980) argues that because a linguist can find "meaningful decomposition" in the comprehending process, then we shouldn't object to a theory based on meaningful decomposition of the perceiving process. A linguist would object to a direct theory of comprehension, one asserting that "our auditory system is tuned to directly pick up their meanings. Similarly, the perceptual psychologist should be dissatisfied with the claim that a property like rigidity is directly picked up" (p. 377). This simple example reveals two key theoretical assumptions: that a cognitive mechanism is necessarily a set of interacting (preexisting, well-defined) parts and that comprehension and perception involve the same kind of mechanism.

I have argued that people can always find a causal story (at some level of objects and events) and therefore use descriptive modeling to show how something is assembled from preexisting parts. But despite the obvious seriality of behavior, even phenomena such as speech could occur by direct, hierarchical coupling between perceptions and conceptualizations (as in the relation between conceiving a paintbrush's operation and talking about pumpoids in Chapter 10). Our perceived organization of the product, the grammatical forms of speech, is not proof that the *descriptions of the patterns* participated in their production, any more than a taxonomic description of phenotypes participates in populating a plant or animal species. We must also consider that descriptive models may appear to replicate human problem solving because rule and algorithm explanations need only relate the categories we have devised for describing inputs and responses in our experimental protocols. The fit is especially good for conceptual processes involving speaking and writing because the products are discrete and serial. But again, it is information processing theory itself that views speech as receiving and producing *words*. When the product is viewed in terms of conceptually coordinated activity (e.g., being an artist-researcher; Chapter 1), the beginning and ending are less clear. Similarly, the ineffectiveness of descriptive models for instruction in perceptual-coordination processes – such as judging paper pulp by its smell and feel, swimming the butterfly stroke, or changing your accent – suggests that describing and inferring are inadequate for guiding learning and hence inadequate for explaining all cognitive processes.

To conclude, Ullman's summary of the commentators' reactions to his presentation provides a useful window into what is confusing him. His arguments questioning direct perception may be grouped into two parts:

- *Variations on the nature of "indirectness":* verbal descriptions in inferential arguments; "internal processes" between "the stimulus and final percept" or an "interplay between perception and action" (which is not a refutation because this interplay is part of the theory of direct perception).
- *Variations on the role of conscious activity:* "explicit conscious processes" or "reasoninglike activity" – perception in lower animals may be direct ("direct recording of information"), but inference in humans is not (which omits the role of perception and coupling during inference).

Ullman's analysis is pervaded by the view that information is descriptive and exists as a static, referential entity, exemplified by his idea that a visual stimulus contains all the information "to specify its source" uniquely. These dilemmas are grounded in the idea that categorizing is necessarily referential and hence that knowing is inherently *conceptually* knowing *about* some *thing*. The idea of *source* is relevant to the private investigator, not the frog. Fodor and Pylyshyn's analysis, which I detail later, makes crystal clear how descriptive models of symbolic inference assume that *conceptual meaning* (reference and intentionality) is the foundation of all cognition. The consequence of this assumption is that the categorical status of reference and intentionality is not related properly to perceptual categorization, and hence reference and intentionality are not understood.

Gibson's interpreters respond

Having reviewed Ullman's arguments, I now present a selection of the commentary his analysis evoked. These comments are especially useful in explaining and elaborating Gibson's ideas. The ideas distinguish between different kinds of mechanisms:

- State variables versus a process-memory incorporating a history of interactions
- *Symbolic* calculations versus adaptive resonance
- Flow of signals versus active perception

- Matching descriptions versus becoming attuned to feedback invariances
- Encodings versus functional indicators

Together these commentaries provide an initial theory of how a coupling mechanism works.

Shaw and Todd: Abstract machine theory

Although the debate about direct perception tends to focus on the picking up of information "in" stimuli, there are two other phases in the descriptive approach that can be addressed: the capturing of information in intervening variables and the subsequent "integration of current inputs with background information" (Fodor and Pylyshyn, 1981, p. 183). Just as information is viewed as sitting in the environment to be sampled or extracted, background information is viewed as sitting in memory, waiting to be matched and reassembled. Thus, in the descriptive approach, the constructive aspect of categorizing is always working on *representational parts* of transducer-produced encodings (intervening variables) and stored descriptions (background information).

In their commentary on Ullman, Robert Shaw and James Todd (1980) rigorously present the opposing position, using a simple notation from abstract machine theory. Because their presentation is so lucid and incisive, I present it in detail. They begin by characterizing the debate in terms of *intervening variables*, indicated here as Q(t):

The typical cognitive rendition of perception in machine theory is as follows: $R(t + 1) = F(Q(t), S(t))$ where $R(t + 1)$ is the perceptual response (output) which arises at time $t + 1$ as a function F of some stimulus (input) S at time T and some "internal state" of the machine Q at time t. (p. 400)

Illusion disambiguation suggests to Ullman that perception is determined by stimulus input plus internal representations:

Ullman's major complaint against what he takes to be Gibson's theory of perception is that it omits the state variable and reduces simply to perception being a function of stimulation, that is, $R(t + 1) = F(S(t))$. (Ibid.)

Could some other mechanism provide the same formal functionality as a state, and might it be construed theoretically as "something other than a reified 'internal state' which causally mediates perceptual affects?" Yes, if the response function depends on a *history of transactions*, H(t):

Let us assume an animal (machine) A with some history of interaction with an environment E, then let H(t) represent the history of the state of affairs concerning A's transactions with E up to some time t. This means that H(t) includes all the effects of A's relationship with E, such as the inputs received, and the outputs afforded. Then, following Minsky (1967), assuming that the (perceptual) state of affairs in which A participates up to t constrains its next response r, at t + 1, there must be some relation, F, of the form, R(t + 1) = F(H(t), S(t)).

Notice in the above formulation, no state term Q(t) is needed, in the sense of an "internal" state, which somehow imparts meaning or enriches the input. Rather the term H(t) refers to the entire history of transactions of the animal with its environment. The reason that this conception of abstract machines is not ordinarily used by computer scientists is that any relation involving an entire history of transaction "would be hopelessly cumbersome to deal with directly" (Minsky, 1967, p. 15). Nevertheless, the most general conception of a machine with a history in no way requires the notion of "internal states," Q(t), but invokes such variables only as a convenience for designing and programming man-made devices, such as computers. For this reason, a computational scheme over Q(t) (a program) is but a convenient means of providing a device, which has no history in a natural environment, with an artificial "history." The variable Q(t) has no meaning of its own, except what is derived from the history term H(t).

However, even if one adopts this convenience, it is by no means necessary to reify Q(t) as an "internal state." For, as Minsky (1967) rightly observes, any "internal state" that has no external consequences is irrelevant to the description of a machine's behavior. Since a canonical definition of *machine* need not incorporate such irrelevant states, "it might be better to talk of our classes of histories [internal states] as 'external states'" (Minsky, 1967, p. 16). (Shaw and Todd, 1980, p. 400)

Hence Q(t) and H(t) might be viewed as internal (cognitive) or external (behavioral)–complementary views with explanatory power. Yet neither view alone may be adequate; we need a dialectic mechanism:

In fact, the ecological approach to perception ... proceeds upon the assumption that they must be treated jointly and that they entail a mutually defined, integral unit of analysis whose "states" are neither internal nor external. Although it may be useful for methodological reasons to focus temporarily on a single interpretation in isolation, one cannot lose sight of their reciprocal nature without losing something essential. (Ibid.)

The issue is not only how to interpret Gibson's theory, but how to understand the nature of machines in terms of *alternative kinds of mechanisms*. This is what abstract machine theory provides. Descriptive cognitive models reify H(t) in neurobiological processes as discrete snapshot events, thus decomposing the overall representing function of the mechanism into representations of objects and properties of the environment, formulated as the intervening variables, Q(t):

The existence of so-called "internal states," Q(t), is nothing more than a convenient fiction of contemporary computer science methodology, which allows the programmer, in lieu of evolution and learning opportunities, to provide machines which have no natural histories, H(t), with artificial ones. ... Algorithmic models of perceptual phenomena ... may provide a useful summary of the complex histories of animal–environment transactions by which the perceptual systems under study might have become attuned. On the other hand, such theorists should be admonished to be circumspect and not take the "internal state" description fostered by this methodological tool as being a blueprint of the ghostly states of mind. ... (p. 401)

If such cognitive (indirect) models of perception are neither formally nor theoretically necessary, then how should one conceptualize perceptual systems in terms of machine theory so as to capture their essential nature, namely, their ability to become attuned in design and function through evolution, development, and experience? (Ibid.)

Shaw and Todd show how the direct (ecological) approach suggests an alternative formulation in abstract machine theory, specifying how Response and Stimuli are dialectically (reciprocally) related:

Notice that in the traditional abstract machine conception as given by $R(t + 1) = F(H(t), S(t))$, there is no necessary reciprocal relation between inputs S, and outputs R, to express the mutuality of constraint postulated by the ecological approach to exist between perception and action. To wit: the things that an animal perceives constrains what it does, and what an animal does constrains what it perceives.... Action enters as a variable into perception no less than perception enters as a variable into action. All of this suggests, moreover, that there is an intrinsic mutual compatibility between an animal and its environment, which is, after all, the fundamental premise of Gibson's theory. As a rough first pass, this mutuality of constraint between the animal, as actor and perceiver, and environment, as acted upon and perceived, minimally requires the following machine theory formulation (cf. Patten 1979):

$R(t + 1) = F(H(t), S(t))$ as before and additionally, $S(t + 1) = F(H(t), R(t))$.

In accordance with the earlier discussion, there is no necessary sense in which any of the above variables should be taken as being "states" *in* an animal. Rather the animal as actor/perceiver is more aptly thought of as being functionally defined *over* the constraints specified by these dual equations. Furthermore, since the environmental terms $R(t + 1)$ and $S(t + 1)$ (the action consequences of perceptual histories and the perceptual consequences of action histories, respectively) directly specify each other, then no "between" variables are causally or epistemically required to mediate this mutual relation. It is for this reason that both action and perception may be said to be direct.... (Ibid.)

Randall Beer provides a diagram that usefully depicts the relation of R and S as dual relations, specifying how the environment and agent influence each other (Figure 12.1). The function R corresponds to "motor response." An example of the dynamic, dual nature of perception–action and E–A coupling is sustaining a trajectory when walking on a rolling boat. Recall that in Steels's analysis of emergence in terms of types of variables (Chapter 8) an emergent behavior involves an uncontrolled variable, which represents the resulting reciprocal relation between the stimuli and the motor response. In particular, on the boat one keeps moving to avoid hitting a bulkhead or being tossed over the side, yet the resulting (perhaps S-curved) path is not strictly controlled.

Ullman's (1980) response to Shaw and Todd's commentary is revealing. He summarizes it by saying that there is an "interplay of perception and

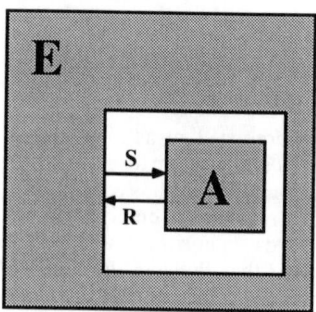

Figure 12.1. "An agent and its environment as coupled dynamical systems." (Adapted with permission from Beer, 1995, Figure 2, p. 182.)

action" – focusing on the outer feedback loop (cf. Figure 9.6) rather than the internal coupling, $S \Leftrightarrow P \Leftrightarrow M$. He claims that his "main objection to the 'history function' formulation is not that it is descriptively incorrect, but that it is unsatisfactory as a psychological theory of perception" (p. 412). By definition, consistent with his interpretation of Marr, he requires a mechanism involving "meaningful decomposition and internal constructs." That is, a psychological theory *must be* an algorithmic account (i.e., a program with intervening variables modeling the world and behavior). Thus, he views Shaw and others as denying "the legitimacy of internal constructs"; that is, they are behaviorists.

But the real issue is not whether the organism is empty or even immediacy per se (which suggests a distinction of time or amount of processing). The distinction highlighted by Shaw and Todd is between *kinds of internal constructs*, namely, states that symbolically represent experience ($Q(t)$) versus a coupling mechanism that arises out of historical relationships ($H(t)$) (in Bartlett's terms, how the parts have worked together in the past).[5] Examples of mechanisms based on history functions are Freeman's chaos-attractor model and Edelman's classification couple in TNGS. By comparison, systems with direct electromechanical linkages, such as mercury thermostats and toilet bowls, which are often used to contrast descriptive models with *analog* or *nonrepresentational* models, lack a history function. They illustrate something simpler – how current state may be embodied in physical relationships rather than encoded as variables in a descriptive model.

Of course, categories $Q(t)$ do exist in inferential mechanisms; but again, $Q(t)$ in human inference are categorizations, not necessarily descriptions (the topic of Chapter 13).

Grossberg: Adaptive resonance

Stephen Grossberg (1980) explains how Ullman's interpretation of Marr's levels is inconsistent with a *resonance mechanism*:

The perceptual event is an activity of the whole system as it manifests resonant properties. Ullman's view of computation does not seem to embrace the idea of resonance, and Gibson's emphasis on the resonant event has caused him to underestimate the functional substrates from which resonances emerge. In making these statements, I have carefully avoided the words "algorithm" and "computation," because these words are often used in a way that deflects the study of internal representations from directions wherein Gibson's intuitions can be mechanistically understood. (p. 385)

Grossberg is interested in how a stable mechanism develops. The concept of *stability* emphasizes that a subsystem is *doing something all the time* (Bartlett's emphasis) and forms (stable) relations by virtue of functioning. Grossberg focuses on how *functional substrates* organize or emerge. These substrates may involve or be replicated by a mechanism of local computations. The mechanism is described as forming "in real time":

[S]o the boundary between mechanism and algorithm is vague, which Ullman might dislike. The theory also exemplifies the fact that a variety of functional transformations work together to compute perceptual events, which Ullman might like. However, the perceptual events in the theory are in, a literal mathematical sense, resonances, which Gibson might like. (p. 386)

Grossberg turns the computational approach inside out. Rather than viewing arithmetic operations as what the person does, he views computation as something the mechanism does, but in a distributed, mutually constrained, dynamic system. To put Grossberg's analysis in the perspective of TNGS, an adaptive resonance computational system is more like a population, in Darwinian terms, than a program that flows. Local computations are in some sense like particular individuals; the resonance is like the species in its niche:

The "computations" that go on in my networks might never change, but in different environments, and as time goes by, the networks' resonances can change drastically. In this limited sense, local computations are irrelevant. In a profound sense as well, many neural potentials and signals, which are derived by perfectly good local computations, are perceptually irrelevant until they are bound together by resonant feedback. Only then does a perceptual event occur. In this framework, one does not find process and "still more processing". Rather, certain processing ends in resonance: and other processing does not. . . . Infinite regress is replaced by a functional rhythm between resonance and rest. (p. 386)

Thus, Grossberg views adaptive resonance as a mechanism for tuning of a perceptual system mentioned by Gibson:

I find Ullman's particular levels, notably the algorithmic level, unnatural for me, even misleading, in that they tend to point away from the truth in Gibson's insight that the perceptual system "resonates to the invariant structure or it is attuned to it" (Gibson, 1979, p. 249). (p. 386)

Debates about alternative mechanisms are often framed by descriptive modelers in terms of whether the mechanism is computational or not. This is actually a reformulation of the argument about inference, suggesting instead that *symbolic* means that some kind of computation-equivalent process is occurring somewhere in the system.[6] But the central claim of the descriptive modeling approach is that a *particular kind of computation* is occurring: inference on symbols using a stored associative memory. Computations that are local, *subcognitive* (within and between neuronal groups in TNGS) and sometimes *irrelevant* (they don't affect results) constitute an entirely different kind of mechanism than we find in Aaron, Mycin, or Soar. The idea of adaptive resonance in a system whose activations embody H(t) begins to explain how representing might emerge and function within coordination circuits.

Reed: Perceiving is an act

Edward S. Reed (1980) provides another way of understanding why a theory of perception must be psychophysiological, that is, *both* psychological *and* physiological:

It is not the case that Gibson held that pickup was an unanalyzable primitive construct. . . . According to Ullman, Gibson's theory of information pickup is a variant of S–R psychology. Ullman says that, for Gibson, perceiving is based on "direct coupling" between stimuli and percepts, directly analogous to reflexes which can "probably be though of as prewired, immediate coupling between stimuli and responses." Reflexes and information pickup are both primitive constructs as far as psychological theories are concerned, because they can only be analyzed meaningfully in physiological terms. (p. 397)

To understand Reed's point, consider how the idea of an information processing psychological theory – of a mechanism consisting entirely of meaningful descriptions and their associative relations through and through, with nothing left unexplained – is at odds with other scientific theories. For example, chemistry isn't this way: One needs electromolecular and quantum theories to understand everything from heat/energy requirements and products of reactions, inertness, temporal patterns of phase shifts, and so on. Expecting psychology – dealing with knowledge, belief, perception, emotion, and so on – to explain the origin and interaction of such constructs is as incorrect as expecting that chemistry omitting molecular theories – dealing only with palpable substances and their combinational properties – could explain why the halides are so intensely reactive, why potassium chloride can be substituted for table salt, why a flash of light is produced by fireflies, and so on. Whether one aspires to replace one level by another (chemistry by physics) or to make one level stand on its own (psychology without physiology), the effect is reductionism. Again, the reconciliation is a *both-and* theory, Wilden's dependent hierarchy of explanations (Figure 10.1).

On the matter of reflexes, Gibson (1979) acknowledges that he presented an S–R theory of perception at one time (during the 1950s) but clearly refuted this:

> I thought I had discovered that there were stimuli for perception in much the same way that there were known to be stimuli for sensations. This now seems to be a mistake. . . . I should not have implied that percept was an automatic response to a stimulus, as a sense impression is supposed to be. For even then I realized that perceiving is an act, not a response, an act of attention, not a triggered impression, an achievement, not a reflex. (p. 149)

Hence, although in some sense indirect means inferential, direct doesn't mean reflex – the descriptive modeler's view of noninferential – an automatic S–R production. Rather, direct means coupled, and coupled means in a sensory-perception-motor circuit. Reed (1980) continues:

> Gibson's theory of perceptual activity is anything but the reflexive pairing of stimuli with percepts that Ullman claims it is. Ullman argues that, since indirect theories of perceptual activity hold that perceiving involves an indirect computation of percepts out of stimuli, a direct theory of perception must hold that percepts and stimuli are directly coupled. This is very misleading: *DVP (direct visual perception) theory does not involve inverting indirect theories of perception*, but rather involves rejecting their basic assumptions and hypotheses. (p. 397; emphasis added)

Reed elaborates on the idea that energy patterns are detected as invariant relations over time. This brings together the analyses of Turvey and Shaw (Chapter 11) and Grossberg, in which adaptive resonance is a mechanism by which time dependency enables a circuit to settle into a mutually stable adjustment:

> Perceiving is not based on stimuli or even on the transmission of excitation along afferent nerves to sensory cortex; rather, perceiving starts with purposively functioning animals exploring their environment. Because ecological information exists within the environment in energy patterns which are relatively large in space-time, it cannot be registered by a receptor. . . . A pattern of peripheral stimulation cannot be information because it cannot specify its environmental source. Ullman takes this to imply that perception requires computations to "recover" meaningful information, whereas Gibson takes this to imply that proximal stimulation is not the basis of perception, although stimulus *information*, which is specific to its source, is the basis of vision. . . . Information does not flow along afferent-efferent channels the way excitation does; indeed, when information is being picked up, the mutual adjustments of a perceptual system's organs require that excitation be flowing centrifugally and centripetally, horizontally as well as vertically throughout the CNS. (Ibid.)

Notice that here *information* is what is available in the optic array by excitation (S). What is picked up (the formation of a classification couple, represented by S ⇔ P) is determined by activity. Perceiving is not based on receptor stimulation as a sort of reflex or as inference – two variants of the flow of information metaphor. Rather, perceiving is an activity, an accomplishment of and in the service of the whole system (S ⇔ P ⇔ M). Picking up is not "recovering" information missing from the stimuli. Rather, the operations of scanning and other attentional *behaviors* arise within purposefully organized activity (browsing plants, stalking prey, grooming, etc.). Perceiving is thus not just an internal transformation, but a systemic event, a matter of detecting something of interest while engaged in some activity – not a mere input event, like passively receiving a package at the front door.

Prazdny: The symbolic account is more eccentric

K. Prazdny's perspective provides another way to understand why Gibson used the term *direct* and argued against intervening variables. Specifically, Prazdny (1980) characterizes the descriptive, inferential account of perception in terms of a "cue theory . . . because it views space or depth perception as equivalent to static space perception . . . in which perception is a process of stitching together or comparing a sequence of static snapshots" (p. 394).[7] Hence, information processing is

a kind of detective work on the part of a visual system attempting to solve a gigantic jigsaw puzzle by patiently creating, testing, and rejecting hypotheses proposed mainly by an already established context, until one of them prevaile[s]. . . . (Ibid.)

In cue theory, perception is viewed as occurring in *stages* operating on *views*. Indeed, Minsky's (1977) presentation of frame theory says: "different frames of a system describe the system from different viewpoints, and the transformations between one frame and another represent the effects of moving from place to place" (p. 355).

But because change is not named, but occurs and is detected by resonance coupling, "the classical cue theory has very little, if anything, to say about perception in kinetic contexts" (Prazdny, 1980, p. 395). The information takes form within the feedback of movement:

Gibson correctly pointed out that the excessive reliance of most theories of visual perception on various forms of cognitive or semilogical processes was brought about by their preoccupation with static images. These are inherently ambiguous. He argued that this ambiguity is reduced enormously, or even disappears, when the observer moves, as the spatiotemporal structure of the ambient array affords information specifying certain aspects of the environment uniquely. (Ibid.)

Gibson's hypothesis that *all perception* works this way "has proven almost correct in the case of frogs . . . but almost certainly incorrect in the case of man." This is because the theory overstresses the role of invariance and *physical action* at the expense of conceptualization. Prazdny credits Ullman for recognizing that the nature of the information within the mechanism (as opposed to the psychologist) is pivotal:

> Ullman . . . is right in asserting that the relevant problem is not whether the information in the optic array and the corresponding perceptions are expressible in terms of invariants or whatever other *theoretical constructs*, but rather in terms of what the information is, and how it is used and processed by the visual system. This is a nontrivial remark, for all too often the structure of "input" information has been taken to be determined by the requirements of the representations containing a priori cognitive (or higher-level) information with which it was designed to interact. (Ibid.; emphasis added)

In summary, on the one hand, we must be careful in injecting a scientist's conceptual constructs into the mechanism; on the other hand, we need a theory of perception that is integrated with conceptualization.

Bickhard: Functional indicators

Mark Bickhard and D. Michael Richie wrote a book responding to the direct perception debate, *On the Nature of Representation* (1983). Their ideas inspired and gave form to much of my analysis. Unlike the other participants, they focus on the idea of *encodings*, a particular kind of representation that appears, for example, in expert systems and descriptive cognitive models. They characterize Gibson's theory as arguing against an encoding model of perception: "Gibson's basic insight was that it is possible to derive information about an environment from interactions with that environment without encoding anything from that environment" (p. 17).

Bickhard and Richie present a theory of *representing* in which perceptual categorizations are *indicators* based on feedback. Hence they call these representations *interactive outcomes* and *functional indicators*. As Maturana emphasized, these are internal distinctions:

> [The] two basic aspects of serving as a ground for apperception [keeping the "situation image" current] and of potentially transforming the world are present in all interactions. . . . Interactions with the environment . . . yield internal outcomes, and . . . outcomes yield internal indications concerning possible future interactions. Inputs to the system are generated by the sense organs, of course, but the significance of those inputs concerning the environment resides only in their participation in an overall (perceptual) interaction. (p. 19)

Hence the system constructs *interactive recognizers*, such that *knowledge of what is represented* is constituted in terms of what *further* patterns of potentialities are indicated by the occurrence of a *given* (implicitly defined) pattern, rather than in terms of the epistemically circular "knowledge of what is encoded." (p. 82)

Rather than an encoding based on correspondence – which is what people assemble in the knowledge bases of expert systems and descriptive cognitive models – perceptual coordination develops an indicator of potential interactions.

Bickhard and Richie's analysis is distinctive in its attempt to relate the debate about direct perception to the idea of symbols in descriptive models. They outline an interlevel neural architecture in which nonrepresentational processes control and coordinate interaction and thus provide the substrate for functional distinctions to emerge:

From an interactive perspective, however, there is at least one level of emergence *between* the material and the representational: the level of interactive control structures. Representation, then, is an emergent functional property of certain forms of goal-directed interactive control structures, which in turn, are emergent properties of certain patterns of material processes. (p. 57)

This approach begins to explain how animals conceive and can be apparently goal directed – without having language, a means of modeling (encoding) their world and experience. Bickhard and Richie postulate that the goal-directed coordination processes emphasized by Newell and others (Chapter 3) must not depend on encodings; rather, language develops from the interactional control structures that make physical behavior possible:

In present-day information processing or computational approaches . . . the level of interactive control structures and processes that is properly *between* the material level and the representational level has instead been moved *above* the level of encoded representations, leaving the level of encodings hanging in midair with no grounds for explication. (Ibid.)

Situated cognition research in the context of children's learning, animal cognition, and neural dysfunctions provides an especially rich basis for exploring the idea of "interactive control structures."[8]

Fodor and Pylyshyn: Perceiving as knowing *what* you know about

Shortly after the appearance of *The Behavioral and Brain Sciences* debate organized by Ullman, Jerome Fodor and Zenon Pylyshyn published a detailed analysis of Gibson's ecological approach: "How Direct Is Visual Perception?" (1981). Here we find most of the miscommunications I have already described (summarized in Table 12.1).

Table 12.1. *Summary comparison of Gibson's theory of direct perception and the descriptive, inferential approach*

	Gibson	Inferential model
Information	A coupling indicator: invariant attunement	Any structure-pattern consisting of symbols
Representation	Variable, trace (engram)	Something that *stands for* something else
Information processing	Picking up	Any inference
Symbolic	Something meaningful	Any representation
Inference	Mental act	An associative relation
Association	Matching, comparing	A kind of inference
Memory (remembering)	Reactivation (not retrieval)	A reinstantiation or reinstatement of a symbol structure or execution of a procedure
In a nutshell	Perception is special; but perhaps conceptualization is like it	Perception is like conscious inference, except that it is subconscious

But Fodor and Pylyshyn (F&P) also have an insight that Gibson isn't concerned about, namely, the nature of inference. They are struggling to relate *directness*, of which some aspect is necessary, and *reasoning*, as two aspects of cognition that need to come together. In particular, they are confused (openly and honestly) about how an organism can detect information about something, that is, have knowledge, without having *beliefs*. Probably, after all I have said about dragonflies and sensorimotor coordination, it is obvious that F&P are dealing with a different kind of cognitive phenomenon, namely, the reasoning of a physician, the judgment of an artist, or the creative theorizing of an inventor. Steeped in such a complex variety of human thought, in which *cognition* is tantamount to *human*, it never occurs to Fodor and Pylyshyn to consider how a rabbit smells food, how the owl monkey knows which finger is touched, or how a horse jumps over a creek. The split between perception and cognition has been not just a theoretical confusion, but an interdisciplinary barrier. In this section I discuss how F&P view correlation as always a semantic (conceptual) relation and thus how they wrongly view perceptual categorizations as beliefs about properties.

Correlation as a semantic relation

According to F&P, in Gibson's theory the notion of information is unexplicated because he provides no account of how one thing X can be about another thing Y:

The fundamental difficulty for Gibson is that "about" (as in "information about the layout in the light") is a semantic relation, and Gibson has no account *at all* of what it is to recognize a semantic relation. (p. 168)

F&P conflate the operation of a perceptual system with a *person's recognizing* that there is a semantic relation between the layout in the light and the information detected. Their notion of recognizing is semantic or *conceptual*, not a perceptual categorization alone. Indeed, only a scientist would recognize the relation they describe. There is no need for the frog to recognize any semantic relations at all! Cognitive operations of referring, knowing that you have an idea about something, knowing that something stands for something else, or knowing that you are seeing one thing as another are *conceptual*. There is no need for the frog to have such thoughts, to categorize its perceptions and categorizations as being about anything. Recognizing a semantic relation is a second-order categorization (at least), *a categorization about a relation.* The frog doesn't know that its categorization refers to a fly because it isn't categorizing its categorization of the blob. *Knowing that* or referring requires a higher-order categorization – a conceptualization of reference.

The distinction between direct perception and conceptualizing reference is so basic that to say it at first appears very odd, like saying that Mycin's rules are only a representation of knowledge and not knowledge itself. In fact, it is the same kind of confusion: identifying a scientist's claims about what a perceptual system *accomplishes* with how the perceptual system *operates*. F&P are on firm ground when they describe human conceptualizing; the mistake is to attribute such understanding to perceptual systems:

[I]t seems plausible that recognizing X to be about Y is a matter of mentally representing X in a certain way; e.g., as a premise in an inference from X to Y. And it is, of course, precisely the notion of mental representation that Gibson wants very much to do without. (p. 168)

They are right on both accounts. A frog needn't represent a perceptual categorization of a blob *as being a fly.* According to Maturana and others, a frog has no categorization "fly," just "blob-contrast-in-motion-I-could-eat." Contra frame theory, the frog's characterization of the fly is not "I see a blob with characteristics A, B, C" and that matches my stored fly-frame concept. The fly is not making inferences at all. Recognizing a semantic relation entails recognizing that a categorization is a potential match and inferring that it fits. Gibson does without the inferential mechanism because he doesn't need it. We might turn the tables on F&P as follows:

[I]t seems plausible that recognizing X to be an indicator of activity Y is a matter of coupling X in a certain way to Y; e.g., as a classification couple relating X and Y. And it is, of course, precisely the notion of learning nonconceptual categories that F&P want very much to do without.

Table 12.2 *Two relations, S1 and S2, in analysis of vision*

| S1 | Pick up light | Light → S | "Mapping between various aspects of the environment and some spatio-temporal patterns of the visual array" (Ullman, 1980, p. 373) |
| S2 | Directly perceive layout | S → P | "Mapping between stimuli and perceptions" (Ibid.) |

Let's step back a bit and look at F&P's argument in more detail. Table 12.2 summarizes perception from a perspective that Gibson and his opponents generally agree on. Two aspects, S1 and S2, are correlated by (visual) perceptual processes. The trick is to understand how these aspects are *relations* (not information-carrying descriptions) and how the correlation (a coupling or *corelation*) works.

The very way in which F&P phrase their notion of information shows a top-down view – from category to sensation – as if perceiving is indeed working like a detective from candidates (S2) to evidence (S1): " 'Information' is a defined construct for Gibson; S1 contains information about S2 if, and only if, they are correlated states of affairs." This is especially ironic, for the whole thrust of the ecological theory is that S2 contains information about S1. But F&P place the little man inside, peering down from cortex to optic nerve, "learning about the layout" from descriptions of features and categories stored in memory:

We learn about the layout by inference from the detected properties of the light. What we detect is not the information *in* S1 but rather the informative properties *of* S1. Then what we learn about S2 in consequence of having detected these informative properties depends upon which inferences we draw from their presence. (p. 166)

Again, F&P and ecological psychologists talk about S1 in similar ways: "informative properties of the medium . . . are correlated with the properties of the layout." But Gibson views properties as part of a *theorist's description*; F&P view properties as *beliefs* represented in the mechanism. When F&P consider how the perceptual system gets from S1 to S2, they need to know how the detecting mechanism works; it is not sufficient for a theorist to say merely that the properties are correlated: "The fact that the frequency of the light is correlated with the color of reflecting surfaces cannot itself cause a state of a detector." Rather than a mechanism that correlates (e.g., by adaptive resonance) with constructed features, F&P start with the features and seek a mechanism that somehow *relates them*: "How (by what mental processes) does the organism get from the detection of an informative property of the medium to the perception of a correlated property of the environment?" Hence, to F&P one first knows (from prior learning) that a *property* is informative (S2) and then must relate this to a property in the environment (S1). They miss that a property couldn't be informative – indeed, no categorization would form – unless it were functionally relevant. Detecting a distinction in the layout array is detecting a difference that makes a difference. As discussed in Chapter 11, distinctions are affordances in the sense that Bickhard and Richie referred to "indications concerning possible future interactions," summarized as follows:

> *Medium* (environment) ⇐(S1: sense impression, stimuli)⇒ *layout (e.g., optic array)* ⇐(S2: categorization)⇒ *percepts* ⇐(interactive control structures)⇒ *actions*

(double arrows indicate coupling; feedback between action and sensation is not shown).

In many respects, F&P's summary of their dilemma is an apt character-ization of why the descriptive approach, which postulates knowing about a correlation and relating it mentally through inferences, is untenable:

To summarize: Gibson has no notion of information over and above the notion of correlation. You can, no doubt, pick up properties of S1, and, no doubt, pick up properties of S2. But you cannot pick up the property of being correlated with S2, and it is hard to see how the mere existence of such a correlation could have epistemic consequences unless the correlation is mentally represented, e.g., as a premise in a perceptual inference. (p. 68)

Because F&P see information as contained in stimuli, they need to postu-late that the organism has some kind of knowledge for mapping or matching stimuli to perceived categories. But the correlational (coupling) perspective doesn't require information to be explicated to the organism. The organism isn't correlating what's in the layout with stimuli or with what is perceived. Picking up and acting arise together, the one providing the possibility for the other: The blob affords eating. Whipping out the tongue is an act of categorizing. There is one coordination:

> sensing ⇔ blob categorizing ⇔ tongue whipping

The organism doesn't "get from" S1 to S2 or vice versa (cf. Table 12.2); S1 and S2 are codetermined relations. That's what a corelation is (cf. Figure 7.1).

F&P acknowledge that "it is incorrect to assume that the only way that one can perceive change is by detecting and comparing two instantaneous states, at least one of which is retained in memory" (p. 175). But all they can place between stimuli and categories are transducers, such as speedom-eters. (Indeed, beyond this, they miss the possibility that some categoriza-tions are not even functioning as referential symbols.) Viewing information as something that can exist in itself, F&P postulate that correlations may exist that are not viewed as informative: "It is perfectly possible that an organism should pick up a *de facto* informative property of the light but not take it to be informative, e.g., because the organism does not know about the correlation." Of course, this violates almost every tenet of ecological psychology. F&P wrongly suppose that information exists independent of function, that the organism can create categories that make no functional distinctions (uninformative), and that categorizing is "knowing about a correlation" as opposed to simply *correlating*.

Knowing about a correlation is knowing that there is a relation between perceptions and *ideas*. This is possible in people because we can know that we are categorizing (have an idea), hold multiple categorizations active, and categorize the relation of categories we are holding active. I know there is a correlation between a flash of light and the angle of the sun against the hood of my car because I have conceptualized a relation between my categorizations of angle, sun, and reflection. Unlike a scientist, a frog is not *concerned* with correlations; it is detecting blobs. A frog doesn't take a property to be informative because it doesn't *take* anything (but flies on its tongue). *Taking* some experience to be informative is a mental act that is part of having ideas, forming hypotheses, and conceiving evidentiary relations – the work of the detective or the epistemologist, not the work of a frog.

In short, F&P's analysis is pervaded by the descriptive modeling view that knowing (in this case, perceptual categorizing) is "knowing *that*" or "*knowing what* you know about." In ecological theory, perceptions and actions arise in a coupled, coordinated relationship such that *knowing* is not a kind of knowledge of the world in the sense of a model, but coordinating a relation, a change, of interest, a change that has implications for potential action (Figure 11.1).

Aboutness is a higher-order categorization (cf. the composition of categories in Figure 7.4 and Table 7.2). F&P miss this because they suppose *every categorization* to be a symbol that is referential for the organism. But perceptual categorizations are not (necessarily) used as pointers or names; they need not function referentially to be functional.[9] The "mentally represented" relation that F&P mention involves a special kind of conceptual categorization that two categories, say S1 and S2, are related, such that one refers to or provides information about the other. Examples of referential categorizations include a relation between an instance and a type, a property and an object, or an event and an idea about the event. On the basis of referential (semantic) categorizations, as F&P suggest, one would then have constructed the perceptual categorization to stand for something else or to be part of something else, such that it could function as a reference within a serial, *inferential* relation.

To repeat the main point: A categorization functions referentially when the organism categorizes it that way. The distinction between a "bare" categorization and a referential one is a matter of *structural composition* (Bateson's ladder of logical types, such as the "name of the name," discussed in Chapters 10 and 13) and also a matter of *content,* in the sense that each *stands for* (*represents*) categorization is a learned, conceptual relation.

Relation of perception to beliefs, inference, and judgment

We have now seen the key differences between the ecological and descriptive perspectives and may have a glimmer of how to bring them together. The idea that only some categorizations function as referential symbols is so different from the simple view that "it's symbols all the way down" that I would like to use F&P's analysis of the idea of *properties* to show further how the descriptive approach imputes referential function to what are only couplings.

The essential idea – what separates the two points of view – is how the properties cited in the scientist's report are manifest in perceptual systems. From the Gibsonian perspective, F&P talk fast and loose about properties: "Consider again the property of being a shoe. This is clearly a property that we can perceive things to have, hence it is property we can directly perceive" (p. 145). In effect, they make no distinction between correlations and conceptualizations. Their view is often implicitly top-down, from language to perceptual event, as if to say, "Look, does that object appear to be a shoe?" Indeed, the conceptual relation imputed is even more indirect, for they do not talk of perceiving shoes or detecting shoes but of "the property of being a shoe." I claim that the categorization of "being a shoe" is conceptual; "the property of being a shoe" is a higher-order categorization yet, a relation between something categorized to be an object and the concept of "being a shoe." Strictly speaking, we do not *perceive* a thing to have a property. Rather, we *conceive* that there is a relation between something we perceive and our conception of a property.

Throughout, F&P give examples of conceptual entities, namely, da Vinci artwork, shoes, and grandmothers, in an argument that "what's perceived" is undefined by Gibson. But he means *ecological properties* (pp. 145, 152) – affordances, functional distinctions, categories-in-action. Indeed, F&P's discussion suggests that the distinction between perceptual and conceptual categories is fundamental to understanding ecological theory.[10]

For example, they have a long discussion about whether *sentencehood* could be a perceptual property. In part, their descriptive habit of converting every distinction into P's and Q's is responsible for this puzzle: Categorizing and coordinating are leveled and tokenized, and the question becomes whether we could "directly perceive" the description Q. F&P thus call both color and sentencehood *properties*. They conclude that some perceptions may be mostly transduced (color) and that others require inference (sentencehood). But sentencehood is a *conceptualization*, not a perceptual categorization. Through practice, sequential conceptual relations may become coupled (the so-called compilation or chunking effect of practice), but they are still higher-order categorizations (Chapter 13).

One must admire F&P for their consistency and doggedness. They clearly interpret *pick up* to mean *encode* (Bickhard and Richie, 1983, p. 44) and rigorously follow through how "perceptual properties" – whether they are colors or shoes – can be constructed from stimuli. Their pervasive assumption is that cognition operates therefore only on stimuli and properties (encodings, descriptions). Thus, in contrast to an ecological account in terms of energy and activity, the descriptive account begins with the scientist's notion of properties and asks how they come to be formed in the subject's mind. Thus they view *their descriptive decomposition* as being the parts the cognitive system must be putting together. As Ullman says, this entire research program is driven by the assumption that a scientific theory requires an inventory of properties and causal interactions.

What is missed is that the representational structures in the cognitive system do not necessarily correspond to an observer's descriptions of the world. The assumption that cognition involves *manipulating a model* of the world reduces all cognitive operations to manipulations of descriptions of the world and behavior. The ecological approach also decomposes the perceptual-motor system, but along different lines. As Bickhard and Richie (1983) say, "Interactive models . . . are also decomposable, though not necessarily in any way involving encodings or inferences" (p. 39). A decomposition in terms of meaningful properties (what is perceived) is circular, for it assumes that what needs to be created is simply *transduced* (ironically, the kind of one-step directness that Gibson is attacked for!). Bickhard and Richie say, "The attempt to define transduction, of *any* properties, is internally incoherent" (ibid.) – incoherent because it suggests picking up *encodings*. The descriptive approach is therefore a kind of "direct encoding" model.

One may also take another tack, which I have begun in this section, namely, to point out that conceiving a property is a higher-order categorization involving what is technically called *intentionality*. Although a scientist may give a third-person account – talking of how an organism "detects a property," the categorization of "being an object" or "being an object having such-and-such a property" – such a representation is more than perceptual categorization accomplishes. Indeed, F&P (1981) say this: "*property* is an *intentional* notion" (p. 191). Their analysis is limited because they don't distinguish between "property" qua scientific distinction attributed to a cognitive system (a description), "property" qua perceptual categorization (a coupling), and "property" qua conceptualization (referential categorization). In F&P's terms, Gibson is only interested in "extensional perceptual relations (seeing, hearing, tasting, etc.)" (p. 188) – not the conceptual *judgments* of art collectors, scientists, engineers, or cooks. F&P say that they want to focus on how "perceptual transactions with the world affect what we know and believe" (p. 189). But (based on present evidence) a frog has no beliefs, for it conceives of nothing. It has no *ideas* at all. It is not aware that it is categorizing because it is not categorizing *that* it is categorizing.

Ironically, F&P hit the nail on the head: "To do cognitive psychology, you must know not just what the organism perceives, but how it takes what it perceives." The essential distinction that they never make is that *taking* has many forms. An organism may "take" a perceptual categorization to be about something (e.g., evidence for a hypothesis), or "take" it in a certain modal way (with doubt, with surprise, in fear), or "take" it with a grain of salt, so to speak, as being indeed only tentative or misleading, and so on. Thus "taking what is perceived" may be referential, modal, and/or conceptual. But a frog doesn't *take* the blob to be anything, except *literally* "a-thing-I-could-take-with-my-tongue."

Similarly, F&P are puzzled that Gibson "sometimes denies . . . that what you see when you look at the sky are stars." But "seeing a star" is not just a perceptual categorization, but a conceptualization that "that *thing* . . . is a star." Birds may see the same lights, but obviously, they don't conceive of them as stars. Even mistaking a planet for a star requires *conceiving* it that way. At least three conceptual relations (stars, the property of being a star, and that something has a property of being a star) are involved in referring to something as a star. If "being a star" is ecological, an affordance, which we (as scientists) describe as "being-a-blob-that-I-could-navigate-by," then it is perceptually categorized *in* such a coordination relation, not as a stand-alone property of a thing. Cognitive psychologists traditionally talk about "perceiving properties"; but as I have said, strictly speaking, one *conceives properties* and perceives *differences* of interest. Attributing properties to things is a conscious act, which requires conceiving a relation between a conceptual categorization and categorized stimuli – an *act of attribution*.

Again, F&P have already described attribution as a mental coordination: "One's theory of intentionality will have to postulate two of *something* if it is to account for the two ways of seeing Venus. The Establishment proposal is that we postulate two different *mental representations of Venus*" (p. 192). They need only go one step further to acknowledge that two categorizations are being coordinated. They need to move from their focus on the stuff in the world (as observers) to imagining how the brain is holding multiple categorizations active, categorizing them *as views*, and conceptualizing the relation of these views. Every step along the way requires particular kinds of conceptualizations: that a categorization can be a view (a way of taking the world), that two views may be different ways of the same object (a way of taking what is perceived). In effect, these higher-order categorizations provide ways of coordinating categorizations, and this coordinating occurs as an activity in what we commonly call *mental operations* (cf. Figure 9.4).

The miscommunication between F&P and Gibson arises because F&P are obviously focusing on conceptual, mental operations and Gibson is focusing on perceptual, nonconceptual categorization. We can bring these two points of view together by showing, as I have sketched here, that inference in the human brain is more than chaining descriptions together; it also involves structural coupling. The mental or cognitive operations that production systems model are *physical* coordinations, real actions, performed by a cognizant person. These may be acts of the imagination (in our reading or silent musing) or outwardly manifest in speech and writing. In frogs, coordinated action is presumably all nonconceptual, but in people coordination is perceiving-conceiving-acting at the same time.

My analysis provides some leverage for resolving dilemmas about appearances and reality. For example, F&P talk about the "(perceptual) inference from appearance to edibility." By my analysis, a *conception of edibility* is quite different from the categorization of "something-green-I-could-eat." F&P are interested in illusions because they hold to a correspondence view of truth, following from their presumption that perception is a conceptual relation: "Things that are misperceived to be edible *do* have the property of being *apparently* edible, and the problem for a theory of misperception is to explain how things could be taken to have properties that in fact they do *not* have" (p. 153). By viewing perception as detecting what is in the world (properties) – "What you see when you see a thing depends on what the thing you see *is*" (p. 189) – F&P are puzzled about how perception could construct an image of what is not there. Indeed, illusions reveal the standard case: What is perceived is a relation between stimuli and action. Perceiving is this relating, not constructing a mapping between the world and subject.

Hence F&P construe "apparently edible" as an objective property residing in the thing, rather than a categorization, that is, "seeing as edible." Again, when they say "perceive edibility," they mean "conceive edibility." Obviously, *edibility* is the concept of a botanist, an ethologist, or perhaps a chimpanzee. Most animals in the wild don't take a thing to have a *property* at all; they perceive an affordance and act (though it is an open question whether the deer in Portola Valley dream about walking on my decks and devastating my flowers). Similarly, F&P use the phrase *perceptual judgments*, as if perceiving a fly, avoiding red berries, and diagnosing diseases are all judgments. Again, they have flattened categorizing, so there is no distinction between a perception and a conception, between a physical coordination and having an idea, or between subconscious coupling and (inferential) deliberation.

The idea of properties is also often traditionally expressed in terms of propositions. By my analysis, a proposition is a conceptualization, an idea, what is called a belief in the descriptive account. In these terms, by the ecological account, the browsing deer or tongue-whipping frog is not forming and relating propositions about the world. F&P do acknowledge having read about this distinction:

Turvey and Shaw (1979) suggest that we should cope with the issue of perceptual error by "tak(ing) perception out of the propositional domain in which it can be said to be either right or wrong . . . and relocat(ing) it in a nonpropositional domain in which the question of whether perception is right or wrong would be nonsensical". (p. 182). Apparently, this means either that we should stop thinking of perception as eventuating in beliefs, or that we should stop thinking of beliefs as having truth values. Turvey and Shaw describe this proposal as "radical", but "suicidal" might be the more appropriate term. (p. 154)

Actually, Turvey and Shaw would advocate both conclusions: Direct perception doesn't involve forming beliefs. And if we take a belief to be a conceptual categorization that is known about the world or action, then only referential conceptual categorizations are beliefs (in particular, categorizations that function as symbols in inferences). "Having truth value" to the agent is (like "having a property") a higher-order conceptual relation. *Conceiving the possibility of error* in one's conceptions requires conceiving that there is a relationship between conceptions and experience (categorizations), that is, simply put, *knowing that one has a belief.* That is, having a belief is not having a certain kind of categorization per se, but categorizing a categorization as functioning as a model of the world. Knowing that categorizations function as models is quite different from merely categorizing at all. Indeed, by this analysis, an animal could have beliefs and make inferences without conceiving the idea of belief or inference.[11]

More basically, in a coupling, forming and sustaining a categorization is a *functional* differentiation, not dependent on *veridicality*. But F&P keep interjecting descriptions where only couplings may be needed: "The cognitive (and hence the behavioral) consequences of what you see depend on how you represent what you see" (p. 190). Thus they conflate seeing (a process of representing) with representing *what is seen*. Wittgenstein (1953) took pains to elucidate this point:

> I meet someone whom I have not seen for years; I see him clearly, but fail to know him. Suddenly, I know him, I see the old face in the altered one. . . . The very expression which is also a report of what is seen, is here a cry of recognition.
> What is the criterion of visual experience? – The criterion? What do you suppose?
> The representation of "what is seen." (pp. 197–198)

An artist represents what he or she sees by drawing. A journalist represents what he or she sees by describing. Such representing is properly called *commentary*, a second-order form of representing. The same mistake is often made in imputing knowledge representations to an expert or a student (cf. Figure 3.1). Being knowledgeable about the world doesn't necessarily mean representing knowledge (what knowledge engineers do), but *knowing* or *representing*.

Ultimately, F&P acknowledge that there is something to the distinction Gibson is talking around:

> Even theories that hold that the perception of many properties is inferentially mediated must assume that the detection of *some* properties is direct (in the sense of *not* inferentially mediated). Fundamentally, this is because inferences are processes in which one belief causes another. Unless some beliefs are fixed in some way other than by inference, it is hard to see how the inferential processes could get started. Inferences need premises. (p. 155)

But the issue is not that "some beliefs are fixed," but rather that some categorizations become "objects of thought"; they become beliefs by functioning as premises (a physical coordination process we have barely described, let alone explained in neural terms). For F&P, the noninferred perceptions are not perceptions at all – because anything not inferred is transduced, not based on what the organism learns and knows. Transduced properties, in their account, are not learned or based on experience, but hardwired relations between sensory and perceptual processes. Hence, all learning must occur by inference. By the theory of structural coupling, categorizations may be learned that are not functioning as referential representations, let alone being constructed from inferences.

F&P's correspondence view, locating information (properties) in the world, makes adaptive resonance neither necessary nor sufficient. Because information exists in the world, it need only be converted by the sensory system: "Transducers are technically defined as mechanisms that convert information from one physical form to another" (p. 157). But then the formation of premises requires some kind of combination of categories: "The output of the complex property detector must be *constructed* from primitively detected subfeatures" (p. 186). On the ecological account, premises are indeed constructed (conceptualizations), but perceptions are not assembled from features in the way arguments are assembled from premises (cf. the opening quotes of this chapter). As we saw in Part II, features are themselves developed by perceptual systems (see summary Table 8.1).

Coupling is a kind of transformation relation, but it is never clear whether F&P understand that *tuned* means categorical learning. The kind of integration of "subfeatures" F&P appropriately cite (texture, discontinuities, intensity) does not require inferential mediation, as they say, because such aspects are not detected independently and then correlated. In particular, the integration accomplished by a classification couple in TNGS is a dialectic relation, a *mutual organization* of (sub)features, not an assembly process.

In summary, the view that perception is inference fails to make several distinctions that biology and ethology suggest. First, perceptual categorizations are nonconceptual, functional distinctions, not conceptualized properties (of reified and distinguished *things*). Second, understanding how experience is objectified in reasoning (modeling the world and behavior) requires making a distinction between subconscious processes and conscious operations. Intentional (mental or symbolic) categorization, that is, having beliefs (forming propositions), involves higher-order conceptual categorization of reference and modality. Together these distinctions provide a different interpretation of what a symbol is, beginning to suggest what leverage categories functioning as referential symbols provide over structural coupling alone. Indeed, no better summary can be provided than F&P's statement: "the meaning of a representation can be reconstructed by a reference to its functional role" (p. 192). We are now ready to reconsider the functional roles of perceptual categories, of indexical conceptualizations (viewing an entity as a-thing-I-could-interact-with-in-special-way, e.g., how a dog relates to its owner), and of propositions in descriptive models. In the next chapter, we reconsider how diverse phenomena such as smoke signals, tokens in a descriptive model, and ideas function as symbols in different ways, and thus how the ideas of encoding, calculation, and human reasoning relate.

13   The varieties of symbol systems

[T]he most fundamental contribution so far of artificial intelligence and computer science to the joint enterprise of cognitive science has been the notion of a *physical symbol system*, i.e., ... systems capable of having and manipulating symbols, yet realizable in the physical universe.

[I]t becomes a hypothesis that this notion of symbols includes the symbols that we humans use every day of our lives. . . . (p. 135)

Nothing to speak of is known about "continuous" symbol systems, i.e., systems whose symbols have some sort of continuous topology. (p. 179)

Allen Newell, Physical symbol systems, 1980

The last chapter focused narrowly on the relation of stimuli, perceptual categorization, and action. I showed that Gibson's arguments are compatible with a coupling mechanism, and argued that the resulting categorizations become symbols in the sense intended by the physical symbol system hypothesis (PSSH) when they are functioning referentially, particularly in inferences. This referential functioning requires a higher-order *categorization of reference*, a categorization by the organism that a particular perceptual categorization or conceptualization bears some relation (e.g., part of, property of, or about) to a conceived object or situation. This is to say that a symbol in human reasoning (in imagination) is not a unit or physical thing in isolation, but a complex *conceptual relation functioning as* a marker or pointer. I pursue this hypothesis further in this chapter to show that the tokens in our descriptive models are not equivalent to the symbols in human reasoning because the latter are *coupled* to other categorizations; this coupling enables the "grounding" and nonverbal understanding that people experience but that purely descriptive cognitive models lack. However, I take Newell and Simon up on their offer to view symbols broadly, and suggest that we engage in a taxonomic study of varieties of *denotation* in cognitive systems, an effort I begin here.

Reformulating the physical symbol system hypothesis

In the philosophical literature of cognitive science, the term *symbol* has been used to refer to DNA, *molecular encodings* for proteins, program *tokens* in descriptive models, retinal *stimuli* patterns, and *neural categoriza-*

302

tions. Various attempts have been made to develop a unifying definition, under the hypothesis that the processes being described amount to the same thing, *symbol systems.* The common idea, articulated most clearly by Newell, is that a symbol works because it provides "access" to something else:

A PSS is simply a system capable of storing symbols (patterns with denotations), and inputting, outputting, organizing, and reorganizing such symbols and symbol structures, comparing them for identity or difference, and acting conditionally on the outcomes of the tests of identity. Digital computers are demonstrably PSSs, and a solid body of evidence has accumulated that brains are also. The physical materials of which PSSs are made, and the physical laws governing these materials are irrelevant as long as they support symbolic storage and rapid execution of the symbolic processes mentioned above. . . . (Simon, 1995, p. 104)

In this section, I review in some detail how Newell (and especially Simon more recently) tried to make this a clean, precise, and inclusive definition. I then show how the definition doesn't work to the extent that coupled neural processes don't have the defining properties of stored descriptive models (inherent stability, composability, sequential interpretability). I then try to bring things under one umbrella by characterizing the mechanisms by which patterns may functionally denote. That is, I characterize the different kinds of symbol *systems.*

Symbolic meaning versus distal access

To begin, it is useful to emphasize, as Newell did, that *symbol* does not necessarily mean *symbolic* in the sense of something whose meaning is open to semantic interpretation. We encountered this distinction in the discussion of Mycin's rules (Chapter 2), in which we indicated that Mycin works as a symbol system without examining what the terms in it mean. Furthermore, in the discussion of sematosensory maps in the owl monkey (Chapter 3) we found that neural representations need not be conventional linguistic distinctions (e.g., such as the terms in Mycin's rules). To include both descriptions in a computer model and neural maps, Newell (1990) restricted the meaning of the term *symbolic* to refer to certain kinds of *structures:*

Symbolic could be defined to be essentially synonymous with representational. Anything that represents exhibits symbolic function. I choose not to do this, because this usage obscures an important issue that is closely bound up with what are normally called symbols, which are things that occur in expressions or other media. Symbols are certainly used to represent, as when "cat" in "The cat is on the mat" is used to represent a specific cat. But there is more going on than just that. (p. 72)

What is going on, which for Newell is the essence of a symbol, is the general ability to access a structure at some other location, a process he calls *distal access.* A symbol is *any pattern* that provides access.

At this point, one could examine what is meant by distal access or denotation. A published debate about Newell's *Unified Theories of Cognition* took that form.[1] However, I believe that with all we have considered about perceptual categorization and situated robots in this book, the argument can move from a difficult philosophical analysis to a more direct taxonomic study. To begin this, it is useful to consider the argument for defining symbol in such a broad way and why it is believed to work, as articulated in another recent published discussion led by Alonso Vera and Herb Simon (1993).

Vera and Simon (V&S) start by repeating the essential definition that symbols are patterns that denote:

The case for regarding sensory inputs and motor outputs (whether human or computer) as symbol structures is that they are patterns and they do denote. Being patterned and denoting are the two properties generally taken as defining symbols, and this is the definition that is used consistently in the literature associated with the physical symbol-system hypothesis. The definition makes no reference to the linguistic or nonlinguistic character of the patterns. They can be either. Sensory inputs denote (however complex the language of denotation) the scenes and sounds that they record. . . . (p. 123)

Thus, according to V&S, a pattern of sensory stimuli can be viewed as being a symbol because it denotes, that is, it *records* a scene or sound, presumably in the manner of a data structure. That is, they agree with the view of Fodor and Pylyshyn (Chapter 12) that information is derived from external objects and flows into the system via the senses, and this information, because it is an *encoding*, is denotational:

We have categorized retinal images as . . . symbols, which may strike some readers as stretching the term "symbol" intolerably. Similarly, it may seem extravagant to regard portraits, photographs, or images in a mirror as symbols, for they encode so literally and "mechanically" the information derived from the objects they denote. But retinal images lie along the path leading to the more intricately encoded symbols in the central nervous system that designate the external objects. . . . As one moves upstream in the visual system, increasing levels of abstraction and combination are found in the representation of an image. It is wholly arbitrary to call one step in this sequence symbolic, but deny its label to its predecessor. All these processes are distinctly symbolic: They involve patterns that denote. And they are wholly different from the "direct" apprehension of the environment. . . . (p. 124)

This admirably clear description of the symbolic view is based on the idea of denotation as a kind of pointer in which reference is a mapping. All of this would be correct if perceptual categorization worked in this manner. But we saw in the debate about direct perception (Chapter 12) that it is inappropriate to refer to stimuli as encodings because the relation between stimuli and perceptual categorizations is not that of a flow of information, but a correlational (codependent) coupling. Furthermore, the relation of selected stimuli to the world is not a mapping of features in the world, or a "recording" from which information flows downstream, but a *selectional process* of constructing functionally relevant features (Chapter 7). No "language of denotation" is involved because there is no categorical designation (referential) process involved in perceptual categorization. Indeed, V&S reveal that they do not understand the coupling process of direct perception when they contrast the existence of internal patterns with "'direct' apprehension."

But V&S's discussion goes further to include various physiological processes as symbolic phenomena. They begin by emphasizing that to be a symbol a structure must be representational, which here means that the pattern "carries interpretable information":

Symbols include some types of signals, such as those on the retina. . . . As long as the abstracted pattern or representation encodes information that will be interpreted (and which has a functional role of carrying interpretable information) to generate action, then it is a symbol. Hemoglobin in the circulatory system actually carries oxygen; it does not just represent it, nor do the recipient cells interpret it. Antibodies and DNA, on the other hand, lie in a fuzzier area with respect to the symbol–signal distinction. These biological processes involve physical patterns that are interpreted, albeit in a low-level mechanical way. In this respect, these latter systems are more like thermostats than hemoglobin. They interpret a physical signal pattern according to a predetermined symbol system (e.g., a sequence of amino acids or a scale of voltage values) to generate a representation (be it of a protein molecule or of current room temperature). This is the essence of the PSSH. (p. 356)

Thus, the notion of interpretation in the PSSH is syntactic, based on the structures' forms. The forms change or are assembled according to the other forms or processes they represent (e.g., a protein or a temperature). The denotational function is what Newell meant by "something else is going on," and as a general functional concept it is worth pursuing. To this end, V&S argue that their critics have adopted too narrow a notion of *symbol*:

[Touretzky and Pomerleau's] characterization of many biological processes as nonsymbolic also derives from a too-narrow definition of symbol. When people burn their fingers and a subcortical reaction causes them to move their hand quickly, the single (evolutionarily derived) function of the nerve impulse is to indicate that bodily damage is occurring. The nerve impulse does not carry the burn in any sense; it communicates its occurrence. This symbol denoting the event is transmitted to the spinal cord, which then transmits a symbol to the muscles, which contract to pull the hand away. Although subcortical, this process is a good example of a PSS at work, much like a thermostat. (Vera and Simon, 1994, p. 358)

If we define symbols . . . as patterns that denote, then connectionist systems and Brooks' robots qualify as physical symbols systems. (Simon, 1995, p. 104)

[S]ymbols may be as readily processed subconsciously as consciously. (Vera and Simon, 1994, p. 359)

Now, grouping DNA, expert systems, connectionism, thermostats, situated robots, and conscious activity such as interpreting Aaron's drawings is too much for an engineer or a biologist focusing on the various *mechanisms* involved here. How can we sort out the different levels of categorizing or clarify the distinction between coupling and inferential processes if we simply lump everything together as being symbol systems? In fact, V&S (1994) provide an approach, although they don't carry it through: Adopt the view that these are all symbol systems and then ask "What are the different kinds of symbol systems?" The first step, responding to the claim that their definition of symbol is "so broad as to be vacuous," is to

[point] to the many examples of patterns that do not have denotations, hence are not, by our definition, a symbols. We can begin with snowflakes, and proceed through the whole vast collection of nondenotative patterns exhibited by natural (and artificial) systems: the wind ripples on lakes, the shapes of birds, the masses of clouds, crystals, the grain in wood, a Jackson Pollock painting.... Therefore, to say that a particular pattern denotes, hence is a symbol, distinguishes it from most other patterns in the world, and says something quite strong about its functioning. In particular, a symbol in a physical symbol system (PSS) can be manipulated to obtain information and to draw inferences about the thing it denotes.... (pp. 355–356)

V&S play fast and loose here with the ideas of *information, drawing inferences*, and *denotation* – and this is why their definition of symbol system is inadequate. But if one focuses on how *distinctions* (not just patterns) are created and what kind of functional role they play in *differentiating transactions*, then the notion of denotation can move from something that is imbued with conceptualization of reference and inference to something more basic that does cover biological, computational, and reasoning systems. Then, on this basis, we would have additional leverage to articulate how computer models differ from human knowledge in terms of *pattern creation* and *denotational mechanism*.

How to develop a broader view of symbol systems

V&S's argument with Touretzky and Pomerleau suggests that it's not useful to argue whether something is a PSS or not. PSS is an analytic notion, and one can't argue about definitions in isolation. As V&S point out, there are many varieties of phenomena that we may find useful to characterize as being a PSS. A typical scientific approach would therefore be to *study the varieties* that have been initially grouped as PSSs. What are their forms and operation and the relative roles they play within larger systems? That is, if a variety of patterns are characterized as *denoting*, what are functionally the different ways in which denoting *develops within a system* and how does denoting work to change behavior?

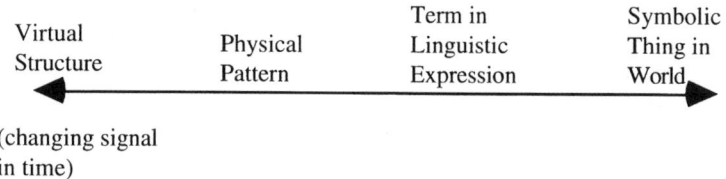

(changing signal
in time)

Figure 13.1. The variety of symbols.

Can we taxonomize types of PSSs and study the nature of symbols? We can use italics throughout to remind ourselves that analytic terms such as *symbol* are buckets for phenomena that we may wish to distinguish, both for understanding and for engineering artificial systems. Our goal is not to formulate a precise definition per se, but to find dimensions for relating patterns and *denotation*. Among the distinctions we may find useful are these: Are the symbols patterns in a conventional vocabulary? Are they stored? Are their forms continuous and changing over time (as in sematosensory maps) or are they fixed and discrete? Are they perceived and descriptively interpreted in a kind of commentary? Is this interpretation essential to their role? Do the symbols combine recursively to form new *symbol structures*? Do they encode names or attributes of what they represent (i.e., are they part of description-expressions)?

These questions are, of course, motivated by the diversity of examples provided by V&S and by our own analyses of Mycin, the message from Nice (Chapter 9), neural models (Chapters 6 and 7), and so on. The nature of denotation and interpretation changes in these examples, as does the involvement of perceptual categorization, motion, and language. Roughly speaking, we find that there are *levels of representationality* relative to the role of the distinction in affecting the system's interactive behavior in time. To elaborate this intuition (which parallels Schön's levels in Chapter 9), I examine a number of examples, and in later sections make some longitudinal (across-systems) and latitudinal (within-systems) comparisons.

To begin, a tentative spectrum of kinds of symbols is given in Figure 13.1. At one extreme, we have smoke signals and probabilistic-topological maps (owl monkey) – organized processes within a behavior system. At the other extreme, we have Mycin's tokens, the Nice message, and Aaron's drawings – perceived entities in the world that an agent views as a model or representation of experience. (Such entities can be arranged on another spectrum from formal encodings to artistic, aesthetic expressions.)

To draw an essential distinction: In the example of the Nice message an agent is using perceptual categorization to decide what constitutes a symbol *thing* in the world. Obviously, this is at a higher level than perceptual categorization alone, as in the example of the frog snatching a fly. The complexity is most clear when we, as observers, ask, "What is the relation of the symbol found by the agent in the world and the patterns in the brain?" I suggest that this question is either confused or unnecessary at this point. A more pertinent observation is that *levels of categorizing are required* in perceiving a symbol in a written message and then conceiving that it designates something (recall the levels of Figure 7.4). The essential point, for the moment, is that such denotation involves a *conceptual relation,* to be contrasted with the low-level mechanical relation between DNA patterns and proteins (indicated as physical patterns in Figure 13.1).

Furthermore, detecting that a symbol exists may involve a mixture of perception and conception in time. For example, a sequence of smoke signals would constitute a symbol to an agent perceiving them in time and then conceptually coordinating their relations to "parse" them into tokens. Thus again, finding symbols may involve relating transient and changing forms. Consistent with V&S's definition, a symbol is not only a physical structure that statically describes something, but a pattern of structural changes, such as a varying signal over time. In this respect, the signals in the layers of Brooks's robots are symbols even though perceptual categorization is not involved.

To summarize, once we adopt the broad view that a symbol is "that which refers to or represents something else" (the definition in *Webster's New World Dictionary*), our work becomes to distinguish the varieties of reference (Newell's *denotation*) that may occur. The distinction between *direct-causal mechanism* (as in DNA, neural classification couples, signals, and program pointers), *conceptualization of reference,* and *commentary about meaning* suggests that Newell's *distal access* is too broad. In general, denotation is not about physical access to a referred entity (as in mental planning about tomorrow's events). The term *representing* may be more useful: patterns that are (functionally) representing. The idea of *pattern* also needs to be examined. The term *distinctions* may be more useful: Are distinctions tautological or conventional? (G005 in Mycin is arbitrary because its physical form is direct-causal, with tautological meaning, not conceptual interpretation.) If the distinctions are stable physical forms, are they *sustained relations* in a coupled dynamic system, such as in sematosensory maps, or are they fixed tokens, as in descriptive models?

These are the kinds of distinctions an engineer considering different mechanisms needs to know about. Some variations may be viewed as functionally equivalent as first approximations (in descriptive cognitive models, tokens represent human conceptualizations). Some symbolic systems may replicate others if they are tuned over time (as may be the case for Freeman's model of olfactory categorization). In effect, the claim that PSSs are not equivalent across the board – that human cognition is situated – leads now to a study of *representing* that includes programs of various sorts, robots, biological processes of various sorts, animals, and people. Calling them all PSSs is a first step, and Newell and Simon deserve credit for adhering to a simple definition. But understanding the difference between biological cognition and what our machines do – following a means–ends approach to advancing cognitive science – is now necessary. We can begin with a taxonomic study and then move to an engineering study of what different kinds of representing require. The broad range of what we will find is foreshadowed by an initial consideration of what *system* is being described. Is the environment included (as in writing systems)? Is perceptual or conceptual categorization required? Does action creating representations require iterative refinement over time (as in writing)? Are multiple agents involved in creating and using the symbol system? Is the functionality driving the agent's interpretations *conceptual*, with respect to the agent's role within a *social system*?

Diverse examples of symbols

Table 13.1 brings together different examples of patterns that denote what we have considered in this book. To taxonomize these examples, we need some terms for distinguishing them. To begin, I have indicated how the example would be commonly named, as well as whether it exists as a physical entity apart from an interpreting process, whether the symbol is perceptually constructed, and whether its reference is conceived (usually involving inferential steps). I attempt to describe the functional role of the symbol in the system.

By ordering the table according to the presence of perceptual categorization and conceptualization in the symbol system, we can clarify that in certain cases, although we refer to some artifact in the world as being a symbol, it functions this way to the agent only because the agent is conceiving a semantic relation – the stuff in the world is parsed and ordered *as being a symbol* (e.g., a smoke signal message). At the other extreme, structures engaged in direct causal-coupling relations, for example, DNA and perceptual categorization in the frog, are not referential categorizations to the agent (let alone categorized as *being symbols*). These extremes correspond to the first-person and third-person views: In the case of structures conceived as being symbols, the symbols are functioning as *representations* from the agent's point of view (e.g., the token SIGNIFICANT in Mycin's rules from the doctor's point of view). In the case of structures whose forms are codetermined by the system, the symbols are *representing* from the

Table 13.1. *Diverse examples of patterns that might be called symbols*

Pattern that denotes (symbol)	Common name	Exists apart from its interpreting mechanism?	S ⇔ P (symbol is constructed)	⇒C (reference is conceived)	Representing (third person) or representational (first person)	Functional (denotational) role
DNA	Code				Third	Direct encoding
Light pattern on retina	Stimuli (layout)				Third	Part of a perceptual categorization coupling
"Blob-contrast-I-could-eat" category in frog	Perceptual categorization		√		Third	Differentiates possible action
"Fuzzy thing" categorization in Darwin III	Category	√ (Wired to motor mechanism)			Third	Classification couple (triggers action)
Pengi's the-block-that-I-just-kicked	Indexical representation	√			First	Dynamic pointer name

CULTURE-1 (to Mycin)	Token	√			First	Pointer name in SSM
SIGNIFICANT (to Mycin)	Token	√			First	Pointer name in general model
Bee dance	Message	√	? (Iconic motor activation)		First	Organizes group behavior
Aaron's drawing (to human)	Picture	√	√	√ (Described)	First	Evokes aesthetic response
Smoke signal	Signal	√	√	√ (Named)	First	Coded message (artifact)
SIGNIFICANT (to human doctor)	Word	√	√	√	First	Coded model (artifact)
Nice message	Text	√	√	√	First	Natural language message (artifact)

observer's point of view (e.g., the classification couples in Darwin III). I claim that this is a primary distinction; in effect, the first-person view corresponds to *symbol* proper, the representations used in descriptive models and in human reasoning. The symbolic function in other systems is only attributed by an observer because only the observer is conceiving a denotational relation between the symbols and what they are accessing, referring to, or carrying information about. Munsat (1990) summarizes the distinction:

> We can (and do) speak of these [neural network] structures or patterns as "representing" this feature, but again, the internal structure doesn't work by representing in the sense of "standing for" or "symbolizing" for the purpose of a computation: it is physically activated by the physical presence of some feature in the input. (The height of the ball in the toilet can be spoken of as "representing" the height of the water to the mechanism, but a toilet doesn't work by using a representation.) (p. 503)

Thus, "using a representation" means that the system is categorizing a categorization entity as referential, as representing something.

Recalling Gibson's use of the term *mental*, the distinction between representing and categorizing reference allows us to understand Agre's interpretation of the symbols in Pengi (Chapter 5). Referring to names like "the car I am passing," Agre (in preparation) says, "These names are conveniences for the theorist, not mental symbols of any sort. Although they look like definite descriptions, they are not descriptions that agents represent to themselves as linguistic entities" (p. 52). Although these expressions are not text that the agent reads, they still could be symbols of *some sort*. As Agre says:

> They designate, not a particular object in the world, but rather a role that an object might play in a certain time-extended pattern of interaction between an agent and its environment. . . . The concept is not that of linguistic reference, since symbolic representations are not necessarily involved. If an entity refers to a certain object on some occasion, then that object is said to be assigned to that entity. (Ibid.)

Designation through assignment in Pengi (what others call *registration*) is a form of coupling in a perceptual-motor system (a role in a pattern of interaction). The token is a physical entity that is viewed as operating directly, causally, within a system, and this function gives it the properties we ascribe to it. Interpreting what the token means – categorizing it as referential – occurs in Agre's interpretation and is manifest in his descriptions ("symbolic representations"). The table lookup in Pengi that effects the designation is a means of *implementing the coupling mechanism* in a digital program; such lookup is not interpreted by Agre as being a model of referential categorization ("linguistic reference").

Another primary distinction, which Table 13.1 does not make, is that in coupling relations, symbols do not exist in isolation. In particular, one cannot point to a retinal layout and say that it is a symbol that "carries interpretable information." On this point, the language used by V&S is misleading and violates their own objective of adopting a universal notion of symbol systems. In order to broaden the definition of *symbol systems*, we cannot use the notions of *structure, information,* and *interpretation* in uniform ways. In particular, we cannot point to one aspect of a structural coupling and claim that it is a symbol, in the same sense that a token in a descriptive model is a symbol. As I have taken pains to explain (Chapter 12), the coupling is a relation that coorganizes its components; indeed, coupling makes unorganized materials into *functional components* (such as the areas in the owl monkey's brain). To take a simple example, if we view knocking at the door as being a symbol, then the knocking without a sound does not function in the same way (carry the same information), nor does a sound of knocking without an agent hitting the door. Knocking and sound must occur together. Similarly, the examples of signals or stimuli given by V&S are not phenomena functioning in isolation; they are symbols only because they are part of circuits.

On the other hand, Newell and Simon's (1981) definition of designation is that "an expression designates an object if, given the expression, the system can either affect the object itself or behave in ways depending on the object" (p. 40). Hence, we might say that stimuli and perceptual categorizations "designate" one another because they behave in ways that depend on one another. That is, they are symbol duals; they provide access to one another in that they coactivate each other (in the manner of a classification couple in TNGS or coupled chaotic attractors). A stimuli, is of course, not an expression, or a stable token, so further distinctions need to be made. In short, what we are uncovering is that how a structure is organized so that it *functions as a symbol* varies considerably, and these mechanisms are precisely what the biologists and engineers want to know.

At this point, we are accumulating quite a few distinctions, which I need to make explicit. Here are other essential ways, besides the first-person–third-person distinction, in which symbol systems thus broadly conceived may vary:

Pointer versus categorization. Broadly speaking, Mycin uses tokens like CULTURE-1 as *pointers*; they thus function referentially (first person). In contrast, in human inference, ideas and perceptual details – the topics of an argument – are *categorizations*. This distinction becomes essential for understanding how human reasoning is different from symbolic calculators like Mycin (see the later section on heuristic coordination). In circuits in which the symbols are not separate from the interpreter (such as the signals in Brooks's robots, Figure 5.1), this distinction is irrelevant: The symbol is neither a pointer nor a categorization; it is just a change in time that directly causes changes to the system's behavior. Thermostats and toilet bowls are similar (although they incorporate arms and dials that enable a human to read their internal state).

Internal versus external denoting. Pointers in Mycin and molecules in DNA refer to other structures internal to the operating system. That is, the referent is directly accessed, perhaps through an interpreter (e.g., Mycin's explanation program uses tokens stored by the consultation program to access other records). In other systems, the symbols refer to something outside the system (from either the first or third person point of view).

Coupled existence versus flowing of information. In traditional information-processing systems, as in descriptive models, the information carried by symbols is viewed as flowing. Under the broader reformulation of symbol systems, information comes into existence via a coupling relation or by an interpretation process (such as Mycin's applying its rules or looking up records in the situation-specific model). Newell characterizes interpretation as a process designated by an expression; we can broaden this to allow the symbol and the process to arise together, as in the case of sensorimotor circuits.

Composed expression versus part of a system. Newell and Simon say that a "symbol structure is composed of a number of instances (or tokens) of symbols related in some physical way (such as one token being next to another)" (1981, p. 40). One might view a sensorimotor map as a symbol structure in this sense. On the other hand, in a topological map, the relations are codefined (recall how the entire map will become rearranged if one portion is lesioned). Thus, in coupled systems the symbols are not merely composed independently into new units; a set of symbols is composed as *one functioning system.* The idea of an *expression* or *composition* must be broadened to include dynamic, *tautological* relations.

Stable versus dynamic structures. Symbols may be relatively fixed or may adapt in relation to one another. The forms may constitute a vocabulary (or alphabet) in a *conventional language,* a conceptual system (e.g., a belief system), a topological network developed by adaptive resonance, and so on. Again, the different ways in which symbols *form* in relation to the existing system is of the utmost interest to the study of biological and robotic systems. Newell and Simon's original definitions suggesting relatively static tokens must be accordingly broadened.

Tim Smithers (1995) provides a useful summary of the shift required if we are to understand how third-person symbol systems develop. He argues that the great success of digital computers is based on the separation of the logic circuit and device levels from the logic behavior and knowledge levels:

This separation of the logical behaviour of computers from the physical behaviour of the implementing devices is what produces the formal medium that Newell sees as enabling the "Great Move" from what he calls *analogical* representational systems, which depend on the physical and dynamical properties of the representational media, to a neutral stable medium that is capable of being organised in all the variety of ways required and supporting further composition. (p. 150)

But this "liberation of the representation builder" comes at a cost:

We now have to specify explicitly all the necessary constraints on a representational system for it to meet its needs. This includes the general problem of controlling the formal inferences that our representational system can support so that only those beneficial to the agent's ongoing goal-achieving activities are actually made. (Ibid.)

In fact, in the brain there is still an important separation between neural "implementation" and representational function, as is obvious in the variety of ideas a person may think. However, what is not separate in people is the *development* of the representational distinctions and the operating (functioning) of the system. In this manner, as I have explained throughout this book, concepts are coupled to perceptual categorizations and both are coupled to potential actions – the essence of situated cognition. From the perspective of the variety of symbol systems, this means that the symbols in a descriptive cognitive model must be elaborately designed and have a *dual first-person designation* – as designators of conceptualizations for the human reading the expressions and as pointers for controlling internal processes for the program itself. (This shows why we can replace G0009 in Mycin's rules without changing its referential function for the system but we will violate its referential function for the designers.) In contrast, the symbols in a neural system, whether insect or human, are always developed as part of the functioning of the system in a kind of tautological relation – the designators are categorizations and always designate one another or are derived by inference from existing distinctions within the system. A great deal needs to be said here about consistency, independence of conceptual modalities, and so on. But the essential point is that, as designators, the neural symbol system is always constructing distinctions for itself, so the symbols constitute a certain kind of *system of relations*, which in a *designed* system such as Mycin or Aaron cannot be attained without great and careful work.

In summary, I began this inquiry some years ago with the view that symbols should be viewed as tokens, as in programs, and rejected the idea that neural structures are symbols. Finding that conceptual categorizations of reference do function as symbols in inferences (from the analysis of Fodor and Pylyshyn's arguments in Chapter 12), I decided that *categorization of reference* should be the required distinction; hence, tokens in programs are not symbols after all! This equivocation suggested that a broader view of symbol systems was warranted (as V&S advocated). Broadening the definition to include all the examples V&S give requires broadening the notion of reference to include pointers (such as Mycin's tokens, aka Newell's *distal access*) and then realizing that *perceptual categorization functions as representing* from a third-person, scientific point of view. To properly include direct-coupling systems, I indicated that we must broaden the view of *designates* to allow for corelations and broaden the view of *expression* to allow for structural organizations operating dynamically in circuits.

I conclude that the question "What is a symbol and what is not?" is relatively unfruitful because it dichotomizes kinds of cognitive systems. It is more interesting to begin by grouping what appears to be similar – despite obvious superficial differences – and inquire about the varieties of symbol *systems*: What are the ways in which symbols relate developmentally to one another? What are the varieties of mechanisms for coordinating behavior? The idea of *functional differentiator* (from Mark Bickhard) is perhaps the most useful reformulation of *symbol*. A symbol is thus any indicator or "a difference that makes a difference" in Bateson's sense. Crucially, we can characterize that difference either in terms of the system's *operation* or in terms of an outsider's view of what the system is *accomplishing* with respect to its environment. Adopting the broad perspective that V&S advocate therefore requires being more careful of statements like "Information is about something" or even "A signal carries information," which do not distinguish between first- and third-person denotation or how distinctions develop.

All of this adds up to the claim that symbols in descriptive models always functionally designate (refer to) other *symbols*, whereas categorizations in the conceptual symbol system of the human brain functionally designate *other categorizations*. What are the implications of this claim? The remainder of this chapter reconsiders human knowledge and computer representations from this point of view.

Reconsidering human reasoning

Until now, my investigation in this chapter has been longitudinal (across different kinds of PSSs); this section provides a latitudinal survey (within the human PSS). Having lumped everything together, we can now go back and differentiate varieties of *distal access* in the human PSS to articulate the spectrum of distancing and interpreting that may occur:

- *Structural coupling*: Two areas of the system mutually activate each other, codefining what constitute internal parts or processes.
- *Categorical reference*: The system conceptually categorizes another categorization as bearing the relationship of part, property, name, and so on, of a conceptualized thing in the world.
- *Symbolic interpretation*: The system recategorizes the references of (interprets) its own prior *descriptions*, often by rearranging these descriptions and reinterpreting the juxtapositions and flow (e.g., an artist modifying a drawing).

On the one hand, we have the ecological view of perception and action; on the other hand, we have the social view of knowledge construction and participation. One way to link the ecological and social views of situatedness is to carry the idea of categorization throughout the system, as hypothesized by Edelman's model of consciousness, in which the brain categorizes its own functioning (Figure 7.4). Do these neural levels of processing and self-organizing structure build on one another in the way that molecules build compounds and complex objects in the world? I pursue this approach in the somewhat speculative analysis of this section.

We might begin by reminding ourselves that different levels of organization are of different *logical types*, so again, talk about flow of information or control will be misleading. We will be depicting a *dependent hierarchy*, not necessarily a mechanism with the separated representation–implementation relations of digital computers.

My approach is also inspired by Bateson's (1988) theory of communication. The theory uses the idea of logical typing (which comes from Bertrand Russell) to explain how levels of coordinated process and naming (description, more generally categorization) are constructed in living systems. By this analysis, the levels constitute a "zigzag ladder of dialectic between forms and process" (p. 211). Wilden's diagram (Figure 10.1) relating inorganic systems and culture is an example (inverted, with increasing complexity at the bottom). The hierarchy is maintained by feedback between levels. Information becomes more abstract and its "sphere of relevance" broadens as more complex organizations are constructed to include simpler organizations. For example, Bateson presents the example of a policeman using radar to detect that a motorist is speeding; the law he is enforcing was set by the town council, which "acted self-correctively" with an eye on the voters (p. 216). But information used by the council is not necessarily relevant to the policeman; there is a *change in the logical type* of information as we move through the hierarchy. The arrest of a motorist will be viewed differently by the governor than by the local mayor. What constitutes information (an *event* in contextualist terms) and how it operatively affects behavior depends on the sphere of influence. Again, a "sphere of influence" is dialectically formed: The context of "possibilities for action" is co-determined by the operational distinctions developing at the next lower level.[2]

Here is a first-cut summary of the logical levels of representation in human knowledge:

- *Topological maps*: Analog relations ("coarse coding"), as in the hierarchy of maps coupled to the visual retina (five or six layers deep, with "jumpers" to three or even four levels down). In these maps, "internal structure derives from internal structure of referents" (Phillips, Hancock, and Smith, 1990, p. 505). Coupled to categorizations in sensorimotor circuits, they constitute *features* (e.g., Pierce and Kuipers's model).
- *Coupled categorizations*: As in TNGS.
- *Referential categorizations*: *Grounded symbols* participating in inferences.
- *Conceptual hierarchy*: Type-instance conceptualization, nonliteral "seeing as."
- *Descriptive modeling of objects and events*: Names, qualities, actions, modality (necessity, sufficiency, possibility, negation), and so on.
- *Coordinate system*: Descriptive formalization of conceptual relations according to a dimensional analysis (e.g., metric system, natural language grammar, dictionary, knowledge representation language).

This particular dependent hierarchy attempts to relate mental processes and descriptive modeling. Another approach is to focus on the internal relations of categorization; for example, how do behavior sequences form and perceptual categorizations become recategorized? How do behavior sequences become coordinated conceptually, such that behavior becomes "grammatical"? (An exercise for the reader.)

The varieties of conceptual relations

One way of simplifying the many dimensions of representational organization in human knowledge is to consider only how conceptual relations relate categories:

- *Coupling relation*: A categorization of correlation between concepts; unarticulated, as in the conceptual relation of pumpoids and paintbrushes, there is just one idea (the left side of Figure 13.2).
- *Categorization of relation*: A distinction about the kind of relation (Figure 13.2, center). For example, C1 is like C2, C1 is adjacent to C2, and C1 is part of C2. In the coupling (metonymic) relation we may have "ball

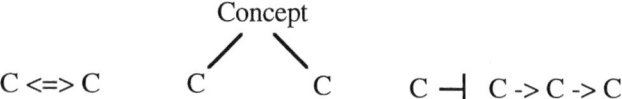

Figure 13.2. Coupling corelation of categories (C), categorization of a relation between categories, and categorization of a sequence.

⊂ play," so for the dog, seeing the ball is equivalent to playing. In the categorization of the relation, there are categorized entities that interact in the event; so, for the person, the ball is conceived as something the dog will fetch.

- *Categorization of a sequence of categorizations*: Categorizing a coordinated sequence of perceptual and motor events (Figure 13.2, right). In animals this includes conceptualization of feeding, grooming, nest building, and so on. The sequence is not merely chained by serial activation (each categorization activating the next); an overarching categorization of the sequence makes it a unit or chunk. Hence, there is the idea (conception) of feeding, playing, and so on, manifest as goal-oriented behavior in which alternative means of accomplishing "steps" are explored without losing the thread or overall intention. Specifically, the overarching sequence is held active, such that substitution in the sequence is possible.

I will say more subsequently about temporal relations. For the moment, I want to emphasize a few points. First, conceptualizing a *coordination* may be primary and may develop prior to conceptualizing kinds of relations between included things and events. So-called *concepts* in descriptive cognitive modeling are a combination of different kinds of categorizations: couplings, dependent hierarchies, goal sequences (routines), and linguistic orders (named *hierarchical relations*). What is most ignored is that nonverbal conceptualizations – ways of coordinating behavior sequences in time *without describing them*, such as sounds, images, and rhythm – are crucial in animal behavior. Furthermore, the understanding modeled by descriptive cognitive models (especially expert systems, student models, and models of natural language) requires conceptualization of *type*, *instance*, *variable*, and so on. That is, to understand the relation between "a culture" and CULTURE-1, a person must conceive objects ("thing"), indexical references ("that thing") and types ("a thing like that"). Indeed, in human knowledge the concept of *type* is coupled to the concept of *situation*. Conceiving a name for a type requires categorizing temporal and spatial relations that distinguish here and now from there and then so that different events are categorized in terms of different times and places. After relations are conceived as entities, naming can become a deliberate activity. That is, the agent conceives that symbols exist. The past and present and what is not perceptually present are tokenized and can be related in names, stories, and causal theories.[3]

The relation of names and meaning has, of course, been raked over by linguists and philosophers of language. My interest here is to highlight that conceptualization formalized in descriptive models relies on and could only have evolved from more basic forms of categorization, and these categorical relations – of thing, event, and situation – appear to be coupled in our understanding. That is, beyond the limitations already shown in modeling perceptual categorization descriptively (Chapter 12), the analysis of conceptualization in terms of kinds of categorization (Figure 13.2) suggests that a descriptive-inferential mechanism (a descriptive cognitive model) cannot replicate the dynamic relations in our understanding of concepts, especially their relation to our direct experience.[4]

The ideas of coupling, sequence, and conceptual relation of multiple categorizations suggest that how categorizations are activated in time with respect to one another is a defining characteristic of a coordination mechanism. The very idea of coupling is that activations are contemporaneous, such that multiple areas in the brain, connected by neural paths, become organized at the same time.[5] (This is most obvious in visual shifts that occur in illusions such as the Necker cube.) Conceptualizing a sequence (Figure 13.2) requires that somehow the beginning and end must be related by a neural (global) mapping. The conceptualization of reference requires that (at least) two categorizations are held active; inference obviously requires not merely chaining of categorizations, but the conceptual coordination of instances in a *premise* – a whole complex of entities, properties, and their relations.

Strikingly, descriptive cognitive modeling takes activation relations for granted: A typical knowledge modeling language gives us for free the notions of variables, buffers, registers, pointers, stored sequences, inheritance, and so on. All of these are now known to be prerequisites for modeling human reasoning, but they are not taken as the mechanistic capabilities that must be explained. In effect, this is the connectionist research program. But rather than focusing on the network as a place where stuff is lodged and interacting, my analysis suggests that the manner in which *coordinating processes* organize one another, sequence, and compose is primary. Some of the possible mechanisms have already been formulated: Freeman's chaotic attractor model suggests how different neural "modules" may simultaneously organize each other; Edelman's TNGS model can be extended to allow for global maps to activate each other sequentially (constituting the kind of subsumption hardwired into Brooks's robots), and Edelman's model of consciousness as reentrant categorization suggests how awareness of internal processes occurs.[6]

Put another way, distinctions important to understanding the temporal sequencing and composing of categorization are perhaps useful for understanding the origin of consciousness. On this basis, we can formulate some of the next steps in building situated robots (Part II), including the categorization of identity and the reification of objects and events into individuals and types (not requiring a predesigned ontology). Situated robots do form symbol systems around features and simple classification couples. But they do not yet conceptualize. Hence, we appear to be some distance from inferential mechanisms that work together with coupling mechanisms (as is evident in the reasoning of the paintbrush inventors in Chapter 9). One way to bridge the gap is to look again at animal behavior to characterize how behavior can be coordinated without a modeling language (but possibly including inference). This is a rather large undertaking in itself, beyond the scope of this book.[7] Another approach is to look again at our programs to relate their architecture to what we have learned about perception and conceptualization, the topic of the next section.

Heuristic coordination

Many expert systems, and descriptive cognitive models in general, incorporate taxonomic classifications, such as the disease and antibiotic taxonomies in Mycin. The "reasoning" of these programs fits the general pattern of (1) abstracting descriptions of situations in the world, (2) heuristically (by cause, frequency, or preference) relating these abstractions to a second classification, and then (3) refining the second description to a level suggesting particular actions. This inference pattern is called *heuristic classification* (Clancey, 1985). For example, in Mycin these phases include the following:

- *Abstracting patient characteristics* (e.g., the patient's elevated temperature implies "fever," drug consumption implies a "compromised host").
- *Heuristically associating patient abstractions* to the organism-disease taxonomy (e.g., a compromised host may be infected by organisms that normally are found in the body).
- *Grouping features in laboratory results* and matching them against properties in the organism-disease taxonomy (e.g., the shape and staining characteristics of an organism growing in a sputum culture imply that it is a pneumococcus).
- *Refining initial organism-disease classifications* (e.g., the combination of "normal organism," symptoms of an infection, symptoms of respiratory infection, alcoholism, and laboratory results suggest bacterial-pneumococcus infection in the blood).
- *Heuristically associating the organism-disease classification* with antibiotic classifications (e.g., pneumococcus might be treated by penicillin and related antibiotics).
- *Refining the initial antibiotic classification* (e.g., the combination of the

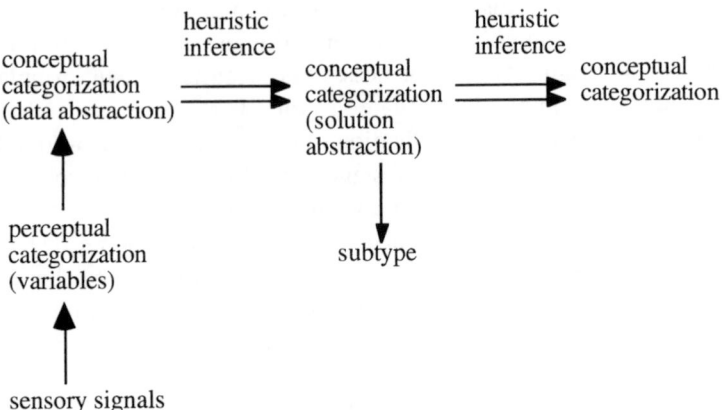

Figure 13.3. Heuristic coordination: Heuristic classification reformulated in terms of perceptual and conceptual categorization.

patient's allergies and laboratory information about organism resistance suggests that another drug must be substituted for penicillin).

The inference pattern of heuristic classification (HC) – consisting of repeated data abstraction, heuristic association, and classification refinement – has been shown to fit a wide variety of descriptive models in engineering, medicine, and business. Until this pattern was articulated, many of these programs were characterized in terms of the representation language (e.g., rules versus frames). Until the advent of heuristic modeling, most cognitive psychologists studied how people classified objects and events in isolation (Bruner, Goodnow, and Austin, 1956). The HC pattern suggests that the distinctions people make – their conceptual structures – are chained and hence *functionally defined*. For example, the descriptions and level of detail in a medical diagnosis are defined with respect to the alternative therapies available. In particular, viral meningitis is treated by orange juice and rest; distinguishing the kind of virus is irrelevant. Hence, the HC pattern is consistent with the idea we have developed throughout this book that categorizing occurs within a perceptual-action circuit. The HC pattern is thus a better psychological model of human knowledge than classification or semantic networks viewed in isolation.

We are now posed to relate the HC pattern to what we have learned about perceptual categorization (Figure 13.3). The diagram shows that the initial data abstraction in a program is actually describing the human perceptual categorization process plus the conceptualization of features. These conceptualized features (e.g., "the shape of the organism") are represented in the descriptive model as parameters (variables) by which the data classification hierarchy is organized (e.g., types of patients, types of cultures, and organism growth characteristics). From this point, descriptions (named *categorizations*) are chained to descriptions according to a conception of cause, preference, or perhaps habit ("what I do when"). The analysis I have presented to this point suggests that descriptive models fitting the HC pattern may differ from human knowledge and reasoning processes in several ways:

- Perceptual categorizations may be coupled to conceptual categorizations (e.g., recognizing a Delicious apple via the bumps on the bottom); that is, it is not always necessary for a person to generate intervening descriptions of data (properties) in order to relate sensory experience to conceptualizations.
- Perceptual features may be coupled and hence simultaneously categorized, as in the conceptualization of chess board configurations. Again, intervening description is not necessarily required to generate an integrated conceptualization. (Because concepts are uniformly reified in models as descriptions, such recognition is often characterized as *perceptual*, although again, the distinction is with respect to the action intentions of the player and is hence conceptual. The simultaneity of multiple feature integration is often reformulated as *distributed representation* in connectionist architectures.)
- A heuristic association description (if-then rule) may suggest that the person is relating descriptions, but the associational process may be a coupling (bidirectional, codefined relation). Put another way, the meaning of one classification (such as a diagnosis) may be with respect to its function in differentiating a subsequent classification or action. For example, the triage diagnostic sorting in emergency situations is completely based on the "potentiality for action."
- In human knowledge, subtype relations may form a dependent hierarchy; taxonomic descriptions of inherited and distinguishing properties may reify structural relations that are actually emergent and contingent on newly conceived situations. In particular, the refinement step in HC may be modeling novel conceptualization that is occurring during the problem-solving event itself.

Given these clarifications, Figure 13.3 reformulates the HC structure of descriptive models as a more general model of *heuristic coordination*. The HC pattern characterizes a mechanism involving temporal relations and coupling that is reified into named properties and concepts and linearized into if-then associations in expert systems and descriptive cognitive models.

We must also consider the possibility that during inference, coupling relations form between named categories (functioning as symbols proper in inferences) and other categories. That is, multiple *dimensions of organizing* may be occurring – not just sequential coordination of inferential chains, but also relational couplings of images (e.g., adjacency), rhythm, and sound. Specifically, similarity, proximity, rhythmic correlations, and auditory cor-

relations may be constraining each other, serving to supply further categorizations on which inference may operate. This process is illustrated by the
combination of looking, categorizing, and naming occurring in both the
paintbrush inventors and message in Nice examples (Chapter 9). Although
these additional categorizations are shaped in part by the interest of the
inferential process (such as gaps in an argument, questions about cause and
ordering in a theoretical story), what additional relations we perceive and
conceive are not bound by the already formulated ontological distinctions
of our inquiry. Rather, new features and new ways of relating objects and
properties (across modalities) may form. Inferential materials are thus not
restricted to the beginning set of distinctions. Indeed, inference is a fine way
of generating new, productive distinctions, by virtue of constraining
categorizing, in pursuit of distinctions that will now function within an
argument, to make a story whole, to explain what happened, or to project
a future event.

The common experience of recalling a name illustrates how inference
and coupling are related. When we are trying to remember the name of
a person, for example, we are failing to conceptualize the relation between
the conceptualization of the person (CP) and the name categorization
(NC). That is, we know that we knew a conventional referential categorization, NC (the name of the person), for a conceptualization, CP (our
idea of who the person is), and we know that we are holding the referent,
CP, active. In some respects, this tip-of-the-tongue (TOT) phenomenon
suggests that our CP is incomplete because surely NC is part of
our understanding. But this detail, a reification of the person – a label –
eludes us.

TOT illustrates how conceptualization may be active without having the
benefit of its name. We are holding categorizations active and inferring
perhaps some properties of the person (e.g., where or when we met them).
These categorizations are *coupled to* other categorizations of events
(images, gestures, feelings). We often adopt the strategy of describing these
categorizations to help focus the remembering process ("he is someone I
knew in school"), and on this basis we may *infer* some other properties ("it
must have been in Texas"). We may even conceptualize TOT itself as an
experience in which certain strategies may be useful ("I should just quit
trying and it will occur to me later"). Obviously, the NC isn't acting here as
the "symbol for access," but something else that is not a name or token can
function to create and constrain the conceptualization (CP). The example
of TOT thus strongly contrasts the operation of descriptive models of
memory (hence, recognition and inference) to the mechanism of human
reasoning. The essential distinction, again, is that coordination is possible in

the brain via coupling of categorizations, not requiring intervening descriptions or special indices (the point of Chapter 7).

Ironically, TOT in human experience is the inverse of the "symbol grounding" shortcoming of descriptive models. In TOT the conceptualization we are forming is grounded, but because it lacks a name it appears to be incomplete. In contrast, descriptive models like Mycin have no internal conceptual relation between the tokens (e.g., CULTURE-1) and their referents: There are names but no meanings! Why is it so irksome to not remember a name? Because the name, as a referential categorization for the concept, encapsulates the meaning, as if everything we want to know is accessible from that starting point. It feels as if the name is the root, the head of the idea. The meaning of the name is the conceptualization itself.

In short, coupling and inference (on descriptions) interact in human reasoning. We may proceed directly from perception to conceived action without intervening description. Or we may proceed through a complex interactive process of perceptual categorizing, describing, inferring implications, interpreting pros and cons of alternative situation models and plans, and then acting. In transactional analysis, acting includes reshaping materials, looking in different ways, and so on in the service of generating useful descriptions. Hence, descriptive modeling, as a tool in human inquiry, and perceptual-action coordination interpenetrate; they shape each other (Figure 9.6). This means that human planning, for example in engineering design, involves both Fodorian formal symbol manipulation (in the manner of expert systems) and Searlian reconceptualization of reference; how we carve up the world, the relevant properties, and the meaning of terms and relations may change during the inquiry. Thus, for people, distal access involves a coupling of perceptual categorization and semantic interpretation, such that what we perceive and do codetermines what our descriptions mean.

In some respects, human inference directly parallels the steps and results of a descriptive model (e.g., especially in mathematics and engineering). In other respects, inference may proceed in jerks as implications are conceived, and even before they are described, we have rejected the idea and thought of another, complicating constraint. That is, the everyday phenomenon of thinking suggests that inference and coupling are occurring together, such that the steps are not discrete landings with well-formulated, punctuated encapsulations, but more like islands that cover and connect, often tentative and tacitly known to be incomplete. Coupling and inference may interpenetrate so much that the person thinking aloud to us never utters a complete sentence but haltingly does move forward in his understanding. Thought in this respect is neither serial nor parallel, but a mixture of apparent attractor basins (de Bono, 1969) and sequential relations, with matching, gap filling, naming, and probing all working together to formulate a point of view.

In summary, human reasoning (cf. Figure 13.3) differs from the operation of descriptive cognitive models in four ways:

- In *sensory-perceptual coupling*,
- In *conceptual coupling* (heuristically or in dependent hierarchies),
- In *interpretive reconceptualization* of the appropriateness of a calculated or inferred model/plan, and
- In the *overarching conception of an inquiry-activity* that coordinates the processes of observing, describing, shuffling materials and representations, and reevaluating the product.

Together these differences constitute the essence of situated cognition, and this is perhaps the best single statement that delivers on my objective in this book of contrasting human knowledge and computer representations. Much more remains to be said. For example, the idea of *conceptual closure* needs a mechanistic explanation; the idea that a self-organizing system of couplings is based on tautological relations is perhaps a good start. The idea of *knowledge compilation*, by which sequences become chunked (e.g., reading comprehension becomes *perceptual recognition*), suggests that inferential processes may be transformed into coupled subsystems (such that action triggers "move forward" from intervening description to perceptual categorization). And of special interest is how different conceptual orders integrate, such that we can play the piano while singing or speak grammatically while articulating a new idea we are creating at that moment. I agree here with Dewey that coordination is the essential mechanism we must understand if we are to relate human creativity to the regularities we observe.

14   Reformulated dilemmas

What is the relation between the kinds of semantic structures that artificial intelligence researchers and cognitive psychologists postulate in long-term memory and the structures linguists refer to as deep structure? We have learned something . . . about what might be going on in syntactic processes, but we have not learned very much about the relation of these processes to nonlinguistic representations of meanings.

Herbert A. Simon, How to win at twenty questions with nature,
1980, p. 545

Several theoretical dilemmas raised in the course of AI research originate in the assumption that human knowledge and memory consist of stored descriptions of the world and behavior. Once we become aware that non-verbal conceptual organizers ("nonlinguistic representations of meanings"), based on coupling mechanisms, underlie some of the regularities of human behavior, we can reformulate these controversies. Often a reformulation suggests a third alternative, showing that the original dilemma is a false dichotomy.

The procedural–declarative controversy

To start with a simple example of a false dichotomy, consider the controversy that arose in the mid-1970s concerning whether knowledge is *procedural* or *declarative* (Winograd, 1975). In fact, these are two versions of the stored-description assumption. The *procedural view* holds that knowledge about the world is expressed as a body of rulelike associations and procedures for manipulating the world: Knowledge is of the form "what to do when." The *declarative view* holds that knowledge is memory expressed as facts (propositions or statements) about the world. On the one hand, the effect of repeated performance, which makes behavior faster and less consciously controlled, is evidence that knowledge becomes "compiled" or packaged in procedures. On the other hand, the ability of people to recite many apparently isolated facts about objects and events, and then productively combine them into models and plans that can be interpreted to guide behavior, is evidence that some knowledge is stored in independent units. As we saw in Chapter 3, the contextualists add the twist that the apparent independence of factual knowledge is an illusion, an artifact of experimental protocols; the independent existence of facts is a property of descriptive models, not the neurological mechanism of memory.

The procedural–declarative debate is often subtle and reveals an underlying, unexpressed intuition that is poorly captured by the way the question has been posed. In effect, the debate recapitulates Gilbert Ryle's well-known distinction between *knowing-how* and *knowing-that*. But in descriptive modeling, knowing-how can only be a *description of what to do* and knowing-that can only be a set of *descriptions of what is true*. By the contextual-situated analysis I have presented in this part of the book, knowing-how is fundamentally conceptual and may be nonverbal – not descriptive at all. Knowing-that (following Ryle's distinction) involves facts, histories, and theories – propositions (descriptive claims) about the world and behavior. Knowing-how involves conceptual organizers in different modalities, including images, sounds, and gestures.

By this view, nonverbal conceptual knowledge becomes reified as described objects, events, and properties through writing, drawing, and speech. The compilation view may be right that comprehending descriptions involves a transformation into conceptualizations – which are inherently "potentialities for action." Hence, descriptions are "compiled" into procedural capability (indeed, this occurs in the imaginative process of understanding, a kind of action that does not change the physical environment). But the traditional compilation view fails to explain how descriptions are produced in the first place from nonverbal form (i.e., how procedural capabilities become reified as factual distinctions). For example, a better story of the forms of knowledge would account for how already functioning perceptual distinctions become named features and qualities of things in the world.[1] Descriptive cognitive models fail to account for reification because the categorizations are incorrectly viewed as already being descriptions of objects and properties.

Elementary deliberation: Serial versus parallel, thinking versus reflexes

As I have indicated, the serial–parallel distinction is based on a false dichotomy: Both alternatives assume that modules exist independently of one another. But coupled subsystems may organize each other in real time. Most researchers have assumed that the issue is simply speed: Parallelism allows checking or combining many things at once, whereas serialism constrains processing to sequential, ordered form. Most representational languages require all processing to be serial, so processes that are generally acknowledged to occur in parallel, such as perceptual chunking involved in recognizing a chess board, are implemented as serial processes. The speed differences matter less as computers have gotten faster. But coupled parallelism is essential for timing and ordering behavior in time in multiple sensorimotor modalities. It is not sufficient to simply process vision, sound, verbalization, and action in turn faster. Conceptual coordination involves *integrating across dimensions during action itself.* Our neurological models of such coupled processes are obviously primitive; my point is that recognizing the false dichotomy has been essential in the search for alternative mechanisms and in broadening the reach of cognitive science beyond the serial, one-dimensional nature of descriptive models.

The problem of timing is also manifest in the dichotomy between thought and reflex action. For robot designers, the question arises in trying to bring together the intellectual modeling and planning phases with physical skills – another false dichotomy that views cognition as primarily intellectual and control of body performance as subconscious and something different from coordination of coordinated control (cf. Figure 3.2, in which action symbols are merely shunted off to motor processes as commands to be executed). One of the most ambitious efforts to unify different aspects of cognition and performance is the Soar system. Soar has been described as "a symbolic architecture for intelligence that integrates basic mechanisms for problem solving, use of knowledge, learning, and perceptual-motor behavior" (Cho, Rosenbloom, and Dolan, 1991; Laird and Rosenbloom, 1990; see also Vera, Lewis, and Lerch, 1993, and Rosenbloom, Lehman, and Laird, 1993). Nevertheless, Soar researchers acknowledge that they have not satisfactorily integrated perception, cognition, and motor behavior; for researchers also say that current robot designs incorporating Soar are "not psychological models of perception and action" (Lewis et al., 1990, p. 1039).

Indeed, coordination in Soar is modeled as three kinds of planning: *extended* (looking ahead by abstracting and selecting goals), *hierarchical* (selecting operators for achieving goals according to a previously learned plan fragment), and *reactive* (selecting motor actions immediately without checking their relevance to the current operator). According to this view, "learning moves knowledge from [extended] planning to the middle level of deliberate action and also to the bottom level of reflexes" (Laird and Rosenbloom, 1990, p. 1028). *Moving knowledge* refers to the process of converting general production rules that refer to plans and goals to *reactive rules* that refer to specific perceptions and actions (a process often called *knowledge compilation* or, in this context, *chunking*).

Newell (1990) contrasts Soar's chunking model of learning to the connectionist approach, which strives to integrate learning with experience and performance (p. 485). He says that neural networks apparently have an "ability to become organized in task-oriented ways just by performing tasks, without requiring programming by an intelligent agent." Here Newell addresses the problem that the meaningful units of descriptive models are initially hand-crafted by people.

But setting aside issues of feature construction and categorization (which I have already discussed at some length), there is a serious problem if the model is to fit psychological timing data. Soar literature cites the "overhead" in requiring the deliberation cycle (with intervening "cognitive productions" shown in Figure 3.2) for every movement: "Existing recognition memory is computationally unrealistic. . . . Current match processes in Soar are computationally suspect" (Newell, 1990, p. 486). With more learning, more productions are available to be matched, further slowing the matching process. But this problem might be ameliorated by restricting expressiveness of production conditions, in the way an RISC architecture is faster by having fewer primitive instructions to be interpreted. That is, a simpler language for "reflex productions" would reduce the amount of work to be done in evaluating the rules available for firing (Laird and Rosenbloom, 1990, p. 1028). Furthermore, to reduce the overhead involved in matching production rules against working memory, methods were developed for "processing of states by continuous modification, rather than discrete copying." This idea is consistent with the notion that neural processes are activated *in place* rather than retrieved descriptions that are modified on a scratch pad and sent off to be executed in some other place in the brain.

More fundamentally, the architecture must allow for a flexible coordination of planned and reflexive behavior. Deliberation must occur when appropriate rather than being fully supplanted by reflex productions. Presumably, the program must not fall into "mindless" reactivity – impasses should arise when reflexes fail. But how is the program to notice that reflexes are not realizing current goals? Reflexive action in Soar is always uncontrolled, without tuning to the ongoing goals and plans. In contrast, the theory I have presented posits that conceptual coordination involves ongoing recategorization, even as inference or environmental interaction is occurring. Such dynamic recoordination is evident in the experience of an artist (Chapter 1) and an inventor (Chapter 9).

In effect, by appropriately focusing on real-time interactions involving frequent attention to the environment, Soar researchers have rediscovered the fundamental dichotomy between physical skills and cognition in the stored-schema approach. When cognition is viewed as solving abstract problems like cryptarithmetic, the problem of coordinating ongoing interaction with cognition is avoided. In attempting to put the pieces of perception, cognition, and motor operations back together in robots that must not only reason intellectually but also coordinate this reasoning with real-time interactions in some environment, it is unclear how to make reflexes sensitive to cognitive goals.

In short, in Soar and related models the notion of *attention* is identified with *deliberate*, and hence cannot be related to reflexive or nonmediated behavior. This dichotomy arises because deliberation is opposed to, and in the architecture disjoint from, immediate perception–action coordination. Rather than viewing immediate perception–action coordination *as the basis of cognition*, cognition is supposed to supplant and *improve on* "merely reactive" behavior. Deliberation is viewed as a kind of system stasis, existing, for a few microseconds at least, in the juncture between perceiving and moving, independent of activity.

But deliberation is not a kind of "time out from action" (Suchman, 1987). As Dewey emphasizes, even when we are stuck – trying to figure out what kind of situation we are in – we are always acting, as we look about, utter possibilities to ourselves, and try to visualize alternative configurations. Again, *deliberation occurs as perceptual-motor experience*, as coordinated activity, not prior to it or between perceiving and acting. Deliberation is not a higher-level process in the sense of control, but in the sense of organizing how we are looking at, ordering, and making sense of previously created materials and experiences (Bamberger and Schön , 1983). Essentially, descriptive analysis classifies certain sequential aspects of behavior as "deliberation" – as, for example, when I am sitting and mulling over possible courses of action – and then posits that process as something that occurs *inside each act* in the series (Ryle, 1949).

The theory of structural coupling posits that every act of deliberation occurs as an immediate behavior. That is, every act of speaking, every motion of the pen, each gesture, turn of the head, or any idea at all is produced by the cognitive architecture as a matter of course, by the very process by which coordination develops at a neurological level. The contrast is not between *immediate* behavior and *deliberate* behavior (Newell, 1990, p. 136). The contrast is between an integrated, ongoing coordination – what Dewey called *a circuit* – and the results of a sequence of such circuits over time, which observers perceive, name, classify, and rationalize. From the perspective of a more complex neurological view with both coupling and inferential mechanisms, the stored production system model of Soar ironically retains too much of the stimulus–response analysis of behaviorism. Structural coupling processes are nonlinear and codependent, not strictly of the form that input causes output.

One useful approach for critiquing and improving the Soar model, as pursued by Newell, is to consider what is known about the relative speed of human behaviors. For example, Newell (1990) states that elementary deliberations, in which "the answer appears to *pop out*," require about 100 milliseconds (ms). Newell concludes:

One consequence of the minimality of the deliberation is that the action that is taken by the elementary deliberation cannot be a composed operation – that is, cannot be composed as part of the elementary operation. There is no way to have deliberated over what parts to put together, because the system is already down at the bottom level. (p. 135)

In saying that elementary deliberation cannot be composed, Newell is claiming that he conceives of composition in terms of *serial* manipulation of symbolic structures. "Deliberating over what parts to put together" means matching, specialization, chaining, and construction of descriptions encoded from perceptions and decoded into motor commands.

Working with a storehouse memory paradigm, Soar runs out of time:

The temporal mapping implies there can't be any subsymbolic level – there isn't enough temporal space. The symbolic memory access is already at the ~~10 ms level, according to this mapping. There is no way that any substantial level could get in between this and the neural level. . . . (p. 488)

That is, the speed of the computer is irrelevant; Soar is modeling actual steps that are hypothesized to occur in the brain. How long each "step" takes in human behavior is empirically known. If Soar must go faster, then the steps it is trying to do are unnecessary or too complex. On the other hand, Newell acknowledges that a lower "connectionist" process could operate "below" the deliberative level:

However, it would be possible (attending to just this constraint) to posit that behavior up to ~~100 ms is a connectionist system, and that it produces a higher level organization above it (~~1 sec and up). (Ibid.)

But then what is Soar today? A description of the higher-level organization that emerges from these lower-level organizations? This opens the possibility that the lower-level operations are more flexible than Soar describes, allowing for recategorization and multimodal correlations. But Newell holds to the view that the connectionist system would be selecting from "prepared possibilities." Creating new coordinations, he believes, requires deliberation or "full problem solving," that is, manipulating descriptions:

That full cognition [working in a real problem space with composed operators] exceeds by one system level the ~~1 sec limit set for the emergence of cognition presents something of an anomaly. It does not show that cognition cannot be attained within the ~~1 sec limit. Rather, it shows that cognitive behavior does not arrive all at once, full blown. It is first limited in being primarily a selection from prepared possibilities. But if full problem solving is required then it takes longer. (p. 146)

Newell is right to emphasize that what we typically call cognition, involving creating and weighing alternatives, is constructive, involving *cycles of perception and action* (e.g., in at least the 1- to 10-sec range). But he is probably wrong to characterize each act as "selection from prepared possibilities." The stored-schema model fundamentally fails to acknowledge or explain that new ways of seeing, talking, and coordinating perception and action are always being composed, as observed by Bartlett (1932):

Every day each normal individual carries out a large number of perfectly well-adapted and coordinated movements. Whenever these are arranged in a series, each successive movement is made as if it were under the control and direction of the preceding movements in the same series. Yet, as a rule, the adaptive mechanisms of the body do not demand any definite awareness, so far as the change of posture or change of movement is concerned. (p. 198)

The traditional production system model (Figure 3.2) fails to relate properly the attentive, deliberate creation and use of descriptive representations, with the sense-making, coordination process that occurs with every behavior below the 100-ms level. Nevertheless, the Soar model is an important abstraction, built on notions of impasse and hierarchical organization that are consistent with Bartlett's data and theories. It is possible that neural organizations constructed and remaining activated during the 1- to 10-sec range are transient, functional relations between perception and action and are well described by the productions in Soar.[2]

The frame problem

How should a robot modify its model of the world as a result of its actions or what it learns about other events? How does a robot know that if it moves the saucer, it moves the cup? That after you eat a ham sandwich you are still in the same place? That you needn't check for a potato in your car's tailpipe before driving to the airport? Viewed in terms of a memory of descriptions, the *frame problem* appears to be a problem of keeping a database up-to-date or, when retrieving a fact from memory because you need it, knowing that it might no longer be true. The frame problem begins by assuming that the agent's model of the current situation is inherently descriptive or declarative, a network of facts about the world.

The preceding examples fit what I have called *conceptual coordination*. Knowing that the cup moves with the saucer may be conceptual and hence tacit. Perception, conception, and movement may be adaptively coordinated in time without intermediate description of all the facts. (At another level, causal relations come for free; the cup moves with the saucer even if you forget about its existence. However, if the cup is too full or if the environment is rocking about, as on a plane or boat, the liquid will not come with the cup – you must coordinate your motion more attentively.) Knowing how to conceive a situation – what kinds of things to worry about – can develop within the transaction itself. Impasses of different kinds, past and present, influence how attention subconsciously organizes action and what must be explicitly checked. In this respect, an impasse is a conceptual *discoordination*. The neural architecture must be inherently capable of interrupting a (reconstructed) action sequence and coordinating a repair process – stitching together and composing a new orientation. In terms of TNGS, this is part of the neural activation and classification coupling that creates global maps. It also must be part of the behavior-sequencing process.

Thus, the frame problem is real in the sense that we need to understand strategies for organizing and sustaining coordinated activity, which develop through experience. In part, these conceptions are the *knowledgeable content* of active learning processes (such as the paintbrush inventors' deliberate experimentation with different brushes). Most attempts to understand and resolve the frame problem posit additional metadescriptions that control perception and action, such as the nonmonotonic axiom "If a fact is true in a situation, and it cannot be proven that it is untrue in the situation resulting from an event, then it is still true." Attempting to solve the problem of keeping descriptions up-to-date, by postulating *yet more inference rules* to be learned and applied, completely misconstrues the coupling mechanism by which behavior is physically and conceptually coordinated.[3]

Symbol grounding

Related to the frame problem is the puzzle of how symbols in the brain can refer to things in the world. Stevan Harnad (1993) and others have characterized this problem as symbol grounding: "The interpretation of symbols [in computer programs] . . . is not intrinsic to the symbol system: It is projected onto it by the mind of the interpreter, whereas that is *not* true of the meanings of the thoughts in *my* mind" (p. 170). I illustrated this problem in the discussion of Mycin by observing that the human designers project meanings onto the tokens (e.g., SIGNIFICANT). Harnad observes that his own use of names and ideas does not require the same additional interpretation; he knows what words mean when he uses them. Harnad's analysis illustrates the honest struggling of scientific debate and is worth examining in some detail.

In considering several papers at a cognitive science symposium in 1993, Harnad discusses common resolutions to the symbol-grounding dilemma and their shortcomings. He poses the possibility that the constraints on symbols might be sensorimotor projections, which on the surface is similar to my presentation of perceptual categorization. Harnad discusses a robot that would pass the "Total Turing Test" (T3) by virtue of being a hybrid system: Symbols (e.g., "CAT") are grounded by being "connected to objects' categories on the basis of their sensorimotor projections." If this idea of connection were structural coupling, then in broad terms, this is the architecture I have sketched. (In particular, it fits the ongoing, mixed nature of inference and coupling I described in Chapter 13.) However, Harnad defines symbols as "arbitrary category names"; he doesn't mention the possibility that categorizations themselves could function as symbols without having *names*. Harnad also moves rather quickly from perceptions to descriptions and verbal models in suggesting that the target is to have "grounded symbols that can be combined into symbol strings that are systematically interpretable as propositions about the world."

On the other hand, Harnad does allow that an agent's causal interactions could be coherent, without the agent ascribing meaning to the symbols per se, giving an example of a robot picking out cats; this directly parallels the idea of perceptual categorization without referential categorization (people looking inside ascribe third-person referential correspondence to the robot's operation, but the robot doesn't experience a first-person conception of reference; Chapter 13). Harnad evidently supports the interpretation of Gibson I have given (Chapter 12) because he calls these representations *sensorimotor invariance detectors* and, paralleling my critique of Fodor and Pylyshyn, says, "It's a mistake to assign semantics to a feature-detector" (more strictly, a mistake to assign first-person semantics). Harnad supports Fodor and Pylyshyn's more recent idea of *systematicity*, which appears to correspond to the tautological nature of a *system* of codetermined discriminators (i.e., all distinctions are relational; Chapter 12). This discussion harks back to the criticism of NETtalk (Chapter 6) that supplying symbols as input to a connectionist net ignores the problem of symbol grounding (the symbols were created by the human experimenters and are meaningful to them).

One could justify Harnad's analysis of symbol grounding as being primarily about language: How are names and propositional models connected to the world? This is the view looking backward from Mycin to the world. But one could also start with animals and human experience, move forward without encountering names and propositions, and still raise issues about symbol systems. For example, Harnad discusses Lakoff's advocation of a connectionist solution,[4] making the distinction between "sensory projections" and "descriptions," which I have stressed. Harnad emphasizes that he wants to reserve the term "symbol grounding" for relating descriptions to the world; hence, he calls Regier's connectionist spatial analyzer "situated" and says it uses *ungrounded spatial descriptions*.

Here the terminology thicket becomes a bit dense. Harnad says that "concepts . . . are surely stronger constructs than symbols," appearing to suggest that conceptualization depends on reference. But in my analysis (Chapters 12 and 13), reference is a conceptual relation; indeed, the notions are coupled: To have a concept of a word or an image is to be conceiving a reference. But if *symbol grounding* concerns language (names and propositions), as Harnad defines it, then he is wrong: conceptualizing must *precede* a symbol-grounding capability.[5]

The preferable resolution is to broaden the meaning of *symbol* to include nonlinguistic categorizations (Chapter 13) and broaden *grounding* to mean *coupling* rather than just propositions commenting on meaning (semantic interpretations). That is, *symbol* and *grounding* would be defined as functional *relations*, not structural constructs of a certain kind (names and propositions). Thus, as aspects of cognitive mechanisms, *symbol* and *grounding* would no longer concern interpreting forms or keeping forms causally related to the world (a variant of the frame problem), but constructing discriminators that function within a perceptual-conceptual-motor system. If a categorization is a relation, then one needn't (and perhaps shouldn't) attempt to locate categories in particular structures; and indeed, the evidence is that sensorimotor projections are dynamic networks with spatial characteristics, not immutable forms (Chapters 4 and 6).

Searle's Chinese room

John R. Searle's (1990) famous thought experiment asks: Could a man (assumed to be Searle) in a closed room plausibly respond to inquiries in Chinese passed through a window by processing rules (a set of written instructions) without otherwise understanding the language? The apparent paradox is that "Searle plus rules in a room" would appear to be speaking Chinese, but Searle himself can't interpret the meaning of these rules or inquiries. The markings aren't symbols for him. Like Harnad, Searle defines symbols as entities with a first-person interpretation: "There are no physical properties that symbols have that determine that they are symbols" (1995a, p. 210). Searle is playing the part of Mycin's inference engine.

Searle's intended argument about meaning is generally consistent with what I have said about the frame problem and symbol grounding. But his thought experiment is fundamentally flawed and has consequently produced more debate than insight. Instead of focusing on the idea of a person being inside a computer, we should *start by rejecting the assumption* that "Searle plus rules in a room" (shown as ⒮ in Figure 14.1) would appear to

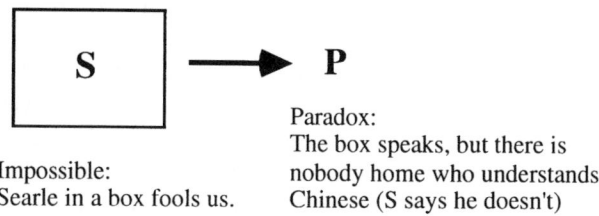

Figure 14.1. Reformulating Searle's paradox: Recognize that the thought experiment begins by assuming the impossible.

be speaking Chinese. Once we realize that Ⓢ would fail to understand Chinese, that is, that Searle-in-a-box *can't* speak like a Chinese person, then there is no paradox. Searle (S) says he doesn't understand Chinese, and indeed, Ⓢ does not appear to understand. Arguments about how Ⓢ *could* understand Chinese are pointless, yet that is where the vast majority of commentators begin.

Our focus should be on why Ⓢ fails to understand Chinese, that is, why rules, a dictionary, and so on are inadequate for simulating a Chinese speaker. The tipoff is the rigidity of the system, its inability to deal with ambiguity and understand subtle changes in the initial set of definitions. For example, could Ⓢ converse as one of the painters in Schön's example (Chapter 9)? If Ⓢ isn't involved in perceptual tasks that involve using language to articulate new conceptual relations within an activity, then we are operating with an impoverished view of what "understanding Chinese" means. Within a closed domain, we can tune the system Ⓢ to function like an intelligent kiosk. The issue is whether Ⓢ can participate in a changing, inventive community whose interests, perceptions, and theories are redirected and interpreted in everyday discourse. Ⓢ won't be able to participate because it is a system that lacks a conceptual foundation for coordinating perception and action, for conceiving reference, and for conceiving social choreographies of role, time, and place (Figure 1.2).

George Miller's experiments with children attempting to use word definitions to construct sentences provide related evidence for my claim that the assumption of the thought experiment is impossible (Ⓢ won't understand Chinese). The children know what they want to say, but they apply the words strangely. They write statements like "I was meticulous about falling off the cliff" (Miller and Gildea, 1987). A knowledge engineer can describe meaning and context, but what a skilled speaker knows cannot be inventoried or replaced by rules and definitions. Miller's experiments show that merely manipulating definitions in the dictionary does not make you speak like a native. Speaking isn't translating meanings into words, but *reconceiving* what the words and phrases mean within reconceived contexts.

When Searle says he "doesn't understand Chinese," he means that when he is making translations, he doesn't conceive what he is saying as meaningful: A comprehension process is missing. That is, for $\boxed{S}$ there are two separate tasks: generating text and understanding text. But for the human speaker, speaking and understanding what one is saying occur together. I know I am making sense, and I adjust what I am saying as I go along. The nature of the feedback is such that I am conscious that I am making sense. Searle (1980) does argue that referring is a kind of awareness in which symbols have *intentional content* (what I called *referential categorization* in Chapters 12 and 13):

> To interpret the symbol as meaning egg foo young . . . he would have to have, for example, some awareness of the causal relation between the symbol and the referent: but now we are no longer explaining intentionality[6] in terms of symbols and causes but in terms of symbols, causes, and intentionality. . . . Fodor's only answer to this is to say that it shows that we haven't yet got the right kind of causal linkage. But what is the right kind? . . . It is any form of causation sufficient to produce intentional content in the agent, sufficient to produce, for example, a visual experience, or a memory, or a belief, or a semantic interpretation of some word. (p. 484)[7]

This argument was generally not understood because Searle didn't explicate the mechanism of intentionality. I have claimed that the categorization mechanism of classification coupling and reentrant classification described by Edelman begins to describe how referential categorization (intentionality) is possible.

Although Searle's conclusion is right, the Chinese room argument fails to be convincing as a thought experiment. Searle intends the paradox, **P** ($\boxed{S}$ understands even though S does not), *to refute the premise* that $\boxed{S}$ could understand. But the proponents of the descriptive approach didn't see **P** as paradoxical. If they had, they would no doubt be perplexed about other programs. They'd be scratching their heads at the oddity that Mycin, for example, which understands none of its rules, could act like an expert physician. Or they would refer to Aaron as "the incredible, blind artist." But descriptive cognitive models are evaluated in the contexts for which they are designed; the designers experience no paradox because the boxes do appear to speak and understand.

In circumscribed domains, especially where people are formulating the inputs and interpreting the output (i.e., ensuring symbol grounding in Harnad's sense), we can usefully view the symbolic calculator plus the human team of users as speaking and understanding medicine. G009 or "SIGNIFICANT" are texts as well as part of a mechanism. Unless we see this dual aspect, we do not understand how our tools work – this is a dubious starting point for improving them. Indeed, our experimental protocols, such as the formal evaluations of Mycin (Buchanan and Shortliffe, 1984), are themselves jury-rigged to test intended functionality. If we presented Mycin with a first-year medical exam, it would of course fail (and Aaron is incapable of selecting drawings for its shows).

These arguments are well known in the AI community. For example, Drew McDermott (1981) eloquently called his AI colleagues' attention to how the descriptions of programs and internal naming conventions obscured their capabilities. He recommended that a program be called G0034 instead of "UNDERSTAND," or alternatively, that the programmer use "a name that reveals its intrinsic properties, like NODE-NET-INTERSECTION-FINDER, it being the substance of his theory that finding intersections in networks of nodes constitutes understanding." Rather than calling a program the "General Problem Solver" (GPS), it should have been called the "Local-Feature-Guided Network Searcher." In this way, McDermott was suggesting that AI researchers could have promoted the *qualitative modeling techniques* that were used to describe reasoning and create tools rather than attributing to the program the human ability they hoped to mimic. The implications of this confusion for science, practical application, public relations, and funding are, of course, profound.

In conclusion, rather than focusing on the paradox, Searle should have demonstrated empirically why Ⓢ lacks the ability to participate as a Chinese person, why a nonlinguistic coordination process is necessary to account for meaning, and how we as interpreters and suppliers of text strings attribute intelligence to our programs.

What transfers?

I conclude by briefly considering the issue of *learning transfer*, which has arisen repeatedly in the debate about situated cognition. An enduring puzzle in education is how to relate learning about theory to everyday practice. For example, should medical students sit in a classroom for 2 years before they begin to follow physicians in the hospital? Does knowledge transfer from one situation to the next or is it highly particular and unique? Again, distinguishing between descriptions and knowledge – while adopting a both-and perspective – is helpful.

Human behavior is always adapted. So, strictly speaking, theories and instructions are never literally applied. Even when the descriptions themselves are not explicitly reinterpreted in new descriptions, tacit reconceptualizations adapt our understanding. As part of ongoing *concep-*

tion of our activity – our role, resources, trade-offs, values, and so on – we reconceive the problem situation and action possibilities. Knowledgeable action is not rotely applying a scientific theory, a plan or design, or a policy in a situation: Descriptions must be related to other conceptualizations, both at lower levels in multiple sensory modalities and more abstractly with respect to the conceptualization of identity. When we say that knowledge is constructed, we mean that in activity *new coordination generalizations are forming* even when our activity appears smooth and untroubled. Thus, there is mechanistically no process of strictly or merely applying a rule, although an observer may describe behavior as *fitting* a single rule in multiple situations.

Theories (descriptions) generate action in computer programs but not in the same direct, "programmatic" way in people. No situation is ever the same as one that occurred before, although it may be categorized as being familiar. What "transfers" from the classroom (besides the books and notes we store in our offices) is theoretical language and heuristic procedures, or better, *ways of talking* about and hence *ways of guiding* what you are doing on the job. For Dewey, the curriculum is a map, a means of orientation.

In short, the argument about transfer has been partially an argument about applicability ("Are languages and models of value in multiple situations?") and mechanism ("Does knowledge strictly carry over?"). Theoretical *descriptions* do transfer, but knowledge does not. We need not argue whether knowledge could be applicable in multiple situations. The fact is that *it is not available in this form*; it is always reconstructed and hence adapted. But here there may be a middle ground: Categorizations as relations may be stable and reactivated (as is obvious in our naming and syntactic speech). One may say that the coordination strategies especially do transfer (and here is an intriguing way of understanding the discoordinations that occur when a person joins a new social group and finds the thinking and interactive styles to be out of joint). What transfers especially well and provides a broad basis for human action are *social conceptions*, including our understanding of conversation, dress, employment, and so on. Once again, the focus of the study of transfer should not be on the transfer of descriptions per se, but of *functional distinctions*, ways of relating within an already organized activity in which one begins to participate (cf. " Choreographed Participation in Activities" in Figure 9.6).

To narrow the study, to consider *how* instructions or curricula transfer, we will need to understand, at a neuropsychological level, how speaking recoordinates what we see, how we pay attention, and how we resolve conflicting ways of ordering our behavior. Theorizing could then be understood as a *coordination tool*, both in the physical domain of engineering and in the social domain of participation. The still prevalent educational focus on packaging and disseminating descriptions would fade into the background, and the role of theorizing in repairing impasses and building a foundation for new invention would be enhanced.

Conclusions: Lessons for cognitive science

By assuming that the intelligence of a carpenter, a cook, a clerk, a concert pianist, a comic, a chemist, a call girl, a college professor, a capitalist, and a crook are of the same kind of intelligence is a rank impertinence, denying each their rightful degrees of freedom to be different in kind. To rank them on a single scale is indeed so silly that we should seek some psychological explanation for this most famous error of psychologists.

Richard L. Gregory, The future of psychology, 1995, p. 139

All behavioral science and all analysis of mental processes are liable to fall on their face when logical typing is ignored.

Gregory Bateson, The birth of a matrix, or double bind and epistemology, in Sacred unity, 1977, p. 203

Now at the end of this introductory book about situated cognition, it is evident that all I have laid out is just a new beginning for cognitive science and the engineering of robots. This is a good time to review briefly some of the ideas I have sought to clarify and then to take stock in the broader issues. In the past decade, I have been repeatedly struck by the fact that the difficulties of the situated cognition debate reveal something important about the nature of the conceptualization process, and especially the rhetorical pitfalls we are prone to repeat. I have reformulated the pitfalls as research heuristics. I conclude with some brief remarks about the proper use of descriptive models as scientific and practical tools.

Clarifications about situated cognition

Situated cognition is a research approach, spanning many disciplines and objectives, that relates social, behavioral/psychological, and neural perspectives of knowledge and action. Situated cognition is a both-and framework; it shows how different views can be reformulated in terms of different causal influences (producing levels of organization that Bateson calls different *logical types*) that depend on each other. The following are some possible misconceptions I have sought to clarify in this book:

1. *Situated cognition is not merely about an agent located in the environment, strongly interactive, or behaving in real time*, but also a claim about the internal mechanism that coordinates sensory and motor systems (and how a similar coupling mechanism is the foundation of conceptualization).
2. *Representing occurs in the brain* (e.g., imagining a scene or speaking

343

silently to ourselves), *but "having a representation" from an agent's perspective involves intentionality:* conceiving a categorization as being a thought, conceiving categorizations as being about something (referential), and conceiving the thinking process itself as being part of an activity. Thus, a distinction is drawn between *processes of representing* in sensorimotor systems (which may also be conceptually ordered, as in some animals) and *inferential reasoning* (which may require a modal language for descriptively modeling the world and behavior). Conceptualization is a coordination (action-organizing) mechanism first and foremost.

3. *Situated cognition in itself is not a prescription for learning* (situated learning), *but rather a claim that learning is occurring with every human behavior.* Through physical coordination – and the very nature of memory – actions are always at some level improvised. This improvisation is situated with respect to perceptual coupling of sensation and motor actions (inherently interactional), but also with respect to conceptual coupling of timing, sense of place, role, and choreographies of participation (inherently social). Hence human knowledge is located in physical interaction and social participation. Expertise is more than scientific models and heuristics; it also comprises knowledge of other people and a tacit, conceptual understanding of "how to behave when" (social knowledge).

4. *Planning plays a role in everyday human life*; a situated perspective seeks to explain how plan descriptions are created and interpreted in *already (conceptually) coordinated* activity. Specifically, the creative flexibility of human speaking and comprehending depends on nonverbal conceptualization.

5. *Descriptive models are essential for cognitive psychology.* Situated cognition seeks to explain how *regularities* described in semantic networks, heuristic rules, and task hierarchies develop in the course of everyday practice from previously formed coordinations. Related to this, situated cognition seeks to reveal how descriptive models can't step outside prestored ontologies and in what ways human behavior is more flexible (because inference is coupled to nonverbal perceptual and conceptual processes).

In summary, the term *situated* emphasizes that perceptual-motor feedback mechanisms causally relate animal cognition to the environment and action in a way that a mechanism based on logical (descriptive) inference alone does not capture. Embodiment is more than receiving signals from the environment or modifying the environment (such as a process control program in a manufacturing plant). Being situated involves a causal, in-the-moment coupling *within* internal organizing (forming new coordinations) and *between* internal and external organizing (changing stuff in the world). Hence, *new ways of seeing* and *ways of making changes* to the world develop together. Time sensitivity (reactiveness) doesn't mean just reasoning about events – reasoning itself exists as physical activity in time (even in the imagination), and *past reasoning experiences* are causally influencing reasoning as it unfolds in time. We could just as well use the expression *situated reasoning*, but the broader notion of interactivity and feedback carries over to other, noninferential forms of animal cognition, as occurs in navigation, nest building, and food gathering. All told, this is a far broader view of cognition than *symbolic reasoning* suggests. Most important, we have found evidence that perceptual mechanisms we didn't previously understand are also occurring in human conceptualization, and these mechanisms are quite different from sequential, inferential matching of descriptions.

Of course, much more could be said about the details we have learned about situated robots, symbol systems, contextual memory, and so on. But this summary is a good starting place for understanding different facets of situated cognition and the implications for future research. Implicit in the preceding list are certain kinds of mistakes that have been made in presenting and interpreting situated cognition during the 1980s, the topic of the next section.

How to participate in a scientific controversy

Arguments about situated cognition have produced so much passion, expressions of certitude, lengthy publications, born-again rhetoric, and the like that it would appear that cognitive scientists could learn something about how conceptualization works (in its social manifestations) by examining the kinds of arguments people have produced, and especially where those arguments have been unproductive or insightful. I have collected examples over time and here present an abstracted list, in the form of heuristics for participating in such a debate. Afterward, I speculate on what these heuristics suggest about conceptual processes. The subsections that follow are loosely ordered in terms of advice pertaining to mechanisms, conceptual strategies, and mental styles.

Beware an either-or mentality

The most striking and most often self-destructive form of expression I have encountered is the either-or view of the world (cf. Chapter 10). I have repeatedly fallen into this trap myself. It appears to be especially prevalent during the initial formation of positions. Consider, for example, the following remark by Winograd and Flores (1986): "We introduce much of Maturana's terminology, without attempting to give definitions (indeed our own theory of language denies the possibility of giving precise definitions)" (p. 40). Notice how the theoretical perspective they are attempting to formulate is applied as a means of presenting that perspective, as if a consistent, black-and-white view were paramount. Of course, the impossibility of giving *precise* definitions (whether true or not) does not preclude giving *useful* definitions at all! Similarly, Winograd and Flores fall into the same rhetorical trap when they say that we "cannot model" how a cognitive system constructs operators:

The effects of different "operators" cannot be fully described or anticipated when they elicit responses by people (or even by other computer systems). We can define the domain of perturbations (the space of possible effects the interaction can have on the system), but we cannot model how the system's activity will engender them. (p. 53)

We can, of course, describe anything, if we understand it at least a little; the issue is whether *this kind of computational model* could functionally substitute for the biological mechanism it describes.

Gibson's (1966) theories are difficult to understand because he has littered his presentation with either-or statements: "Resonance to information, that is, contact with the environment, has nothing to do with the present" (p. 276). In attempting to be clear, to distinguish his position against a common misinterpretation, Gibson overstates his case; obviously, present stimulation plays a role. Edelman's title, *The Remembered Present*, better expresses the distinction Gibson is attempting to make – a both-and concept: The experienced present is a reconstructed relation. In general, the difficulty of understanding that a theory of perception must be psychophysiological (see the discussion of Reed in Chapter 12) stems from an either-or perspective.

In short, after making initial statements that appear to articulate a new sharp insight (e.g., "knowledge is in the environment, not in the head"), try reexpressing the statement as "both ... and" and see if that is a better formulation of your idea.

Try both narrow and broad interpretations of terms

Terminology can be narrowly or broadly defined. Part of the difficulty in the debate about the physical symbol-system hypothesis is that some people want to define *symbol* narrowly, whereas others adopt a universal, but looser interpretation. For example, Harnad wants *grounding* to refer only to the relation between an interpretable entity (symbol, name, token) and what it refers to. For him, *symbol* is a technical term that should have no broader interpretation than the entities in the engineered artifacts that it was coined to name. Other researchers, such as Vera and Simon, want *symbol* to be a theoretical construct (like *concept*), that is, a name for a wide variety of *natural and artificial phenomena* that need to be sorted out. On the narrow interpretation, there are no symbols in simple connectionist networks; on the broader one, categorizations may be functioning as symbols, but nonreferentially. In some respects, the narrow view prefers to define symbol as a structural entity (an *arbitrary shape* that can be interpreted), whereas the broader view favors a functional definition (*distal access*).

Debates about symbols become arcane when they are actually debates about whether to adopt a narrow or a broad definition. A name is needed both for the stuff in programs and for the phenomena in nature that appear to have the same functionality. One approach, which I adopted in Chapter 13, is to take advantage of conceptual broadening, the proclivity to generalize terms to make them more inclusive (Chapter 2). Group the phenomena that appear similar on the basis of functionality, view them as systems, and then *study the varieties of the systems.* In particular, the history of the debate shows that one doesn't get far by asking whether something is a symbol or not. Rather, one should adopt the view that the phenomenon being studied is a symbol system and ask how it is different developmentally, interactively, and dynamically from other symbol systems. In this respect, I endorse Vera and Simon's inclusive interpretation because it has variety built in. But I reject their research strategy of assuming that all the systems are isomorphic; I assume that they are different and ask how. (This is again my preference not to say that programs are intelligent and leave it at that, but to ask, what are the varieties of intelligent systems? Cf. the chapter-opening quote by Gregory.) Just as we don't argue about whether both a jet and a glider are aerodynamic systems, we can view DNA, Mycin, and human reasoning as physical symbol systems. But understanding how the systems work and replicating their functionality requires making distinctions about the internal mechanisms.

In short, allow a concept to be broadened, but then carry out a taxonomic study of the different systems that fall under that umbrella.

Given a dichotomy, ask what both positions assume

Scientific communities rally around dichotomies; they are the debating points that make for good theater and provocative reading. Newell and Simon point out that the cognitive psychology community formulated dozens of binary oppositions (e.g., short-term versus long-term memory) that became the questions experiments were designed to answer. But if the binary oppositions are false dichotomies and the experiments replicate the same assumptions (especially about the nature of inputs and outputs), further questioning and investigation won't be enough to resolve the issues: "matters simply become muddier and muddier as we go down through time" (Newell, 1973, pp. 288–289, cited in Simon, 1980, p. 536).

One approach is to study the binary oppositions – procedural versus declarative, serial versus parallel, stored versus reconstructed – to see whether there are *common assumptions that both sides take for granted.*

Donald Broadbent (1991) described this approach in reflecting on his debates with George Mandler:

There is a lesson about looking for the core of the debate rather than the periphery. We spent most of our time debating correction factors in scoring, or the danger of drawing conclusions from the absences of significant differences. We each assumed we knew why the other wanted to make certain claims; "obviously" George had a strength model, and "obviously" I was reintroducing S–R theory. The irony in this case is that we were both ultimately after the same thing; more usually, but just as unprofitably, one person may be after a goal at right angles to that of the antagonist, rather than incompatible with it. (p. 128)

The key oppositions in AI assumed that processes exist independently, as if modules in the brain are things that can be stored, substituted, turned on and off, and so on like programs in a digital computer. The difficulty is moving orthogonally when such a move is required; often the supposed reformulation (e.g., parallel instead of serial) retains aspects of the original understanding (e.g., relational information localized in space). For example, in discussing coupling versus inference (Chapter 13), I deliberately considered whether inference could mixed with coupling and found the TOT example. I suspect that most of my understanding of coupling is pervaded by notions of flow and hierarchical location that I find difficult to change because I cannot easily visualize the adaptive resonance or chaotic attractor organizers as processes operating in time.

Beware imposing spatial metaphors

The either-or view is concretely manifest in spatial metaphors that pervade scientific reasoning. The ideas that memory is a place, that concepts are things located somewhere, or that knowledge can be captured, stored, and disseminated have pervaded cognitive science. The root assumption is that the study of intelligence is actually the study of stuff called knowledge. But a biological perspective reveals that neurological organizations are not immutable forms but dynamic relations, networks with spatial characteristics (Chapter 4). Indeed, we are reminded of the lesson of relativity in physics: Spatial extent is not an absolute, but relative to (created by) movement (cf. Prometheus in Chapter 7). With our everyday, two-feet-on-the-ground perspective, these are difficult ideas to comprehend.

Beware locating relations

The spatial metaphor (and the substance view of knowledge) has been most misleading in viewing *meaning* or *understanding* as being a thing. Indeed, the very idea that a category is a thing is misleading. Once we adopt the view that categories are relations and develop in multimodal coordinations, the very idea of *representing* changes from manipulated stuff (representations) to functional differentiators and coordinators. This is a far cry from the literature of the 1970s, which so often discussed the meanings "in" representations or proposed languages for encoding meaning (e.g., the conceptual dependency notation for representing semantics of natural language).

One consequence of the nonlocalizability of meaning – it cannot be "captured" – is that understanding a model requires a commentary about what the notations mean. For example, Agre's commentary about what the tokens in Pengi mean (cited in Chapter 13) is necessary to understand his model. Other observers may make equally interesting and valid interpretations (from the perspective of observable behavior). We need to know what parts of the mechanism are placeholders, which ones are irrelevant to the claims being made, and so on.

Try viewing independent levels as codetermined

The spatial metaphor is also manifest in the distinction between *content* and *mechanism*. Taking the architecture of computer systems as a hypothesis for how intelligent behavior is organized in the brain, researchers have almost universally adopted the content–mechanism (or representation–implementation) distinction: Knowledge is the changeable component, and the neural architecture is the engine in which the knowledge is stored and manipulated. But in the brain we apparently find a mechanism that is not merely a *substrate*, but an integration of "content" with "hardware." Consciousness has been difficult to understand precisely because such a self-organizing mechanism provides the possibility for a certain kind of self-referential content – the conceptualization of "my role-behavior-goal in this enterprise," which is arising with and coconstructing the physical, perceptual, and conceptual content of behavior as it occurs.

Sperry (1995) summarizes the advance and the challenge: "The cognitive revolution, as here conceived, involves radical changes in, not just one, but in *two core concepts*: namely, *consciousness* and *causality*" (p. 37). The causal notion is that levels described as independent may codetermine each other – and this is how consciousness is both an emergent categorization of what is happening internally and a controlling influence. Indeed, it is by virtue of being both an *effect* and a *cause* at the same time that consciousness has the quality of both the "epiphenomenal" product as well as the essential driver of attentive processes.

The lesson about independent levels applies more generally to the relation between phenomena studied by neurobiology, psychology, and social sciences (Table 1.1). These levels can now be productively related, and indeed need to be related, if we are to resolve old dilemmas about knowledge, representations, and consciousness. Indeed, throughout science today the insight about hierarchical, Janus-faced (codependent) processes is influencing new theorization about evolution, economics, social problems, and so on (Gould, 1987; Koestler, 1964; Schön, 1987).

Don't equate a descriptive model with the causal
process being described

Possibly the most specific lesson is that scientists must beware of equating a *descriptive abstraction* of a causal process with a *causal mechanism*. Again, because descriptions of program behaviors do map onto the manipulations of descriptions *inside* programs and because knowledge is viewed as a body of descriptions, it is easy to assume that descriptions of cognitive processes might be isomorphic to neural processes (the stance adopted by Vera and Simon). Probably no other science besides cognitive psychology and its partner, instructional design, has been so prone to this gloss, that "models equal the phenomena being studied," rooted in the view we all learned in school that "models equal knowledge." We saw this in Ullman's (1980) presentation as he searched for a particular kind of perceptual theory, one expressed in "psychologically meaningful terms" (p. 412). He equated explanatory adequacy with descriptions of a certain sort, not realizing that the sensorimotor mechanism might not be built out of descriptive blocks and mortar. *How to describe* reasoning became equated with *how to build* a reasoning mechanism. This is the predominant interpretation of Marr: An explanatory psychological theory = an algorithm = part of the mechanism. Probably no other assumption in the past few decades has been more fruitful or damaging.

But in addition, psychology has a special problem – how to distinguish the scientist's model of the subject from the subject's model of the world. This is where the first- and third-person views are useful: Is the categorization made by the agent (first person) or attributed as an explanatory relation by an observer (third person)? Psychological models require both aspects. But models of knowledge need to distinguish carefully between what the subject is actually *doing* and what the subject is *accomplishing* within interactive behavior (through use of tools, as an agent embedded in some environment). Even here, we need to be careful about what a mental process is accomplishing versus what the subject is actually categorizing (the idea that referential categorization may not be necessary for causal coupling between perceptual categorizations and objects in the world, as in the story of the frog snatching a fly).

The frame of reference analysis (Chapter 8) suggests that two models be created and related in an engineering analysis: the *mental model* created within a mechanism of a robot and the *total system model* created by the engineer, which includes a descriptive model of the world and functional goals attributed to the robot, understanding of feedback dynamics, and the robot's mental model. Specifically, in building expert systems, we need to distinguish the psychological *performance model* attributed to the human expert and the *scientific model* of the domain (Menzies, 1995). The first explains cognitive processes, the second physical processes in the world that reasoning is about. A third model (at least) is required to place the expert system in the interactive-social context of use. The design of programs like Mycin merged these, making commitments to medical science alone but relying on psychological fidelity (e.g., the rule system must be constructed by and understandable to people) and taking the value of automation for granted (if you build it, they will come).

In short, there are different views of what constitutes a good modeling language: the robot builder's, the psychologist's, and the physical scientist's. Despite the focus on the perceptual-conceptual-motor mechanism in this book, robot engineering must build on descriptive cognitive models and be complemented by better models of the physical-social environment (e.g., see Hutchins, 1995a, 1995b).

Recognize that first approximations are often overstatements

It is helpful to recognize that breaking with the Establishment often requires making sharp distinctions, and this may result in overshooting the mark. Gibson's work exemplifies the risk:

> Gibson was a pioneer, and like all pioneers he oversimplified and disregarded pieces of evidence in order to accentuate his principal proposition: that visual perception is primarily a function of the structure of the ambient array and not of (acquired) knowledge. It is not accidental that his view shifted from what was called a psychophysical theory of visual perception to what he called ecological optics. He never ceased to emphasize that the analysis of the structure of information contained in ambient light logically preceded any statement about how it is, or could be, processed. In this respect, Ullman correctly points out that Gibson chose to disregard the processing and representational problems by calling perception "direct" and "immediate." One cannot do much better as a first approximation. (Prazdny, 1980, p. 395)

Gibson had an insight that needed to be heard. But the shift in emphasis, perhaps because it was unbalanced, was interpreted as an either-or claim:

> One wonders why so much criticism has been made of Gibson's theory, apparently only because it overstressed the first [finding out what information is available],

and deemed as psychologically (N.B. not computationally) irrelevant the second stage of investigation [whether and how the information is used by the visual system]. (Ibid.)

Gibson's statements were overstatements because if you try to ground your theory in an analysis of stimuli alone, then it's difficult to explain higher-order processes. The organism must be changed by past experience, and the idea of *knowledge* was the contribution of information processing theory. The mistake of descriptive modelers was to assume that cognition could be fully explained in terms of stored knowledge and reasoning. Where did referential representations (in the brain or on paper) come from? The information processing simplification was just the dual of Gibson's and neither was more scientifically astute than the other; both were pointing to an essential characteristic, and both needed to defend their turf against the other's simplifications.

I saw the same kind of conflict as a graduate student as the AI community was inventing rule-based and frame-based representation languages. I concluded then that ideas need a protective space – a community – so that they can be elaborated and taken to their natural limits. As a student, I thought this seemed wasteful and delayed.

A wiser view is that discrepant views can be brought together later; there is no rush. The benefits of well-developed, multiple scientific views will make up for the delay. The confusion is painful to experience but better in the long run.

While in the middle of a controversy like "rules versus frames" or "direct perception versus inference," it would help to raise one's head periodically and acknowledge: "My group has just one view; we don't know how to relate to what those other (respected, intelligent) people are saying." The first rule should be to respect your colleagues. Given that most participants in the debate were graduates of top universities with advanced degrees, it is probably better to assume that those (unintelligible, suddenly insane) people are on to something.

Of course, it is helpful to recognize that understanding is often first inarticulatable, "nonoperationable," a hunch, a direction, an insight in action. Give your incomprehensible colleagues some space and time. Recognize that it might take 10 years or more before they find productive examples, experiments, and theoretical terms. But also recognize that in clarifying their own past and future, getting your attention, and expressing their ideas with passion, they are prone to overstate their case. They see the world now through new glasses, and these glasses have blinders attached to hide the old ways of thinking that otherwise continue to distract them.

Be aware that words sometimes mean their opposites

As if we didn't have enough problems in formulating ideas, language itself often gets in the way. I have been repeatedly struck by the fact that many key terms are given opposite interpretations. The following examples have been presented in this book:

- *Functionalism (Dewey's instrumental interactivism) versus functionalism (symbolic AI's compartmentalism):* A functional analysis has very different results, depending on whether it is applied to characterize the organism-in-its-environment or the characteristics of modules. The first is an emergent, instrumental *adaptation*; the second is an *ascribed purpose*. The first view is organic, developmental, and evolutionary; the second is the view of the designer. The manner in which AI researchers talked about the "teleology of computer circuits" and the "teleology of nature" ignores the distinction between self-organizing systems and designed systems.
- *Symmetric theory (both-and) versus symmetry (either-or):* Like the word *dual, symmetric* could mean "coorganized" or "split into two independent, interlocking parts."
- *Closed system (structurally) versus open system (developmentally):* Attempts to locate information get stuck when we consider whether a system is open or closed to information. Maturana's point was that in a structural coupling a system's components are tautological relations (not input), but the system is open to structural change and indeed sustained by transactions with the environment.
- *Interactive (Newton) versus interactivism (Bickhard):* Newton's idea of interactivity was a collision of preexisting entities; Bickhard's *interactivism* argues that the components come into being through the productive (functional) interaction of the whole system in its environment. The first is an event at a spatial-temporal *point*; the second is a closed-loop (adaptive feedback) *system* whose form incorporates its history.
- *Control (Wiener) versus cybernetics (Bateson):* The idea of control followed two paths in information processing theory, one based on localized functionality (a control module) and the other on coorganization. In Bateson's cybernetics, coordination is an adaptive response, not a designed or inherent property of some part of the circuit.
- *Coded variety (Ashby/Wilden) versus encodings (Bickhard):* Wilden, following Ashby (1956), uses *code* the way Simon uses *symbol:* as a broad, all-inclusive term that is not restricted to linguistic systems. In Bickhard's writing, *encodings* refers to meaningful symbols in some representational language (like Morse code or Mycin's parameters).
- *Constructive ("inferential," Gibson) versus constructive ("new," Bartlett):* In perhaps the most surprising double meaning, we find ecological psychologists viewing cognitive science theories of higher-order, symbolic reasoning as constructive (because they show how pieces are assembled in mental models and plans); at the same time AI theorists are viewing "subsymbolic" processes as constructive (because they show how pieces are invented). *Creating features* (or *information*) is similarly confusing: It might mean creating the world (bad idea) or creating representational relations (good idea).

The duality of meanings is all the more pronounced because in most cases two proponents of situated cognition are using the same term in different ways. Why does this happen? Different notions of causality pervade the distinctions, but this is perhaps inevitable because the arguments are all about causality. I believe that lurking in all these distinctions are the localized view and the codependent view – pointing to the parts versus pointing to the developmental history that makes the parts what they are.

Enduring dilemmas are possibly important clues

The dilemmas I discussed (Chapter 14), if properly viewed, might have led to quicker progress. The problem is that the dominant view (which is easily measured by examining the commentary on Ullman or a book on the frame problem) is louder; the ground-breaking insights are not understood or even visible. A good heuristic would be to sort through the commentary and find a subgroup of people who appear to speak the same language and who are incomprehensible to the rest. Invite these people to give a panel presentation at a conference, to organize a workshop, or to write their own book. Encourage subgroups to organize themselves and to find ways of communicating their ideas better. The idea that such discussion is "just philosophy" is destructive, although such a pessimistic view is supported by the fact that sometimes the majority is wrong, so a dialogue is non-productive. The role of philosophical debate is surely proved by the advance of situated cognition in the 1980s (both in the manner of the development in print, such as the commentary I have cited and the content of the theory as foregrounding the role of conceptual understanding in scientific theorizing).

Periodically revisit what you have chosen to ignore

For the past 50 years, most cognitive scientists have recognized that perception is special. As an undergraduate learning about AI in the early 1970s, I was struck that the early work emphasized *classifier systems* and pattern recognition. Was this a subfield that lost, got moved into electrical engineering, and merely continued to hang on until the practitioners retired? Marvin Minsky, one of the most famous founders of the AI field, abandoned his work on "Perceptrons" in the 1960s, so nobody I knew bothered to even read what he wrote about them. In retrospect, the focus on perception in connectionism was not a reactivation, but a spreading of ideas that were never actually dormant.

Periodically, old-timers are invited onto the stage and asked to list the most important unsolved problems. The founding of the Cognitive Science

Society in 1979 was marked by a series of papers outlining unsolved problems. Don Norman prominently listed perception. When I produced a
similar list (1993), I decided it was better to mention specific phenomena
(e.g., figure–ground illusions) rather than broad categories of research (e.g.,
learning). We need to focus on specific examples of what people experience
or do that is not replicated by our robots and models. That is, be explicit
about the gaps in the data, not just about areas needing research. Every
researcher should have a favorite list of unexplained phenomena with some
sort of theory about what is wrong with state-of-the-art models. Of course,
there is a problem of balance here; if we were all writing essays about
why a 5-year-old child can tie his shoes but a computer can't learn as
much, we would not make any progress at all. Simon (1995) is right that
experimentation and building things must be the primary activity of the
community.

Another approach might be to round up the dilemmas and look for
patterns. The difficulty of relating inference to coupling (Chapter 12) was
manifest as the problems of symbol grounding, semantic primitives, direct
perception, ontological boundedness, ill-structured problem solving, the
frame problem, and learning transfer. Lost in this maze, we didn't realize
that it was all one problem. We might have asked: What do these problems
all take for granted? What assumptions should be converted into hypotheses and pursued directly?

Another aspect of the walling off of problems was the implicit definition
of *cognition* as being something inherently human and not a phenomenon
of animals in general. The separation of psychology from ethology was
heuristically useful, but it damaged both parties. Of course, this separation
is manifest as the cultural bias that humans are special, so studies are
oriented to proving that we have something that other animals do not
(language, tools, etc.). If we had a research oversight committee, it might
have set up another community whose aim would be to show ways in which
the cognition of humans and other animals is similar. In this respect, the
combination of a self-organizing community at the national level and functional silos in university departments inhibits progress.

Beware of building your theory into the data

Probably the most important implication of ignoring evidence about perceptual processes was presenting subjects with text as "problems" to be
solved (Lave, 1988). The idea that this was a *framework* for studying cognition became lost; cognition became synonymous with problem solving.
Refuting the sufficiency of descriptive modeling then becomes synonymous
with falsifying the framework, which is impossible within its own terms and

assumptions (e.g., see the discussion by Morton and Bekerian, 1986, p. 44). From the perspective of another framework, the first framework may appear to be imposing the wrong constraints in how it defines data. Hoffman and Nead (1983) explain this lesson from contextualism:

> According to Jenkins, the failure of cognitive science to obtain unification of principles is because not enough constraints are being used in theorizing and the wrong kinds of constraints are being placed on research strategies. Most of the constraints on experiments come from theoretical considerations about specific phenomena:
>> Thorndike's cats could not be anything but "trial and error" learners, Tolman's rats learned cognitive maps, and so on. . . . I do not want to suggest that the experiments are "untrue." Obviously they do tell us that subjects can behave in certain ways under certain circumstances. This will be of interest to us if the circumstances are interesting, or important, or highly frequent. But if the circumstances occur only in the laboratory, the experimenter must take on a considerable burden of justification. . . . (Jenkins, 1980, pp. 218–222). (p. 524)

Thomas Dietterich's (1986) analysis of *knowledge level learning* (based on Newell's characterization of a level of content more abstract than the symbolic representation used for encoding) was a breakthrough because it showed how learning programs often rearranged or redescribed contents for more efficient access – they didn't learn new content but were able to find, assemble, and apply stored descriptions more effectively. Dietterich's analysis is just a step away from recognizing how conceptual change in people is different from what descriptive models are accomplishing when they "learn." However, refuting the descriptive view of learning requires jumping outside the description-based framework to show that pre-articulated meaning or primitive descriptions don't exist.

The impossibility of refuting the descriptive modeling approach in its own terms must be recognized; otherwise, the debate will go in circles. Consider, for example, the modeling process when creating individual student models for instructional programs. We start with a problem-solving protocol; we describe it in some formal language, explaining behavior in terms of facts, rules, and procedures; then we examine additional cases to test and elaborate our model. Because we are working within a language and a problem-solving framework that we used to define the data, we are highly likely to find some set of descriptions (a story to tell) that fits the subject's behavior. As necessary, we assume that the subject had additional background facts of knowledge and add that to the model. If you can assume arbitrary background descriptions stored in memory, anything can be explained.[1]

The limitations of predescribed problems are well known, and naturally the right first response was to work within the framework. For example, recognizing the role of problem instructions on a subject's representation and approach to solving a problem, John R. Hayes (1974) experimented with how subjects learn instructions – thus staying within the "problem as description" paradigm. When subjects can't understand instructions, one assumes that they lack the stored knowledge to decode the meaning. But the very idea of a controlled experiment of this sort is to predefine the problems within the experimenter's vocabulary. That is, the psychologists start with a descriptive model of the domain. The work involved in inventing new meanings and theories is thus not explored (cf. Chapter 9).

Of course, all scientists work within a descriptive framework in which problems are cast. The trouble is that cognitive science aims to study how theories themselves are formed, and thus must consider the origin and modification of frameworks, too. In my experience, the best work in breaking out of this vicious circle has been done by Donald Schön and Jeanne Bamberger in their studies of policy interpretation and children's learning.

Locate your work within historical debates and trends

The past trend you now lampoon possibly contains the germ of an idea you require to resolve your theoretical impasses. As a graduate student, I was implicitly led to believe that two ideas were especially wrong-headed and should be stamped out at all costs: behaviorism and the even more controversial gestalt psychology. I didn't know quite what to make of cybernetics; it appeared respectable but was obviously ignored by my teachers. Indeed, all literature before 1956 was ignored. I was taught that the computational approach was "totally new" and contained the solution (in itself) to all our scientific questions. But when Newell asked me a question at a talk about parameter optimization (which reminded me of operations research), I suddenly realized that our seniors knew more than they were teaching in introductory classes.

My presentation in this book exemplifies how older sources can be read and drawn on for insights. Obviously, the work of Dewey and Bartlett has many more nuggets than I have yet brought out for view. Equally, you must read with a certain preunderstanding of what you are looking for. You don't start with a theory, but you do start with a point of view. Once you discover that Dewey and Russell were arguing about *discursive models* and knowledge 60 years ago, you view contemporary debates in a different way. In particular, my horizons broadened remarkably when I discovered Israel Rosenfield's *Invention of Memory* in the Stanford bookstore; after we met several times, I realized that my allies were in many different fields throughout the world.

In general, I would like to highlight the stereotypic way researchers are inclined to talk about past work. They don't view a proper understanding of the history of ideas as part of their intellectual development. I was struck in particular by how several people have cited Kenneth Craik's work to me, as apparently contradicting what I was saying about Bartlett: If Bartlett's student's work appeared to support the descriptive modeling view, then perhaps I was misreading Bartlett. Resolving such questions requires research. I found the following in an obituary that Bartlett (1946) wrote for Craik (who died in a car accident at the age of 31):

> The only completed study of any length which he published was his small book on *The Nature of Explanation* (Cambridge University Press, 1943). In this he appeared at first sight to be taking up a position diametrically opposed to that of his earlier essay. He argued that perhaps the human mind and body operate exactly according to the mechanical principles of the complex calculating machine or certain developing forms of servomechanisms, regulating its output not only according to the quantity but also according to qualitative features of the input supplied by its appropriate stimuli. . . . He seemed to be trying to see them [machines] as evidence that in so far as they are successful, they show how the mind works, *not in inventing the machines and using them*, but in actually solving the problems. . . .
>
> These inferences are dubious. Both seem a far cry indeed from the earlier essay which asserted that "the mind is . . . a fit instrument for any research, and something to be treated with a reverence that we can never feel for what may turn out to be a novel and complicated kind of engine." (1946, p. 114; emphasis added)[2]

Ironically, Craik's work, which Bartlett here explicitly disavows, is one of the few pre1956 books that one finds cited in the AI literature.

"It's not new" doesn't refute a hypothesis

Diverse threads of ideas and issues run through research communities; they are neither homogeneous nor isolated. What's news for one person is accepted wisdom for another. For this reason, one should be careful in using the objection "it's not new." Consider, for example, the response of a psychologist to Ullman's presentation of Gibson:

> Gibson's earlier stress on perception as a function of stimulation was not new. . . . Nor was Gibson's stress on higher-order variables new. Stimulus relationships, ratios, invariants, and the like were basic factors for Gestalt psychology. . . . The direct pick-up of information provided by the optic array is not a completely new departure. (Zuckerman, 1980, p. 407)

This researcher is generally sympathetic to Gibson's points, so much so that he takes for granted what the majority of AI researchers questioned. Of course, there are similarities between direct perception and gestalt psychology – and that's precisely what the community at large needs to understand (even at this very moment!). I have never quite understood what "it's not new" was intended to say; all it reveals to me is that the speaker is unaware of the fragmentation of the research community. A related response is to call the view being attacked a "straw man." Of course, the people who do believe the straw man theory (such as Fodor and Pylyshyn in Chapter 13) tend to hear the ideas (which are new to them) as "throwing the baby out with the bathwater."

Because one doesn't know precisely the history of other fields and what other people are trying to accomplish, scientists in different disciplines should be careful, respectful, and generous in their judgments. One should avoid belittling the effort required to cross disciplines and the lack of generosity evident in this response: "The compiled detector story may be a revolution in the psychology of perception, but it is not a *Gibsonian* revolution" (Fodor and Pylyshyn, 1981, p. 187). A related defense is to require that a new idea replace the entire edifice of a developed theory: "He has suggested no alternative to the proposal that the process comes down to one of drawing perceptual inferences from transducer outputs: in the present state of the art that proposal is, literally, the only one in the field" (ibid., p. 166). Such responses fail to recognize that a research community works with a proposer to develop a new theory; it is a rare contribution that is delivered whole. Hypotheses develop and are refined in practice. A little encouragement, rather than dismissal, is helpful for a process that may take a decade or more.

Beware of errors in logical typing

Bateson, like Gilbert Ryle and Bertrand Russell, warned us to be careful of confusing different levels of description. The *category error* is one form of either-or thinking in which abstractions, emergent relations, and components get confused (e.g., "you have shown me the playing fields, the classrooms, and the provost's office, but where is the university?"). Two logical typing errors are prevalent in the situated cognition literature. The first I would call *suprareductionist*, in which an antireductionist denies the existence of subsystems within a whole. For example, in his critique of AI, Rom Harré (1995) says, "There is no hypothesis testing [in language learning] because there is no *individual* process of learning" (p. 312). Harré's rejection of descriptive cognitive modeling illustrates dismissiveness that indeed *does* throw the baby out with the bath water. In the service of better explaining human language, he leaves no explanation for computer languages – actually the reverse flaw of descriptive modeling!

The second common error in logical typing is to equate a paradigm with a field of study. For example, in referring to AI as cognitive science, Searle (1995b) says, "It was a doomed research project." But a cognitive science (human-oriented) approach might be based on many different hypotheses, any one of which would spawn multiple research projects. I found the same tendency in my own early writing, in referring to "AI" as if it were a particular idea (a theory of stored-schema memory). Possibly the dominance of the AI/cognitive science field by one point of view (until recently) led to this category error.

Recognize conceptual barriers to change

The study of conceptual change may allow scientists to anticipate difficulties in conveying new theoretical ideas and hence to head off fruitless debates. Unfortunately, the study of conceptual change is still mostly at the taxonomic level of organizing concepts that are difficult to learn (Chi, 1993, p. 317) or *knowledge shields* people use to handle discrepant information (Feltovich, Coulson, Spiro, and Adami, 1994). We do not yet have good pedagogical heuristics that address the problem of conceptual change.

To illustrate the challenge cognitive science faces in applying its own theory to heuristically improve research progress, consider the following example. After more than 15 years of regular dialogue with AI researchers, Searle (1995b) writes the following:

> The problem with Strong AI and Cognitivism is that computation is not a causal process. Computation is an abstract mathematical process that happens to be implementable in a hardware system. But the only causal features of the implemented computation are the specific features of the hardware, and they have no intrinsic connection to computation. (p. 293)

In the same article, Searle heads off the common misconception in the 1980s that he was saying that only neural processes could causally produce consciousness. The "causal power of the brain" he refers to is not the brain per se, but the *nature of causality* in the brain – the idea of coupling and codetermination (which I describe throughout Part III). The problem is that Searle doesn't present a mechanism (as Freeman and Edelman do) or argue from biological data (as Maturana and Gibson do), but rather tries to describe how computation differs from what the brain is doing. The argument flounders because computation is a defined term, not a natural phenomenon. Computer scientists are rightfully quick to attack the idea that computation is "an abstract mathematical process" rather than a *system* of software plus hardware (a definition of *process* the U.S. Patent Office would recognize).

It would help if Searle related his analysis to Brian Smith's extensive writing on the nature of computation (after all, both are philosophers, and Smith is a recognized insider with the ear of the community). Another approach would be to develop Chi's taxonomy of physics concepts

Table 15.1. *Summary of theories in terms of what researchers were against*

What Gibson is against	What Ullman is against
Storage, traces	Nonexplanatory theory (needs a mechanism)
Perception as conscious processing (operations on propositions)	Antirepresentational/anticomputational
Integrating discrete events: mapping of locally assembled engrams or linear collections of senses somewhere	Anti-internal states
Antirealism	

to show that there are different forms of causal processes in relation to matter (different notions of *implementation* or relationships between levels of organization). Using the approach of Feltovich et al., we could describe methods for sweeping discrepancies under the carpet (e.g., using "partly legitimate subsumption," one can recognize that the brain plays a different role in reasoning than silicon hardware; but lacking an understanding of how the process is different, conceptual change doesn't occur).

To understand an incomprehensible position,
start with what the person is against

The recurrence of binary opposition, overstatement, either-or thinking, category errors, and so on suggests the heuristic of understanding what idea the proponents are trying to *preserve* by examining what they are *against.* Rather than bolstering the disparaged point of view (being defensive), try to understand what is *problematic.* For example, this is how to approach the early writing of Brooks, Agre, and Chapman (Chapter 5), where new concepts were first painted as contrasts: "There are no variables . . . no rules . . . no choices to be made" (Brooks, 1991, p. 149).

Similarly, Gibson's and Ullman's language characterizes problems they perceived in each other's theoretical positions (Table 15.1). Ullman needed to focus more on Gibson's arguments about storage; Gibson needed to relate his theories explicitly to mental states in conscious reasoning. Table 15.1 appears to be indirect ("against anti-"), but it shows the form that arguments actually take. One needs to outline the arguments and then turn them inside out. For example, Ullman is against attacks on explanatory theories. One then must investigate what he is trying to preserve about explanatory theories and help him understand a complementary approach.

Recognize that the "born again" mentality
conceives sharp contrasts

In examining the development of individual thought, one finds a striking pattern in which researchers are "born again" and adopt a diametrically opposed point of view. This is well known in the work of Ludwig Wittgenstein, for example, who moved from the logical-positivist view of his teacher, Bertrand Russell, to essentially the view that gave birth to situated theories of language and categorization (manifest especially in the work of George Lakoff and Eleanor Rosch). Within the cognitive science community itself, we have witnessed similar shifts by Hilary Putnam,[3] Terry Winograd, Rod Brooks, and myself.

Two patterns are striking: First, the shift is accompanied by considerable passion and even fanaticism. The rejection of the past self appears to be accompanied by an either-or full rejection of the past consistent with a figure–ground conceptual reorganization. The points of view are first conceived as dichotomies, with sharp outlines (leading to overstatements and category errors). Apparently there is resistance to forming radial categories, as if the new conception needs to be protected and isolated (perhaps because it is conceptual, inarticulate, supported by few examples, incomplete, and prone to redescription in old terms). Most likely, both nurture (early exposure to the two points of view before either is entrenched) and nature (a proclivity to make figure–ground reconceptualizations) play a part in the born-again experience.

The second pattern I can only pose as a question: Was anyone born again in the other direction, from an emergent, self-organized view to a descriptive, linear view of nature? Or does the shift parallel the dominant view of Western culture (what is taught in schools) and the development of an alternative mathematics, physics, and causal framework in this century? Hence, does one learn the formal view in school and then overturn it after getting an advanced degree?

Recognize how different disciplines study and use as tools
different aspects of intelligence

Most of my colleagues at the Institute for Research on Learning are social scientists, predominantly anthropologists. In relating ethnography to computational modeling, I have been struck by how the former attempts to construct insight (tied to conceptual relations) and the latter to construct descriptive precision (tied to definitions). In practice, these methods are in opposition. More specifically, cognitive psychology and AI tend to be mathematical cultures – self-consistent, logical, thorough, attempting to be well defined. These goals limit applicability and require blinders to incommensurate data. At worst, this scientific approach defines away basic phenomena like consciousness and tends toward social irrelevance. On the other hand, the social sciences, exemplified by anthropology, aim for broad applicability and inclusiveness. Researchers are trained to find fault in generalizations, to show the particularity (uniqueness) of every situation and event. But rejecting generalizations leads to difficulty in working with models and hence to difficulties in collaborating with engineers. At worst, this mindset produces inconsistency or even hypocrisy in social behavior (attempting to be inclusive while protecting one's own turf). The heuristic is to recognize that, as professionals, our methods cut in different ways and that a well-rounded study of intelligence is helped by using complementary techniques.

In particular, AI researchers should avoid physics envy. Impressed by the fundamental advances of physics and the apparent advantages of a community consensus that allows "big science," AI researchers have a tendency to compare themselves to physicists. They envy the mathematical rigor of physics and the respect the discipline commands as a real, serious science. But this attitude leads to several misconceptions and mistakes. The first mistake is the tendency to ignore the mechanism of biological phenomena and to treat *intelligence* as a universal property like energy or an abstract mechanical-physical relation like aerodynamics. The second mistake is to commit the same errors as physicists in assuming that properties *reside* in stuff rather than being dynamic relations, created during interactive processes.[4] The third mistake is to only look down (like physics), emphasizing the neural without understanding the social influences that organize and pervade human behavior. Cognitive science does have something to learn from other disciplines, but it can also lead the way in showing how to be inherently multidisciplinary, humanistic, and useful to society.

Recognize the different mental styles of your colleagues

In the published debate about situated cognition, one rarely finds a dispassionate observer. Participants fall broadly into two camps (okay, a useful dichotomy!): the defenders and the enthusiasts. The defenders (e.g., Vera and Simon, Hayes and Ford) are located squarely inside a territory whose boundaries are well defined to them. They are the conservatives. They subsume new ideas under previous (now redefined) terms. They want *representation, computation, symbol,* and so on to cover whatever we ever discover about the mind. In this mental style, there is nothing really new under the sun. They write, "Someone has already done this in our field already" and even refer to "good old-fashioned connectionism" (Andy Clark, private communication). Poetically speaking, these people stay at home and stick to their knitting. They defend the family and emphasize the importance of civility and quiet.

The enthusiasts (e.g., Winograd, Brown, Greeno, Brooks, Agre and Chapman) are explorers. They know where the boundaries are, too, and are most happy to be outside them on the range. Explorers thrive on stimulation; they are on the lookout for something new. When an idea appears to tie together many puzzles, they proclaim a "radical breakthrough." Emotionally, they feel a major shift has occurred. They sense that nothing will be the same again. They are overwhelmed by a sense of change and revolution: The field must be overhauled! We must throw away our mistakes and clean up! (The family conscious conservatives reply, "Don't throw out the baby!") Explorers are driven by personal experience and intuition. They are amazed at how much we don't know and the extent of ignorance in human history (Rocks falling from the sky? Another land across the sea?). These people are prone to have born-again experiences.

Possibly in the situated cognition debate, people are showing their mental styles as much as anything else. Some people are born again; others adopt a conservative, dug-in orientation. The study of these styles could be an important clue to the nature of conceptualization; very likely, the emotional response to change will prove important. For the moment, as writers and reviewers, we have to respect the diversity of our audience and aim for a balanced, gracious presentation.

Reflecting more generally on the list of pitfalls I have now described, I see a repeated problem of understanding *distinctions*: They get overstated, linearized, viewed as independent opposites, and so on. It behooves cognitive science to explain why argumentation develops in this way. Is each view a *partition* of sorts (and hence incomplete)? Is the pattern of dichotomization a conceptual-cultural *strategy*, inherent in the nature of conceptual *systems*, or an *artifact* of the neural "implementation" of human cognition? My analysis of the born-again phenomenon suggests that a figure–ground process, familiar in perceptual processes, plays a role in the construction of new conceptualizations. Perhaps the basic transformational process for constructing a new concept is inherently an either-or sharpening of contrast, whereas the system of well-integrated concepts is necessarily a dependent hierarchy (both-and, based on codevelopment). That is, to break out of a dependent hierarchy, one needs to define differentially, to make a contrast and hence form an opposition. My speculations are obviously incomplete, but they illustrate the door opened by this broader view of conceptual processes – the idea of a *system of distinctions* based on Piagetian notions such as order, correspondence, and negation.

A proper treatment of descriptive modeling

In their attempts to build intelligent robots and to model human knowledge, AI researchers and cognitive scientists have produced something between mechanical insects and symbolic calculators. We are a long way from the wisdom of diplomats. The one-dimensional view of descriptive cognitive models – although indeed revolutionary and potentially of great value to society – ignores evolutionary theory, contradicts what is known about animal cognition, and denies the very nature of human creativity and the experience of consciousness. My approach in this book has been to focus on the nature of human memory and perception and to clarify how the best programs relate to everyday human abilities.

With these conclusions in mind, how shall we practically employ the symbolic view? To what heights can symbolic calculators aspire? How does situated cognition change our understanding of policies, plans, and tools?

Cognitive science is, of course, a mixture of enterprises in which situated cognition will play itself out:

- Situated robotics (including synthetic biology).
- Qualitative modeling tools for science, design, and policy interpretation (usually identified with knowledge engineering).
- "Autonomous" control systems in manufacturing, telescience, and so on (put a model in a box and let it run).
- Cognitive-social simulations (scientific modeling of neuropsychological processes).

In the coming years, we can expect descriptive modeling and computers to be as pervasive in engineering, business, and science as ordinary mathematics and the slide rule before desktop computing.

With respect to ultimate impact, the knowledge engineers out there with their hammers wonder how far they will get if they just keep hammering. They ask, "Could we create a plan follower that's indistinguishable from humans?" Our experience so far indicates that we might approximate human capability over time in relatively closed domains. For example, Mycin's ability to associate symptoms with appropriate therapy might become indistinguishable from an expert physician's if diseases don't change rapidly or in unpredictable ways. But, of course, this supposes that we are concerned with predominantly verbal behavior. As neural net modeling emphasizes, descriptive modeling is obviously inadequate for explaining how we recognize accents, voices, faces, and even artifacts like typefaces. But even here, a simple connectionist stored-descriptions approach may work if forms in the world are slowly changing or predictably novel.

The problem of *generativity* – stepping outside the designer's ontology – is not just in constructing novel verbalizations, but in coordinating the behavior of *nonverbal* modalities in time. The difficulty of describing different smells, except by example ("it's like pine"), illustrates the multiple modalities of experience and the futility of basing a cognitive mechanism on descriptions alone. Few people have tried to get a robot to dance or draw from experience; situated robots are just the first step in developing mechanisms that could couple perception and action in rhythmic motion in time. The different strategies of patients studied by Oliver Sacks for constructing an identity in time reveal as well the obvious limitations of today's descriptive cognitive models in explaining obsession, depression, and other emotional disorders. These dysfunctions suggest that robots will appear to be very strange characters indeed if they lack the ability to coordinate their experiences in time. Their musings and interests may seem nerdish. As personalities, they may be confabulators or eerily lost in time.

Perhaps the most obvious first step in developing robots with subjectivity is to extend theories of cognitive tasks to relate expertise to the conception of the self as a social actor (Figure 1.2) – the expert as a persona on a stage, whose interactive setting shapes interests, constrains actions, and provides an overarching choreography. That is, we must recognize that the overarching *content* of thought is not scientific models, but coordination of an identity (Clancey, in press-a).

Given that today's models cannot *replicate* human capability in general, how should knowledge bases be used? Knowledge engineers should certainly continue developing and using descriptive modeling techniques. To use today's programs wisely, we need to build on our understanding of how descriptive models *complement* human capabilities. In this respect, knowledge engineering could be significantly broadened:

- Rather than excluding numeric models, because "that's not how the expert thinks," *incorporate whatever techniques are useful* for building a practical tool.
- Rather than striving for an omniscient program, *build tools that provide information by failing to model a situation.* Help people detect and cope with unusual or emergency situations rather than modeling only what is routine and well understood. Inform people who are monitoring or auditing complex systems about nonroutine events (what doesn't fit the ontology).
- Rather than attempting to build into the program everything an expert knows, design programs that act as *active media for facilitating conversations* between people. For example, allow people to post, annotate, and argue about different descriptions of what is true in the world and what they should do.
- Rather than conceiving of a "glass box design" as an objective, inherent property in the structures of a program, *integrate tool development into the process by which people modify and reinterpret their own models every day.* Transparency is a relation that is accomplished through people's participation in the design process (Greenbaum and Kyng, 1991; Wenger, in preparation).

- Rather than exploiting the technology for knowledge capture and delivery in training, follow Dewey by making model construction and interpretation the focus of instruction. Instead of viewing an expert system's knowledge base as material to be *transferred* to students, teach the *process* by which practitioners access, modify, share, and interpret such theories in their everyday lives.

In short, situated cognition (and its relative, the sociology of knowledge) implies a dynamic, transactional view of expertise and tools. The focus is on facilitating knowledge construction by facilitating conversations, using modeling tools so that people can express their point of view, carry through logical implications, and compare alternatives. Placing robots that actually control events *in our lives* requires addressing the warnings of Weizenbaum, and of Winograd and Flores, about responsibility and commitment. To participate fully in human society requires an ability to reconceptualize; unfortunately, it is not obvious to everyone that symbolic calculators are unable to judge because they cannot conceptualize at all.

Finally, the shift in our understanding of how plans, and in general all descriptions, relate to human activity enables us to understand better how organizations learn and change:

- Policies are not rules to be stored in human heads and implemented but resources for promoting conversations. Explaining variance from plans is not only *justifying what you did*, but also *creating new theories* to organize future behavior.
- Capabilities of groups can transcend individual control and awareness, so we can speak of "group knowledge" and understand that this *coordination capability* is not predescribed in any individual mind. (And especially, "corporate memory" is not a body of descriptions such as an e-mail database.)

Because conceptions form with respect to social choreographies, planning and judging often involve *projections of social ramifications*, based on knowledge of what other people know and how they will behave. Social values are themselves tacitly conceived with respect to previous activity and emotional experience, such that the conception of there being a problem or a situation arises with respect to these remembered and imagined judgments.

Without these shifts in point of view, descriptive models of work and knowledge have limited applicability. Organizational learning and change isn't only giving classes, distributing a solution that jumps out of a box, or bringing individuals up to speed, but also *changing culture*. Unless knowledge is appropriately related to learning in a culture, psychology has limited value for designing instructional materials and job performance aids or, more generally, improving competitiveness. For example, AI researchers seeking to apply their technology to education lament decades of delay, never addressing the central problems of changing the practice of instructional design (Clancey, in press-b). Tools can change a culture, but the evolution of innovation must be addressed. Now I seem to remember that Bartlett wrote something about that. . . .

Notes

Introduction: What is situated cognition?

1. Throughout this book, I use the term *descriptive model* to refer to what is commonly called a *symbolic model* in the literature. This distinction is important in explaining how categories, concepts, symbols, and words are related. In particular, I will explain how programs built out of labels people can read (*symbols*) are different from neural symbol systems. Thus, I refer to the *descriptive approach* rather than the *symbolic approach* to make clear that I am referring to a particular view of knowledge, memory, and reasoning and not to the idea of symbols or representations per se. Throughout this book, a *description* is an expression in some grammatical language, such as a statement in natural language or a computer program. In the literature, descriptions are also called *propositions* and *verbal representations*.
2. The approach and results are summarized well in Buchanan and Shortliffe (1984).
3. See especially the articles and commentary in *Behavioral and Brain Sciences*, e.g., Donald (1993).
4. Drew McDermott made a similar observation 20 years ago (reprinted 1981). He claimed that the use of terms like *deduction* in resolution theorem proving led many AI researchers to assume "that deduction, like payroll processing, had been tamed." The same could be said for *diagnosis* and *explanation*. He argued that explanation programs should be called *network inference record retrieval*. "And think on this: if 'mechanical translation' had been called 'word-by-word text manipulation', the people doing it might still be getting government money today."

1. Aaron's drawing

1. Nonaka (1991) discusses activities of inventing in a business context; Wynn (1991) provides an excellent introduction to the contrast between formal views of work and tacit context. I develop these ideas further in Chapter 9.
2. Chapter 10 considers more broadly the either-or logic that often obscures these debates.
3. The self-referential mechanism I refer to here is presented in some detail by Edelman (1992); see also Dennett (1992). I present these issues in detail in my book *Conceptual Coordination* (in preparation).

2. Mycin's map

1. This is an early version of Mycin's neurosurgery rule.
2. There is no single general model; many different levels of abstraction may be possible. The distinction is between *types*, which indicate no specific time, place, or things in the world, and *instances*, which are situation-specific, a description of particular objects and events.
3. See Clancey (1986, 1992) for more details about various kinds of descriptive models for representing processes of reasoning, communication, and the domain.

4. Lewis Johnson (1994) has explored ways in which a program can explain its behavior not by just retrieving rules from memory that map 1-1 to program actions, but also by reconstructing how the behavior relates to the original goals and data. Thus, the explanation process is itself a learned procedure.
5. See also the discussion of Searle in Chapter 14.

3. Remembering controversies

1. *Neural reconstruction* refers to an automatic process of physical coordination, which is not to be confused with the conscious verbal process of recollection, namely, remembering by reconstructing events in a story. That is, there are two senses of reconstruction, occurring simultaneously on two levels. Broadly speaking, because the neural process is not retrieval but a reconstruction, the recollection process is always partially improvised.
2. However, Piaget (1970) still held to a correspondence view of knowledge: "Knowing reality means constructing systems of transformations that correspond, more or less adequately, to reality" p. 15. He still viewed knowledge as being about reality instead of being somehow grounded in the organism's functioning. For related discussion, see Bickhard (in press, p. 7) and Bickhard and Terveen (1995).
3. See the related discussion of the color phi phenomenon in Dennett (1992).

4. Sensorimotor maps versus encodings

1. See Bickhard and Terveen (1995) for discussion of *implicit differentiation*. They distinguish this notion of representation from the scientist-observer's linguistic process of coding (naming) such structures and processes. See Chapter 12.

5. Navigating without reading maps

1. For example, see the special issues of *Artificial Intelligence*, "Computational Research on Interaction and Agency," 72(1–2) and 73(1–2), January and February 1995. See also *Proceedings of From Perception to Action Conference*, Los Alamitos, CA, IEEE Computer Society Press, 1994.
2. J.A. Effken and R.E. Shaw (1992) provide a brief survey of the development of the synthetic approach, dating it to "the electronic tortoises built by Grey Walter in the late 1940s and 1950s" (p. 253).
3. Regarding information gradients, see the discussion by Effken & Shaw (1992, p. 259) of Kugler, Shaw, Vicente, and Kinsella-Shaw (1991), "The Role of Attractors in the Self-organization of Intentional Systems."
4. Beer (1995, p. 179) gives a useful tutorial introduction to the concept of dynamic systems. A dynamical system is any system that may be characterized in terms of state variables that change over time. Examples include systems described by recursive functions, first- or second-order differential equations, and state transition networks. A dynamical system is nonlinear if state variables change by some nonscalar relation over time. The states of a dynamical system may converge to a set of points constituting an invariant; such stable invariants are called *attractors*. A chaotic system is one in which sensitivity to initial conditions is such that "no matter how closely two unequal initial states are chosen, their resulting trajectories can diverge exponentially even while remaining bounded on the attractor until they become completely uncorrelated."
5. The cognitive map idea of J. L. Gould (1986) is refuted by Cartwright and Collett (1987), who use path integration (vector addition), similar to the path length and positional averaging of Toto. The difference between these representations is discussed by Jamon (1991).

Adopting a skeptical view, Jamon suggests that salmon are doing a random walk, not deliberately finding their home; less than 20% are recaptured (pp. 164–165), which can be attributed to chance. Dyer and Seeley (1989) are similarly skeptical of the stored maps and directional memory theories. They suggest that "broad features of the landscape" are used for orienting flight; that is, landmarks are seen from afar and flown to, rather than recognized when encountered, as in Toto. But Toto's design is inspired by evidence that the hippocampus may represent locations in terms of movements (Mataric, 1991a). Finally, it must be noted that pigeons appear to be using magnetic gradients, like Steels's robots. In short, there may be multiple mechanisms used in combination: coordination memory (bearings and durations), external fields (magnetic and polarized light), landscape sighting, and revisualization of a path (mental model). These debates are just the first steps in distinguishing internal memory from behavior in insects, birds, mammals, humans, and robots. The ecological psychology of Turvey and Shaw (1995) formalizes the physics of gradient detection in the motion of insects (Chapter 11).

6. Because Mycin is designed to create and compare multiple disease hypotheses, it may comment on its certainty. A Mycin procedure could comment on how an early hypothesis was mistaken and why. The kind of error detection I am referring to steps outside of a frame of reference; for example, what is required in redesigning Mycin to prescribe therapy on the basis of circumstantial evidence only, to handle infections without positive cultures.

6. Perceiving without describing

1. This list elaborates material from Turvey and Shaw (1995, p. 163).
2. See also Beer (1995) for a tutorial-level presentation of these concepts.

7. Remembering without matching

1. As we saw in Chapter 4, Maturana goes a step further, insisting that in labeling phenomena as signals, an observer is partitioning a single interactive process into "inside" and "outside" components and events. Such partitioning is an important aspect of scientific study, but it should not suggest that the analytic categories exist apart from the observer's ontology and purposes (for discussion, see Winograd and Flores, 1986, and Dell, 1985).
2. "Recognizes" appears in scare quotes here to emphasize that the process is not a comparison, but actually a novel construction based on previous constructions. *Reconstructs* is better. Note also that in referring to a "previous interaction," we adopt an observer's point of view. I avoid saying "previous experience" because at the lowest levels the process is cognitively impenetrable (although conscious experience may be indirectly shaping what develops). Similarly, I don't say "previous situation" because a situation is a complex *categorization* of a configuration of recognized objects or events. In effect, the theory seeks to explain how an "encounter" is a construction of the organism-in-action.
3. *Topobiology* "refers to the fact that many of the transactions between one cell and another leading to shape are place dependent"(Edelman, 1992, p. 57). This theory partially accounts for the nature and evolution of three-dimensional functional forms in the brain. Movement of cells in epigenesis is a statistical matter (p. 60), leading identical twins to have different brain structures. Special signaling processes account for the formation of sensory maps during infancy (and in some respects throughout adolescence). The intricacy of timing and placement of forms helps explain how great functional variation can occur; this diversity is "one of the most important features of morphology that gives rise to mind" (p. 64). Diversity is important because it lays the foundation for recognition and coordination based exclusively on selection within a population of (sometimes redundant) connections.
4. Calvin (1988) emphasizes these two steps of development and selection should be a

recurrent "two-step." Overlapping development and experiential selection during childhood fits the Darwinism model better.

5. Calvin (1994, pp. 105–106) describes six properties of a Darwinian machine: "it must operate on patterns of some type; copies are made of these patterns; patterns must occasionally vary; variant patterns must compete to occupy some limited space; relative reproductive success of the variants is influenced by their environment; the makeup of the next generation of patterns depends on which variants survive to be copied." The ideas of mating and reproduction are not essential parts of the more general ideas of population thinking and recognition. By analogy, the reactivation of a neuronal group corresponds to copying of a new individual with inherited relations from its activation within previous maps. Randomization of genotype of individuals in a species corresponds to changes in the strength of synaptic connections of neuronal groups within a map (Edelman, 1992, p. 94). A simple evolutionary analogy might suggest viewing an individual as an *instance* of a species. Instead, we view a species as a coherent collection of *interacting* individuals (here, a map of neuronal groups). Thus, the connections, not the individual neurons, define the population. Furthermore, selection occurs on multiple levels of form – neuronal groups, maps, and maps of maps.

6. Formation of synaptic connections (primary repertoire) and neuronal groups (secondary repertoire) can be intermixed (p. 85). The extraordinary threefold increase in human brain size after birth (Leakey and Lewin, 1992, p. 159) may be related to the formation of reentrant loops between the conceptual cortex and perceptual categorization, enabling primary consciousness (Figure 7.1).

7. See Reeke, Finkel, Sporns, and Edelman (1990a) for comparison of reentry to recursion.

8. Here Edelman is describing the simulated robot, Darwin III, hence the scare quotes around "hand-arm" and "eye." The relation between striped-bumpy and flailing is hardwired as a practical matter because of available computer resources at the time (George Reeke, private communication). Such a reflex can be assumed to have evolved in animals adapted to this niche. In later work, the categorization-response loop was trained by conditioned associative learning (cf. Verschure's model in Chapter 5). See Reeke, Sporns, and Edelman (1990b) for further discussion of limitations, experiments, and extensions.

9. I elaborate this theory in some detail with many examples in the book *Conceptual Coordination.*

10. This program shouldn't be confused with Calvin's "Darwin machine" (Calvin, 1990, p. 372), which was proposed 5 years after the initial work by Reeke and Edelman.

11. Illustrating the notion of a complete circuit of activation, "perceptual categorization occurs only when, after disjunctive sampling of signals in several modalities (vision, touch, joint sense), Darwin III activates an output through its reentrant maps" (Edelman, 1992, p. 93). Edelman says that Darwin III "categorizes only on the basis of experience, not on the basis of prior programming." This means that the association between built-in sensory detectors (e.g., bumpy, striped) and movement is constructed in the global mapping, not stored as schemas or rules. At the lowest level, values relating to light and visual centers lead the robot to sample its environment and to target objects for contact.

12. I discuss consciousness in detail in *Conceptual Coordination.*

13. For example, see Edelman (1992, pp. 69, 86–89).

14. Internal categorizing allows awareness of changing categorizations within a temporally sensitive relation (coordination). Edelman has elaborated this into a theory of consciousness that is summarized by book reviews in Clancey, Smoliar, and Stefik (1994).

15. See the examples and discussion in Chapter 13.

16. I am grateful to Stephane Zrehen's suggestions for improving my presentation.

17. De Bono's (1969) speculative analysis and diagrams clearly present the basin attractor model of memory, which appears much later in Freeman (1991) and in Zrehen and Gaussier's probabilistic maps.

18. Edelman (1992) and Zrehen (1995, Chapter 5) model appetitive/survival internal drives in terms of levels of brain subsystems, incorporating value signals such as pain, hunger, and fatigue.

8. Engineering transactional systems

1. Anderson's (1988) *rational analysis* is consistent with situated cognition in this respect; he asks us to separate our theorist's perspective ("focusing on the information processing problem") from what is going on in the agent ("the information processing mechanism").
2. For provocative, scholarly discussions of alternative perspectives on the nature of mechanisms, see especially Varela (1995), Kauffman (1993), and Prigogine (1984). Bateson's *Mind & Nature* (1988) is a good primer.
3. I am indebted to Jozsef Toth for calling this work to my attention. See also Toth (1995).
4. Strictly speaking, a distinction is sometimes drawn between associations that are inferential and those that are couplings. The associations in Table 8.1 are all forms of couplings; that is, the aspects work together, not sequentially.
5. In studies of people, sensation is sometimes wrongly viewed as a "raw" form of perception, that is, something *experienced* (Gibson, 1966, p. 48). In these robots, sensation refers to signals detected by sensors, which Gibson terms *stimulus information*.
6. This point is highlighted by Tim Smithers (1995), who provides a useful summary of how situated robot designs differ from descriptive models.
7. See Varela (1995 p. 220) for further discussion of recursive coupling in causal trains.
8. See, for example, Iran-Nejad's (1990) model of self-regulation and emotion.
9. See also Varela (1995) for further discussion and Bateson (1991, p. 221).
10. Bickhard (in press) emphasizes the need for the organism to sense its own errors. To summarize the distinctions more formally: Supervised learning supplies as an information source both input and output: [I + O]; reinforcement learning supplies a signal after an I/O sequence: I→O,[S]; TNGS selectionism involves a set of I/O relations competing for activation {I→O}. In this notation, [X] means that X is given to the robot by a person.
11. This is Maturana's point about frogs: "Frogs don't have fly-concepts" (Cussins, 1990).

9. Transactional experience

1. Commentary in response to Fodor (1980). Shaw and Turvey's (1980) methodology for *ecological science* is concisely presented in outline form on pages 95 and 96. But the points are opaque to many cognitive scientists. Fodor responded, "I admit to understanding almost none of this" (p. 107).
2. Unless otherwise indicated, all quotes in this section are from Schön (1979, pp. 258–260).
3. Note that I might have said "given meaning by statements that represent what is happening. . . ." This phrasing is more common but shifts from viewing describing as coupled perceiving-conceiving-description creating to locating meaning in statements, making description manipulation appear to be the only mechanism and conflating the distinction between different kinds of internal categorization and statements.
4. Indeed, consciousness of a lower order is part of apparently referential processes in other animals. See Edelman (1992), Griffin (1992), and Tomasello, Kruger, and Ratner (1993).
5. Bickhard indicates that Piaget's model is similar but assumes correspondence between concepts of actions and "potentialities in the environment." He also indicates that Drescher's (1991) model focuses on pragmatic error, "a momentous advance," but omits representational error.

10. Dialectic mechanism

1. By *mechanism* I mean any process or system having a functional role with respect to some broader operational perspective. Describing a system as a mechanism is an analytic perspective, not a commitment to any particular kind of device or machine. Some people consider the term *mechanism* inherently reductionistic, equating all mechanisms with a particular kind of machine and theory of causality, especially clockwork. Some philosophers of psychology reject the idea of mechanism entirely because they reject particular causal theories of behavior (e.g., the idea of a *defense mechanism*). But this interpretation is an anachronism, like equating "computer" with a particular kind of program. Indeed, in using the term *mechanism* in the context of AI, I mean to emphasize that we need to invent a *new kind* of machinery (or a new kind of "program") based on an understanding of causal interactions, physical parts, and development in biological systems (Clancey, 1995). I call this kind of functional process, which we do not yet understand, a *dialectic mechanism.* Thus, my view of a mechanism is similar to Calvin's (1990, 1994) in referring to a "Darwin machine," which operates on the principles of selectionism. Maturana (1978) adopts the same stance in defining an *autopoietic machine* as "a network of processes of production, transformation, and destruction of components that produces the components, which, through their interactions and transformations, regenerate and realize the network of processes (relations) that produced them" (p. 135; commas added).
2. Here I use the term *interactive* according to the framework of Altman and Rogoff (Chapter 8). The interactive system of Bickhard and Terveen (1995) is what Altman and Rogoff call *transactional.*
3. Awards have been given at the AI conferences for inventing notations and deductive methods that can represent both-and relations within an either-or descriptive framework. For example, the paper by Etherington and Reiter won a prize in 1983.
4. On the one hand, the system is structurally determined by its history and hence informationally closed in Maturana's sense; but the system is functionally open because its historical dependence, its actual configurations, arise only within interactions with its environment. As Dewey pointed out (Chapter 9), in a conceptual system this environment can arise in imagination, but imagination over the long run develops historically as actual agent-environment experience and usually functions as action-oriented projection.
5. For example, Bickhard and Terveen (1995) argue that, considering timing, a Turing-equivalent computer is not adequate.
6. For example, see Hofstadter's discussion of the role-filter blur in analogical reasoning (1995a, p. 78) and Fauconnier (1985).

11. The ecological approach to perception

1. "Knowing about" is not to be confused with Ryle's (1949) "knowing that." Knowing about is a dynamic relation, described in a scientist's theory of nonverbal categorizing in the organism. Knowing that involves a verbal description that the organism itself constructs. In effect, knowing about is a transactional account of Ryle's "knowing how"; skillful performance is characterized as categorization-in-action.
2. Just as psychologists in general study different kinds of behavior, ecological psychologists are concerned with certain phenomena. The ecological psychology of Barker (1968) is more concerned with sociology than with biology. Barker studies social settings, in contrast to niches, and communication in contrast to energy transformation. The ideas are related, but as throughout this book, my concern is with the neurobiological, not the social aspect of situated cognition. In the final analysis they are related, but this is the first analysis.
3. See also the discussion of Maturana's structure-determined system in Chapter 4.
4. For a conceptualizing organism, what constitutes the environment includes internal con-

structions, so we must similarly give a physical account of how categorizations occurring inside a brain are knowable by the organism itself. In Edelman's TNGS, awareness of ongoing categorizing is explained in terms of reentry at the level of maps of maps. I will return to this point at the end of this chapter.

5. Wilden shifts to the substance view when he says "carried by." It is difficult to describe a hand clap in terms of a single hand.

6. I discuss the difference between symbolic (referential) and real (directly perceived) information in Chapter 13.

7. I use the term *mutuality* where Turvey and Shaw say *duality* because it is too easily confused with *dualism*. That is, Turvey and Shaw are in favor of duality but against dualism.

8. There is a subtle shift in wording here: Descriptions are not stored, and neither are nonlinguistic perceptual categorizations.

9. Bickhard and Richie (1983) say that Gibson abandoned this initial consideration of memory and eventually developed a metatheory that appeared to make his approach untenable.

12. Coupling versus inference

1. In this chapter and the next, I don't systematically replace the term *symbolic* by *descriptive*, as I have elsewhere in this book. In particular, like Fodor and Pylyshyn, I use the term *symbolic inference* to refer specifically to multiple-step human reasoning.

2. Here *encoding = symbol processing* and *interactive = transactional*.

3. Runeson (1980, p. 400) also points out that in Ullman's analysis of addition, the inputs and outputs are already in numeric form, hence a *symbolic, computational* process is dictated.

4. Arguments about whether all programs are algorithms are irrelevant here; the point is that the mechanism is assumed to include a descriptive model (characterized by variables and stored data structures – representing objects and events in the world or the organism's behavior – which are inspected and modified by comparison and combination operators).

5. This is a good time to review Chapter 4, particularly the section on autopoietic systems.

6. West and Travis (1991) provide an historical survey of the computational argument as a metaphor. Pylyshyn (1980, 1984) argues for a precise definition, such that "cognition is computational" is a literal scientific hypothesis.

7. Prazdny points out that within the Gibsonian community, the symbolic, information processing account (*descriptive modeling*) is called *constructivistic*. This is especially ironic given that some forms of situated cognition attempt to reformulate information processing by introducing constructiveness, especially in theories of learning.

8. For example, see Bamberger (1991) and Thelen and Smith (1994). I present a descriptive model of interacting modalities of organization (e.g., image, sequence, rhythm, sound) in *Conceptual Coordination*.

9. Throughout this discussion, I am developing a notion of a category functioning as a symbol in human reasoning. How this notion of *symbol* relates to the tokens in descriptive models is the topic of the next chapter.

10. Thus nonconceptual or perceptual categorization is what Adrian Cussins (1990) called *nonconceptual content*. See also the discussion of Cussins's ideas in Bickhard and Terveen (1995).

11. If one takes the "we" in the second alternative ("we should stop thinking of beliefs as having truth values") as referring to F&P, then this alternative is not strictly rejected insofar as beliefs are attributed by the scientist.

13. The varieties of symbol systems

1. See the reviews of *Unified Theories of Cognition* in Clancey et al. (1994).
2. Annette Karmiloff-Smith has developed a theory of *representational redescription* in her book *Beyond Modularity* (1992): "implicit information *in* the mind becomes explicit information *to* the mind" (p. 18). She speaks throughout the book about information and storage in the traditional way. However, focusing on the process of rerepresentation strikes me as basically right. But the term *description* shouldn't be applied to nonverbal representations.
3. Merlin Donald (1991, 1993) provides an especially broad theory of the evolution of representing in brain and culture.
4. For example, see Rosenfield's (1992, pp. 110–111) discussion of Creole learning.
5. Dennett (1992) examines the subtle issues of "at the same time" relative to conscious awareness of events.
6. In Edelman's (1989) model of primary consciousness, a map of maps is reactivated and coupled to the present perceptual categorization (C(W)) and the categorization of internal activity (C(I)) ("intereoreceptive input – autonomic, hypothalamic, endocrine activity"). "The step leading to primary consciousness involves a comparison of this memory, which is critically determined by self events leading to C(I), with fresh categorizations of world events C(W) which have not yet been related to value" (p. 157). The interaction and comparison of these categorical systems, C[C(W) • C(I)], constitutes accumulated categorization of the generalized relation between C(W) and C(I). A distinction is therefore drawn between the present categorization C(W) and the higher-order generalization of previous correlations, C(W) • C(I). This comparison allows for a categorical relation of *degree of match* or *identity*. In short, conceptualization involves the categorization of the change from previous categorizing, and as such, a (recursive, categorical) comparison between the self's history and the present experience constitutes the experience of primary consciousness (pp. 155–159).
7. I discuss animal conceptualization and inference in *Conceptual Coordination*.

14. Reformulated dilemmas

1. Zuboff's (1987) study of expertise in a paper mill provides an example of this interplay between sensory know-how and theoretical explanations of performance.
2. Excellent related analyses of the *Unified Theory of Cognition* appear in *Contemplating Minds* (Clancey, et al., 1994). See, for example, Dennett's discussion of serial behavior, Pollack's comments on "non-symbolic control," Arbib's discussion of serial behavior and neural lesions, and Purves's argument in favor of considering brain structure.
3. The examples here come from Drew McDermott (1987). Arguments by Haugeland, H.L. Dreyfus, and S.E. Dreyfus and others in Ford and Hayes's collection are consistent with my claim that the paradox arises in viewing knowledge as a body of descriptions. Jozsef A. Toth (1995) provides a thorough, incisive review of this collection and the problem, building on the interaction–organismic distinction of Altman and Rogoff (1987), which I presented in Chapter 8.
4. Based on the work of Terry Regier (1991).
5. See Edelman's (1992) discussion of concepts and names.
6. I believe Searle means "explaining meaning" here.
7. See also Natsoulas' response (1980, p. 440): "knowing that we are knowing subjects. . . ."

Conclusions: Lessons for cognitive science

1. Thus modeling the learning of an entire curriculum places an important constraint on the learning theory (vanLehn, 1987).

2. To be fair, Crick's mention of servomechanisms is insightful; but this is not the idea descriptive modelers cite.
3. See the discussion by Edelman (1992, pp. 223ff).
4. Discussing the relation of situated cognition and the proper interpretation of quantum mechanics requires a book in itself; for example, see Bohm (1980), Gregory (1988) and the philosophy of Bohr (Petersen, 1985) and Heisenberg (1962).

References

Agre, P. E. in press. *Computation and human experience.* Cambridge: Cambridge University Press.

Agre, P. E., and Chapman, D. 1987. Pengi: An implementation of a theory of activity in *Sixth national conference on artificial intelligence*, pp. 268–272. San Mateo, CA: Morgan Kaufmann.

Altman, I., and Rogoff, B. 1987. "World views in psychology: Trait, interactional, organismic, and transactional perspectives" in D. Stokols and I. Altman (eds.), *Handbook of environmental psychology*, pp. 7–40. New York: Wiley.

Anderson, J. 1988. "The place of cognitive architectures in a rational analysis" in K. vanLehn (ed.), *Architectures for intelligence: The twenty-second Carnegie Mellon symposium on cognition*, pp. 1–24. Hillsdale, NJ: Erlbaum.

Arbib, M. A. 1981. Visuomotor coordination: From neural nets to schema theory. *Cognition and Brain Theory*, IV(1, Winter): 23–40.

Ashby, W. R. 1956. *An introduction to cybernetics.* London: Chapman and Hall.

Bamberger, J. 1991. *The mind behind the musical ear.* Cambridge, MA: Harvard University Press.

Bamberger, J., and Schön, D. A. 1983. Learning as reflective conversation with materials: Notes from work in progress. *Art Education* (March): 68–73.

Bannon, L. 1991. "From human factors to human actors" in J. Greenbaum and G. Kyng (eds.), *Design at work: Cooperative design of computer systems*, pp. 25–44. Hillsdale, NJ: Erlbaum.

Barker, R. G. 1968. *Ecological psychology.* Stanford, CA: Stanford University Press.

Barresi, J., and Moore, C. 1996. Intentional relations and social understanding. *Behavioral and Brain Sciences*, 19(1): 50.

Bartlett, F. C. 1946. Obituary notice: Kenneth J. W. Craik. *British Journal of Psychology*, XXXVI (May, pt 3): 109–116.

Bartlett, F. C. [1932] 1977. *Remembering: A study in experimental and social psychology* (reprint ed). Cambridge: Cambridge University Press.

Bateson, G. 1972. *Steps to an ecology of mind.* New York: Ballantine Books.

Bateson, G. 1988. *Mind and nature: A necessary unity.* New York: Bantam Books.

Bateson, G. 1991. *A sacred unity.* New York: Cornelia & Michael Bessie.

Beer, R. D. 1995. A dynamical systems perspective on agent–environment interaction. *Artificial Intelligence Journal*, 72: 173–175.

Beer, R. D., Chiel, H. J., and Sterling, L. S. 1990. A biological perspective on autonomous agent design. *Robotics and Autonomous Systems*, 6(1,2): 169–186.

Bickhard, M. H. In press. "Is cognition an autonomous subsystem?" in S. O'Nuallain (ed.), *Computation, cognition, and consciousness*, Philadelphia: John Benjamins.

Bickhard, M. H., and Richie, D. M. 1983. *On the Nature of Representation: A Case Study of James Gibson's Theory of Perception.* New York: Praeger Publishers.

Bickhard, M. H., and Terveen, L. 1995. *Foundational issues in artificial intelligence and cognitive science: Impasse and solution.* Amsterdam: Elsevier.

Boekhorst, I. J. A., and Hogeweg, P. 1994. "Effects of tree size on travelband formation in orang-utans: Data analysis suggested by a model study" in R. A. Brooks and P. Maes (eds.), *Artificial life IV: Proceedings of the fourth international workshop on the synthesis and simulation of living systems*, pp. 119–129. Cambridge, MA: MIT Press.

Boesch, C. 1991. Teaching among wild chimpanzees. *Animal Behavior*, 41(0003-3472, March, Part Three): 530–532.

Bohm, D. 1980. *Wholeness and the implicate order.* London: Ark Paperbacks.

Braitenberg, V. 1984. *Vehicles: Experiments in synthetic psychology.* Cambridge, MA: MIT Press.

Bransford, J. D., McCarrell, N. S., Franks, J. J., and Nitsch, K. E. 1977. "Toward unexplaining memory" in R. E. Shaw and J. D. Bransford (eds.), *Perceiving, acting, and knowing: Toward an ecological psychology*, pp. 431–466. Hillsdale, NJ: Erlbaum.

Bredo, E. 1974. Reconstructing educational psychology: Situated cognition and Deweyian pragmatism. *Education Psychologist*, 29(1): 23–35.

Bresnan, J., and Kaplan, R. M. 1984. "Grammars as mental representations of language" in W. Kintsch, J. R. Miller, and P. Polson (eds.), *Method and tactics in cognitive science*, pp. 103–136. Hillsdale, NJ: Erlbaum.

Broadbent, D. 1991. "Recall, recognition, and implicit knowledge" in W. Kessen, A. Ortony, and F. Craik (eds.), *Memories, thoughts, and emotions: Essays in honor of George Mandler*, pp. 125–134. Hillsdale, NJ: Erlbaum.

Brooks, R. A. 1991a. "How to build complete creatures rather than isolated cognitive simulators" in K. VanLehn (ed.), *Architectures for intelligence: The 22nd Carnegie Mellon symposium on cognition*, pp. 225–240. Hillsdale, NJ: Erlbaum.

Brooks, R. A. 1991b. Intelligence without representation. *Artificial Intelligence*, 47: 139–159.

Brooks, R. A. 1995. "Intelligence without reason" in L. Steels and R. Brooks (eds.), *The artificial life route to artificial intelligence*, pp. 25–81. Hillsdale, NJ: Erlbaum.

Bruner, J. S., Goodnow, J. J., and Austin, G. A. 1956. *A study of thinking.* New York: Wiley.

Buchanan, B. G., and Shortliffe, E. H. (eds.). 1984. *Rule-based expert systems: The MYCIN experiments of the heuristic programming project.* Reading, MA: Addison-Wesley.

Calvin, W. H. 1988. A global brain theory. *Science*, 240(4860, June 24): 1802–1803.

Calvin, W. H. 1990. *The cerebral symphony: Seashore reflections on the structure of consciousness.* New York: Bantam Books.

Calvin, W. H. 1991. Islands in the mind: Dynamic subdivisions of association cortex and the emergence of the Darwin machine. *The Neurosciences*, 3: 423–433.

Calvin, W. H. 1994. The emergence of intelligence. *Scientific American*, 271(4): 100–108.

Cariani, P. 1991. "Emergence and artificial life" in C. G. Langton, C. Taylor, J. D. Farmer, and S. Rasmussen (eds.), *Artificial life II*, pp. 775–797. Reading, MA: Addison-Wesley.

Cariani, P. 1993. To evolve an ear. *Systems Research*, 10(3): 19–33.

Cariani, P. Unpublished. *Strategies for sensory evolution in artificial devices.* Technical Report. Boston: Massachusetts Eye and Ear Infirmary.

Cartwright, B. A., and Collett, T. S. 1987. Landmark maps for honeybees. *Biological Cybernetics*, 57: 85–93.

Chapman, D. 1992. Intermediate vision: Architecture, implementation, and use. *Cognitive Science*, 16(4): 491–537.

Chi, M. T. H. 1993. Barriers to conceptual change in learning science concepts: A theoretical conjecture in *Proceedings of the fifteenth annual conference of the Cognitive Science Society*, pp. 312–317. Hillsdale, NJ: Erlbaum.

Chi, M. T. H., Glaser, R., and Farr, M. J. 1988. *The nature of expertise.* Hillsdale, NJ: Erlbaum.

Cho, B., Rosenbloom, P. S., and Dolan, C. P. 1991. Neuro-Soar: A neural network architecture for goal-oriented behavior in *Proceedings of the Cognitive Science Society*, pp. 673–677. Chicago: Erlbaum.

Clancey, W. J. 1985. Heuristic classification. *Artificial Intelligence*, 27: 289–350.

Clancey, W. J. 1986. "Qualitative student models" in J. F. Traub (ed.), *Annual review of computer science*, pp. 381–450. Palo Alto, CA: Annual Review, Inc.

Clancey, W. J. 1992. Model construction operators. *Artificial Intelligence*, 53(1): 1–124.

Clancey, W. J. 1993. Situated action: A neuropsychological interpretation (response to Vera and Simon). *Cognitive Science*, 17(1): 87–107.

Clancey, W. J. 1995. AI: Inventing a new kind of machine. *ACM Computing Surveys*, 27(No. 3): 320–323.

Clancey, W. J. in press-a. "The conceptual nature of knowledge, situations, and activity" in P. Feltovich, K. Ford, and R. Hoffman (eds.), *Expertise in context*, pp. 241–291. Cambridge, MA: AAAI Press.

Clancey, W. J. in press-b. "Developing learning technology in practice" in C. Bloom and R. Bowen Loftin (eds.), *Facilitating the development and use of interactive learning environments*, Hillsdale, NJ: Erlbaum.

Clancey, W. J., Smoliar, S. W., and Stefik, M. J. (eds.). 1994. *Contemplating minds: A forum for artificial intelligence*. Cambridge, MA: MIT Press.

Cliff, D. 1991. "Computational neuroethology: A provisional manifesto" in J.-A. Meyer and S. W. Wilson (eds.), *From animals to animats: Proceedings of the first international conference on simulation of adaptive behavior*, pp. 29–39. Cambridge, MA: MIT Press.

Cohen, H. 1988. How to draw three people in a botanical garden in *Proceedings of the seventh national conference on artificial intelligence*, pp. 846–855. San Mateo, CA: Morgan Kaufmann.

Cussins, A. 1990. "The connectionist construction of concepts" in M. A. Boden (ed.), *The philosophy of artificial intelligence*, pp. 368–440. Oxford: Oxford University Press.

Cytowic, R. E. 1993. *The man who tasted shapes*. New York: G. P. Putnam's Sons.

Davis, R., and Lenat, D. 1982. *Knowledge-based systems in artificial intelligence*. New York: McGraw-Hill.

de Bono, E. 1969. *The mechanism of mind*. Middlesex, England: Penguin Books.

Dell, P. F. 1985. Understanding Bateson and Maturana: Toward a biological foundation for the social sciences. *Journal of Marital and Family Therapy*, 11(1): 1–20.

Demazeau, Y., Bourdon, O., and Lebrasseur, M. 1989. Contours et illusions de contours: Un Gabarit Elastique pour l'extraction de formes, in *Workshop Regional de Sciences Cognitives, Rapport LASCO1*, pp. 244–261, Grenoble: CNRS–LASCO3.

Dennett, D. C. 1984. "Cognitive wheels: The frame problem of AI" in C. Hookway (ed.), *Minds, machines, and evolution: Philosophical studies*, pp. 129–151. Cambridge, MA: Cambridge University Press.

Dennett, D. C. 1992. *Consciousness explained*. Boston: Little, Brown.

Dewey, J. 1934. *Art as experience*. New York: Minton, Balch.

Dewey, J. 1938. *Logic: The theory of inquiry*. New York: Henry Holt.

Dewey, J. [1896] 1981. The reflex arc concept in psychology. *Psychological Review*, 3: 357–370.

Dewey, J. [1902] 1981. *The child and the curriculum*. Chicago: University of Chicago Press.

Dietterich, T. G. 1986. Learning at the knowledge level. *Machine Learning*, 1(3): 287–316.

Donald, M. 1991. *Origins of the modern mind: Three stages in the evolution of culture and cognition*. Cambridge, MA: Harvard University Press.

Donald, M. 1993. Precis of origins of the modern mind: Three stages in the evolution of culture and cognition. *Behavioral and Brain Sciences*, 16(4): 737–791.

Drescher, G. L. 1991. *Made-up minds*. Cambridge, MA: MIT Press.

Dyer, F. C., and Seeley, T. D. 1989. On the evolution of the dance language. *The American Naturalist*, 133(4): 580–590.

Edelman, G. M. 1987. *Neural Darwinism: The theory of neuronal group selection*. New York: Basic Books.

Edelman, G. M. 1989. *The remembered present: A biological theory of consciousness*. New York: Basic Books.

Edelman, G. M. 1992. *Bright air, brilliant fire: On the matter of the mind.* New York: Basic Books.

Effken, J. A., and Shaw, R. E. 1992. Ecological perspectives on the new artificial intelligence. *Ecological Psychology*, 4(4): 247–270.

Elman, J. L. 1989. Structured representations and connectionist models in *The 11th annual conference of the Cognitive Science Society*, pp. 17–23. Hillsdale, NJ: Erlbaum.

Etherington, D. W., and Reiter, R. 1983. On inheritance hierarchies with exceptions in *Proceedings of the national conference on artifical intelligence*, pp. 104–108. Los Altos, CA: William Kaufmann.

Evans, D., and Patel, V. 1988. *Medical cognitive science.* Cambridge, MA: Bradford Books.

Fauconnier, G. 1985. *Mental spaces.* Cambridge, MA: MIT Press.

Feltovich, P. J., Coulson, R. L., Spiro, R. J., and Adami, J. F. 1994. *Conceptual understanding and stability and knowledge shields for fending off conceptual change* (Technical Report No. 7). Springfield, IL: Conceptual Knowledge Research Project, Cognitive Science Division, Southern Illinois University School of Medicine.

Flavell, J. H. 1979. Metacognition and cognitive monitoring: A new area for cognitive-developmental inquiry. *American Psychologist*, 34: 906–911.

Fodor, J. A. 1980. Methodological solipsism considered as a research strategy In cognitive psychology. *Behavioral and Brain Sciences*, 3(1): 63–109.

Fodor, J. A., and Pylyshyn, Z. W. 1981. How direct is visual perception?: Some reflections on Gibson's "ecological approach." *Cognition*, 9: 139–196.

Foelix, R. F. 1982. *Biology of spiders.* Cambridge, MA: Harvard University Press.

Ford, K., Hayes, P., and Adams-Webber, J. R. 1993. The missing link: A reply to Joseph Rychlak. *International Journal of Personal Construct Psychology*, 6: 313–326.

Freeman, W. J. 1991. The physiology of perception. *Scientific American*, 264(2, February): 78–87.

Gardner, H. 1985a. *Frames of mind: The theory of multiple intelligences.* New York: Basic Books.

Gardner, H. 1985b. *The mind's new science: A history of the cognitive revolution.* New York: Basic Books.

Gaussier, P., and Zrehen, S. 1994a. "Complex neural architectures for emerging cognitive abilities in an autonomous system" in P. Gaussier and J.-D. Nicoud (eds.), *From perception to action conference*, pp. 278–289. Los Alamitos, CA: IEEE Computer Society Press.

Gaussier, P., and Zrehen, S. 1994b. "A constructivist approach for autonomous agents" in D. Thalmann (ed.), *Artificial life in virtual reality*, pp. 1–16. New York: Wiley.

Genesereth, M. R., and Nilsson, N. J. 1986. *Logical foundations of artificial intelligence.* Los Altos: Morgan Kaufmann.

Gibson, J. J. 1966. *The senses considered as perceptual systems.* Boston: Houghton Mifflin.

Gibson, J. J. 1979. *The ecological approach to visual perception.* Boston: Houghton Mifflin.

Gleick, J. 1987. *Chaos: Making a new science.* New York: Viking Press.

Goldstein, I. P. 1982. "The genetic graph: A representation for the evolution of procedural knowledge" in D. Sleeman and J. S. Brown (eds.), *Intelligent tutoring systems*, pp. 51–78. London: Academic Press.

Gould, J. L. 1986. The locale map of honey bees: Do insects have cognitive maps? *Science*, 232(4752): 861–863.

Gould, J. L., and Marler, P. 1987. Learning by instinct. *Scientific American*, 256(1): 74–85.

Gould, S. J. 1987. *An urchin in the storm.* New York: W.W. Norton.

Greenbaum, J., and Kyng, M. 1991. *Design at work: Cooperative design of computer systems.* Hillsdale, NJ: Erlbaum.

Gregory, B. 1988. *Inventing reality: Physics as language.* New York: Wiley.

Gregory, R. L. 1995. "The future of psychology" in R. L. Solso and D. W. Massaro (eds.), *The science of the mind*, pp. 137–143. New York: Oxford University Press.

Griffin, D. R. 1992. *Animal minds.* Chicago: University of Chicago Press.

Grossberg, S. 1980. Direct perception or adaptive resonance? *Behavioral and Brain Sciences,* 3: 385–386.

Harnad, S. 1993. Symbol grounding is an empirical problem: Neural nets are just a candidate component in *Proceedings of the fifteenth annual conference of the Cognitive Science Society,* pp. 169–174. Boulder, CO: Erlbaum.

Harré, R. 1995. Great engineering: Pity about the psychology! *The World & I,* (July): 309–317.

Hayes, J. R., and Simon, H. A. 1974. "Understanding written problem instructions" in H. A. Simon (ed.), *Models of thought,* pp. 451–476. New Haven, CT: Yale University Press.

Hayes, P. J., Ford, K. M., and Agnew, N. 1994. On babies and bathwater: A cautionary tale. *AI Magazine,* 15(4): 15–26.

Hayes-Roth, F., Waterman, D., and Lenat, D. (eds.). 1983. *Building expert systems.* New York: Addison-Wesley.

Head, H. 1920. *Studies in neurology.* London: Oxford University Press.

Heinrich, B. 1993. A birdbrain nevermore: When put to the test, ravens display insight. *Natural History,* 102(10): 50–58.

Heisenberg, W. 1962. *Physics and philosophy: The revolution in modern science.* New York: Harper & Row.

Hinton, G. E. 1980. Inferring the meaning of direct perception. *Behavioral and Brain Sciences,* 3: 387–388.

Hoffman, R., and Nead, J. 1983. General contextualism, ecological science and cognitive research. *The Journal of Mind and Behavior,* 4(4): 507–560.

Hofstadter, D. 1995a. A review of mental leaps: Analogy in creative thought. *AI Magazine,* 16(3): 75–80.

Hofstadter, D. 1995b. *Fluid concepts and creative analogies: Computer models of the fundamental mechanisms of thought.* New York: Basic Books.

Hutchins, E. 1995a. *Cognition in the wild.* Cambridge, MA: MIT Press.

Hutchins, E. 1995b. How a cockpit remembers its speed. *Cognitive Science,* 19(3): 265–288.

Iran-Nejad, A. 1987. "The schema: A long-term memory structure or a transient functional pattern" in R. J. Tierney, P. L. Anders, and J. N. Mitchell (eds.), *Understanding readers' understanding: Theory and practice,* pp. 109–127. Hillsdale, NJ: Erlbaum.

Iran-Nejad, A. 1990. Active and dynamic self-regulation of learning processes. *Review of Educational Research,* 60(4): 573–602.

Jackendoff, R. 1987. Consciousness and the computational mind. *Behavioral and Brain Sciences,* 18(4): 670

James, W. [1892] 1984. *Psychology: Briefer course.* Cambridge, MA: Harvard University Press.

Jamon, M. 1991. "The contribution of quantitative models to the long distance orientation problems" in J.-A. Meyer and S. W. Wilson (eds.), *From animals to animats: Proceedings of the first international conference on simulation of adaptive behavior,* pp. 160–168. Cambridge, MA: MIT Press.

Jenkins, J. J. 1974. Remember that old theory of memory? Well, forget it! *American Psychologist,* 11: 785–795.

Johansson, G., von Hofsten, C., and Jansson, G. 1980. Direct perception and perceptual processes. *Behavioral and Brain Sciences,* 3: 388.

Johnson, W. L. 1994. Agents that learn to explain themselves in *The twelfth national conference on artificial intelligence,* pp. 1257–1263. Menlo Park, CA: AAAI Press.

Karmiloff-Smith, A. 1992. *Beyond modularity: A developmental perspective on cognitive science.* Cambridge, MA: Bradford Books.

Kauffman, S. 1993. *The origins of order: Self-organization and selection in evolution.* New York: Oxford University Press.

Koestler, A. 1964. *The act of creation: A study of the conscious and unconscious in science and art.* New York: Dell.

Kolodner, J. 1993. *Case-based reasoning.* San Mateo, CA: Morgan Kaufmann.

Kugler, P. N., Shaw, R. E., Vicente, K. J., and Kinsella-Shaw, J. 1991. "The role of attractors in the self-organization of intentional systems" in *Cognition and the symbolic processes: Applied and ecological perspectives,* pp. 387–431. Hillsdale, NJ: Erlbaum.

Laird, J. E., and Rosenbloom, P. S. 1990. Integrating execution, planning, and learning in Soar for external environments in *Proceedings of the eighth national conference on artificial intelligence,* pp. 1022–1029. Menlo Park, CA: AAAI Press.

Lakoff, G. 1987. *Women, fire, and dangerous things: What categories reveal about the mind.* Chicago: University of Chicago Press.

Langer, S. [1942] 1958. *Philosophy in a new key: A study in the symbolism of reason, rite, and art.* New York: Mentor Books.

Lave, J. 1988. *Cognition in practice.* Cambridge: Cambridge University Press.

Lave, J., and Wenger, E. 1991. *Situated learning: Legitimate peripheral participation.* Cambridge: Cambridge University Press.

Leakey, R., and Lewin, R. 1992. *Origins reconsidered: In search of what makes us human.* New York: Doubleday.

Lehman, J. F., Lewis, R. L., and Newell, A. 1991. *Natural language comprehension* (Technical Report CMU-CS-91-117). Pittsburgh: Carnegie-Mellon University.

Lehnert, W. G. 1984. "Paradigmatic issues in cognitive science" in W. Kintsch, J. R. Miller and P. Polson (eds.), *Methods and tactics in cognitive science,* pp. 21–50. Hillsdale, NJ: Erlbaum.

Lewis, R., Huffman, S. B., John, B. E., Laird, J. E., Lehman, J. F., Newell, A., Rosenbloom, P. S., Simon, T., and Tessler, S. G. 1990. Soar as a unified theory of cognition: Spring 1990 symposium in *Proceedings of the twelfth annual conference of the Cognitive Science Society,* pp. 1035–1042. Hillsdale, NJ: Erlbaum.

Lloyd, D. 1989. *Simple minds.* Cambridge, MA: MIT Press.

Mandler, G. 1962. From association to structure. *Psychological Review,* 69: 415–427.

Mandler, G. 1984. "Cohabitation in the cognitive sciences" in W. Kintsch, J. R. Miller, and P. G. Polson (eds.), *Method and tactics in cognitive science,* pp. 305–315. Hillsdale, NJ: Erlbaum.

Marr, D. 1981. "Artificial intelligence: A personal view" in J. Haugeland (ed.), *Mind design,* pp. 129–142. Cambridge, MA: MIT Press.

Mataric, M. 1991a. "Navigating with a rat brain: A neurobiologically-inspired model for robot spatial representation" in J.-A. Meyer and S. W. Wilson (eds.), *From animals to animats: Proceedings of the first international conference on simulation of adaptive behavior,* pp. 169–175. Cambridge, MA: MIT Press.

Mataric, M. 1991b. Behavioral synergy without explicit integration in *AAAI spring symposium on integrated intelligent architectures,* pp. 130–133. Menlo Park, CA: AAAI Press.

Mataric, M. J. 1992. Integration of representation into goal-driven behavior-based robots. *IEEE Transactions on Robotics and Automation,* 8(3): 304–312.

Mataric, M., and Brooks, R. A. 1990. Learning a distributed map representation based on navigation behaviors in *Proceedings of USA–Japan symposium on flexible automation,* pp. 499–506. Kyoto.

Maturana, H. R. 1975. The organization of the living: A theory of the living organization. *International Journal of Man-Machine Studies,* 7: 313–332.

Maturana, H. R. 1978. "Biology of language: The epistemology of reality" in G. A. Miller and E. Lenneberg (eds.), *Psychology and biology of language and thought: Essays in honor of Eric Lenneberg,* pp. 27–64. New York: Academic Press.

Maturana, H. R. 1980. "Biology of cognition" in H. R. Maturana and F. J. Varela (eds.), *Autopoiesis and cognition: The realization of the living.* Boston: Reidel.

Maturana, H. R. 1983. What is it to see? ¿Qué es ver? *Archivos de Biologica y Medicina Experimentales,* 16: 255–269.

Maturana, H. R., and Varela, F. 1987. *The tree of knowledge: The biological roots of human understanding.* Boston: New Science Library.

McClelland, J. L. 1991. "From association to structure, revisited" in W. Kessen, A. Ortony, and F. Craik (eds.), *Memories, thoughts, and emotions: Essays in honor of George Mandler*, pp. 42–44. Hillsdale, NJ: Erlbaum.

McCorduck, P. 1991. *Aaron's code: Meta-art, artificial intelligence, and the work of Harold Cohen.* New York: W. H. Freeman.

McDermott, D. 1981. "Artificial intelligence meets natural stupidity" in J. Haugeland (ed.), *Mind design*, pp. 143–160. Cambridge, MA: MIT Press.

McDermott, D. 1987. "We've been framed: Or, why AI is innocent of the frame problem" in Z. Pylyshyn (ed.), *The robot's dilemma*, pp. 113–122. Norwood, NJ: Ablex.

Menzies, T. 1995. Limits to knowledge level-B modeling (and KADS) in Yin Yao (ed.), *Eighth Australian joint conference on artificial intelligence*, pp. 459–465. Canberra, Australia: World Scientific.

Merzenich, M., Kaas, J., Wall, J., Nelson, R., Sur, M., and Felleman, D. J. 1983a. Topographic reorganization of somatosensory cortical Area 3B and 1 in adult monkeys following restricted deafferentation. *Neuroscience*, 8(1): 33–56.

Merzenich, M. M., Kaas, J. H., Wall, J. T., Sur, M., Nelson, R. J., and Felleman, D. J. 1983b. Progression of change following median nerve section in the cortical representation of the hand in Areas 3B and 1 in adult owl and squirrel monkeys. *Neuroscience*, 10(3): 639–666.

Michalski, R. S. 1992. "Concept learning" in S. C. Shapiro (ed.), *Encyclopedia of artificial intelligence* (Volume I), pp. 248–259. New York: Wiley.

Miller, G. A., and Gildea, P. M. 1987. How children learn words. *Scientific American*, 257(3): 94–99.

Miller, R., Polson, P. G., and Kintsch, W. 1984. "Problems of methodology in cognitive science" in W. Kintsch, J. R. Miller, and P. Polson (eds.), *Methods and tactics in cognitive science*, pp. 1–18. Hillsdale, NJ: Erlbaum.

Minsky, M. 1967. *Computation: Finite and infinite machines.* Englewood Cliffs, NJ: Prentice-Hall.

Minsky, M. 1977. Frame system theory in P. N. Johnson-Laird and P. C. Wason (eds.), *Thinking: Readings in cognitive science*, pp. 355–376. Cambridge: Cambridge University Press.

Moore, C., and Barresi, J. 1996. Intentional relations and social understanding. *Behavioral and Brain Sciences*, 19(1): 166.

Morris, H. C. 1991. "On the feasibility of computational artificial life – A reply to critics" in J.-A. Meyer and S. W. Wilson (eds.), *From animals to animats: Proceedings of the first international conference on simulation of adapted behavior*, pp. 40–49. Cambridge, MA: MIT Press.

Morton, J., and Bekerian, D. 1986. "Three ways of looking at memory" in N. E. Sharkey (ed.), *Advances in cognitive science 1*, pp. 43–71. New York: Wiley.

Munsat, S. 1990. Keeping representations at bay. *The Behavioral and Brain Sciences*, 13(3): 502–503.

Natsoulas, T. 1980. The primary source of intentionality. *The Behavioral and Brain Sciences*, 3: 440–441.

Neisser, U. 1976. *Cognition and reality: Principles and implications of cognitive psychology.* New York: W. H. Freeman.

Newell, A. 1973. "You can't play 20 questions with nature and win" in W. G. Chase (ed.), *Visual information processing*, pp. 283–308. New York: Academic Press.

Newell, A. 1980. Physical symbol systems. *Cognitive Science*, 4(2): 135–183.

Newell, A. 1982. The knowledge level. *Artificial Intelligence*, 18(1): 87–127.

Newell, A. 1990. *Unified theories of cognition.* Cambridge, MA: Harvard University Press.

Newell, A., and Simon, H. A. 1981. "Computer science as empirical inquiry: Symbols and search" in J. Haugeland (ed.), *Mind design*, pp. 35–66. Cambridge, MA: MIT Press.

Newell, A., and Simon, H. A. 1972. *Human problem solving.* Englewood Cliffs, NJ: Prentice-Hall.

Nonaka, I. 1991. The knowledge-creating company. *Harvard Business Review* (November–December): 96–104.

Pagels, H. R. 1988. *The dreams of reason: The computer and the rise of the sciences of complexity.* New York: Bantam Books.

Patterson, K. 1991. "Learning by association: Two tributes to George Mandler" in W. Kessen, A. Ortony, and F. Craik (eds.), *Memories, thoughts, and emotions: Essays in honor of George Mandler*, pp. 35–41. Hillsdale, NJ: Erlbaum.

Petersen, A. 1985. "The philosophy of Niels Bohr" in A. P. French and P. J. Kennedy (eds.), *Niels Bohr: A century volume*, pp. 299–310. Cambridge, MA: Harvard University Press.

Phillips, W. A., Hancock, P. J. B., and Smith, L. S. 1990. Realistic neural nets need to learn iconic representations. *The Behavioral and Brain Sciences*, 13(3): 505.

Piaget, J. [1970] 1971. *Genetic epistemology.* New York: W. W. Norton.

Pierce, D., and Kuipers, B. 1994. Learning to explore and build maps in *The twelfth national conference on artificial intelligence*, pp. 1264–1271. Menlo Park, CA: AAAI Press.

Polanyi, M. 1966. *The tacit dimension.* New York: Doubleday Anchor Books.

Polk, T. A., and Newell, A. 1995. Deduction as verbal reasoning. *Psychological Review*, 102(3): 533–566.

Prazdny, K. 1980. How wrong is Gibson? *Behavioral and Brain Sciences*, 3: 394–395.

Pribram, K. H. 1991. *Brain and perception: Holonomy and structure in figural processing.* Hillsdale, NJ: Erlbaum.

Prigogine, I., and Stengers, I. 1984. *Order out of chaos.* New York: Bantam Books.

Pylyshyn, Z. W. 1980. Computation and cognition: Issues in the foundation of cognitive science. *The Behavioral and Brain Sciences*, 3(1): 111–169.

Pylyshyn, Z. W. 1984. *Computation and cognition: Toward a foundation for cognitive science.* Cambridge: MIT Press.

Pylyshyn, Z. W. 1991. "The role of cognitive architecture in theories of cognition" in K. VanLehn (ed.), *Architectures for intelligence*, pp. 189–223. Hillsdale, NJ: Erlbaum.

Reed, E. S. 1980. Information pickup is the activity of perceiving. *The Behavioral and Brain Sciences*, 3: 397–398.

Reeke, G. N., and Edelman, G. M. 1988. Real brains and artificial intelligence. *Daedalus*, 117(1): 143–173.

Reeke, G. N., Finkel, L. H., Sporns, O., and Edelman, G. M. 1990a. "Synthetic neural modeling: A multilevel approach to the analysis of brain complexity" in G. M. Edelman, W. E. Gall, and W. M. Cowan (eds.), *The Neurosciences Institute publications: Signal and sense: local and global order in perceptual maps*, pp. 607–707. New York: Wiley.

Reeke, G. N., Sporns, O., and Edelman, G. M. 1990b. Synthetic neural modeling: The "Darwin" series of recognition automata. *Proceedings of the IEEE*, 78(9): 1498–1530.

Regier, T. 1991. *The acquisition of lexical semantics for spatial terms: A connnectionist model of perceptual categorization* (Technical Report TR-9j2-062). Berkeley: University of California Press.

Rosenbloom, P. S., Lehman, J. F., and Laird, J. E. 1993. Overview of Soar as a unified theory of cognition: Spring 1993 in *Proceedings of the fifteenth annual conference of the Cognitive Science Society*, pp. 98–101. Hillsdale, NJ: Erlbaum.

Rosenfield, I. 1988. *The invention of memory: A new view of the brain.* New York: Basic Books.

Rosenfield, I. 1992. *The strange, familiar, and forgotten.* New York: Vintage Books.

Rosenschein, S. J. 1985. Formal theories of knowledge in AI and robotics. *New Generation Computing*, 4(4): 345–357.

Runeson, S. 1980. There is more to psychological meaningfulness than computation and representation. *The Behavioral and Brain Sciences*, 3: 399–400.

Rychlak, J. 1991. The missing psychological links of artificial intelligence: Predication and opposition. *International Journal of Personal Construct Psychology*, 4: 241–249.

Ryle, G. 1949. *The concept of mind.* New York: Barnes & Noble.

Sacks, O. 1987. *The man who mistook his wife for a hat.* New York: Harper & Row.

Sandberg, J. A. C., and Wielinga, B. J. 1991. How situated is cognition? in *Proceedings of the 12th international conference on artificial intelligence*, pp. 341–346. San Mateo, CA: Morgan Kaufmann.

Schön, D. A. 1979. "Generative metaphor: A perspective on problem-setting in social polity" in A. Ortony (ed.), *Metaphor and thought*, pp. 254–283. Cambridge: Cambridge University Press.

Schön, D. A. 1987. *Educating the reflective practitioner.* San Francisco: Jossey-Bass.

Searle, J. R. 1980. Minds, brains, and programs. *Behavioral and Brain Sciences*, 3: 417–457.

Searle, J. R. 1990. Is the brain's mind a computer program? *Scientific American*, 262(1): 26–31.

Searle, J. R. 1995a. "Ontology is the question" in P. Baumgartner and S. Payr (eds.), *Speaking minds: Interviews with twenty eminent cognitive scientists*, pp. 202–213. Princeton, NJ: Princeton University Press.

Searle, J. R. 1995b. How artificial intelligence fails. *The World & I* (July): 285–295.

Shaw, R., and Todd, J. 1980. Abstract machine theory and direct perception. *Behavioral and Brain Sciences*, 3: 400–401.

Shaw, R., and Turvey, M. T. 1980. Methodological realism. *The Behavioral and Brain Sciences*, 3(1): 95–96.

Simon, H. A. 1980. "How to win at twenty questions with nature" in R. A. Cole (ed.), *Perception and production of fluent speech*, pp. 535–548. Hillsdale, NJ: Erlbaum.

Simon, H. A. [1969] 1981. *The sciences of the artificial* (2nd ed). Cambridge, MA: MIT Press.

Simon, H. A. 1995. Artificial intelligence: An empirical science. *Artificial Intelligence*, 77(1): 95–127.

Sleeman, D., and Brown, J. S. 1982. *Intelligent tutoring systems.* London: Academic Press.

Smith, B. in preparation. *The middle distance: An essay on the foundations of computation and intentionality.* Volume I: *Introduction.*

Smithers, T. 1995. "Are autonomous agents information processing systems?" in L. Steels and R. Brooks (eds.), *The artificial life route to artificial intelligence*, pp. 123–162. Hillsdale, NJ: Erlbaum.

Smoliar, S. 1992. Elements of a neuronal model of listening to music. *In Theory Only*, 12(3–4): 29–46.

Sperry, R. W. 1995. "The impact and promise of the cognitive revolution" in R. L. Solso and D. W. Massero (eds.), *The science of the mind: 2001 and beyond*, pp. 35–49. New York: Oxford University Press.

Steels, L. 1990a. Exploiting analogical representations. *Robotics and Autonomous Systems*, 6(1,2): 71–88.

Steels, L. 1990b. "Cooperation between distributed agents through self-organisation" in Y. Demazeau and J.-P. Muller (eds.), *Decentralized AI*, pp. 175–196. Amsterdam: North-Holland.

Steels, L. 1994. The artificial life roots of artificial intelligence. *Artificial Life Journal*, 1(1): 1–47.

Stites, J. 1995. Ecological complexity takes root: Profile of Jim Brown. *Bulletin: The Bulletin of the Santa Fe Institute*, 10(1): 10–13.

Stone, J. V. 1994. "Evolutionary robots: Our hands in their brains?" in R. Brooks and P. Maes (eds.), *Artificial life IV: Fourth international workshop on the synthesis and simulation of living systems*, pp. 400–405. Cambridge, MA: MIT Press.

Suchman, L. A. 1987. *Plans and situated actions: The problem of human–machine communication.* Cambridge: Cambridge Press.

Suchman, L. A., and Trigg, R. H. 1991. "Understanding practice: Video as a medium for reflection and design" in J. Greenbaum and M. Kyng (eds.), *Design at work*, pp. 65–89. Hillsdale, NJ: Erlbaum.

Thelen, E., and Smith, L. B. 1994. *A dynamic systems approach to the development of cognition and action.* Cambridge, MA: MIT Press.

Tomasello, M., Kruger, A. C., and Ratner, H. H. 1993. Cultural learning. *The Behavioral and Brain Sciences*, 16(3): 495–552.

Toth, J. A. 1995. Book review of Kenneth M. Ford and Patrick J. Hayes, eds., *Reasoning agents in a dynamic world: The frame problem. Artificial Intelligence*, 73(1–2): 323–369.

Turvey, M. T., and Shaw, R. E. 1995. "Toward an ecological physics and a physical psychology" in R. L. Solso and D. W. Massaro (eds.), *The Science of the Mind*, pp. 144–172. New York: Oxford University Press.

Tyler, S. 1978. *The said and the unsaid: Mind, meaning and culture.* New York: Academic Press.

Ullman, S. 1980. Against direct perception. *Behavioral and Brain Sciences*, 3: 373–415.

van Gelder, T. 1991. Connectionism and dynamical explanation in *Annual conference of the cognitive science society*, pp. 499–503. Chicago: Erlbaum.

vanLehn, K. 1987. Learning one subprocedure per lesson. *Artificial Intelligence*, 31(1): 1–40.

Varela, F. J. 1995. "The re-enchantment of the concrete" in L. Steels and R. Brooks (eds.), *The artificial life route to artificial intelligence*, pp. 11–22. Hillsdale, NJ: Erlbaum.

Vera, A. H., Lewis, R. L., and Lerch, F. J. 1993. Situated decision-making and recognition-based learning: Applying symbolic theories to interactive tasks in *Proceedings of the fifteenth annual conference of the Cognitive Science society*, pp. 84–95. Boulder, CO: Erlbaum.

Vera, A. H., and Simon, H. 1993. Situated action: Reply to William Clancey. *Cognitive Science*, 17(1): 117–135.

Vera, A. H., and Simon, H. A. 1994. Reply to Tourtezky and Pomerleau: Reconstructing physical symbol systems. *Cognitive Science*, 18(2 April–June): 355–360.

Verschure, P. 1992. Taking connectionism seriously: The vague promise of subsymbolism and an alternative in *Fourteenth annual conference of the Cognitive Science Society*, pp. 653–658. Bloomington, IN: Erlbaum.

Verschure, P., Kröse, B. J. A., and Pfeifer, R. 1992. Distributed adaptive control: The self-organization of structured behavior. *Robotics and Autonomous Systems*, 9: 181–206.

von Foerster, H. 1970. "Thoughts and notes on cognition" in P. L. Garvin (ed.), *Cognition: A multiple view*, pp. 25–48. New York: Spartan Books.

Vonnegut, K. [1952] 1980. *Player piano.* New York: Dell.

Waldrop, M. M. 1992. *Complexity: The emerging science at the edge of order and chaos.* New York: Simon & Schuster.

Wenger, E. In preparation. *Communities of practice: Learning, meanings, and identity.* New York: Cambridge University Press.

Wertheimer, M. 1985. A Gestalt perspective on computer simulations of cognitive processes. *Computers in Human Behavior*, 1: 19–33.

West, D. M., and Travis, L. E. 1991. The computational metaphor and artificial intelligence: A reflective examination of a theoretical falsework. *AI Magazine*, 12(1): 64–79.

Wilden, A. [1972] 1980. *System and structure: Essays in communication and exchange.* New York: Harper & Row.

Wilden, A. 1987. *The rules are no game: The strategy of communication.* New York: Routledge & Kegan Paul.

Winograd, T. 1975. "Frame representations and the declarative/procedural controversy" in D. G. Bobrow and A. Collins (eds.), *Representation and understanding: Studies and cognitive science*, pp. 185–210. New York: Academic Press.

Winograd, T., and Flores, F. 1986. *Understanding computers and cognition: A new foundation for design.* Norwood, NJ: Ablex.

Wittgenstein, L. [1953] 1958. *Philosophical investigations.* New York: Macmillan.

Wynn, E. 1991. "Taking practice seriously" in J. Greenbaum and M. Kyng (eds.), *Design at work: Cooperative design of computer systems*, pp. 45–64. Hillsdale, NJ: Erlbaum.

Zrehen, S. 1995. *Elements of brain design for autonomous agents.* Docteur és Sciences dissertation. École Polytechnique Fédérale de Lausanne, Département d'Informatique.

Zrehen, S., and Gaussier, P. 1994. "Why topological maps are useful for learning in an autonomous agent" in P. Gaussier and J.-D. Nicoud (eds.), *From perception to action conference*, pp. 230–241. Los Alamitos, CA: IEEE Computer Society Press.

Zuboff, S. 1987. *In the age of the smart machine: The future of work and power.* New York: Basic Books.

Zuckerman, C. B. 1980. What are the contributions of the direct perception approach? *The Behavioral and Brain Sciences*, 3: 407–408.

Author index

Subject index